Alfred Colbeck

A Summer's Cruise in the Waters of Greece, Turkey and Russia

Alfred Colbeck

A Summer's Cruise in the Waters of Greece, Turkey and Russia

ISBN/EAN: 9783337141905

Printed in Europe, USA, Canada, Australia, Japan

Cover: Foto ©Andreas Hilbeck / pixelio.de

More available books at **www.hansebooks.com**

Alfred Colbeck

A Summer's Cruise in the Waters of Greece, Turkey and Russia

ISBN/EAN: 9783337141905

Printed in Europe, USA, Canada, Australia, Japan

Cover: Foto ©Andreas Hilbeck / pixelio.de

More available books at **www.hansebooks.com**

MOSQUE OF ST. SOPHIA.

A SUMMER'S CRUISE

IN THE WATERS OF

GREECE, TURKEY, AND RUSSIA

BY

ALFRED COLBECK

London

T. FISHER UNWIN

26 PATERNOSTER SQUARE

MDCCCLXXXVII

PREFACE.

MORE than thirty years ago, Mr. Curzon, upon the publication of his most entertaining book on "The Monasteries of the Levant," said, "The public is already overwhelmed with little volumes about palm trees and camels, and reflections on the pyramids." Since that *overwhelmed* period, volumes of a similar kind have continued to pour forth from the press, and what condition the public is now in it would be rather difficult for me to say. I would not add to the discomfort of the reading world by increasing the deluge even to the extent of a single drop. Certainly my book is about the East, but not about palm trees, camels, and pyramids. My wanderings led me away from these, on a line not usually taken by travellers, and I hope, therefore, that those who look into my treasury will find things *new* as well as *old*.

In dealing with Constantinople, I have thought well to sketch the rise and spread of Islam, and to describe its ecclesiastical constitution and the phases of its religious life, in order that the character and policy of the Ottoman people might be more clearly understood; and for the same reason with regard to the people of Russia, I have added a chapter on the Russo-Greek Church, and another on that scourge of the Russian national life—Nihilism. To all readers interested in Biblical incident the chapter illustrative of the movements of the Apostle Paul will be welcome. My excuse for an account of Gibraltar must be the importance of the fortress. It was the most attractive feature in the scenery on the way home.

My thanks are due to those authors whose works have largely assisted my observations, and increased the pleasure of my voyage; and I would also most gratefully acknowledge the kindness of Mr. Edward Hain, senr., of St. Ives, Cornwall, and Mr. Richard Hain, of Cardiff, master mariners, and all other friends who contributed to make the voyage, not only possible, but enjoyable.

A. C.

Oct. 1st, 1887.

CONTENTS.

CHAPTER I.

OUTWARD BOUND.

Newport—Fog in the Channel—Bay of Biscay—Whales—Spanish fishermen—Cape Finisterre—Corunna, and Sir John Moore—The minor incidents of war—Service off Vigo—Battle of Vigo Bay—Portuguese trade winds—Sea-sickness and imaginative sounds—Rock of Lisbon—Harbours of refuge—Flag signalling—Cape St. Vincent—Sagras Point—Cuttle-fish—Petrels—Nelson and Trafalgar—Miscarriage of the Smyrna fleet—Mountains of Southern Spain—Roman Catholic ecclesiasticism—Blue waters—North Africa—Cape Bon—Earthquakes—Bed of the Mediterranean—Pantellaria—Sicily—Phosphorescent waters—Greece 1

CHAPTER II.

THE SHORES AND ISLANDS OF THE ÆGEAN SEA.

Navarino—Cape Matapan—Gulf of Laconia—Homer—Lycurgus and his laws—Sparta—Cape Malea, or St. Angelo—The eremite—Eastern Church—Beaticus—Cerigo—The Ægean Sea—Cliffs—Islands—Milo—Serpho and Siphanto—The Cyclades—Deli—Its origin—Its oracle—Confederacy of Delos—Religious festivities—Palm tree—Asylum—Earthquake—Paros—Disgrace of Miltiades—Naxia—Mycone—Tenos—Image of the Virgin—Superstition—Andria—Gyrae—Audacious impiety—Zea and Thermia—Simonides—Byron's Haidee—View from Syra—Marathon—Patmos and St. John—Samos and Polycrates—Pythagoras—Scio—Sharks—Sunset—Lesbos—The

Northern Ægean—The plains of Troy—Tenedos—Lemnos—
Imbros—Thassos—Samothracia—Its grandeur—Worship of
the Cabiri—Deluge—Scenery—Mount Athos and its monasteries 30

CHAPTER III.

SYRA.

The town—Its appearance—Harbour—Public square—The people
—Costumes—Cafés—Wineshops—Market—Trades—Speech
—English in Syra—Italian man-of-war—Visit to country garden—Beautiful evening—Singing on the forecastle—Church
of the Resurrection—Church of St. Nicholas—Woman and
child—Older churches—Sacred pictures—Infirmary—St. Bartholomew's Hospital—Funeral—The observance of Sunday—
St. John's Eve: its bonfires, and their origin—Pherecydes—
The story of Eumæus 86

CHAPTER IV.

THE WATERWAYS OF CONSTANTINOPLE.

The two waterways—Railway system—Isolation of Constantinople
—Scenery of the Dardanelles—Sea-fowl—Chanak—Sestos and
Abydos—Leander—Byron—The army of Xerxes, and its pas-
sage across the Hellespont—Alexander—Julius Cæsar—The
Turkish invasion—Bride of Abydos—Fortifications—Damage
to an English fleet—Turkish boatmen—Œgospotami—The
River Granicus—Gallipoli—Origin of the Janizaries—Boulair
—Sea of Marmora: its shores and islands—Scenery of the
Bosphorus—The Symplegades—The Giant's grave—The
Genoese castles—Therapia—Deep waters—The castles of Asia
and Europe—Cemeteries—Suburbs of Constantinople . . 117

CHAPTER V.

THE CITY OF CONSTANTINOPLE.

Moonlight view — Suggestions — Morning—Origin — Situation—
General description—Population—Old seraglio—Armoury and
Museum—St. Sophia; its construction—Byzantine model—

CONTENTS. ix

Ecclesiastical furniture and service—Mosque—**The** bloody hand—External appearance—The Achmedie—The Suliemanie—The Pigeon mosque—Mosque of Ortakeui—Palace **of** Dolma Bagtché—The Sultan's life—Church of the Fountain—Pera—Galata—Hamals—Old round tower—Genoese—Fires—Atmeidan: its obelisk—Meta—Twisted serpents—The Nika sedition—Triumph of Belisarius—Revolutions, and destruction of the Janizaries—Burnt column—Galata bridge—Mosque **of** the Sultana Validé—Women—Dogs—Beggars—Bazaars—Walls—**Latin** siege—Arab **sieges—Turkish** designs—Bajazet **and** Tamerlane—Turkish siege—**Golden Horn**—Caiques—Story of an English seaman—Leander's tower—Scutari—Selimie barracks and English cemetery 144

CHAPTER VI.

ISLAM.

Origin—Knowledge of Islam important—Condition of the Christian Church—Condition of Arabia—Birth of Mohammed—Personal appearance and character—Hanyfism—Mecca and Medina—Rapid spread of Islam under the perfect Caliphate—A localized religion—National embodiments—Claim of the Sultan to the Caliphate, and to the title of Imaum-ul-Islam—Its influence upon the foreign and domestic policy of the Sublime Porte—The Mahdi—God—The Koran—Prayer—Almsgiving—Fast of Ramadan—Pilgrimage to Mecca—Disallowance of gambling, usury, and the use of wine—War—Slavery—Woman—The royal Seraglio—Paradise—Ulema—Imaums—Preaching—Muezzins—Mysticism—Dancing dervishes—Howling dervishes—Influence of Islam on Turkish life and character . 192

CHAPTER VII.

THE BLACK SEA AND THE SEA OF AZOV.

The Black Sea—Name—Sunset—The hoopoe—Eastern legend—Acalephæ—Porpoises—Rapidity of motion—Crimea—St. Vladimir—His baptism—Massacre of the Tartars—British bravery—Fortifications—Russian officials—Kertch—Green Waters—Straits of Yenikalé—Sea of Azov—Sturgeon—Smaller fish—Pelican—Mosquitoes—Robins—Russian fowls—Dragon-fly—Locusts—Lightning—Mirage 221

CHAPTER VIII.

TOWN AND COUNTRY SCENES IN SOUTH RUSSIA.

The great plain—Flat land around the Sea of Azov—Taganrog—Shallow water—An ice accident—Streets and buildings—Public gardens—The Czar's palace—Death of Alexander—Visit to the palace—Journey to Rostoff—Tumuli—Grain tract—Sunflowers—Hamlets—Kingfishers—The delta of the Don—Horses—The city of Azov—Tamerlane—Turks and Russians—Peter the Great—Rostoff—Circus—Wool-washing—Central Asian route—Selim's attempt to open it—Napoleon and Paul—House of Romanoff 248

CHAPTER IX.

THE RUSSIAN PEOPLES.

Different races—Muscovy and the Muscovites—House of Rurik—Cossacks and Tartars—Cossack troops—Music—No middle class—Artificial government—The *tchin*—Its effect—Personal appearance of the State officials—Lower orders—Contrast between the Russians and the Greeks—Dress—Dhrosky drivers—Recreation—Tea-drinking—*Vatke*—Domestic life—Marriage customs—Woman—Women's rights—Education of women—Development of trade—Jews and Greeks—Russian labourers—Development of particular industries—Cotton—Woollen, silk, iron, oil, &c.—Repressive power of the Government—Domestic policy—Foreign aggression 276

CHAPTER X.

NIHILISM.

Peculiar to Russia—Origin of the name—Misleading term—Its creed: religious and social—Raskolniks and Jews—Political creed—Moderate and advanced sections—Organization—Subterranean press—Conversations—Official converts—Weapons—Adherents—Students—Women—Disaffected aristocracy—Mercantile classes—Peasantry—Veneration for the Czar—

Cossacks—Causes—Characteristics of the Russian peoples—Liberties of Novgorod—Rural Communism—Invasion of Tartars, and rise of absolutism—Introduction of the *tchin*—Political agitation in the early part of the nineteenth century—Peasant revolts—Government interference—The Nihilistic struggle—The Czar—The people—The future of Russia . . 303

CHAPTER XI.

THE RUSSO-GREEK CHURCH.

Introduction of Christianity—The two legends—Olga and Vladimir—Influence upon the nation, and alliance with the Czars—Independence—Michael and Philaret—Splendour of the patriarchate—Nicon—Peter the Great—Suppression of the patriarchate—Synod—Reforms—National Church—Architecture—Cathedral at Taganrog—Clergy—Monks and monasteries—Hermits—Doctrines—Liturgy—Veneration for pictures—Baptism—Confirmation—Chrism: its preparation—Visitation of the sick—Marriage service—Bells—Choirs—Description of a service—Noisy Sabbath—Saints: catacombs at Kief—Martyrs—The persecution of the Uniates—Raskolniks—Starovers—Safeguards against dissent—Constantinople 326

CHAPTER XII.

ON THE TRACK OF ST. PAUL.

Sacred associations—Apostolic authority of St. Paul—His character—Value of geographical observations in confirming the truthfulness of Scriptural incident—Conybeare and Howson's "St. Paul"—Voyage from Malta to Sicily—Castor and Pollux—The Euroclydon in Adria—Drifting of the vessel—St. Paul's behaviour during the storm—Ship's course from Corinth to Ephesus—Ayasaluk—Syra—Priscilla and Aquila—The shorn head—Troubles in the Corinthian Church—Alexandria Troas—The journey thither—Voyage to Philippi—Scenery—Sunrise—St. Luke—Second visit to Troas—Third visit to Troas—Affection for the Philippians—Preaching at Troas, and accident to Eutychus—Walk to Assos, and voyage down the coast—Fourth visit to Troas—Arrest and martyrdom 355

CHAPTER XIII.

THE SENTINEL OF THE MEDITERRANEAN.

Eastern side of the Rock in the early morning—Western side—Clear waters of the bay—Surroundings—Town—Moors—Castle—Name—Capture by the British in 1704—Siege of 1705 —1727—1779 to 1783—Natural strength—Strategical position —Caverns—" Munitions of rocks "—Climate—Inhabitants— Smuggling—A soldier's conversion—Drive to Europa Point— Stranded steamer—Fauna—View from the summit—Current through the Straits—Beyond the "gates." . . , . 385

CHAPTER XIV.

OLD ENGLAND.

Fire on the Spanish land—Sagras Point and Cape St. Vincent— Sea-fowl—Land seen through the haze—Healthy breeze—Bay of Biscay—Old England—The Lizard Lights—Coast of Cornwall—Falmouth Harbour—Home 407

A SUMMER'S CRUISE.

CHAPTER I.

OUTWARD BOUND.

Newport—Fog in the Channel—Bay of Biscay—Whales—Spanish fishermen—Cape Finisterre—Corunna, and Sir John Moore—The minor incidents of war—Service off Vigo—Battle of Vigo Bay—Portuguese trade winds—Sea-sickness and imaginative sounds—Rock of Lisbon—Harbours of refuge—Flag signalling—Cape St. Vincent—Sagras Point—Cuttle-fish—Petrels—Nelson and Trafalgar—Miscarriage of the Smyrna fleet—Mountains of Southern Spain—Roman Catholic ecclesiasticism—Blue waters—North Africa—Cape Bon—Earthquakes—Bed of the Mediterranean—Pantellaria—Sicily—Phosphorescent waters—Greece.

NEWPORT, in South Wales, is not the most picturesque town in Great Britain, and any one embarking there on a voyage to the Mediterranean would do his utmost to hasten the departure. The higher part of the town is the pleasanter part, and, when you get high enough to look inland, an interesting view of wooded hills and valleys stretches temptingly before you. But the desire to ramble is checked when the fact forces itself upon you that the steamer is in the dock, expecting every tide to drop down the river into the channel and bear you away to new and lovelier scenes. The nearer you get to the docks, the more uninviting

Newport becomes. The streets are dustier; traffic increases; dirty men and women, and dirtier children, linger about the shops, and on the doorsteps, and near the public-houses; the rattle of coal waggons is more distinct as they are run to the dock side, lifted by powerful hydraulic machines thirty feet above the vessel, their contents tipped into the hold, and then, empty and rattling still more, run down the incline, while the fine particles of coal blow about in clouds, and settle thickly upon the decks of the vessel, and the wharves, and the offices, and the workmen, and the water.

It was flood-tide at midnight. The docks were silent. The coal dust had all settled. The *Treloske* lay under the electric light, which, from the lantern of the lighthouse, quivered and streamed into the night, burying in denser darkness everything outside its radius, and weirdly illuminating everything within. There was the hurry of departure; men's voices giving and receiving orders, and saying "Good-bye!" amid the noise of ropes and chains, and the hiss of steam; and, when stretched in the berth and wearicdly closing the eyes, these mingled sounds formed themselves into an unusual lullaby.

The morning broke through mists, and right ahead, as if it too were awaking from a sound sleep, and pushing aside its wrappings, was Lundy Island. The dark brown hills rose above a cloud of white vapour that rested upon and mingled with the grey sea. It appeared as much an island in the air as in the water, and seemed every moment inclined to wrap itself in its mists again and go to sleep, which it finally did, so far as our observation went; and so did the hills of North Devon. They had been cautiously peering through the mists, withdrawing here and disclosing there, alternately hiding and revealing their loveliness like some beauteous moving form in gossamer, until at last the mists closed in, and rolled over the grey waters and about the ship; and, at half speed, blowing the fog signal, a dismal operation, we passed along the Cornish coast, vainly hoping that the fog would lift sufficiently to permit a run into St. Ives Bay. Friends there knew we were passing down the coast, and we wished to give them a parting whistle. But no! thicker and thicker grew the fog; the soundings showed twenty-seven fathoms, with a bottom of shells and pebbles, and we judged ourselves off St. Ives Head; later on we had thirty-five fathoms, and toward midnight we heard the warning fog-horn of the Sevenstones lightship off the Land's End, and spake with a Newlyn fishing boat, by which we sent our last message home.

In the morning we were entering the Bay of Biscay. The sky was clear; the sea was calm; the long dark blue billows of the Atlantic were so subdued as to make scarcely any perceptible difference to the motion of the vessel. A large sailing ship, the *Winnifred*, with sails all set, was gently rising and falling with the swell of the sea. Several passengers, among whom were women and children, were moving about the deck, some of them perhaps impatiently, for she made little, if any, progress, and we steamed past, and speedily lost her as she dipped below the receding horizon. The Bay of Biscay was on its very best behaviour. The boundless expanse of azure overhead appeared to deny the possibility of roaring thunders and sweeping rains; but, in the long majestic swell of the indigo deep beneath, subdued as it was, there was the suggestion of magnificent and irresistible billows before which the boldest mariner might quake, and in the midst of which no ship could live. What tales of terror; what exhibitions of fortitude and bravery; what loving attempts to rescue friends from peril, and to rescue "nearer and dearer" ones still, attempts no less loving because wearied and vain; what strange and varied secrets of human life and destiny lie hidden beneath the troubled surface of those dark blue waters, hidden deep enough never to be disturbed by the fiercest storm that blows, and never to be known till the sea shall give up its dead!

Sunday morning brought a fresh wind, with short, white-capped waves, and haze in the distance. Half a mile off the starboard bow whales were spouting, the columns of water rising thirty feet, and falling in fountain-like spray, while the troubled sea in their track brought to mind the description of Job's leviathan, " He maketh a path to shine after him ; one would think the deep to be hoary." And yet the whale, notwithstanding his bulk, is not half so terrible as Job's leviathan, but a timid and inoffensive animal, contented with his food of living jellies, and quite peaceable if only let alone. Spanish fishermen were out, looking very cold clad in shiny oilskins in the grey morning, their anchored boats tumbling uneasily upon the tide, but quite alive to business, Sunday as it was, and indicating in various ways their desire to barter fish for any other commodity we might have on board suitable to their needs or fancy. Among the rest we refused the tempting offer of a large live flat fish, held aloft at arm's length, and wriggling to and fro; and passed on to view Cape Finisterre looming through the haze and growing more distinct with every turn of the propeller.

To the north-east of Cape Finisterre the land runs out to the picturesque and memorable town of Corunna, the scene of a gallant struggle during the Peninsular War, and where,

" Like a warrior, taking his rest,
With his martial cloak around him,"

lie the remains of Sir John Moore. The retreat of his small army closely pressed day by day by an overwhelming host under the personal command of Napoleon ; the unselfish sacrifice of treasure (£25,000 having to be thrown over a precipice, and left behind as a worthless impediment on the weary march); the cold, and hunger, and death ; the harassing charges of the French cavalry among the frost-bitten stragglers, who fell trodden beneath the horses' hoofs, or sabred, or were made prisoners; and, withal, the orderly movement, the patient endurance, the calm fortitude of the men, inspired by the example of their general, won the warm commendation of Napoleon and Soult, and led Napoleon to exclaim—not having yet proved the genius of Wellington—that Moore was the only general living worthy to contend with him. And when, at last, 20,000 veterans of the French army reached Corunna at the same time as the English fleet appeared in the offing, the 14,000 English remaining after that devastating march faced about, and bought a dear victory by the death of their commander; for while the French were falling back everywhere before the impetuous fighting of desperate men, Sir John Moore was dashed from his horse by a cannon-shot, and carried away with broken ribs and flesh torn and mangled to die in a foreign land.

> "Lightly they'll talk of the spirit that's gone,
> And o'er his cold ashes upbraid him;
> But little he'll reck if they let him sleep on
> In the grave where a Briton has laid him."

Who shall chronicle the minor incidents of war? We remember the great men, and the broad outlines of every important struggle; but the private has a personal history. The woman and child, who once followed the camp because the husband and father was in the ranks, felt the keenness of the struggle; and the woman and child, who now wait, expectantly fearful and trembling, at home, also feel the keenness of the struggle. The misery of war is not confined to the march, and the camp, and the battle-field. It extends far beyond. The nobility of its personal incidents is not always recorded in the fleeting records of our newspapers, in the permanent pages of our literature, in the imperishable marbles of our national mausoleums. Many noble incidents remain unknown. During that fearful retreat through the snow in the north-western portion of the Spanish peninsula, an officer, overcome with fatigue, perishing for lack of food, persuaded that his end was come, turned aside into a wood to die unseen, and there, laid upon the ground, nearly dead, was a soldier's wife, protecting as best she could her little babe, and, with a last effort, she besought him to take the babe and save its life. Her appeal was like the infusion of new strength. He took the infant and rejoined his comrades, and, sustained by the trust of the dying woman, continued the march, carrying the infant upon his back, and never forsaking it until he had safely seen it in tender hands on board a transport in Vigo Bay. Surely this is not a solitary instance! Our records of human life would be very much richer if incidents such as these—the minor incidents of war—were gathered together; and beneath the terrible aspect of war, an aspect which all its pretended glory cannot soften and commend to right thinking men, we should see that chivalry exists—that often they who have little to do with its wickedness, and much to do with its hardship and agony, are men of noble spirit, generous sympathy, and loving hearts.

Cape Finisterre, the European Land's End, and, before the days of Columbus, thought to be the western extremity of the earth, is not a picturesque promontory. Its rounded hill and detached rocks, cold and sombre in the morning light, the rising sun shining behind them and throwing them in the shade, were passed quickly; and we steamed along beneath a beautiful sky, and through the dark blue waters, until the late afternoon brought us off Vigo. There, under an awning aft, we held a service, joining in the praise of Him whose the sea is, and who made it; and meditating upon the charity which springs from Him, wide, and free, and all-encompassing as the sea, and which, embodied in human life, as the mainspring and chief glory of human character, never faileth.

Other than songs of praise have been heard in these waters. Other than feelings of heaven-born charity have animated men's hearts. Songs of warlike triumph have rung from lips blackened with powder, or reddened beyond their wonted redness with warm, fresh blood. Feelings of slaughter have burned in the bosoms of English and Dutch, anxious to crash in through the formidable boom protecting the French navy and Spanish merchantmen in Vigo Bay. It was years ago, in the early days of Queen Anne, when Louis XIV. claimed the Spanish crown for his grandson, and thereby reopened a struggle with England and Holland, whose combined arms, under the indomitable Prince of Orange, he had learned both to respect and dread; and the English and Dutch, then the bravest sailors afloat, fearing no foe, and shrinking from no danger on that element which had become their second home, made straight for Vigo, where lay the wealthy Spanish galleons under the convoy of the French men-of-war. The first vessel to strike the boom, which was nearly 500 yards long, and moored at each end to heavy ships, was the *Torbay*, and through the rending timbers she went, only to find herself between two vessels who swept her right and left with their thundering cannon, and speedily set all her rigging aflame. But on came the rest, the Dutch admiral alone, however, entering the breach with his vessel. The others, the wind having died away, had to lower their boats, and send their men eagerly clambering to the fray over the shattered boom. The Dutch admiral rendered timely aid, and the *Torbay* was saved, not so much by him as by one of those freaks of war that sometimes happen; for the vessel she was engaged with had been a merchantman, and so hastily fitted up for warfare that her cargo had never been removed; and her cargo consisted of snuff, which, when the vessel blew up, extinguished the fire. The flames were literally *snuffed out*, and the gallant *Torbay* saved. The fight was fierce and terrible. No less than eight vessels were burned, and four were sunk; and much treasure in silver coin and plate, and costly merchandise, enriched the combined victorious fleets.

The seas roar, and the floods clap their hands; but there is One who "stilleth the noise of the seas, the noise of their waves, and the tumult of the people." To-day the seas were calm; no trace of conflict lingered on the deep; all thought of conflict was hushed by our sweet evening hymn; the sun was sinking in the western ocean, wrapped in soft and many-coloured clouds, which, reflected in the ocean, transformed it into a pavement of sapphire suffused and chastened with amber, and emerald, and amethyst—a quietude of splendour, the counterpart of that to be produced by God's all-obliterating, all-conquering, never-failing charity, when it shall cover the earth with heaven's eternal peace.

By the next day we were fairly within the compass of the Portuguese trade winds. These winds are very helpful to sailing vessels proceeding south, and as great a hindrance to those going north. The current sets southwards too, and merges itself in that current which incessantly flows through the Straits of Gibraltar into the Mediterranean.

Sea-sickness, of a very slight nature, had already disturbed me, and was here renewed; and it appeared as if the inability to poise the body, and walk steadily along the ship's deck, were not only an aggravation, but a partial cause, of the sickness. The loss of the body's equilibrium seems to have some direct relation with the stomach's distress; qualms of sickness pass over one when the foot strikes the deck sooner or later than the mind reckons upon; and, certainly, sickness is almost, if not altogether, overcome by the acquirement of what are popularly known as "sea-legs." When a man gets his sea-legs on he may defy sickness. But when, under stress of weather, old Neptune robs him again of his sea-legs, sickness once more creeps over him, and he longs for *terra firma*.

When suffering from sickness, a peculiar phenomenon of the imagination several times presented itself, for which I could not account on the grounds of association, or in any other way. One day I heard the sounds of horses' hoofs and the interminable rattle of traffic in busy streets; another day I heard birds singing, and could distinguish from among the rest the notes of the thrush and the cuckoo. Both these imaginative phenomena I became conscious of in the Bay of Biscay. Again, off the African coast, in the neighbourhood of Algiers, while seated reading on the forecastle, I heard the sound as of a brass band playing in the far distance; and next day, near Cape Bon, as I lay in my berth, the ringing of church bells, subdued by distance, fell pleasantly upon my ears. The sounds were present with me, in the imagination, before I became fully conscious of them, and upon becoming fully conscious, and in the effort to distinctly realize them, they faded away. They belonged to a half dreamy mental attitude induced by the slight sickness, and were never present except at such times. There was nothing in the ship, or on the sea, or about the appearance of the African land to suggest these sounds by way of association; and, if the current of my mind happened to be in the direction of busy streets or bird-haunted woodlands, martial music or calls to prayer, and my imagination was quickened thereby to apprehend these sounds, I was not at the time aware of it, nor can I recall it now.

The Berlings, a group of dangerous rocks, or small islands, off the coast of Portugal, came within view. About their bases the blue sea was breaking into white rolling surge, and from the largest rock, a white lighthouse, like a calm and lonely sentinel, overlooked the snowy tide. This rock is fortified, and used by the Portuguese Government as a State prison. The coast of Portugal here runs in a south-westerly direction towards the towering Rock of Lisbon. This mountainous promontory, the seaward termination of the Serra de Estrella, forms the most westerly point of the European continent. The scenery in the neighbourhood of the Rock of Lisbon is charming. The interest grows as you approach the rock. Village succeeds village, half hidden in vines; a large monastery crowns the fertile slope, and, through its hundred windows, looks over the white villages to the distant purple sea; the vivid green of the vineyards becomes more and more largely interspersed with greens of darker shades, and groves grow into woods, and woods into forests clambering up the steep sides of the promontory; here and there are chasms, where the shadows gather deep and thick, and the water leaps, in a thousand cascades, to the roaring torrent below, while over the chasms, on either side, rise the straight pines; and these same pines, overtopping the other trees, still clamber upwards to where the face of the hill is broken by the bare rocky precipice, and stay not there, but, above the precipice, planting their feet on its verge, still clamber upwards, attempting, and yet vainly attempting, to reach the summit; for the stately hill lifts its brown head far above the pines, and woos the clouds, floating in from the Atlantic, to stoop and kiss it, and linger about it, and bathe it in their virgin dews, before proceeding on their mission of mercy to remote and less favoured lands.

As we left the Rock of Lisbon, and came within sight of the broad estuary of the Tagus, we descried, almost in a straight line, and moving westward, seven French ironclads. The efficiency of the French navy is said to be rapidly increasing, and certainly these very fine vessels were a proof of it. Nevertheless, her naval forces are much inferior to those of England, and reasonably so, because England's need of naval forces is much greater than the need of France. In another and more peaceable form of marine equipment, where still the greater need is that of England, France has shown herself the wiser nation by providing all along her coast harbours of refuge for the safety of her seamen, while yet the coast of England, notwithstanding every winter's tale of peril and death, remains in great part unprotected by such harbours. Are not the lives of our mercantile marine, our coasting sailors, our hardy fishermen, worth the careful consideration of the Government? And would not the erection of a few harbours of refuge along our eastern and western coasts, two or three of which would cost no more than one first-rate ironclad, be money wisely spent, even if we had to do with an ironclad the less? Succeeding governments may leave these harbours of refuge to private enterprise, but, in the meanwhile, thousands of valuable lives are being lost, hundreds of homes are made desolate; and private enterprise only tardily moves, when it moves at all, in a scheme which is really national, and the successful development of which is not for any merely private, but for the national, good. France is wiser than England. She has seen her need, and tried to meet it. The need of England cries out loudly every winter with the despairing voices of drowning men, with the tender and pleading voices of bereaved women and children, and England is almost deaf to the cries. Her charitable people furnish lifeboats for the noble work of rescue, but her Government stirs not to make this noble work of rescue,—noble, because always so perilous, and frequently so disastrous as to demand severe self-sacrifice,—unnecessary, by providing harbours into which her vessels might run and be safe.

There is a signal station at Cape Espichel, and another at Cape Carveoiro. We reported ourselves at the former place by means of the universal signal code. This is a simple and ingeniously designed method by which any vessel may communicate with any other vessel upon the high seas, that is, if they possess the signals, and most vessels do, the code having been adopted by nearly all the maritime nations of the world; or, by which any vessel may communicate with any signal station ashore. If the vessels are of different nationalities, if the signal station is in Portugal, or Denmark, or the Cape of Good Hope, the meaning of the communication is not in the least affected. In every language the signals mean exactly the same. So that at sea a Dutchman may talk with an Italian, and a Norwegian with a Spaniard, although ashore they would not be able to understand each other at all. Ashore they would be *at sea*, and they would be more *at home* at sea than ashore.

This universal code of signals, which is based upon a code previously used by the British navy, consists of eighteen flags, representing the consonants—there are no vowel flags—and the pennant expressing the desire to communicate, or the fact that the communication has been understood. The code is divided into four parts, namely, Brief signals, Vocabulary signals, Distant and Boat signals, and the signal indicating the name, port, and owner of the vessel to which such signal has been attached. Where quick dispatch and immediate attention are necessary, as in cases of leakage, or mutiny, or drowning, only two flags are used; where inquiries are made and answered concerning time or geographical position, three flags are used; and four, where the communications are less important, or more involved, and requiring longer search in the vocabulary for each separate word. The flags are of different shapes and colours, and capable of multitudinous combinations—indeed, astounding as it may seem, the combinations possible are no less than seventy-eight thousand, six hundred and forty-two. Of course, the primary object in the adaptation of this code is to meet purely nautical wants; but so efficient is it, that with a little patience general communications may be made, and even conversation indulged in. A word somewhat similar, or analogous, in meaning to the correct one, has sometimes to be substituted for the correct one, not unfrequently with a rather laughable result, as in the case of a vessel in the Mediterranean some years ago, which, wishing to convey to the British fleet the intelligence that there was a majority for the Government in favour of the disestablishment of the Irish Church, signalled this: *Irish Church dislocated, her Majesty's Government surplus.* Mistakes are made through carelessness in signalling, and unfamiliarity with the code, but the mistakes are not many, and will naturally become less. The Board of Trade requires every candidate for an officer's certificate to pass an examination in code signalling, and, if other national authorities insist upon the same, the code will not only come into more general use, but will be more efficiently worked. The assistance which one vessel may render to another, assistance peculiarly valuable at sea, will thereby be largely increased, and the perils of the sea diminished in proportion; while this international intercourse must tend to bring the world nearer together, because it cannot but assert the brotherhood of the race. In common dangers we feel our unity, and the unity must be all the more deeply felt when, in one series of dangers, we can employ a common language.

The universal code of signals can only be used in the daytime. No method of communication during the night has yet been devised so simple and efficient as to meet with, or even hope for, universal adoption. The perils of the sea are doubly increased by the darkness, and he who could invent a code of night-signals, easy and rapid to work, either by flashing lamps or otherwise, would be a real benefactor of the race.

Cape St. Vincent stood out clear and sharp in the grey morning. On the high, perpendicular cliffs, a man's figure, like an active black shadow, was moving hither and thither, apparently endeavouring, by the aid of a rope, to capture something half-way down the cliffs, or to lift something from the shore. Where the cliffs meet to form the Cape, a large convent stands, its walls running up from the very edge of the cliffs themselves—a square-towered, small-windowed, storm-beaten, time-worn old place, perched in picturesque solitude above the billows, and looking directly out upon them. Very few places are so situated as to have the sea for an organ, and the winds for a choir; very few worshippers hear the music of the mass intermingled with the music of the tides, and sing their vesper hymns to the accompaniment of ocean zephyrs whistling round the gables and about the lofty towers; but how terrible must the music be sometimes! When the grand organ is on, the thundering tones of the ocean breaking over the rocky keyboard; when all the stops are out, the mighty winds roaring from the depths of the sky, human voices must be overawed, and worship sink into silent reverence and adoration of the Almighty Power. Who can listen unmoved to the music of God's majesty? For it is not only the tumultuous noise that impresses, but the truth that is underneath: "Thy way is in the sea, and Thy path in the great waters, and Thy footsteps are not known."

To the south-east of Cape St. Vincent the cliffs are lower and broken, running round in a semicircle to Sagras Point. The semicircle is fringed with spray, for here the waters rush over sunken reefs, and awaken the echoes in the many caverns into which the cliffs are broken; while innumerable sea-birds find these broken cliffs and caverns a secure haunt, and this semicircular bay an almost undisturbed fishing ground.

Sagras Point, even more than Cape St. Vincent, is a dangerous headland, and many ships have gone to grief in the attempt to round these two promontories, and pursue their way northward. Three weeks after we passed, a singular catastrophe occurred here. An English steamer, in the night, went straight upon Sagras Point, but managed, by a sudden reversal of the engines, to back off into deep water. She was so seriously damaged, however, that her captain and crew, fearing she would immediately sink, transferred themselves to another steamer which happened to be then passing. In the commotion and hurry no one thought of the engines and helm. The helm was hard down, the engines were working, and as soon as they were aboard the other steamer, she disappeared in the darkness. They never thought to see her again. They fully expected that in a very few minutes she would be at the bottom of the sea. But she floated, and her engines continued to work, and she answered her helm by describing a circle, and, to the consternation of those who had just left her, she came crashing with her bows right amidships the vessel on which they then were, and made such a serious breach in her that they had to take to the boats to save their lives. Both steamers were lost, and some went down with them, but the majority saved themselves by the boats, and were picked up and conveyed to Gibraltar.

When Sagras Point had been rounded, and we were steaming towards Trafalgar, I began to perceive the difference in the shortness of the evenings. The twilight was brief, and darkness rushed on quickly after the setting sun. The waters, too, had another hue. The indigo had vanished and a lighter blue had taken its place, not the lovely ultramarine of the Mediterranean, but a blue between that and indigo. The waters were smooth as oil; not a ripple was on them; and near the ship they had the appearance of blue ink. Moving away from the ship's track, by the aid of its long arms, and peculiar propelling apparatus—an apparatus by which it can draw the water into a bag, and then by contraction of the bag, and forcible ejection of the water, push itself along—was a sandy-coloured cuttle-fish, an interesting object enough when surveyed from a ship's deck, but a dread enemy when within reach of its horrible suckers and insatiable maw. To have a cuttle-fish fastened about one, and feel the intolerable stinging and the irresistible drawing of its formidable arms, is, according to the testimony of the few who have passed through it, and been rescued from it, the most terribly sickening sensation imaginable; and the sudden death by the shark's jaw must be much preferable to the slow agony inflicted by this monster of the deep.

When in the Bay of Biscay, a flock of petrels, generally known as "Mother Carey's chickens," had gathered in the wake of the ship, and followed us every day since, and continued to follow us along the Mediterranean until we approached the shores of Greece. There they left us, and there they joined us again on our return, and continued in our wake until we sighted the shores of England. When the darkness fell they were following, when the morning broke they were following, always on the wing, always darting hither and thither across the waters troubled by the propeller, a flight like that of swallows when hunting for food, and never resting for a single moment, except when the steward threw some greasy liquid into the sea, which they would flutter over, and hastily dip up, and continue their flight again. Their sustaining power in flight must be extraordinary. These must have slept on the wing, if they slept at all, for certainly they never rested on the sea, and they never rested on any part of the vessel. They are small birds, dark feathered, and with white-tipped wings; and when snared, as they may be by simply allowing a few long threads to hang from the stern of the vessel, among which, in their flight backwards and forwards, they become entangled, they are found to be almost bare of flesh, mere feathers and bones, and nearly as light as the air itself. Within their stomachs an oily secretion is found, to increase which, perhaps, they follow the vessels and feed upon the grease thrown overboard, as well as upon the small molluscs, and other tiny sea creatures, their proper food, turned up by the propeller. They never fly far on either side of the troubled waters, but keep constantly crossing the turmoil, and watching it with eager eyes. The name *petrel* is a diminutive of *Peter*, and may have been given them in honour of the fisherman apostle and patron saint of all "who do business on great waters." Petrels are regarded as friendly to sailors, and their presence is taken as one sign of a prosperous voyage. They have been called, and with more appropriateness, *sea-runners*, because of their quickness and precision upon the wing, skimming the surface of the tumbling waters, sweeping in and out of the hollows of the tide, never failing to accommodate themselves to every motion, as if the sea had given them birth, tossed them like animated spray from its bosom, that it might play with them as a mother with the children in her lap.

With the light of Cape Trafalgar on the port bow, growing more distinct as the darkness deepened, we moved on through the waters where occurred the memorable naval fight of Trafalgar. The very name *Trafalgar*, to an Englishman, means *duty*, and the name is never uttered in English ears without calling up visions of the gallant Nelson. The fame of the one-eyed, one-armed hero is as fresh to-day as when he fearlessly engaged the French and Spanish fleets in Trafalgar's Bay.

"For those bright laurels will not fade with years,
Whose leaves are watered by a nation's tears."

A more inspiriting signal to true-hearted, patriotic men was never given than Nelson's signal, "England expects every man to do his duty;" and a more decisive naval victory than Trafalgar was never won. And it must ever be a deep satisfaction to Englishmen to know that the signal came from the commander's heart. Previous to the engagement, and during the engagement, Nelson was impressed with two thoughts—Duty and Death. He felt that he must render to his country his utmost service, and he felt that in the rendering of the service he would die. An old friend of his, Captain Hallowell, had presented him with a coffin, which was deposited in an upholsterer's place in London; and, upon receiving his orders from the Government, he called to say that the coffin might be wanted upon his return. While the English fleet was bearing down upon the enemy, he was in his cabin penning the document in which he committed himself and his cause to the care of God, and his daughter and relatives to the generosity of the nation. When he left the cabin for the deck he scrupulously dressed himself in his full uniform, and wore upon his breast his numerous decorations. He was advised to put them off, that he might thereby not become conspicuous, and endanger himself unnecessarily by attracting and directing the enemy's fire. "But," said he, "in honour I gained them, and in honour I will die with them." When Captain Blackwood left him, with the expressed hope that a speedy return would find him possessed of many of the enemy's vessels, he replied, "God bless you, Blackwood! I shall never see you again." He had a strong presentiment that he would die. And yet interwoven with this presentiment was the feeling of duty. When the ball struck him he said to his friend Hardy, "They have done for me at last." "I hope not," said Hardy. "Yes!" he replied, "my backbone is shot through." And so it proved. And yet the feeling of duty did not forsake him. He lingered in the midshipmen's berth, constantly asking for the results of the battle, brightening as the crew overhead rung out cheer after cheer when they beheld now one and now another vessel strike her colours, until he became too feeble to ask further questions or even to smile, and then, with a dying effort, he said, "I have done my duty—praise God!" and quietly passed away. He was made of stern stuff thus to face what he felt certain would be death, and face it with such a steady and unflinching courage; but mingled with his sternness, as we often find in men like him, was much tenderness of heart, much sympathy with the suffering of others. When shot his thoughts were of his men, not of himself, and lest they should be grief-stricken and dismayed by his appearance, he drew his handkerchief over his face and decorated breast, that he might pass along the decks, and through the cockpit, unrecognized. Well might the sailors who lowered him into the vault in St. Paul's Cathedral, inspired by one common wish, simultaneously rend into fragments the flag, his own victorious flag, that covered his coffin; for each one was anxious to possess some appropriate and precious memento of him whom they revered as a hero, and loved as a friend, and whose face they should see no more.

That reach of sea stretching from Cape St. Vincent to the Rock of Gibraltar has been the scene of many naval exploits. Two or three sea-fights have occurred off Cape St. Vincent itself, and the Rock of Gibraltar has been taken and re-taken again and again. The sea that lies between— like the Netherlands in the history of European armies —occupies a prominent position in the history of European navies, and may almost be considered the naval battle ground of modern Europe. More important engagements have occurred here, but, save Trafalgar, no engagement ever produced a deeper impression upon England than that known as the miscarriage of the Smyrna fleet. The English and Dutch merchantmen had been gathering for months in the Thames and the Texel, afraid to move out without a convoy, fearing that the French fleets in Brest and Toulon would intercept and rob them of their precious cargoes; and when the cries of the merchants, who were losing money every week by the delay, became loud and imperative, and their ships had increased to nearly four hundred, the English Government and the States General provided together a convoy of one hundred armed vessels to see them safely beyond the reach of the French fleets. But the English and Dutch commanders had no information concerning the movements of the French fleets. They thought them safely in Brest and Toulon, and never imagined that they had effected a junction, and were waiting for their prize near the Straits of Gibraltar. Therefore, after seeing the merchantmen beyond Ushant, the convoy, notwithstanding the strong opposition and remonstrances of Rooke, left him, with only twenty vessels, to see them into the Mediterranean. Rooke went forward, innocent of the peril awaiting him. A swift cruiser was despatched, if possible to come up with him, and warn him (for news of the movements of the French fleets had by this time reached England); but he was far away beyond the hope of warning, and discovered, too late, when rounding Cape St. Vincent, the trap into which he had been drawn. What could he do, with twenty ships, against the entire, magnificent naval forces of the French Empire? He had simply to abandon the merchantmen, and run for Madeira. Only sixty of the immense wealthy fleet reached that place with him. Some escaped to Spanish ports, some found their way to Ireland, some were scuttled in the Bay of Gibraltar. The rest were taken, or sunk, or wrecked. The news of the disaster filled England and Holland with consternation. Strong men were broken beneath the blow. It was the sharp and sudden blow of financial ruin for many of them, and the ruin was aggravated by the news of the battle of Landen that followed in a few days. The fortunes of England and Europe were at a low ebb. French domination appeared likely to become supreme. And if the throne of England had not been filled by a wise and mighty prince—a prince whose statesmanship held together the coalition of European forces, and whose generalship, like that of most truly great men, enabled him to transform defeats into victories—Louis XIV. might then have turned the whole course of European history, deferred the progress of liberal ideas, and crippled the influence of the Protestant religion for many, many years. William III., the Prince of Orange, was never more formidable than in the hour of defeat. His defeats made him a great man, and won for him lasting honour and gratitude.

We passed through the Straits of Gibraltar in the night, and in the morning found ourselves steaming along the southern coast of Spain, with Malaga in the receding distance. There is no finer, more beautiful, or more imposing coast in Europe than the southern coast of Spain, provided you keep at sufficient distance to take in the splendid range of the Sierra Nevada in the background. The Sierra Nevada, as their name implies, are snow mountains, and their highest peak, Mulhacen, is the loftiest land in the Spanish peninsula. You may have the range in full view, and yet not miss the towns of Agra and Almeria at their base. Their grey roofs and towers may be seen peeping above the blue waters. Behind the hills rise, and higher hills behind them, lifting themselves above the seaward plain and the landward valleys amid a vast garden of fruitful luxuriance, and clad with verdure to their summits; and still behind, browner and barer the higher they go, are towering mountains, throwing their shadows athwart each other, revealing their impassable chasms and frowning precipices, standing like a band of giants to guard the land beyond; and yet they themselves are flanked and dwarfed by higher mountains still, mountains that run up into the pure sky, and expose their eternal snows to the sunlight, impressively calm, silently majestic, appearing so near heaven as to be invested with heaven's peace.

But they are never twice alike. In returning, as we steamed round the low-lying land that forms the plain of Almeria, and came within full view of the mountains, they were under a cloudless sky; all their outlines were softened in a warm haze of blues and purples, and the snow was glittering on their summits—a beautiful sight, but not so beautiful as that morning on the way out, when the mists were rolling about them, and gradually vanishing beneath the warmer rays of the sun. There was no haze. The outlines of the mountains stood out in all their rugged grandeur, except here and there where the outlines above were cut off from those below by white, swathing mists that rolled uneasily up and down, and became thinner and thinner as they were slowly drawn away into the deep valleys. The snow did not glitter. It was like a spotless mantle thrown over the top of the mountains. The whole scene was lovely. But it was that kind of loveliness which might be appropriately called *intense*. With the bluest of blue seas in the foreground, sufficiently broken in its surface to give it pleasing variable motion; with well-defined grey roofs and towers beyond, to supply the human element, to take away from the solitude of the scene; with the greens and browns of gardens and pasture lands behind, sweeping up into the darker browns of the rising hills; with moving mists, soft and white, enveloping the peaks, wreathing themselves round rocky projections, drawing themselves out into long thin bands across the faces of the cliffs, and vanishing in the valleys; with the towering heights, and all their cracks and chasms, save where the moving mists were spread, clear and distinct as if they were only a mile away; with the lofty ridge above all, snow-clad, a spotless, unwrinkled garment with fringes where the snow had drifted and filled up the fissures below the ridge itself;—all this, in the pure morning light, ere yet the heavens were too bright, and the rosy blushes of the dawn had quite departed, made up a scene of surpassing beauty not easily forgotten, and full of inspiration to the mind and heart.

Almeria, *the conspicuous*, as the Moorish name means, was, under the Moorish domination, a town of great importance, vying in population and influence with Granada itself; but since the swarthy conquerors were themselves conquered, and driven over the flood to the African shores, it has steadily sunk into its present humble position. And yet now, with quite an insignificant trade in fruits and wine, and with a population not much more than one-tenth of the population of its palmiest days, it is considered sufficiently important to give its name to a province, and to take its place as a leading provincial town. But Spain, the entire country, is only a shadow of what she once was; the mere ghost of a power; a spirit dumb amid the councils of Europe, where, three centuries ago, her voice was heard above all others. And what is the cause of her decline? With an extensive sea-board well adapted for eastern and western commerce; with healthy table-lands and fertile valleys; with mountains richer in minerals than any in Europe; with a law-abiding, industrious, cheerful-hearted people, and a people not only patriotic but successful in colonization,—what is the cause of her decline? The answer is an involved one. Many causes enter into the grand cause. But the clue to the grand cause is supplied by the action of Spain in the Reformation and post-Reformation period, when the adamantine fetters of the Roman Catholic ecclesiasticism were more securely fastened upon and over her national life; and all the more securely, as it would seem, in proportion to, and because of the strength with which other nations had burst those fetters, and entered upon the larger and freer life, lest this favoured priestly place, this happy hunting-ground of the inquisition, and the confessor, and the miracle worker, and the seller of indulgences should also burst them, and become larger and freer too. The Roman Catholic ecclesiasticism—for it is well to distinguish between that and the religion of the Roman Catholic peoples—has a firmer hold upon the national life of Spain than upon the national life of any other country in Europe; and in that, more than in anything else, although in something else are to be found minor causes, may be found the major cause of the retarded progress, inactivity, and almost stupor with which Spain has been long afflicted. But Spain will wake up by and by. The movements preparatory to returning consciousness are visible, and when she is sufficiently roused to throw off the incubus of this oppressive ecclesiasticism, she will once more take her place, not the chief place, but an honourable place, and a place to which her people, her history, her geographical position entitle her, among her sister communities in Europe.

These thoughts occupied my mind as Almeria, the *conspicuous*, hid its *diminished* head beneath the plain. We lost sight of it, and rounded the low-lying seaward termination of the plain, and approached Cape de Gata in the late afternoon. This is the rocky south-eastern promontory of the Spanish peninsula. It faded from our view as we plunged forward into the twilight, and next day we were in the middle of the western basin of the Mediterranean,

"An empty space above, a floating field around."

The sky was cloudless. The sea was ruffled beneath a gentle north-eastern breeze. Both sky and sea were blue, the sky lighter in tint than the sea, and the sea of that wonderfully deep, rich ultramarine peculiar only to the Mediterranean. There are no waters in the wide world that will compare in colour with these waters. They are like animated sapphire. The whole ocean is a glowing, moving gem of liquid blue, except where the ship breaks it, and then it is broken into leaping, flashing diamonds.

A variety of causes combine to produce this beautiful colour. The clear atmosphere, "the ambient air," has something to do with it; and the specific gravity of the waters something more. For the specific gravity of the waters of the Mediterranean is greater than that of the waters of the Atlantic. The bed of the inland sea, too, may have something to do with its lovely hue, although not much, because its bed is variable, rock and sand and coral prevailing in different parts; and the sea is generally so deep that its bed must be largely hidden in impenetrable darkness. We were then sailing over 10,000 feet of water, and to the east of Malta the Mediterranean reaches a depth of 15,000 feet. In winter its waters are sometimes lashed into tremendous fury, especially across the mouth of the Adriatic; but its billows are shorter than the billows of the Atlantic. There is not the same mighty mass of moving water; and storms are not frequent. Then the Mediterranean is practically a tideless sea. Nowhere does it ebb and flow more than three feet, and there is no perceptible tide movement along most of its winding shores. And this comparative stillness, this undisturbed surface of the water, may add its little to the causes combining to produce that deep, rich colour which is its greatest charm.

There is nothing very attractive about the North African coast. A succession of low barren hills, with white drifted sands reaching almost to their summits, and crowned with long coarse grass—these were almost everything visible. We had occasional visitors from the shore in the shape of gorgeous butterflies, and one or two small birds; and the ocean was represented by a large yellow turtle swimming ungainly out of the ship's track toward the coast. But for hundreds of miles the same monotonous reach of sand-hills stretched away, until near Cape Bon the outline became bold and broken, with high detached rocks and a really fine promontory. This headland was once the lordly sentinel of Carthage, long the chief maritime power of the Mediterranean, and the haughty rival of Rome. Now Carthage is only a name. Its glory is sunk beneath the blue waters upon which its armaments proudly rode. But Carthage will never be forgotten. If only by that inimitable fourth book of Virgil's "Æneis" Carthage will never be forgotten. But her history is too closely interwoven with the history of Imperial Rome, and too well was the wish and prophecy fulfilled which Virgil put into the lips of dying Dido, to be forgotten:

> "These are my prayers, and this my dying will;
> And you, my Tyrians, every curse fulfil:
> Perpetual hate and mortal wars proclaim
> Against the prince, the people, and the name.
> These grateful offerings on my grave bestow;
> Nor league, nor love, the hostile nations know!
> Now, and from hence in every future age,
> When rage excites your arms, and strength supplies the rage,
> Rise some avenger of our Libyan blood;
> With fire and sword pursue the perjured brood:
> Our arms, our seas, our shores opposed to theirs;
> And the same hate descend on all our heirs!"

From Cape Bon to the coast of Sicily is the ridge of

coral that divides the eastern from the western basin of the Mediterranean. Here the sea is only 200 feet deep, and in one place only 40 feet, dipping suddenly on both sides of the ridge to a depth of 5,000 feet. There is no doubt that here, as well as at the Straits of Gibraltar, the continents of Europe and Africa were connected, and at one time the Mediterranean must have been two large inland seas. Whether the change has been effected gradually by the slow, ceaseless action of the water, and the building up of the rocks, and the shifting of the shores through innumerable ages, or suddenly by some great volcanic upheaval and shattering, we cannot with certainty know. This is an old volcanic region. And the seismic forces are by no means spent. From the sea-board of the Levant, across the Ægean, through the Balkan peninsula, across the Adriatic, in Italy and Sicily and the South of Spain, and even to the Atlantic sea-board so far north as the Rock of Lisbon, the whole region is volcanic, and never safe from seismic disturbances; while some of the most appalling catastrophes that have ever afflicted mankind have occurred along this line. Lisbon has had one terrible visitation. Herculaneum and Pompeii were directly in this volcanic course. Smyrna, at its eastern extremity, has been shaken to ruins several times. Chios, the neighbouring island, has suffered greatly within the memory of living men. The entire Grecian Archipelago appears as if some mighty volcanic force had shattered another Levant and let in the seas, and left its mountain-tops a group of beautiful islands. It was the opinion of the ancients that Sicily was once joined to the mainland.

> "The Italian shore
> And fair Sicilia's coast were one, before
> An earthquake caused the flaw: the roaring tides
> The passage broke, that land from land divides;
> And where the lands retired, the rushing ocean rides."

And perhaps the Mediterranean itself, as we now know it,

with its two basins, its Atlantic outlet, and its opening into the Black Sea, is the result of some sudden volcanic change so vast as to sink into insignificance all the changes of historic times.

If the Mediterranean were dried up, and we could look along its bed, it would appear like two enormously deep valleys, divided by the ridge running between Cape Bon and Sicily,—valleys as deep as from the summit of Mont Blanc to the Lake of Geneva, broken here and there by rugged peaks, and studded with mountains higher than any in Europe; the eastern valley connected by a long narrow gorge with another valley, almost as large and deep as itself, and quite as large and deep as its western neighbour. These three valleys are filled with water, and we call them the Mediterranean and Black Seas, and together they form one of the most wonderful sheets of water in the world—wonderful in its vast area, enclosed as it is by three continents; wonderful in its historical memories, for on its shores civilization was cradled and nursed to strength and beauty; wonderful in its influence upon human life, for its mid-land situation has marked it out for many centuries as the chosen highway of commerce, and the medium of international relations; wonderful in its beneficent effects, for also to its mid-land situation is largely owing the salubrious climate and abundant fertility of Central and Southern Europe.

The island of Pantellaria is a lofty, conspicuous, barren rock off Cape Bon. It may be seen at great distances. The sight of Pantellaria to vessels proceeding westwards is the welcome sign of approach to the African land. The sight is not only assisted, but sometimes deceived, by mirage, a not unfrequent phenomenon in the Eastern Mediterranean. Pantellaria may be seen fifty miles away without mirage, but with the assistance of mirage it may be seen at double the distance. It has been seen, and the distance verified by the sextant, 102 miles away.

Very soon after passing Pantellaria, the large, beautiful, fertile island of Sicily comes within view. But we saw it not.

> "For gloomy night descended on the main,
> Nor glimmer'd Phœbe in the ethereal plain :
> But all unseen the clouded island lay,
> And all unseen the surge and rolling sea."

As we returned, however, we came within full sight of Cape Passaro, and passed along the southern coast of Sicily. A long gentle slope ascends, covered with vegetation, cornfields and vineyards with villages interspersed, and flanked by wooded uplands. These uplands are not thickly wooded, like forests, but open, like a far-stretching and continuous park, with large white houses here and there looking through glades, and down sweeping avenues, toward the distant sea. Like an immense peaceful garden Sicily appears from the sea, at least on its southern side, and when Etna shrouds his head in clouds, one would hardly think that this goodly land is the seat of a thundering volcano, and that its smiling surface is rocked by hidden fires. A dangerous land, though pleasant, is Sicily, and ancient tradition teaches the same, for not only

> "There, sacred to the radiant god of day,
> Graze the fair herds, the flocks promiscuous stray,"

but also there, in dens, dwelt the monstrous one-eyed anthropophagi. A fair face the island wears, but destruction lurks within its bosom nevertheless.

Re-crossing the mouth of the Adriatic at eventide the waters broke from the vessel in phosphorescent gleams. The appearance was exactly like that of tiny, sparkling insects playing along the vessel's side, and among the ripples, and upon the breaking waves. This is not usually seen in the Mediterranean. Phosphorescent fish and insects are not near so numerous in the Mediterranean as in some other seas. In the Irish Channel I have seen the waves breaking from the plunging boat like waves of fire. In the South Pacific, and in Mexican waters, during stormy weather, the yard-arms of vessels sometimes appear to be hung with white, gleaming balls. But these in the Mediterranean were only sparkles, little fiery gleams shot off from the vessel, whirling in the eddies, and dying rapidly away. This phosphorescent life is extremely interesting to the naturalist, and will well repay investigation.

We sighted the high lands of Greece, the lofty ridges of Mount Taygetus, bathed in the soft rosy splendours of the western sun; and we traced them stretching away southward toward Cape Matapan. They were a welcome sight, not only because of their peculiar beauty and historical associations, but also because they brought us within measurable distance of our first resting-place. Already we were anticipating the pleasures of *terra firma*, free from the tossing wave, and out of hearing of the engines and propeller.

CHAPTER II.

THE SHORES AND ISLANDS OF THE ÆGEAN SEA.

Navarino—Cape Matapan—Gulf of Laconia—Homer—Lycurgus and his laws—Sparta—Cape Malea, or St. Angelo—The eremite—Eastern Church—Beaticus—Cerigo—The Ægean Sea—Cliffs—Islands—Milo—Serpho and Siphanto—The Cyclades—Deli—Its origin—Its oracle—Confederacy of Delos—Religious festivities—Palm tree—Asylum—Earthquake—Paros—Disgrace of Miltiades—Naxia—Mycone—Tenos—Image of the Virgin—Superstition—Andria—Gyrae—Audacious impiety—Zea and Thermia—Simonides—Byron's Haidee—View from Syra—Marathon—Patmos and St. John—Samos and Polycrates—Pythagoras—Scio—Sharks—Sunset—Lesbos—The Northern Ægean—The plains of Troy—Tenedos—Lemnos—Imbros—Thassos—Samothracia—Its grandeur—Worship of the Cabiri—Deluge—Scenery—Mount Athos and its monasteries.

THE mountains of Messenia, directly north of us, as we approached Cape Matapan, brought to mind Navarino, closely associated with Grecian history from the remotest times. There was the sage and aged Nestor's city, ancient Pyle; there the Athenians and Spartans maintained a long and fierce struggle during the Peloponnesian War, resulting in the victory of Athens, and the exaltation of that city to the climax of her power; and there the combined fleets of England, France, and Russia, under Admiral Codrington, completely destroyed the naval forces of. Turkey, and secured the national independence of modern Greece. These mountains quickly faded as the high range of Taygetus came rapidly within view, the summits of its barren, pyramidal ridges gathering the tinted clouds about them, and some of them lifting themselves up into the clear azure, and displaying, even in midsummer, broad patches of snow.

Taygetus diminishes in boldness and height somewhat rapidly, and its seaward termination, Cape Matapan, the ancient promontory of Taenarium, is a little disappointing. The cliffs are low, rounded, and barren; a much needed lighthouse, only half built when we went by, rises above the point, and will be very serviceable to mariners as soon as it is completed; and there are very few inhabitants where once were thriving Spartan towns. Away from the Cape, on both slopes, and half hidden between the ribbed sides of the mountains, and generally so elevated and distant from the shore as to make them very difficult of access, are scattered villages; below and above them, on the fertile ground, vines are trailing their vivid green leaves, and shooting out their tender, curling stems, and gardens, wildly luxuriant, yield their olives, and pomegranates, and figs, and apricots to the ready hand; while sheep and goats wander over the loftier and rocky ground in search of the sweet herbage, and fatten themselves for the village feast or the distant market. How different all this from the time when Poseidon's grove waved here, in which Pausanius was betrayed by the conversation of his slave, and from which the Helots were dragged to death! A terrible earthquake shook Sparta at that time, overturning her capital and slaying her nobles, and, in their superstition, the Spartans thought that this was a visitation from the earth-shaking deity because his sanctuary at Taenarium had been violated. Now there is no sanctuary to violate. The old heathenism has departed, and her chief glory, Greece,

"In all save form alone, how changed!"

The view after leaving Cape Matapan is a very noble one. The Gulf of Laconia opens up most beautifully. Its semicircular basin is flanked by high hills, between which the Eurotus flows quietly to the sea. Nothing can be lovelier than this mountain scenery softened by the rays of the departing sun. Sometimes in England, in the late afternoon of a hot summer's day, a bluish haze is discernible about the masses of foliage for which her parks and richest landscapes have become renowned, not a mist, but a soft haze, toning and blending the leafy masses, and spreading itself above them, and giving a distinct charm to the picture; and sometimes, in the Scilly Islands, the same phenomenon is discernible, only the haze is purple and not blue, toning the sharp edges of the rocks, and blending their outlines where they happen to overlap, surrounding and seeming to suffuse their very substance, and adding greatly to the beauty of the scene. In Greece this haze effect may be seen to perfection. It is not only blue and purple, but almost every other colour, and sometimes many colours together shading off into each other, which, with the pellucid atmosphere, and the unflecked azure of the sky, invest the landscape with a splendour unknown in more Western climes. The intensely blue water of the Gulf of Laconia was breaking into the purest white foam as the fresh wind swept over its surface, and the hills around, particularly the range of Taygetus, behind which the sun had disappeared, were bathed in soft light. Spaces of blue and purple were spread between and about the foot of the hills, but nearer their summits the purple gave way to crimson and orange, and above their summits the crimson and orange were melted into the golden sky. There was an inexpressible softness, a subdued splendour, a placid beauty about the whole scene, rendering singularly appropriate Byron's simile of the Grecian shores to death newly come upon a young and lovely face,

> "The wild angelic air,
> The rapture of repose that's there—
> The fixed yet tender traits that streak
> The languor of the placid cheek."

Into the head of the Gulf of Laconia flows the Eurotus, and thirty miles up the Eurotus lies the ancient Lacedæmonian capital, Sparta. Helen, decoyed from the roof of her husband by the arts of Paris, left Sparta for a new home in Troy; and from Sparta went forth the messages to the various Grecian States, calling upon them to arm and avenge this deed of treacherous ingratitude, this base violation of the divine laws of hospitality. And so we have the "Iliad" and the "Odyssey," works of human genius, pictures of human life in those far-away times, which, but for these two books, would be altogether lost in impenetrable shadows. Out from the shadows comes one clear figure, an old, blind, wandering musician, the poet-singer of the royal courts of Greece, and he weaves the heroic struggles of his countrymen with another mighty race into graceful measures, and passes them on to others, and they to others again, until they become finally written and treasured in Greece, and through Greece scattered everywhere for the delight of all civilized nations, winning from all an unstinted meed of praise, the immortal wreath only twined about the brows of the noblest of mankind. Homer will live so long as the race lives, and must ever remain associated with Greece as her oldest, and not the least remarkable, among her many remarkable sons.

Another remarkable son of Greece, *and of Sparta*, one who laid the foundation of the Spartan supremacy, and made her for centuries the leading power in Greece, was Lycurgus, exalted by his countrymen into a demi-god, and worshipped as worthy of divine honour. The Delphian oracle proclaimed that if the Spartans would maintain the constitution of Lycurgus they should be everlastingly prosperous. Like a wise man, Lycurgus disappeared from his country, and thereby prevented the overthrow of his constitution by a personal attack upon himself. He left the constitution with them to be observed or not, as they pleased. The absence, the mysterious departure, the unknown whereabouts, practically the death of Lycurgus—a death which amounted to a sacrifice for the good of his country—must have impressed his countrymen very deeply, and predisposed them to the acceptance of his laws. They are wonderful laws, only possible, perhaps, in a small State like Sparta, and under conditions similar to those of the Spartan State, where the mass of the people were serfs of the soil, cherishing an inveterate hatred towards those above them, and requiring to be kept down by military force. The nominal government was a hereditary monarchy under two monarchs, who shared the throne together, but a very limited monarchy, the real power being vested in the hands of five men, who, in process of time, and by a necessary development of the system, became absolute. There was also a Senate of thirty members and a larger assembly of the people. But the peculiarity and value of the constitution of Lycurgus was not in its political combination, but in the severe military discipline to which every Spartan was subjected in order to fit himself for victorious warfare. It was an embodiment of the principle, and of the principle carried to its utmost limit, that the people exist for the State, not the State for the people. Everything was made subordinate to State requirements. Birth, education, marriage, domestic life, social relations—all were made to serve State purposes. Weakly and misshapen children were exposed at birth to perish on Mount Taygetus. The youths were trained to suffer the greatest hardships without a murmur. Marriage under thirty years of age was disallowed, and, practically, there was no domestic life. A public table was provided by the public purse, and men lived together, not in families, but in companies, as members of the State. In many respects it was a very cruel custom, nevertheless the principle of subordination was boldly embodied, and it resulted in the creation of a State unconquerable, irresistible, the most compact and strongest State, considering its size and population, the world has ever known. For all Laconia was less than many an English county. It made Thermopylæ possible. It has given us a new word for firmness, hardihood, courage with a marble front and feet like adamant, courage which never fails—the word Spartan.

Sparta never became so famous as Athens. She could not, by reason of that very national constitution and discipline which was the secret of her military strength, but which effectually hindered the cultivation of poetry and philosophy, architecture, sculpture, and painting. Yet it would seem as if Sparta, in the early Grecian times, were a rich and well-built city, and, about the description of the palace of Menelaüs, there is a suggestion of barbaric splendour, although there may be little suggestion of grace and refinement.

> "Prodigies of art, and wondrous cost !
> Above, beneath, around the palace shines
> The sunless treasure of exhausted mines :
> The spoils of elephants the roofs inlay,
> And studded amber darts a golden ray."

This is doubtless an imaginary picture, but the imagination rested on a solid basis. Sparta was a fine city. While war remained the chief art and calling of men, Sparta led the van, and from her most southern position, almost girt about and quite cut off from the rest of Greece by her barrier of hills—natural disadvantages—attracted all eyes, and commanded universal respect. But when men began to see there was something better to live for than conquering and enslaving each other, when the pen, and the chisel, and the brush were employed to embody ideas which were struggling for expression and permanency, and thereby developing a higher intellectual life, and, to some extent, a purer morality, Sparta fell into the background, Sparta became simply a memory; and she remains a memory to-day, while Athens is a real power, influencing human thought and human activity throughout the civilized world.

The eastern boundary of the Gulf of Laconia is formed

by the magnificent promontory of St. Angelo. The Zarex mountains here terminate, not disappointingly, like the range of Taygetus at Cape Matapan, but in a fine, bold headland rising high above the flood, and looking proudly over the channel that separates it from the island of Cerigo. This promontory was known as Cape Malea by the ancients, and is so marked on many of our modern maps and charts, but some maps and charts and most seafaring men give it the name of Cape St. Angelo. Its former name, Cape Malea, is a sufficient indication of its dangerous character. It was considered the most critical part of the coast in the circumnavigation of Greece. Sailors might dismiss anxiety from their minds after clearing Cape Malea, but so difficult was it to clear, and so numerous were the disasters in attempting, that the Greeks had a proverb, "When rounding Malea forget your home,"[1] or, *bid good-bye to your home.* The proverb implies that it is doubtful if you will get round, or, should you succeed in getting round, it is doubtful if you will get back, and therefore you had better settle your affairs, and leave your home as if it were the final departure.

Cape Malea was the promontory where several of the Grecian heroes, returning from the siege of Troy, are said to have first met with the calamities which delayed their arrival home. It seems to have been *the* place where calamities must come in. Nestor, relating the voyage home to young Telemachus, tells how he and Menelaüs came safely onward in company, until, as soon as he saw

> "Malea's misty tops arise,
> Sudden the Thunderer blackens all the skies,
> And the winds whistle, and the surges roll
> Mountains on mountains, and obscure the pole.
> The tempest scatters, and divides our fleet."

Menelaüs wandered far and wide, and gathered many treasures; and, by a divinely revealed stratagem, at last seized

[1] Μαλέας περιπλέων ἐπιλάθου τῶν οἰκάδε.

Proteus, the various god, who endeavoured to elude him by running through a whole series of transformations, and who, upon finding himself fast held, during every change, by the hero's powerful arms, condescended to reveal his future travels, and his safe arrival home. He also gave him information concerning other Grecian warriors, companions at the siege of Troy, and particularly concerning the voyage and cruel murder of his brother, Agamemnon. Here again Malea plays its calamitous part.

> "The watery vast,
> Secure of storms, your royal brother pass'd,
> Till, coasting nigh the cape where Malea shrouds
> Her spiry cliffs amid surrounding clouds,
> A whirling gust tumultuous from the shore
> Across the deep his labouring vessel bore."

That wise man, Ulysses, after his arrival in Ithaca, and while preserving his feigned character as Æthon, the shipwrecked wanderer from Crete, invented a story for Penelope's ears; and the better to beguile and cheer the wife who knew him not, spoke of himself (Ulysses) as having been driven to Crete.

> "For elemental war, and wintry Jove,
> From Malea's gusty cape his navy drove
> To bright Lucina's fane."

So that Malea was not misnamed. It had a traditionary bad character. This character was sustained when tradition merged itself in history; and now, to sailing vessels, Malea is an awkward point, which it is well to avoid sometimes by running to the south of Cerigo. The height, together with the narrowness, of the promontory are sufficient to account for its dangerous circumnavigation. The wind gathers and sweeps down from its summit suddenly and furiously, as from other high lands near the shores and on the islands of the Ægean; and, rather than venture round Cape Malea, many mariners, in ancient times, dragged their boats over the isthmus of Corinth. Attempts have been made to prevent rounding Cape Malea, by piercing the isthmus and joining the Corinthian and Saronic Gulfs.

Why has the name of this frowning promontory, this rugged headland lifting itself majestically out of the deep sea, been changed from Cape Malea to Cape St. Angelo? Probably because it has become the solitary home of an eremite of the Eastern Church, a venerable father who has retired to this most lonely place, in order that he might devote himself to a religious life, altogether undistracted by the presence of his fellow-men. A quieter, and more solitary, and more unapproachable residence there is not in the wide world; and if there is any virtue in asceticism, and if spiritual ascendency can be gained by voluntary exile from all human intercourse and an entire surrender of the life to prayer, surely this virtue must be possessed, this ascendency must be gained by the eremite of St. Angelo. His little hut is under the precipice, on a plateau surrounded by a low wall; and the wall also encloses a patch of cultivated ground where he may grow the simple vegetable foods he requires to keep up the slow waste of his physical system. An ass was tethered within the enclosure, as we went by, and cropping the scanty herbage within reach; a very useful animal, but rather a dull companion, nevertheless better than no companion at all. This plateau, containing the hut and small garden, is on the western side of the Cape, and looks across the channel to the island of Cerigo, about six miles away. There is no vestige of human habitation within view. The northern part of the island of Cerigo, which is the only part visible, is rocky and unpeopled, adding rather to the solitariness of the situation than otherwise; and to the westward of Cerigo, stretching away to the horizon, is the lovely blue sea.

A short distance from the hut, to the eastward, and more directly under the precipice, built upon a projecting rocky ledge where the water has worn away the cliff into a gorge or chasm, is a small chapel. It has the distinguishing dome of all Greek places of worship, although, from the smallness of the building, almost in miniature; it is entered by folding doors; on one side cloisters are cut in the solid rock, the evidence of long and patient skilled labour, and on the other side, perpendicular with the chapel wall, the cliff descends sheer into the sea. The chapel is cleanly whitewashed, like the hut on the plateau, and is approached from the hut by a narrow path winding between huge rocks, and now and then tunnelled through the rocks, for only by these means could a safe approach be made to the ledge on which the chapel stands. All this was distinctly visible through a powerful glass as we passed by, both going and returning. The waters here are very deep, and will permit of a close approach to the shore. Very seldom, however, will the holy man himself appear, although passing steamers blow their whistles in the endeavour to attract his attention. But we may suppose he is above the influence of such sublunary things as whistles, and has long since stifled any curiosity he may have had concerning the doings of the outside world. Sometimes he may be seen on his way to the chapel, or on his way home. We were fortunate in obtaining a good view of his venerable figure, tall and thin, clad in a long brown gown, with a band round the middle, and his cowl thrown back, fully exposing his face—a well-moulded, grey-bearded face. He moved along quickly, passing between the large rocks, and through the passages in them, finally disappearing near the chapel, into which he entered, and engaged in his solitary devotions.

This eremite, in his absolute retirement, in his undisturbed and changeless worship, is a faithful picture of the Eastern Church. As it was a thousand years ago, so it is now. The peculiarities of the Eastern life are in it. Quietude, repose, and some might say deadness, prevail throughout all its branches. The activity of the West is unknown, and may be impossible. Monasticism in the West was always very different from monasticism in the East. The East knows nothing of those great brotherhoods which have devoted themselves to art and literature, to teaching and preaching, to political propaganda in the service of Rome. The monks of the Thebaid, and Sinai, and the Levant, and Armenia, and Mount Athos, and Central Russia, have all been given more exclusively to devotion than the monks of the West, and therefore sometimes to pious extravaganza. We have had no pillar saints [1] and navel souls [2] in the West. The Eastern monks were, and are, ascetics in the true sense of the term, and very few monks of the West have been. The Church of the East is contemplative and mystical; the Church of the West is active and practical. Protestantism arose in the West. The only Protestantism of the East is Mohammedanism, if indeed it can be so called, for it is not a protest, but a revolt, an enemy to Christianity, and seeking to extinguish

[1] Among these examples of religious fatuity, none acquired greater veneration and applause than those who were called Pillar Saints (Sancti Columnares), or in Greek, *Stylitæ*, persons of a singular spirit and genius, who stood motionless on the tops of lofty columns during many years and to the end of life, and to the great astonishment of the ignorant multitude.—*Mosheim*. (See also Tennyson's poem, "St. Simeon Stylites.")

[2] Barlaam, a native of Calabria, a monk of the order of St. Basil, and afterwards Bishop of Geraci, in Calabria, travelling over Greece to inspect the conduct of the monks, found not a few things among them which were reprehensible; but in none of them more than in the Hesychasts at Mount Athos, in Thessaly, who were mystics or more perfect monks, who sought for tranquillity of mind and the extinction of all the passions by means of contemplation. For these Quietists, in accordance with the prescription of their early teachers, who said there was a divine light hid in the soul, seated themselves daily in some retired corner, and fixed their eyes stedfastly for a considerable time upon the middle of their belly or navel; and in that situation they boasted that a sort of divine light beamed forth upon them from the mind itself, which diffused through their souls wonderful delight.—*Mosheim*.

the Christian name. Goethe says, in a beautiful little poem, and with a large charity—

> "The East belongs to God ; the West
> Gladly obeys His high behest ;
> Tropic heat, and Arctic cold,
> His hand in peaceful bond doth hold.
>
> Only God is just ; He sees
> What thing is good for each and all ;
> Call Him by what name you please,
> But praise His name, both great and small."

The Eastern Church is set forth in that lonely little chapel, with its one worshipper, hanging above the tide on the rocky ledge of Cape St. Angelo.

The eremite is a subject of much speculation to sailors. Several stories have been invented to account for his solitary residence, and the story which obtains most credence is that the venerable monk is a Scotchman, who lost his vessel on Cape St. Angelo, and every soul aboard, including his wife and children ; and, in the melancholia succeeding this sad event, he took up his residence here, within view of the watery grave of all he possessed on earth, determined to spend here the rest of his earthly days. How fertile is the human imagination ! With what ease may an ingenious tale be told ! If this is so, the natural end of the eremite of St. Angelo will be suicide ; for under the circumstances mentioned in the story, a man would not long continue without taking the fatal plunge from some convenient rock, and seek again, beneath the deep waters, union with his loved ones sleeping there in the silence and stillness of that majestic sepulchre.

Within Cape Malea, on the western side, is a small island which appears to persons passing to be part of the mainland. Behind the island the coast is rounded into a pleasant bay, whose name, "Beaticus," the blessed, like the name

"Malea," the wicked, is a sufficient indication of its character. It must have afforded shelter to many storm-driven vessels, and obtained thereby from ancient mariners this kindly name. When Sparta and Athens were struggling for supremacy in Greece, an Athenian fleet was sent here, and attempted to establish a fort as they had already done at Pylus, the modern Navarino, but the attempt was not successful. It was not so favourable a place as the bay behind the island of Sphacteria. Malea overlooked it, always a dread object to Grecian sailors; and it was in Laconia itself, the Spartan territory proper, nearer the capital, and likely to be defended with more spirit, and not in the conquered province of Messenia, divided from the Spartan capital by the high range of Taygetus.

Opposite Cape Malea is the Island of Cerigo, the ancient Cythera, dedicated to Venus, sometimes called Cytheræa. The goddess of love, when she sprang from the foam of the sea, was carried to Cythera, and thence to Cyprus, both islands thereby becoming specially sacred to her, and under her powerful protection. To Cythera she snatched away Ascanius, Æneas' son, that, by substituting Cupid, and in this way securing Cupid's approach to Dido, and Dido's fondling embrace, she might shed the poison of love in the heart of the Carthaginian queen. Cythera, or Cerigo, is a fertile island on its eastern and southern sides. Its people inhabit these parts of the island, and almost at its southern extremity are the remains of its two ancient cities, Cythera and Scandia, in the former of which was the most famous temple dedicated to the goddess of love. This island is not commercially important, and, beyond its mythical connection with Venus, has very few interesting associations.

Upon leaving Cape Malea, on the voyage eastward, the mariner fairly enters the Ægean Sea. The name of this famous sea is connected with one of those wonderful and savage myths, which, like uncertain objects in a mist, loom out from the prehistoric period of Grecian life. Ægeus was the King of Athens. He married Æthra, the daughter of Pittheus, King of Troezen in Argos. In Troezen the hero Theseus was born to this royal pair, and resided in Troezen until strong enough to raise an enormous stone, beneath which were his father's sword and sandals, and safely carry the sword and sandals over the Isthmus of Corinth—a dangerous road infested with bold robbers—to Athens, as pledges of his sonship. He arrived in Athens, and was recognized by his father and greeted by the people. Minos, the King of Crete, had imposed a fearful tax upon the Athenian people, because of the murder of his son. Every nine years, seven youths and seven maidens were shipped from Athens to Crete, there to be devoured by a monster with a bull's head and a human body, who had his home in a winding labyrinth almost impossible to trace. Theseus determined to end the tax, and, with the next batch of victims, went himself to Crete. Ariadne, the daughter of Minos, fell in love with him, and explained to him the windings of the labyrinth; the hero penetrated to the den of the Minotaur, and slew him, and delivered the Athenians from his cruel maw. On the way home, when nearing Athens, the pilot, instead of hoisting the white flag as a signal of success, hoisted in mistake the black flag usually carried in token of the sad sacrifice; and Ægeus, regarding the signal as certain evidence of the death of his son, flung himself into the sea which thenceforth became known as the Ægean.

The cliff land from Cape Malea northward into the Gulf of Argos is very fine. The Zarex mountains run very near the shore, and in many places break off abruptly, and descend in precipices to the sea. These precipices are very high, and form an irregular zigzag line all along the coast, and not a few of them are pointed toward their summits, exhibiting those "spiry cliffs" so menacing and terrible in stormy weather. It is by no means an inviting coast, although grandly picturesque, and a formidable defence to the south-eastern part of the Morea.

These cliffs are lost to sight upon entering the Archipelago. The most charming marine scenery presents itself to the enraptured and wondering vision. It was a beautiful and clear morning when we found ourselves among the Grecian Islands. The sea was unruffled; directly above each island a little cloud had gathered, like a vaporous island of the sky corresponding with the more solid island of the sea—a curious and interesting sight, and more interesting on a moving vessel passing close by the shores, and through the channels of the islands, than if seen from some stationary position. A sea of water below, of the richest ultramarine, glowing like a jewel in the morning sunlight, and bearing upon its bosom, as if they were the children of the deep, these numerous and various rocks and islands; and a sea of translucent air above, with its own rocks and islands of the softest white clouds, scattered everywhere, but always opposite to those below, the two seas together presenting a most unique and lovely picture.

The first considerable island, upon entering the Ægean from Cape Malea, is Milo, with its hills rich in iron, and its dales full of vines and flowers. A famous place for honey it once was, and therefrom may have derived its name. Alum abounded here, and plentifully supplied those masters of the old world, the Romans, who flew their eagles over Milo as well as over the other islands of the Archipelago. Long years before they came, however, the Melians lived in peace, and strenuously refused to take sides in the Peloponnesian War, although doubtless their sympathies were with Sparta, because they were themselves Spartans, and, except the inhabitants of Thera, the only Lacedæmonian islanders. Athens could not tolerate neutrality, and subdued the island, murdering every grown male, and selling every woman and child into slavery. Lysander, the Spartan general, avenged the cruel deed, drove out the Athenian colony, and brought the Melians back home. Behind Milo, and separated from it by a very narrow channel, is Cimolis, or Argentière, lofty, rocky, and barren, but containing silver mines, and therefore, if the mines were worked, likely to be an important island.

Passing between Milo and Anti-Milo, a small barren islet to the westward of Milo proper, we entered the channel between Serpho and Siphanto. Serpho is a stony and unfruitful island. Its rugged, precipitous rocks are lifted, like prison walls, frowningly above the sea. Indeed, the Romans made use of it as a State prison, and sent here some of the most notorious offenders against the Imperial law. The island is scantily inhabited. There is sufficient soil in the crevices of the rocks to grow certain foods and fruits, and there are cool, fresh water springs, very valuable and much appreciated in Eastern climes. The barren hills, too, although so uninviting in appearance, are full of metal, particularly full of the magnetic iron ore called loadstone, which would doubtless repay any one commercially enterprising enough to work them. Siphanto, the sister island to Serpho, is one of nature's favourites, blessed with a salubrious atmosphere and a fertile soil; yielding corn, and fruit, and flowers in abundance; possessing several good harbours, and altogether conducive to an easy, careless life. The fierce spirit of the Greeks is in these islanders. Siphanto abounds in lead, and two centuries ago certain Jewish speculators were wishful to farm the mines, and proceeded thither to obtain samples of the lead ore; but the captain of the vessel, probably a Greek, being liberally bribed by the islanders, scuttled the vessel while on the way home, and sent the Jews and their cargo to the bottom of the sea. They wanted no Jews on the island, and were perhaps apprehensive of a life of toil should the lead mines be opened and prove successful.

As we left Serpho and Siphanto behind, we came within view of

"The scattered isles of Cyclades,
That, scarce distinguished, stud the seas."

They presented themselves on every side, some of them small and rocky, others large and fertile, but all very beautiful in the morning sunlight. They were all robed in the soft hues of the sea and sky. Villages were visible, not on the seashore, but half-way up the sloping hills; while about the shore, here and there, were houses and small cots, in the gardens of which the vine, pomegranate, lemon, fig, olive, and various other fruits were growing in profusion. As we rounded the southern part of Syra, other islands opened up to the northward; but the harbour and town of Syra came within view, and engrossed all our attention; and very soon we had the pilot aboard, and were working round the mole, and towards the wharf, where we were securely moored, and immediately beset by a motley group of almost wild-looking Greeks, who had been employed to take out the cargo.

The islands of the Grecian Archipelago are divided into two sets, the Cyclades and the Sporades, the Cyclades because they are supposed to be in a circle round Deli, the Sporades because they are scattered or sown over the rest of the sea. Deli, however, is not in the centre of the Cyclades. Most of the islands are to the south of Deli, yet the group is sufficiently rounded in the various local relations of its islands one towards the other as to justify the name Cyclades. Deli is the name now given to *the large* and *the small* islands anciently called Delos and Rheinea, and separated from each other by a channel only a few hundred yards wide. Rheinea is very small, and Delos itself is one of the smallest and least picturesque islands of the Archipelago. It lies low, and almost hidden between Rheinea and Mycone. It is, nevertheless, the most historically important, and, in many respects, the most interesting island in the Grecian seas. From the earliest times it has been a sacred sanctuary, because the supposed birthplace of Apollo and Diana; and it was most intimately associated with the rise and supremacy of Athens. The confederacy from which Athens derived her maritime power, and by which she achieved her successes, was called the Confederacy of Delos, and the temple of Apollo and Diana on the sacred island was appropriated by the combined States as the safest possible treasury for the depositing of their common funds.

> " An island in the Ægean main appears :
> Neptune and watery Doris claim it theirs.
> It floated once, till Phœbus fixed the sides
> To rooted earth ; and now it braves the tides."

So Virgil refers to the myth which accounts for the origin of Deli, the myth which would have us believe that all the Cyclades were once floating islands, and circled round Deli, until they were fixed by the deities, and fitted for the habitations of men. In the description of the shield of Æneas, that wonderful shield wrought by Vulcan at the intercession of Venus for the valiant use of her heroic son, and prefiguring on its ample front the notable events of his posterity, a conspicuous place is given to the naval fight at Actium. Antony is represented as having gathered "barbarian aids," and,

> " Rich in gaudy robes, amidst the strife,
> His ill fate follows him—the Egyptian wife.
> Moving they fight : with oars and forky prows,
> The froth is gathered and the water glows.
> It seems as if the Cyclades again
> Were rooted up, and jostled in the main."

This myth of the floating islands may have had its origin in the phenomenon of mirage, sometimes seen in the Ægean, and likely to produce a feeling of awe within the minds of a superstitious people. From the mole at Syra, Deli once appeared to me quite an unsubstantial island, lifted above the water, and shimmering in the strong light as if about to pass away.

The oracle of Apollo at Deli was the second most famous oracle of the ancient world. Its fame was exceeded only by the oracle at Delphi in Phocis. It was distinguished from that by the plainness of its answers. The Delphian oracle was almost always ambiguous, and its ambiguity was one source of its great fame; the oracle of Apollo at Deli was simple and more direct, and I suppose, therefore, sometimes mistaken, and suffering in consequence. Its antiquity, however, was sufficient to preserve its fame. Æneas called there soon after leaving Troy, consulted the oracle concerning his future abiding place, and obeyed the directions given him so far as his father, old Anchises, could interpret them; but, although the oracle was plain enough, the mortals went astray, and sought a home in Crete instead of Italy. With Theseus also the oracle is connected. He vowed an annual pilgrimage, with games and sacrifices, to the shrine of Apollo at Deli, if that god would aid him in his attempt to destroy the Minotaur, and deliver the Athenians from the terrible tax of human blood; and the vow was kept. This was the mythical origin of the stated voyages of the Athenians to Deli, and their numerous offerings and regular festivals before the sacred shrine. So important was this pilgrimage deemed that no prisoner was executed in Athens during the four or five weeks occupied on the voyage to and from Deli, and the performance of the religious rites there; and to this custom Socrates owed the thirty days' communion with his friends between his condemnation and his death. The Delians themselves established a quinquennalia in honour of a statue of Venus, the gift of Ariadne to Theseus, and said to have been deposited in Deli by that hero; and at this festival it was customary to dance a peculiar, sinuous, winding dance, supposed to represent in its motion the intricate labyrinth of Crete.

The Confederacy of Delos was the outcome of the Grecian struggles with Persia. This was the most spirited and glorious period of Grecian history, the period of Marathon, Thermopylæ, Salamis, Platæa, Mycalé, and which revealed to the Greeks the necessity of maintaining a well-equipped navy if they wished to preserve their independence. The wealth of Athens; the attention which she had already devoted to the formation of a fleet, and the fortification of the Piræus; the conspicuous skill and bravery which she had displayed at the battle of Salamis, all marked her out as the head of the new Confederacy. Sparta was offended, but for a while she had to submit. Most of the Grecian islands joined the Confederacy, and the temple of Apollo and Diana at Deli was the periodical place of meeting of the confederated assembly, as well as the treasure-house of their accumulated funds. The sacredness of the island was a sufficient guarantee for the safety of the treasure. No one would dare to violate the sanctuary of the gods. A temple of local fame might have been a tolerably safe place for depositing private wealth, but for public wealth the universal fame of the temple must be assured. It must be acknowledged sacred by all the people, and Delos was so acknowledged; and for a maritime confederacy it had the advantage over Delphi of being an island, and in the midst of the States who had entered into a compact to defend their country against the well-nigh overwhelming and inexhaustible forces of a common foe.

That the oracle at Deli was universally revered, and that the island of Deli was held sacred by all the nations, may be abundantly proved. The island was the summer residence of Apollo, and the festival commenced with the returning warmth of the year. This is set forth, as well as the wide-spread fame of the sacred island, in a figurative description of Æneas, by the mention of Scythians from the north and Cretans from the south joining hands before the altars. Æneas is represented as going forth to the chase—

> " Like fair Apollo, when he leaves the post
> Of wintry Xanthus, and the Lycian coast ;
> When to his native Delos he resorts,
> Ordains the dances, and renews the sports ;
> Where painted Scythians, mixed with Cretan bands,
> Before the joyful altars join their hands :

> Himself, on Cynthus walking, sees below
> The merry madness of the sacred show.
> Green wreaths of bays his length of hair inclose;
> A golden fillet binds his awful brows;
> His quiver sounds."

Here we have a view of the religious festivities, the wild play of these children of the world; for humanity was then young, and spake as a child, felt as a child, thought as a child, and had not even dreamed of putting away childish things. Cynthus is only a hillock, but from its summit may be seen all the tiny isle. Further south than Crete, however, had the fame of Deli spread, if we may take the evidence of the massive architectural remains that now strew the island. On the top of Cynthus are the traces of a noble temple, and among its broken marbles have been found the inscription of a vow to Serapis, Isis, and Anubis. There must have been some connection, therefore, between the sacred isle and these Egyptian deities; and we may the more easily believe this, because of the myth that the waters of the fountain at Deli rose and fell with the waters of the Nile. It would appear, too, as if the palm had been cultivated in Deli, as sacred to Apollo. It was certainly a wonder among the islands of Greece, and it may possibly have been introduced by the Egyptians. We have the record of an immense brazen palm tree erected here in honour of Apollo, which, during a violent storm, was thrown down, and overturned in its fall a colossal statue dedicated to Apollo by the Naxians. A part of this statue is said to be still among the ruins of Deli. The brazen palm tree may have been erected after the living plant had disappeared; but that the living plant, in very early times, did exist here, we may conclude from Ulysses' comparison of Nausicaa to the beauty and stateliness of the palm tree, when he met her on the beach at Phæacia, and implored her protection.

> "I never view'd till this blest hour
> Such finish'd grace! I gaze, and I adore!

> Thus seems the palm, with stately honours crown'd
> By Phœbus' altars ; thus o'erlooks the ground ;
> The pride of Delos. (By the Delian coast,
> I voyaged, leader of a warrior host,
> But ah, how changed ! from thence my sorrow flows ;
> O fatal voyage, source of all my woes !)
> Raptured I stood, and as this hour amazed,
> With reverence at the lofty wonder gazed :
> Raptured I stand ! for earth ne'er knew to bear
> A plant so stately, or a nymph so fair."

It would seem by the passage in parenthesis that Ulysses had consulted the oracle at Deli, and, misunderstanding the answer, traced his subsequent sorrows thereto. Other evidences of the wide-spread fame of Deli, and the universal reverence with which it was regarded, may be obtained by searching the ruins, and deciphering on the overthrown and defaced entablatures the names of Philip of Macedon, two or three Mithridates of Pontus, and Nicomedus of Bithynia. The Romans respected its sanctity, and refrained from taxing its people. A magnificent city must have covered a great part of the island at one time. The splendour only remains in its ruins. Everything is overturned. So extensive and cumbersome are the fallen fragments, that the little soil which might have been cultivated is obliged to lie waste. Deli is forsaken and desolate. The oracle is not only dumb, but dead.

We can hardly credit to what extent the sacredness of Deli was observed. The sound of war was unknown in the island. When the Persian fleet, under Datis and Artaphernes, crossed the Ægean, and having subdued Naxia approached Deli, the Delians fled to Tino ; but Datis sent a message after them, to remonstrate with them, and persuade them to return home, for, said he, " I have been commanded by the king to forbear practising any sort of hostilities in a country where two gods were born, or using violence of any kind against the inhabitants or the place." He would not even permit a single soldier to land in the island, but sent by a messenger a large quantity of frankincense to burn upon the altars of the gods. Enemies at war with each other, driven by stress of weather, or other circumstances, into the harbour at Deli, have not only suspended hostilities while there, but have become friends for the time, visiting the temples together, and vying with each other in doing honour to the gods. The Athenians, after purifying Deli by the removal from the island of all dead bodies, and the re-interment of the bodies in Rheinea, passed a law to the effect that neither births nor deaths were to be permitted in the island, if they could be at all prevented; but that all births and deaths were to take place in the neighbouring island. The rights of asylum were also granted to any one fleeing to and dwelling in so sacred a place. Even dogs were refused admittance, in order that birds and hares might not be molested, and that thus the place might be preserved from the pollution of violent death; and for the same reason it is said that animal sacrifices were forbidden, and that only the purer and more innocent sacrifices of fruits and wines, costly vestures and wealth in all its varieties, were acceptable. The place was jealously guarded against the more dread and ghastly rites of heathenism. Gladness was the prevailing feature in the worship at Deli.

The Ægean is in the midst of a powerful volcanic region, and once Deli was severely shaken. It was an unusual occurrence, although common in Mycone, a few miles to the east of Deli; and so awe-inspiring a catastrophe in the sacred island, which, within human memory, up to this time, had been entirely free from these visitations, was regarded as a certain portent of coming misery to the Grecian States. The belief in the portent was strengthened by the agitation then felt throughout all Greece, resulting in the Peloponnesian War, during which, for long years, the Greeks wasted their blood and treasure in a fratricidal struggle. The earthquake in Deli proved to be the commencement of a long series of calamities, for other earthquakes followed in different parts of Greece, and the plague ravaged her cities, and drought and famine oppressed her, as if the powers of nature, in the fulness of their sympathy with so intellectual and artistic a people, were warning them to desist from self-destruction, and unite to meet a coming common foe. But Sparta was too pugnacious, and Athens was too ambitious; and when the Macedonian arose they fell before him, and his successors in their turn fell before the invincible legions of Rome. The opportune earthquake, the apparently preparatory shock in sacred Deli would enhance the reputation of the oracle, and more deeply establish the authority of Apollo from his shrine in the centre of the Cyclades.

In the island of Paros, or Parichia, one of the larger islands of the Cyclades, to the south of Deli, are several very deep caverns, the remains of ancient quarries, whence was dug the world-known Parian marble. The closeness of the grain and the exceeding whiteness of this stone, so well adapted for statuary, secured for the island a prosperous and lucrative trade. It possessed several safe and large harbours, and was blessed with a fertile soil, and therefore became one of the wealthiest islands in the Archipelago. Two famous men were born here, one a poet, the great satirist, Archilochus, who threw his extraordinary bitterness into Iambic measures, and thereby became the father of Iambic poetry; the other a sculptor, Scopas, the remains of some of whose work may now be seen in the British Museum. He specially excelled in single figures, and the beautiful statue of Aphrodite in the Louvre at Paris is supposed to be from his chisel. His groups, however, are very successful, as we may judge from the familiar one of Niobé and her children, represented as fleeing toward each other in surprised terror when about to fall beneath the shafts of Apollo and Diana. The attitude of the figures, the facial expressions, and the entire grouping betray the genius of a master mind. We know nothing of the life of Scopas beyond the fact that he was a Parian. But of Archilochus we know that his mother was a slave, and that he was consequently despised by his countrymen. The daughter of Lycambes was betrothed to him, but afterwards bestowed upon another; and this event feathered the arrows of his genius, and winged them home to the family who had wronged him; and so deeply mortified were they by the stinging shafts that they put an end to their own lives. Archilochus wandered to Thasos to find a social atmosphere more congenial than that of his own country, and wandered from Thasos to other lands, but was everywhere disappointed; and, returning home as restless as when he went away, perished in a fight between his own countrymen and the Naxians.

Paros was connected with the disgrace and ruin of a more famous man than either her own poet or sculptor. The great hero of Marathon, Miltiades, after the battle, when

> " The flying Mede, his shaftless broken bow ;
> The fiery Greek, his red pursuing spear ;
> Mountains above, Earth's, Ocean's plain below ;
> Death in the front, Destruction in the rear ! "

conferred immortal honour on him and Greece—Miltiades, strange to say, degraded himself so far as to obtain from the willing Athenians seventy ships, and, without their knowledge, proceeded to Paros to punish the islanders because of a personal grudge he had against one of their leading citizens. The private and unworthy enterprise miscarried. The Parians were closely blockaded many days, and were delivered by an accidental fire to the wood of a neighbouring island, which was misunderstood to be the signal of approaching help from the Persians. Miltiades had been persuaded, by a priestess of Ceres, to visit the temple in the dead of the night, under the promise that she would then reveal to him how he might succeed in obtaining possession of the island, and, being struck with superstitious fear when within the temple precincts, rushed out, and seriously lamed himself by stumbling over one of the surrounding fences or barricades; and, in this lame condition, with the wound festering beyond all hope of cure, he was carried before the tribunal at Athens, and narrowly escaped the sentence of death. His heroic victory at Marathon saved him. But his misconduct was punished by a fine heavy enough to discharge the expenses of his unlawful expedition, and very soon the wounded thigh put an end to his glory and his shame.

Naxia is a large and very fertile island to the east of Paros, reputed by some to produce the richest wine in the Archipelago, but the general opinion is that Chios and Samos share the honour with Naxia, and certainly we are more familiar with the name Chian, and especially Samian wine.

"Fill high the bowl with Samian wine!"

exclaims Byron, in one of the most exquisite of his Grecian poems, the very spirit of which is embodied in the passionate abruptness of its last line—

"Dash down yon cup of Samian wine!"

Naxia, however, is the supposed birthplace of Bacchus, and it was here he was joined by Ariadne. By his command Theseus left her in the island of Naxia. The Naxians worshipped her under the twofold representation of a favoured and happy goddess, and a forsaken and melancholy wife, celebrating festivals appropriate to each condition at certain stated times. The wine of Naxia was certainly very famous, or else we should not have these stories of its connection with Bacchus; indeed, the Naxians say Bacchus himself taught them how to cultivate their vines, so that we need not wonder to hear the wine of Naxia styled "the nectar of the gods." Naxia is very productive. Not only do vines flourish, but many other kinds of delicious fruits—oranges, lemons, pomegranates, figs, olives, citron, apricots, besides which there is no small amount of pasturage, all conducive to the increase of wealth and population. Its wealth was further increased by the presence of a green marble, spotted white, peculiar to Naxia, and the presence of a still more precious and rarer stone, the emerald, and that of the purest and most costly kind, which has been found in its western hills. In ancient times Naxia was able to bring eight thousand heavy armed troops into the field, and possessed a considerable and efficient navy. Its alliance was therefore coveted in the Persian and Peloponnesian Wars by each contending power. The Naxians distinguished themselves by their extraordinary bravery at the battle of Plataea. They favoured the republican form of government, and were therefore the natural allies of the Athenians; and beneath this form of government they attained their greatest power, even extending their authority over the neighbouring islands of Paros and Andria.

The island of Mycone, to the east of Deli, is very scantily supplied with water, and consequently barren. Numerous earthquakes have shaken the place. Here were buried the fabled centaurs killed by Hercules—at least, so report says, but no one can show their graves. The inhabitants are few, and once were said to be mostly bald—not an undesirable peculiarity in so hot a clime; but, if the peculiarity still exists, we may hope that the priests of Mycone, for the sake of appearances, and the veneration with which they are regarded because of their long hair, and the sanctity mysteriously adhering thereto, do not share this peculiarity with the people. A bald-headed, bare-faced Greek priest would be as great a curiosity as a long-bearded, shock-headed English clergyman.

The pleasant, mountainous, fruitful island of Tenos is to the north-west of Mycone. Neptune was the ancient patron of this island, and was worshipped by the islanders, not only as the god of the ocean, but as an older Æsculapius, the god of medicine. He once brought a flock of storks into the island, and the deadly serpents with which the island was infested had been destroyed by them—a fable setting forth the god's triumph over disease. Neptune is now forgotten, and the Virgin Mary has taken his place. An old image of the Virgin was found many years ago in Tenos. It is by no means flattering to the Virgin's personal appearance. But the principle accepted without question in the East is, the uglier the image the greater the virtue; and therefore this image is surcharged and brimming over with miraculous powers. It is not an idol, but an image, an icon, a sacred picture of the Virgin, with its painted face and its tinsel covering; and for the edification of the healthy pious, and the healing of the generous and penitent sick, the icon is paraded once a year through the streets of the town. Many thousands of people gather from the neighbouring islands, and even from Athens and Smyrna, to see this wonderful image, and take part in the religious festival. The cures are marvellous, according to common report; the veneration is still more marvellous, according to actual vision. Nevertheless, the bulk of the people meet probably because it is customary to meet, a time for holiday-making and general rejoicing; and maybe their feelings differ very little from the feeling of the islanders two thousand years ago when they celebrated the festivals of the earth-shaking, and to them, if not to others, the health-giving deity.

These quiet, beautiful islands of the Ægean have been the home of superstition for long ages. The excrescences of Christianity were multiplied rapidly, and overgrew the original stock, hiding and malforming the reality and truth of the Christian religion. These islands afforded an unmolested sanctuary for all kinds of monkery, and whatever tended to increase the influence and authority of the monks was here developed to its utmost degree. The worship of images was carried to an alarming length in Constantinople, and the people were possessed with a profound veneration for these representations of the Christ, and the Virgin, and the saints; but in the Archipelago worship became rank idolatry, profound veneration became outrageous superstition, and the monks favoured this declension from the purer and more spiritual aspects of religious life, because they themselves were greatly benefited thereby. When Leo, the Isaurian, issued the Imperial edict for the abolition of image worship, Constantinople was thrown into a tumult, but the islanders of the Archipelago were roused to rebellion. They fitted out a fleet, erected their consecrated banners, besought the protection and assistance of their icons, and courageously advanced upon Constantinople. They had made up *their* minds that the hand of the iconoclast should be withered, and that the Imperial crown should be removed from the head of the despiser and breaker of the holy images. Another and a worthier than *he* should wear the purple. So the islanders confidently believed, and steering through the Hellespont and across the Propontis, expected to be put into possession of the Imperial city by a mighty miracle; but there was no miracle, only *Greek fire* from the exasperated soldiers by which both they and their fleet were almost entirely destroyed. This event reveals the spirit of the islanders, as well as their superstition; and, if the veneration for images had been finally and universally condemned, it would have been a difficult matter to have rooted up the evil in these small islands of Greece.

Andros, or Andria, is only one mile to the north-west of Tenos, and runs narrowly forward in this north-westerly direction to within ten miles of Eubœa, now known as Negropont. Like Tenos it is a fruitful and hilly island, but appears to have been poorer than many of the Cyclades. In very early times it belonged to the Pelasgians, given to them, so it was said, as a ransom for Ascanius, the son of Æneas, whom the Pelasgians had made prisoner. It openly favoured the Persians, and for that reason was besieged by Themistocles immediately after the battle of Salamis, who informed the islanders that they must pay a heavy fine for their misconduct, and that in order to obtain the fine he had procured the assistance of two powerful gods, Persuasion and Force. The Andrians were ready with a bold and ingenious answer. "We also," said they, "have two powerful gods, Poverty and Impossibility. They dwell in our island, and are very fond of it, and will not remove to new quarters." We cannot say whether this was exactly correct or not, but the avaricious Themistocles failed to screw anything out of the Andrians, or even intimidate them. The Persians again found them friendly, and apparently could rely upon them until their own power was broken by Alexander of Macedon.

Gyarus, or Gyrae, is a very small island directly west of Tenos. It has the unenviable reputation of being the most barren and desolate island in the Grecian seas, and, like Serpho, was employed by the Romans as a State prison. The very mice of Gyrae, for lack of other food, were said to gnaw the iron ore which had been dug out of the mines —a fable undoubtedly teaching the utter impossibility of subsisting on the produce of the soil. A fine passage in the Odyssey is connected with this island, fine in its concise descriptiveness, and fine in its teaching concerning the results of a loud and proud self-glorification.

> "By Neptune rescued from Minerva's hate,
> On Gyrae, safe Oilean Ajax sate,
> His ship o'erwhelmed; but, frowning on the floods,
> Impious he roar'd defiance to the gods;
> To his own prowess all the glory gave:
> The power defrauding who vouchsafed to save.
> This heard the raging ruler of the main;
> His spear, indignant for such high disdain,
> He launched; dividing with his forky mace
> The aërial summit from the marble base:
> The rock rush'd seaward, with impetuous roar
> Ingulf'd, and to the abyss the boaster bore."

Quite as remarkable a passage, and more artistic, though not so concisely descriptive, illustrating the punishment of audacious impiety, may be found in Virgil's "Æneis."

> " Salmoneus, suffering cruel pains, I found,
> For emulating Jove, the rattling sound
> Of mimic thunder, and the glittering blaze
> Of pointed lightnings, and their forky rays.
> Through Elis, and the Grecian towns, he flew :
> The audacious wretch four fiery coursers drew :
> He waved a torch aloft, and, madly vain,
> Sought godlike worship from a servile train.
> Ambitious fool ! with horny hoofs to pass
> O'er hollow arches of resounding brass ;
> To rival thunder in its rapid course,
> And imitate inimitable force !
> But he, the King of heaven, obscure on high,
> Bared his red arm, and launching from the sky
> His writhen bolt, not shaking empty smoke,
> Down to the deep abyss the flaming felon struck."

There is a deep religious tone in these passages, an unwavering condemnation of irreverence, the outbreathing of the most solemn instincts of our nature ; and atheism, particularly blatant atheism, which sometimes looks back fondly to those far distant ages, and longs for their renewal in the earth, would have stood a very poor chance of a hearing, and no chance whatever of a following, among these simple children of the race. Men have always been religious. Atheism is not only the denial of the deity, but the contradiction of humanity.

Zea and Thermia are the two most western islands of the Cyclades. They lie off the coast of Attica, and are both very fertile. The latter, as its name indicates, possessed several hot springs, more renowned in ancient times than now. On its southern shores lie the remains of a fine and well-built city. The former is the larger and more fertile island of the two, and has obtained wide fame as the first place in Europe where silk was spun and manufactured from the cocoon of the silkworm. It was not like the closely-woven silk of China, but a thinner and more gauze-like material, and was much esteemed by the wealthy ladies, and even the gentlemen, in the effeminate days of the declining Roman Empire. So productive was the soil of Zea, so fine the pasturage, and so plentiful and delicious the fruit, that the inhabitants multiplied exceedingly, and the population had to be restricted by the most unpleasant method of poisoning the people on the attainment of their sixtieth year, with the alternative, however, of permitting them to quit the island at sixty if they so preferred, but then to leave all their goods behind. Surely not many would be found willing to retire to Zea for the quiet enjoyment of the evening of life with the prospect of so abrupt a termination. In all climes men prefer towards the end of life a long twilight gradually deepening into darkness rather than the sudden rush of darkness over the pleasant evening sky. However desirable a residence Zea might be, it must have required a spirit of stoical endurance calmly to choose it in the face of its personally inconvenient, even if publicly beneficial, law.[1]

Zea has had its great men—its physician, Erasistratus; its philosopher, Aristo; its poets, Bacchylides and Simonides, the last-named outrivalling all the others in the greatness of his fame. He lived in Athens' most glorious period, and sang of the great battles of Marathon, Thermopylæ, and Platæa; of Artemisium and Salamis. He was a contemporary of Pindar and Æschylus, but a much older man than they; and long after other men sing their last he sang still, and at eighty years of age gained the prize at Athens for the dithyrambic chorus, which made the fifty-sixth prize taken during his life. His special genius was displayed in the composition of threnodies, poetical lamentations for the heroic departed; and he had a singular aptitude for touching the deep sympathies of his hearers. A remarkable

[1] Mr. Anthony Trollope may have derived the central idea of his pleasant book, "The Fixed Period," from this peculiar Zean law.

story is told, illustrating the punishment of the same self-glorification and impiety as the poetical passages quoted above, of a visit paid in the younger years of Simonides to the court of Scopas, at Crannon, in Thessaly. The proud and wealthy man arranged with the poet for the recital of a poem at a public banquet on his own famous deeds. As the custom was, Simonides introduced into the poem, by way of variety, the exploits of the twin gods, Castor and Pollux. Scopas was dissatisfied. He grudged the praise bestowed upon the heroic divinities. Simonides finished, and was about to receive the promised pay, when the vain man said, "Here is my half of thy pay; the Tyndarids, who have had so much of thy praise, will doubtless furnish the other." The confusion of the poet, amid the rude laughter of the Thessalians surrounding the board, may be well imagined. A message came that the poet was wanted without by two young horsemen. He was glad to go. But upon leaving the hall no horsemen were visible. The twin gods had vanished. And no sooner was the poet clear of the roof than down it fell, and buried the proudly impious man and his vulgar applauders in a general ruin. We may reject the myth while we accept the parable. The feeling of the people who invented, and told, and retold the story is in it, the feeling that the gods will brook no insult, and that profanity is a disgrace to man.

There are other and less important islands of the Cyclades to the south and east. Whether it was one of them, or one we have named where Byron's Haidée lived, and loved, and died, we cannot say. One of the many islands he must have had in view there can be no doubt; and perhaps the basis of his story he heard from the islanders themselves. Which of the Cyclades it was we know not; we only know

> " That isle is now all desolate and bare,
>   Its dwellings down, its tenants pass'd away;
> None but her own and father's grave is there,
>   And nothing outward tells of human clay:

> Ye could not know where lies a thing so fair,
>   No stone is there to show, no tongue to say,
> What was; no dirge, except the hollow sea's,
> Mourns o'er the beauty of the Cyclades."

Syra is in the centre of the northern portion of the Cyclades. The finest view of the "scattered isles" may be obtained from one or another of the heights above the town. There they lie—to the east, Deli and Mycone; to the north, Gyrae, Tenos, and Andria; to the west, Zea, Thermia, and Serpho; to the south, Siphanto, Paros, and Naxia, all clearly visible, with smaller islands and rocks, and in the distance the dim outlines of others, presenting in their quiet and varied beauty one of the loveliest scenes on earth.

> " Eternal summer gilds them yet,
>   But all, except their sun, is set."

A sad reflection, truly, but there is hope of a resurrection, if not to their former splendour, yet to true freedom and affluence, in the restored kingdom of Greece, should Greece be wise to make the most of her opportunities, to cultivate all useful arts, and especially to educate, to draw out the versatile genius still slumbering in the bosoms of her sons and daughters. Of the dim heights visible from the hills of Syra none are more interesting than those opposite the lofty lands of Negropont, away to the north-west, where

> " The mountains look on Marathon,
>   And Marathon looks on the sea."

When we entered the Doro channel, on the return voyage, between the mountains of Negropont and the isle of Andria we were much nearer Marathon, but Pentelicus was then shrouded in darkness, and the memorable plain hidden beneath the evening shades. We passed in the silence of the night, and over the silent seas, but not more silent are they than the plain where ten thousand Greeks met ten times ten thousand Persians, and, in their country's defence, defeated them. So low may a country be brought that its most precious spots will lie uncared for, even violated without rebuke, nay worse, sold for a paltry sum, as the entire plain of Marathon, with its tumulus, where, once inurned, reposed the ashes of the Grecian heroes, was actually offered to Lord Byron for about nine hundred pounds. Any one else might have bought it for the same money. Well might the poet sadly breathe forth his pathetic patriotism for his adopted country—

> " And where are they? and where art thou,
>   My country? On thy voiceless shore
> The heroic lay is tuneless now—
>   The heroic bosom beats no more!
> And must thy lyre, so long divine,
> Degenerate into hands like mine?
>
> 'Tis something in the dearth of fame,
>   Though link'd among the fettered race,
> To feel at least a patriot's shame,
>   Even as I sing, suffuse my face;
> For what is left the poet here?
> For Greeks a blush—for Greece a tear."

Upon leaving Syra for the Dardanelles we passed between Tenos and Mycone, and obtained a clear view of fertile Icaria, and, to the south-east of Icaria, rocky and lofty Patmos. Very small is Patmos, and in itself unimportant and uninteresting, but, among all the islands of that beautiful sea, where will you find one so deeply pathetic in its associations to all who have experienced the inward power of the Christian religion? In this barren islet, this prison surrounded by the deep waters, the beloved disciple received the Saviour's messages for the seven churches of Asia. The shores of Asia were visible in clear weather, and especially the promontory of Mycalé, in the neighbourhood of his adopted city, Ephesus; but the sea lay between. He and his people were separated; and the sea, with its wide spaces, was a symbol of the separation. Sorrow had separated them, the sorrow of persecution; and the sea, with its bitter waters, was a symbol of sorrow. The Church was restless beneath the persecution, and his own life was restless, tossed hither and thither in his work for the Master; and the sea, with its incessant motion, was a symbol of unrest. There was mystery in all this work, in its very restlessness, in the divine permission of persecution, in the spread of the good news through persecution; and mystery in the human life, the life of the world, which this work was designed to uplift and bless, and still mystery in the more than human life of Him who commenced the work, and committed it to His followers,—and the sea, with its fathomless depths, was a symbol of mystery. How comforting it would be to St. John, when, toward the close of his Apocalyptic vision, he beheld the "new heaven and the new earth: for the first heaven and the first earth were passed away; *and there was no more sea!*" The separation, the bitterness, the restlessness, the mystery, all gone; the tabernacle of God with men, and God dwelling with them; no more death, neither sorrow, nor crying, nor any more pain; the former things passed away.

But the sea by which St. John was surrounded on that lonely isle, and which was ever before his vision and within his hearing, furnished him with other symbols. The pavement of heaven was like a sea of glass mingled with fire; the voice of the glorified Christ, and the praises of the heavenly multitude, were like the sound of many waters. These were symbols naturally suggesting themselves to one who was constantly gazing across the glittering deep, and who heard always either the gentle murmuring of the waves or the thunderous roll of the billows upon the shore. It was a desolate situation, a cruel exile for a man of so sociable and loving a disposition as the Apostle John; but where could a more fitting theatre have been found for the display of the mystic marvels which he was commanded to record for the blessing of the churches than the little mountainous island of the Ægean? Jesus Christ knew where to put His beloved one; and the grand oriental imagery of the Revelation with which the Scriptures close,—the beauty and majesty of the book,—would have suffered if St. John had not been in some place like Patmos, where brilliant stars stud the midnight sky and the midday firmament is filled with dazzling glory and the marble cliffs are bathed in the splendours of the sunrise and the sunset and the deep azure of heaven is reflected in the burning sapphire of the sea.

Patmos must ever remain of unique interest as the last place where Christ appeared to the last and most beloved of the apostles. But was it an actual appearance? or was it simply a vision like all the visions which followed? I know not; all I know is that to St. John himself the appearance was real enough. "I was in the Spirit on the Lord's day," he says, and the actual or visionary character of the appearance depends upon what is meant by being *in the Spirit*. In that spiritual condition he saw, sufficiently clear to describe in minute detail, the form of his glorified Lord. Whatever haziness there may be about other sights recorded in the book, this sight of the Master was so vividly impressed upon his vision that we can see Him too. In the midst of the seven golden candlesticks He stands, clad in a long robe, and girt about the paps with a golden girdle; with His snow-white hair, and shining face, and flaming eyes, and glowing feet; seven stars glittering in His right hand, and a bright sword proceeding from His lips; and when those lips opened, a voice like the music of the sea. A most wonderful appearance, and, if only symbolical, well worth the Church's careful consideration as the last recorded appearance of our Lord Jesus Christ upon the earth.

As Patmos withdrew behind Icaria, we came within view of Samos, a large Ionian island near the Asiatic coast.

This island has played an interesting part in Grecian history. Other two islands were also known by the name Samos, one near the Thracian coast, called Samothracia, the other among the group of islands on the western coast of Greece, now known as Cephalonia. The Ionian Samos was by far the most historically important of the three, mainly because of its location, although the Thracian Samos had a religious reputation at one time second to none, and for centuries second only to Deli, among the islands of the Grecian seas. The proximity of Samos to the prosperous towns of Ephesus and Miletus, and the fertile Asiatic shore and the fertility of Samos itself, gave it a high position and importance in olden times; and, under its tyrant Polycrates, one of those remarkably fortunate men with whom everything seems to go well until they are suddenly entrapped and completely ruined, it threatened to become the master not only of all the neighbouring islands, but of a considerable part of the mainland. Polycrates entered into a compact with Amasis, King of Egypt, by which he and Amasis engaged not to attack each other, that they might be free, without fear of each other, to attack the weaker States about them. News of the unhindered success of Polycrates was brought to Amasis, and, under the superstition that such like success boded no good, that a run of fortune without a single mishap was very dangerous in its consequences, that a man rising so rapidly and uninterruptedly to the height of power would be sure to provoke the envy of the gods, he wrote to Polycrates advising him to inflict misfortune upon himself by parting with the object he most prized. Polycrates accepted the advice. He had himself rowed out to sea, and cast from him a most costly emerald, set in gold, and engraved with a peculiar seal; and returned home disconsolate for the loss of his favourite jewel. Several days after a large fish was presented to him, and he had it cooked, and invited to partake thereof the fisherman who had caught and sent it; and behold! when the fish was opened, there was the precious stone. Polycrates despatched a messenger to inform Amasis of the incident, and the superstitious Egyptian was so amazed, and so confirmed in his fear that Polycrates would come to some awful end, that he immediately broke the compact lest he too should be involved in the ruin. As a matter of fact the end of Polycrates was a most miserable one, and in entire contrast with his fortunate career. The cruel Persian satrap of Sardis had been taunted by a brother satrap with the fact that he had not yet subdued the island of Samos, and, because of this taunt, he had conceived a most unreasonable hatred for Polycrates. He watched his opportunity to entrap him, succeeded by foul treachery, and inflicted upon him the torture and shameful death of the cross.

The Samians were bold sailors. Many of them refused to submit tamely to the tyranny of Polycrates. They fitted out a fleet, and sought the help of the Lacedæmonians. Whether the Samian wine had loosened their tongues unduly, or loquaciousness was a natural failing of these islanders, I cannot say, but the Spartans told them, after the recital of their story, that they had forgotten the beginning of it by listening to the end. A truly Spartan answer; but the Samians were ingenious, and the next time they were permitted to appeal, they brought an empty basket, and pointing at it, simply said, " It is empty." Then these inhabitants of Laconia outdid themselves by their laconic reply. They told them that they need not have spoken; the sight of the empty basket was enough. But the siege of Samos by the Lacedæmonians was not successful. The good fortune of Polycrates did not forsake him. And the Samian revolters, after various fortunes in Siphanto, Argolis, and Crete, found their way to Italy, and are said to have founded the city of Puteoli.

Famous men have been born in Samos, the most famous of all being the philosopher Pythagoras. He was a contemporary of Polycrates, but could not endure the tyrant's rule. He travelled much, and finally settled in Italy. Notwithstanding the fact that he committed nothing to writing, or, if he did, nothing has remained (as he intended nothing to remain, according to some authorities), he permanently impressed his character and teaching upon human history, and looms forth from the shadows of the past a truly great man. He studied the science of numbers, and made the science serve the purpose of imparting profound philosophical truths; the universe to him was a *cosmos*, beautifully regulated, and producing in its harmonious movements the music of the spheres; he taught the theory of metempsychosis, or transmigration of souls, one day reproving a man for beating a dog, because he recognized in the dog's howling the voice of a departed friend. The reproof was not very flattering to his friend's vocal powers. In that theory of metempsychosis we have the recognition of the immortal principle, and the confession of a needful spiritual cleansing by some process or another—a recognition and confession sufficient to place Pythagoras far ahead of the men of his own times. His disciples were gathered mostly from among the learned and wealthy classes, and formed themselves into a philosophical, and afterwards into a religious school, and later still into a political brotherhood, which led to its downfall. Two centuries later it was revived, but so corrupted and malformed as to differ greatly from its original. The earlier and purer Pythagorean system and teaching reveal the extraordinary mental gifts and sound moral life of Pythagoras; and Samos may be reasonably proud of having given him to the world.

As we approached the celebrated island of Scio, we discovered, to the westward, the rocky heights of Psyra, and in the afternoon we were passing

"The safer road, beside the Psyrian isle,"

by which the Grecian voyagers from Troy came home. The mainland opposite Scio runs northward, and forms the Gulf of Smyrna. Both Smyrna and Scio contend, with five other places, for the honour of Homer's birthplace; and most probably he was born either at Scio, or one of the two towns that claim him on the Asiatic mainland, namely, Smyrna and Colophon. The probabilities are against any European birthplace. The Scians are very confident in their claim, mainly because in Scio, in very early times, dwelt a poetical brotherhood who called themselves Homerids, and who traced their origin to the great poet, and also because tradition still points out the place of his birth in the midst of the far-famed Arvisian fields where grew the grapes so full of the most richly flavoured wine. Statuary casting in bronze had its origin in the combined skill of the inhabitants of the two islands, Samos and Scio. The Scians were not only good seamen, but very brave. During the naval engagement with the Persian fleet at Ladé, when the Samian and Lesbian contingents basely sailed away, the Scians continued the fight with only one hundred small vessels against the six hundred vessels of the Persians until they were overpowered by the sheer force of numbers. Scio is an island of the most varied scenery, and exceedingly fertile. It would now support a large population, if its resources were developed, and its people allowed to profit by their industry. One disadvantage is its liability to earthquakes. These violent visitations sometimes fearfully destroy human life and property, and spread terror far and wide. Several years ago an earthquake shook the entire island, bringing down its buildings, killing its people, and leaving sad traces of its havoc to this day. This liability to seismic disturbance Scio shares with the contiguous Asiatic shores. Smyrna has been rocked again and again, and thrown into indescribable confusion, but Smyrna continues very populous, and appears to care little for the heaving forces ceaselessly at work beneath its surface. Where nature puts on a smiling face, and pours her plentiful stores into the laps of the people, it is wonderful how soon the people forget her outbursts of anger, and live as heedlessly and joyously as if she would never be angry again.

A notice to bathers had been posted in Syra, a few days before we left, warning them of a shark which had been seen by some fishermen not far from the harbour, and which was doubtless on the look-out for a hearty meal. No less than three of these voracious monsters were within a few boat lengths of the vessel as we passed along the coast of Scio. Two of them were very large, the other a small one; and perilously near them, making the best of its way toward the shore, was a young turtle. Sharks were hardly ever seen in these waters previous to the cutting of the Suez Canal, and are not frequent visitors now. They find their way from the Indian Ocean into the Red Sea, and are tempted forward through the Canal by the chance of securing something from the steamers, and may therefore be seen occasionally in the Eastern basin of the Mediterranean. The dolphins of the Ægean, which are very numerous, must have a lively time of it when the sharks are about, but, in a chase for life, the dolphin would far outstrip his big unfriendly brother, and laugh at him in the distance. The fleetness of the dolphin is most extraordinary, and, to escape his rapid, sweeping course, the flying fish, a dainty morsel, will leave the water like a darting streak of silver, only to fall again when his large pectoral fins are dry. Small chance of escape has he when once fairly set upon, and while I admired his flight through the air, I felt sad at the certainty of his fate. The shark after the dolphin, and the dolphin after the flying pike; as in the sea, so on the land—

> "Nature is one with rapine, a harm no preacher can heal;
> The Mayfly is torn by the swallow, the sparrow spear'd by the shrike,
> And the whole little wood where I sit is a world of plunder and prey."

We had a beautiful sunset between Scio and Mitylene. The sun went down a flashing splendour, and drew, like fleecy curtains, about the golden gate of his departure, a soft purple haze. The sea upon the horizon was a dark indigo. The haze changed from purple to violet, from violet to maroon, from maroon through all the shades of red to the lightest pinks in the mid-sky; and behind the pinks, and visible through them, were masses of the most delicate green, across which, and across the pinks, as if interlacing them, rays of golden light were shot from behind the darker shades below, and from beyond the sea, in the form of an *aurora borealis*. All these colours were peculiarly subdued. They were not gorgeous, but soft, calm, quiet, filling the mind with the idea, and the heart with a deep feeling, of rest.

In the evening we passed the isle

"Where burning Sappho loved and sung."

The pale moonlight was streaming upon it from a cloudless sky. We passed it again afterwards, and beheld it flooded with the glorious light of day. This large and beautiful island is crowded with historical memories. From the "Iliad" it appears that not only Phrygia and the lands adjacent to the Hellespont acknowledged Priam's sway, but also

"All fair Lesbos' blissful seats contain."

And Agamemnon, perhaps with the aid of the other Greeks, subdued the island, and offered, among other things, to atone for the wrong he had done Achilles, and to win back that matchless hero's aid,

"Seven lovely captives of the Lesbian line."

Its fortunes varied with the varied fortunes of Greece, but Mitylene, its chief city, early became a distinguished seat of literature and art, and maintained its reputation through the chequered events of several centuries. Sappho was justly celebrated for her poetic genius, and also her contemporary Alcæus, and between them they carried the lyric poetry of the Æolians to its loftiest height. Pittacus, the Lesbian, was one of the seven sages of Greece, and having been invested with the supreme power, through the confidence of his countrymen, he used it wisely; and when the island, under his government, was reduced to order, he resigned it again into the hands of his countrymen. We may say of him what can be said of very few, that he governed disinterestedly, and embodied in his government the precepts which he taught. His precepts are among the wisest ever spoken by human lips. One of them was, "The greatest blessing which a man can enjoy is the power of doing good." His precepts, with those of the other sages, were inscribed upon the walls of the temple at Delphi. He had a different view of the culpability of drunkenness from that of many, and one which, if legally embodied and faithfully carried out, must have lessened the evil, and would lessen it now, namely, that every wrong committed while under intoxication deserves double punishment. So eminent for its intellectual refinement did Mitylene become, that Aristotle spent two years in the city to profit by the conversation of its learned men; and, when about to appoint his successor, he delicately decided between the rival claims of Menedemus of Rhodes, and Theophrastus of Lesbos, by calling for some Rhodian and Lesbian wine, after tasting which, he said, "The Lesbian is the best." It continued famous as a resort for learned men in Roman times, and Marcellus, having withdrawn here after the downfall of Pompey at the battle of Pharsalia, could not be persuaded, although granted a free pardon, to leave the refined and scholarly Mitylene for the wealthy and powerful Rome. Cornelia, the wife of Pompey, was waiting in Lesbos for the result of the battle which was to decide the fate of her husband and of the Republic; and, after the battle, hither Pompey fled first, and then, with his wife, to Cyprus, and from Cyprus to Egypt, where he met with his cruel and treacherous death. Lesbos is thereby closely associated with one of the world's great events, as well as with the world's ancient learning, and may again become important if the tide of civilization, which has so long rolled westward, and which may be stemmed on the western frontier, rolls back again upon its source.

I was on the bridge at four o'clock in the morning, watching the dawn break over the mountains of Ida, and the light spread itself

> "Far on the ringing plains of windy Troy."

As the morning advanced, a scene of incomparable beauty presented itself. The islands of the northern Ægean were kindled into rosy flame by the rays of the rising sun, Lemnos behind Tenedos, and Samothracia behind Imbros—Samothracia towering high in the pure morning air, a sea-mountain of exquisite loveliness; and far away to the westward, eighty miles away, but clearly visible, a higher mountain still, all glorious with rosy tints, "the most magnificent mountain imaginable, rising in a peak of white marble ten thousand feet straight out of the sea."[1] That sacred mountain, with its white marble surface, looking eastward over the sea, caught and enhanced the glories of the sunrise, and stood forth, robed in them, a mountain of matchless beauty. Athos, under any conditions, is impressive. When the sun sets, and its magnificent heights are thrown into dark relief, projecting its shadow far across the sea, it strikes the imagination with solemn awe; but never is it seen to such perfection as on clear mornings like these, when its marble precipices are illumined by the first rays of the sun, and swathed in the soft rosy colours of the advancing day. Between Athos and the plains of Troy the broad Ægean spreads itself, its spaces broken here and there by the islands; and opposite Athos, right across the Ægean,

---

[1] Curzon's "Monasteries of the Levant."

the rolling Hellespont pours its waters in a troubled stream far into the calm and quiet sea.

Towards the Ægean the plains of Troy terminate in low gravel cliffs rounded into bays, Besika Bay, where an English fleet has anchored more than once, and perhaps in the very place where lay the ships of the Grecian heroes, being the best known, and the most important; and, about the tops of the cliffs, towards Cape Sigæum, are Turkish hamlets, the occupants of which tickle the fertile land with their diminutive ploughs, and make it smile into flowers, and fruits, and waving corn. Behind the cliff tops, however, lies

> "A vast, untill'd, and mountain-skirted plain,
> And Ida in the distance, still the same,
> And old Scamander (if 'tis he) remain:
> The situation seems still form'd for fame—
> A hundred thousand men might fight again
> With ease; but where I sought for Ilion's walls,
> The quiet sheep feeds, and the tortoise crawls."

Towards the Hellespont the plain runs out into flat land, well-watered and well-wooded; but no trace remains, either towards the Hellespont or the Ægean, of the works of the Grecian heroes built for the protection of their fleet. The prophecy is fulfilled—

> "Vast drifts of sand shall change the former shore:
> The ruin vanish'd, and the name no more."

Seven or eight miles off the coast of Troy lies the small island of Tenedos, behind which, after building the wooden horse, the Greeks hid themselves, feigning despair at ever being able to subdue Priam's city, and wishing the Trojans to believe that they had gone home. The stratagem succeeded, and Troy was taken. To Tenedos, after the fall of Troy, the Greeks returned, and offered sacrifices to the gods, and prayed for favourable winds to carry them again to their native shores. Tenedos has always been an unimportant island. A few people lived upon it in early times, and now some two or three thousand are supported mainly by its vineyards. Here and there are remains of defences erected at different times by the world's armies when they have passed this way, in the pride of conquest or in the humility of defeat.

To the west of Tenedos lies the large island of Lemnos, in shape, and in varied scenery and fertility, as in name, not unlike Lesbos, but smaller, sacred to Vulcan, who was hospitably received here when Jove expelled him from the courts of Olympus. Jove had been punishing his lady for her interference with Hercules by fastening anvils to her feet, and suspending her from the vault of heaven, and Vulcan, out of pity for the Queen of the skies in the awkward and humiliating position in which she was placed, attempted to relieve her, and found, to his sorrow, that it was a dangerous experiment to step between Jove and his wife. By Milton, Vulcan is included among the gods of Pandemonium, and he describes his unexpected descent into Lemnos in these graphic lines:

> "He fell
> From heaven, they fabled, thrown by angry Jove
> Sheer o'er the crystal battlements; from morn
> To noon he fell, from noon to dewy eve,
> A summer's day; and, with the setting sun,
> Dropp'd from the zenith like a falling star
> On Lemnos, th' Ægean isle."

Another god had his home in this island, the god of sleep, but how he came, and why he lived here, it is difficult to find out. Juno, again at her deceitful wiles, wished to seal her great husband's eyelids, that she might, unmolested by him, assist her favourite Greeks

> "Taking wing from Athos' lofty steep,
> She speeds to Lemnos o'er the rolling deep,
> And seeks the cave of Death's half-brother, Sleep."

The island is intimately associated with Grecian mythology.

The Argonauts rested here, and were so kindly treated by the inhabitants that they remained two years, and almost forgot their expedition for the golden fleece; and Jason married Hypsipyle, the queen of the island, and left two children behind him from whom sprang the reigning race. It was to one of them Achilles sold the young Lycaon, Priam's son, who was afterwards ransomed, and met Achilles again on the field of battle, this time, notwithstanding his tender pleading, to die by the famous hero's arm. But leaving myths for more reliable records, we find that the Pelasgians, driven from Attica, settled here, and revenged themselves upon the Athenians whenever opportunity occurred, until Miltiades, when despot of the Thracian Chersonessus, reduced both Lemnos and Imbros, drove out the Persian garrisons and the Pelasgian inhabitants, and added the islands to the territory and government of the Athenians.

In Lemnos is found a peculiar kind of white earth, supposed to possess wonderful medicinal properties. It is said to be an effectual remedy for poisonous bites and stings, running sores, and bleeding wounds. In very ancient times this earth was obtained during the performance of a religious ceremony, and at one particular time of the year; and the custom yet remains, or did until recently, of digging for the earth only on the sixth day of August, and amid the monotonous chanting of Grecian priests, all earth obtained except on this particular day, and with this specific ceremonial, being considered valueless. In enumerating the Grecian fleet, Homer mentions the renowned archer, Philoctetes, who

> "lay raging on the Lemnian ground,
> A poisonous hydra gave the burning wound;
> There groan'd the chief in agonizing pain,
> Whom Greece at length shall wish, nor wish in vain."

Was he in Lemnos for the purpose of benefiting by this mysterious earth? Or, is its supposed virtue, both then and now, merely a superstition, then kept up by the priests, and now by the officials. Having exclusive privileges of sale, the officials are not averse to the practice of a little quackery in return for a well-filled purse.

To the north of Tenedos, and separated from it by the rolling current of the Hellespont, Imbros lifts its spiry cliffs above the troubled waters, an island which has generally shared the same fate as Lemnos, and which has been inhabited by the same race. Perhaps the continual commotion of the sea between Tenedos and Imbros gave rise to the myth that beneath these waters was a cave where the steeds of Neptune, brass hoofed and golden maned, were stabled, awaiting the monarch's return from the field of Troy. And beneath the calmer waters, on the northern side of the isle, between it and Samothracia, was another cave, the secret home of Thetis, where,

> "placed amidst her melancholy train
> (The blue-hair'd sisters of the sacred main),
> Pensive she sat, revolving fates to come,
> And wept her god-like son's approaching doom."

The sea all round here, from the Hellespont to Mount Athos, and along the entire Thracian coast, has been sacred from time immemorial; and now, when the ancient deities are no longer revered, the ἅγιος ὄρός, the *Monte Santo*, the Holy Mountain, lifts its magnificent form above the western border of these waters, and looks over them from the windows of its many monasteries, claiming for them yet the name of a sacred sea.

There is another island, called Thasos, in the northern Ægean, hid from the view of sailors passing in and out of the Dardanelles by the towering heights of Samothracia. It lies near the coast of Thrace, and at one time possessed territory on the mainland. The fertility of the soil, and the richness of its gold mines, conferred upon it wealth and importance; and, after a stubborn resistance, it fell beneath the Athenian power. Afterwards, however, it shook itself free, and managed to maintain a somewhat precarious independence, almost without interruption, until the days of all-conquering Rome. The first well-known Grecian painter was born here, Polygnotus by name, a contemporary of Phidias, but, like most other island-born artists, he made Athens his home.

The most important and picturesque island in the northern Ægean, if not in the entire Archipelago, is Samothracia. Except on one side, where it shelves off toward the sea, it rises in abrupt precipices to the height of six thousand feet, and is therefore the loftiest island in the Ægean. Waving woods run up the sides of this steep sea-mountain, and far into the deep chasms by which the mountain is rent, retaining the mists and clouds that float about it, and fill it with mysterious awe; and when the mists and clouds get clear, and rise above the mountain, and dissolve in the azure sky, these waving woods add greatly to its grandeur. They clothe it with a robe seldom worn by these sea-girt heights. Samothracia is the Monarch of the Isles. The scenery on Samothracia, as well as the appearance of the island from the sea, is magnificent beyond description. The gorges; the precipices; the fountains, some of them clear and cold, some of them opaque, sulphurous, and warm; the trees climbing one above another, and overhanging the gloomy chasms, and the deep blue sea; the flowers in vast profusion, and filling the air with the most delicious perfume; the mountain rising with its converging heights toward the three glorious summits; the summits, black with gathering thunder clouds, or wreathed in soft vapours, or beautifully clear and adorned with the varied lights of the changing day; the wonderful views seaward and landward that open with every turn of the path in the ascent, and, when the ascent terminates, the crowning view comprising the islands of the Ægean; the plains of

Troy closed in by the high ranges of Ida; the peninsula of Gallipoli, with the shores of Thrace, flanked by the Rhodope mountains; *Monte Santo* rising grandly above the tide, and, on very clear days, the outlines of the *Monte Santo* of the ancient world, the celebrated home of the gods, Olympus—all these unite to enforce the claim of Samothracia to the supreme scenic position among the islands of the Grecian seas. This mountainous island often attracts the wandering clouds, and from its summits in their centre shoots out the brilliant lightnings, rolls forth the pealing thunder, sweeps the ocean with its stormy winds, like an awe-inspiring, terror-striking, majestic Sinai of the sea. One recent visitor to that island says, "Never shall I forget the sublime grandeur of the storm that, one afternoon towards sunset, gathered its blackness about the peaks of this sea-mountain, and, there enthroned, flashed lightnings over the sea, and hurled thunders in a succession so quick that one peal had not ceased when another burst on the ear with its deafening crack, roll, and reverberation. In a moment the breeze rose into a gale; the waves suddenly swelled into vast rolling mounds that threatened to break on and engulf us; and the rigging became like the strings of a lyre for the fierce song and whistle of the tempest."[1]

The main interest of Samothracia is in its religious associations. It was the centre of the worship of the mysterious Cabiri, and the only place where the worthy could be initiated in the secret sacred rites. The testimony concerning these rites, and the Cabiri themselves, is so very conflicting, that we may well despair of any definite knowledge; but this conflicting testimony is itself an evidence of the inviolable secrecy maintained by all the initiated, no matter from what clime they came. It was a sin even to pronounce the names of the mysterious Cabiri. But mysterious as they were, to the initiated they were supposed to be ever present, ready to deliver them in danger either

[1] "Samothrace and its Gods," *Contemporary Review*, 1882.

from the forces of nature or the toils of their fellow-men. It has been said that the initiation consisted in crowning the candidate with laurel, tying purple bands about his loins, enthroning him in a sacred grove, and dancing round his throne in a mad revel, unseen by the eyes of any but those who had been danced around before. But surely something beyond this was included in the ancient mysterious rites. This may be only a guess at the ceremonies, and a guess based upon the supposition that Bacchus was one of the Cabiri. The greater probability is that Vulcan was one of the Cabiri, if not the chief of the three, for these mystic divinities seem to have had something to do with the underworld and the subterranean fires. The worship of the Cabiri was an old religious freemasonry, the secrets of which we vainly try to penetrate. The secrets are buried in the colossal ruins of the temples scattered about the entrances to the awful ravines of the island. In its antiquity this mysterious worship is unparalleled among the heathenish rites of the East. Before Delos, in the Cyclades, became a sacred sanctuary; before Delphi, at the foot of Parnassus, delivered its oracles through the tripod-seated Pythian priestess, Samothracia was revered,—its groves were regarded with superstitious awe, its majestic cloud-wreathed heights were fearfully gazed upon, and its deep, dark, impenetrable ravines timidly looked into, as the homes of the most dreaded of the gods. A man could bind himself by no more solemn and terrible vow than the vow of the Cabiri.

Whence had this mysterious worship its origin? The oldest tradition of the East of Europe is that once the Black Sea, and the Sea of Marmora, and the Mediterranean were inland lakes, and that the Black Sea, fed by the great rivers, burst its way through the Bosphorus into the Sea of Marmora, and the Sea of Marmora through the Dardanelles into the Mediterranean, and the Mediterranean between the pillars of Hercules into the Atlantic. This influx of waters caused the Ægean to rise and overflow all its islands except one, the island of Samothracia, and the inhabitants found there a refuge from the terrible catastrophe. When the waters had subsided this mountainous refuge was solemnly consecrated to the gods, and henceforward became the sacred island of the Ægean. What Ararat was to Noah and his family, Samothracia was to the Pelasgians; and this tradition, doubtless based upon fact, may be taken as evidence of the Noachian deluge. These two events were most probably simultaneous. Geological and submarine evidences exist of some such catastrophe, the last of the kind by which the earth has been visited. Before this chain of lakes burst one into another, Europe must have been joined to Asia at the Bosphorus and the Dardanelles, and to Africa by a continuation of what are now the Italian and Spanish peninsulas, dividing the Mediterranean into two parts; and our own island then must have been connected with the European mainland. When these vast areas of pent-up water found an outlet, the face of North-Western Europe, as well as its southern and eastern borderlands, must have been greatly changed; and these great changes have influenced human life, and controlled the currents of human history, far beyond what we can realize.

The natural sublimity, the awful grandeur of Samothracia,—its high, tree-clad peaks; its deep, shadow-burdened, torrent-riven chasms; its storm-clouded summits, whence the thunderous peals ring across the heavens, and the vivid lightnings flash over the seas; and the earthquakes that sometimes rock it to its centre, have had very much to do with its consecration as a sacred sanctuary, and with the supposition that it was the dwelling-place of mysterious deities. The very position of its ruined temples, at the mouth of dark and impenetrable ravines, is an indication of the secret character of its rites; and certainly no more fitting place could be found for the worship of the gods of the underworld, the gods whose very names were too terrible to be spoken, the weird Cabiri, than amid the recesses of this magnificent and lonely island.

One of the earliest stories connected with Samothracia is that of Dardanus, who wandered eastward from Italy, and brought hither his household gods, previous to settling on the shores of the Dardanelles. Æneas, after the fall of Troy, sought for these very household gods their permanent resting-place in Italy again. But there are many stories connected with Samothracia. All the great heroes of antiquity, from the mythological heroes onward to men whose careers are not adorned with fable, and the events of whose lives are matters of common knowledge, visited the island, and were initiated in the mysteries; and by all it was regarded as an inviolable asylum. Here Perseus, the last monarch of Macedonia, after his defeat by the Romans, found refuge for a while, and the Romans never attempted to disturb him during his stay on Samothracia. He was safe under the shadow of the gods.

The splendid view from Samothracia is incidentally referred to in the "Iliad." It commanded "fair Ilion's glittering spires," the ample plains of Troy, the Grecian ramparts and navy; and there

> "on a mountain's brow,
> Whose waving woods o'erhung the deep below,"

Neptune sat, and mourned the losses of the Grecian troops. Thence he flung himself in his fury, yoked his immortal coursers to their chariot, and rode to the succour of his favourite heroes. The heroes are all gone; Neptune himself, with his blue eyes, and hoary beard, and scaly armour, only exists in pleasant imagination; but there rises Samothracia, the majestic sea-mountain of the northern Ægean, unchanged in its waving woods, and stormy peaks, and dark ravines, and all its solitary grandeur.

The most conspicuous object in the view from the top of

Samothracia is Mount Athos. The impressive majesty of this white marble mountain, two thousand feet higher even than the sacred isle, can hardly be surpassed. It was a dread promontory to ancient sailors. The navy of the first Persian expedition encountered a fearful storm while rounding this mountainous headland, in which three hundred ships were wrecked and twenty thousand men were drowned. The second expedition, at immense cost, and by three years' continuous labour, cut a canal through the isthmus behind the mountain to avoid the risk always attending a voyage round it, the traces of which gigantic work are still visible. Seventy-five years later a Spartan fleet was entirely destroyed by a storm near Mount Athos; and the individual instances of shipwreck must be innumerable. It is the Cape Malea of the northern Ægean.

While crowding the islands with sacred associations mythology has left Mount Athos free. Not so Christianity. Here, as in other secluded and easily-defended positions, in order to escape from the molestations of its inveterate enemies, Eastern Christianity has found a place of refuge. Mount Athos has become the Holy Mountain to all the eastern part of Christendom, and from every quarter the eyes of the Eastern Church are turned toward Mount Athos as toward the centre of its religious life. The great monasteries of the Eastern Church—Greek, Russian, Bulgarian, Servian, Iberian, &c.—are clustered here. In the most picturesque situations, extensive buildings, sheltering vast religious communities, may be seen, all living under the order of St. Basil, passing their whole time in a round of sacred duties, very rarely visited by the outside world. Curious relics of mediæval and early Christian ages are treasured here: jewelled pieces of the true cross, old paintings by fathers whose names are now forgotten, rare manuscripts which might throw floods of light on ecclesiastical history. Here they lie, jealously guarded, even though seldom understood, by these long-bearded monks, who chant and pray, and burn the holy candles, and kiss the sacred images for the brethren without, as if they could save them by proxy. No female foot is allowed to tread on *Monte Santo*. For hundreds of years, if the monks may be believed, no female foot has trodden that sacred mount. It rears its white marble pyramid untainted and inviolate into the pure air. Nowhere in the East is there so holy a sanctuary, and to no place do the Eastern Christians turn with greater veneration than to the majestic Mount Athos. And, that such a retreat has its charms, we may believe with Byron, who, speaking of the solitude experienced amid unknown crowds, said—

> " More blest the life of godly Eremite,
> Such as on lonely Athos may be seen,
> Watching at eve upon the giant height,
> Which looks o'er waves so blue, skies so serene,
> That he who there at such an hour hath been,
> Will wistful linger on that hallow'd spot ;
> Then slowly tear him from the 'witching scene,
> Sigh forth one wish that such had been his lot,
> Then turn to hate a world he had almost forgot."

CHAPTER III.

SYRA.

The town—Its appearance—Harbour—Public square—The people—Costumes—Cafés—Wineshops—Market—Trades—Speech—English in Syra—Italian man-of-war—Visit to country garden—Beautiful evening—Singing on the forecastle—Church of the Resurrection—Church of St. Nicholas—Woman and child—Older churches—Sacred pictures—Infirmary—St. Bartholomew's Hospital—Funeral—The observance of Sunday—St. John's Eve: its bonfires, and their origin—Pherecydes—The story of Eumæus.

SYRA is built on the margin of the sea, and on two hills rising rapidly above the margin, one of them conical, and surmounted by the partly built Church of the Resurrection, and one of them winding round into an elevated plateau, whence may be obtained one of the finest views of the Cyclades. There is no other large town so near the sea as Syra in the entire Archipelago; indeed, Syra is the only large town in the Archipelago, and one of the largest towns in Greece. The other towns, or villages, of these beautiful islands lie significantly far away from the shore, on the hillsides, and in the secluded valleys, generally difficult of access—significantly, because for many centuries, and until comparatively recent years, piracy was very common in the Ægean, and, by building their huts and tilling the ground along the shore, the villagers would simply have tempted these robbers of the sea. The protection of their own lives and property demanded the choice of distant and not easily approachable sites for their houses, and vineyards, and olive-yards, and sheep, and cattle, and all their worldly wealth. The oldest part of Syra is furthest from the sea. The modern buildings, erected with the rapid growth of the port since the days of Grecian independence, are near the shore —a sign that the exciting occupation of these Ishmaelites of the sea, whose hand was against every man, and every man's hand against them, is gone.

Syra is a picturesque town, with its squarely-built, flat-roofed, lattice-windowed houses crowded together, and rising one above another on its two hills; every house painted or washed with a light colour, and sometimes with two or three colours—white, grey, blue, pink—and the latticed windows generally green; the larger houses with verandahs, and vines climbing about them, and apricots clustering between them, and oranges ripening in their little courtyards; the Church of the Resurrection, with its lofty dome and its fanciful square towers, guarding the town from one hill, and the Church of St. Nicholas, a larger and more substantial structure, from the other; older and smaller churches, one near the wharf, another behind the public square, mingling with the houses; and, along the wharf, a motley line of dwellings, and shops, and mercantile offices, and store-rooms, looking into a small harbour crowded with craft of all sorts and sizes, from large ocean steamers to tiny buoyant caiques. Behind the town are other two hills, conical in shape, very high, brown and bare, between whose clearly defined outlines is the pure, silvery atmosphere only seen above the sea, and which everywhere suggests to the susceptible nostrils the smell of the sea; while, on either side of these conical hills, other high, brown, bare hills rise and sweep toward the town, shutting it in to the right and left, and adding very greatly to its beauty. Under the serenest of skies, and from the bluest of seas, this town presents a most charming picture; and the charm is enhanced upon entering the harbour and coming within hearing of its babel voices, and within sight of its varied and gaily attired people.

The little harbour, formed by a stone jetty yet in course of construction, and enclosing a portion of an open bay, is very busy. Syra is the port of call for all steamers passing between Smyrna and Athens, and for many steamers on their way to Constantinople and the Black Sea. And it is *the* port of the Cyclades, and even of the more distant islands of the Egean, to which the islanders bring their fruit, and sheep, and cattle, and at which they purchase what they require for their simple lives. The Cunard steamers call occasionally, and frequently the Austrian Lloyd steamers, which convey the passengers hereabouts—large boats, well officered by Austrians and Germans, and well engineered by Scotch and Englishmen, crowded with the most curious human cargo imaginable, attired in every kind of colour, Turks, Greeks, Jews, Albanians, Armenians, Egyptians, Italians, Germans, French, English, the last four in small numbers, all mixing together, and talking one to another, each in his own language, and producing a new confusion of tongues. One or more English steamers discharging coal may always be found in the harbour, with a Grecian barque or schooner clean and trim, and, moored to the wharf closely alongside, the smaller boats of the islanders, slenderly built, sitting lightly upon the water, and yet with wide, rounded, capacious hulls, into which may be stored a well-nigh incredible cargo. With the stern as sharp as the stem, and the single mast groaning beneath a huge lateen sail, these old-fashioned craft are capable of sweeping across the shining spaces between the islands at an amazing speed. I watched one of these boats discharge a cargo of sheep in Syra harbour, sheep of a small breed, and, as I afterwards proved, mutton not very juicy or tender, and I was greatly surprised at the number turned out. Where, in so small a boat, all that live stock could have been stowed, was a mystery; but they had been stowed somewhere, for out they came, quite a flock of them, floundering in the water, and bleating piteously upon the quay. These island boats remind one, by their light construction, and rig, and speed, and enormous carrying capacity, of the views on old coins and antiquated pottery, and the descriptions in ancient writings, of the boats of long past ages; and they are substantially similar. Moving across the water, between the larger boats, in every direction are small caiques, prettily painted, not so long and not so elaborately fitted and ornamented as the caiques of the Bosphorus, but well adapted for the rapid work required, and the small space of water available in Syra harbour. The constantly changing scene, and the variety of life represented, the quaint and tinted town rising above, and the hum of voices from its closely adjoining market mingling with the voices of the people about the ships and boats, and all the sounds peculiar to harbours everywhere, invest the picture with considerable interest, and many a pleasant hour may be passed in quiet observation and reverie in this busy little port of the East.

The most favourable time and place for seeing the people of Syra is in the evening in the public square. Those who can sleep through the middle of the summer day do so, and remain awake to enjoy the cool season between sunset and sunrise. During the summer months, towards the middle of the day, the heat in the Grecian islands is very great, and nowhere greater than in Syra, facing the south-east, and closed in on every other side by high hills. Soon after eleven o'clock all labour is suspended; the well-to-do people retire to their homes, the poorer people crouch in the shadow of the porches, warehouses, awnings, corners of the street, everywhere, and go sound asleep; and the town is hushed into silence, and dreaminess, and siesta, until the intense heat has partially passed away. Signs of returning activity are visible about two o'clock. Gradually the town wakes up again, the streets and harbour resume their accustomed sounds, and work and business are prosecuted until the early evening. Then the people pour into the public square. Then the band commences its stirring music. Then the cafés drive a thriving trade. Every balcony is filled with merry groups. Every seat and table under the trees are occupied by eaters, and drinkers, and loungers. Waiters are running to and fro with rich, aromatic coffee in tiny cups; and delicious lemonade in glasses; and large narghilés, the bubbling pipes of the East, their glass receptacles half filled with water, through which, and, to further cool the fumes, through long serpentine tubes, the perfect smoker sucks the burning, fragrant weed. And on the smooth marble pavement of the open square, bounded right along one side by a partly finished handsome public building, several hundred people and many little children promenade arm-in-arm, and speak the word of greeting to friends and neighbours whom they recognize as they pass along.

The Greeks are a good-looking race. Ages of degeneration have not availed to erase the regular lines of beauty, or to crush out the animated intelligence by which the face is lit up. The old lines are there, and the old light is there maybe more distinctly visible since they have again tasted the sweets of freedom, and rekindled, by actual possession of their country, the fire of patriotism which once glowed so fiercely within their bosoms. Activity, both physical and mental, ready and graceful movements of the body and of the mind (if we may speak in this figurative way of their quick receptive and expressive faculties) are the special gifts of the Greek. The rough fellows at work upon our cargo were lithe, busy, talkative, eyes beaming with light, features extremely mobile, always apparently on the point of a quarrel, and yet in the midst of violent gesticulation bursting into loud laughter. The warm, restless, passionate spirit of the old Hellenes was largely possessed by these begrimed and ignorant men, and these men had in them the stuff out of which heroes are made. To see the better class of well-dressed Greeks promenading in the public square could not but prepossess any one in their favour. The men are fairly tall, slim in figure, gentlemanly in bearing; the women are only of medium height, and even less than that, many of them with an almost faultless regularity of feature, full and sparkling dark eyes, a profusion of dark hair, with a few rare exceptions, and pleasingly graceful in behaviour; both men and women dressing in the prevailing Western costumes, and with very good taste. But the most attractive sight in the public square is the great number of little children, with brown, soft cheeks, and large, bright eyes, trotting along in groups, under the care of their parents or nurses, dressed in the most beautiful costumes, and with a perfect blending of colours; and the fact is forced upon you that these children have happy homes, and are well cared for—a fact of the highest importance to the future welfare of Greece. As the band plays, the children and the men and women step unconsciously to the music, and pass an hour or two away in the salubrious evening atmosphere—an atmosphere which it is a simple pleasure to breathe—in healthy exercise and innocent enjoyment.

Only the better class of Greeks dress in Western costumes. The larger number dress in the characteristic voluminous breeches, and small embroidered jackets, and scarlet scarves, fifteen or twenty yards long, twined round and round and round their middles, in which they fold their cash, and fasten their weapons, and hide away everything of importance; and this dress, modified in certain particulars to meet the necessities of a man's calling, is most commonly met with in the narrow, unevenly paved, steep streets of the town, and almost exclusively met with in the country. There are many Turks in Syra, well known by their features and the inevitable fez, except in the rare case of some renowned pilgrim from Mecca calling at Syra on his way home, and wearing in place of a fez, or rather twined round his fez, the coloured turban to which he has become entitled; and Jews and Armenians mingle with the crowd, attired a little different from their neighbours. But the most striking and picturesque costume met with in Syra, and in most other Grecian towns, is that of

> "The wild Albanian kirtled to his knee,
> With shawl girt head and ornamented gun,
> And gold-embroider'd garments, fair to see."

This kirtle is of white linen in multitudinous folds, gathered about the middle, and stiffly projecting in a circle above the knees, giving the Albanian a comical appearance to the stranger. He himself, however, is supremely unconscious of his comical appearance. He carries himself with a free dignified bearing which it would be plainly dangerous to provoke. His manner implies that he is best let alone; and I fear that the man who caught an Albanian would be worse off even than the man who caught a Tartar.

Cafés are very numerous in Syra, and supply nearly all the population with foods and drinks suitable to the climate. White wines, with fruit and bread, are freely partaken of; indeed, the people mainly live upon them, eating very little flesh meat, notwithstanding its cheapness. Flesh meat in so hot a climate would be detrimental, and the people do not require it, fruit and bread fully supplying all nature's wants. The Turkish custom of coffee drinking, and eating sweetmeats, largely prevails—coffee of the rarest kind, and perfectly roasted, served in dolls' cups, out of which all the aromatic liquid might be thrust by inserting the thumb; and sweetmeats as only Turks and Greeks can make them, sugared gelatines which melt in the mouth like honey, and recall visions of *delight* in years long gone by, when such-like delicacies could be more freely eaten, and were certainly much more appreciated. The sale of *rahatlakoum*, or "Turkish delight," is one of the many minor evidences of the Ottoman influence upon the people of Greece; for although the Ottomans were a fierce and warlike people, they imbibed a taste for, and became addicted to, the Asiatic luxuriousness and epicureanism which distinguished the cities of the Caliphs after the riches of Persia and the far East had fallen into their hands. The Ottomans received the recipe for this sweetmeat from the Arabs, and the Arabs trace its origin to the inventive mind and skilful fingers of Fatima, the daughter of the prophet, who concocted the sweetmeat during her honeymoon for the gratification of her husband, the famous Ali. And when we remember that it is a compound of gelatine, the powdered kernels of apricots, and the pulp of grapes, sweetened with sugar, and further sweetened with honey, and all mixed together with rosewater, we may hope that the heart of Ali, her beloved, was entranced, and we may credit his belief that the ingredients of the confection were revealed to his newly-wedded spouse by the houris of paradise. These and many other things the cafés supply, and, in summer, the people make it a custom, in order to save trouble at home, and to enjoy the shade of the trees, or the currents of air through the narrow streets, and perhaps also the conversation of their neighbours, to take their meals outdoors. The busiest thoroughfares are crowded with cafés, and their tables and chairs are set on the pavement without, and in the coolness of the morning and evening the streets are full of groups at their slender meals, chatting, card-playing, bead-counting, and doing all these together sometimes, uniting the maximum of enjoyment with the minimum of religious devotion.

There are many wine-shops, and a moderate amount of drinking, although it is quite an unusual occurrence to behold a man the worse for liquor. The intoxicating quality of the native wines is feeble, and well it is, for if these fiery Greeks were a drunken race, blood would run very freely in the quarrels consequent thereon. The wine-shops, like most of the other shops, are open to the street; that is, the windows are unglazed, and mostly without frames, simply open spaces in the masonry for the admittance of light and air; and at the back of the shops are arranged the tuns of wine, enormous barrels, raised a little from the floor, and reaching to the ceiling, while over the floor a few rough benches are strewn, which is the only furniture these places can boast of. The smell of the wine is not confined to these places. It seems to pervade the whole town. The smell follows you through every street, and does not leave you even upon the vessel. The first day we were there I became conscious of this aroma, and never completely lost it until we left the island. There it was, very faintly perceptible, as if wine were constantly being heated in some part of the town, and the vapour were constantly diffusing itself through the atmosphere.

The market is a little lively place in a narrow thoroughfare leading from the wharf into the public square. The most noticeable commodity is fruit, of which there are various kinds, and in very large quantities. Fruit is sold by the *ok*, equalling about four English pounds, and the finest and most delicious peaches, apricots, and plums can be bought at twopence halfpenny the *ok*, retail. In the season grapes are very plentiful, and wonderfully cheap, obtainable retail sometimes at a farthing per pound. Other fruits, such as olives, pomegranates, figs, oranges, are proportionately cheap, particularly olives, which are largely consumed by the natives, but which pall upon an Englishman's taste, unless by constant use he has obtained an artificial liking for them. Fish are also sold in the market, not large fresh fish, but very small pickled fish, anchovy, and the like, packed in barrels, and sold out by number. These fish, previous to pickling, are of various bright colours, not dissimilar to the ornamental perch of a domestic aquarium; and the young lads will sit on the edge of the wharf, or a moored boat, and assiduously drop their hooks into the water, in the hope of a bite from one of these little creatures, whom they could swallow at a mouthful. One ragged, wrinkled, dirty, venerable Greek crouched daily, for eight days in succession, and nearly the whole day long, on the wharf's edge, with a bit of thread, and hook, and bait, jerking these unwary bits of coloured life out of the water, as if fishing were a mania with him; and he seemed well satisfied with half a score as the result of his day's employment. If these were what he lived on we cannot wonder at his shrivelled and scraggy limbs, and at his hollow-eyed, dried-up, dark yellow old face. Other fish are eaten beside these. One day I watched a fisherman carry home a good-sized octopus. A hook was thrust through its pulpy head, and its long tentacles, with their formidable suckers, were dangling underneath; and this strange and dreaded creature, frequently found in the Grecian seas, was to be cut up, and pickled, that, by its salty flavour, it might add to the relish of the white wine. Butchers in the market are in a great minority. There are two or three, looking like brigands, with a whole magazine of weapons thrust into the leathern pouch attached to their scarf; and their business is mostly done with the steamers and foreign vessels in the port, who want flesh meat, and who can purchase it here, either beef or mutton, any cut, at twopence per pound.

The different trades of the town are carried on in the open. The climate is too hot for any one to work shut up in a room. Tailors, shoemakers, all artizans follow their employments in the streets, or in the open spaces which form the windows of their dwellings. Portering must be one of the most lucrative callings in Syra, and everything is carried on the backs of fine, short-haired, glossy-skinned asses, almost the only beast of burden adapted to wind through the narrow streets, and climb the steep ascents in the higher part of the town. These asses bring the purest drinking water obtainable on the island into the town, in cool, stone bottles, from which the owners sell it in glasses to the thirsty who can indulge in the luxury of a drink so common in England, and therefore not valued, but in Syra more delicious than wine. The appearance of the town is almost entirely Asiatic; in occupation and manner of life the people are half-Asiatic; the port, and the only important port lying *between* the borderlands of Europe and Asia, partakes of the peculiarities of both continents, and reflects the life of the East and the West.

The one language generally understood by the tradespeople, besides their own Romaic, is French. A person well conversant with French may pass, without much difficulty, through any country in Europe. It is not only the diplomatic language of Europe, but the commercial language, and the language for all international conversation. French words and English money are current everywhere. The chemist in the square at Syra could speak French, but not English, and an English prescription was of no use to him until it had been translated into French. Upon asking another gentleman, who could struggle through a little English, if he would accept English coin, he said, "Certainly! Engleesh mooney the best mooney." Over one establishment, in which a hairdresser carried on his trade, was the ostentatious announcement, "Maison d'Angleterre." Thought I, "Here at last are congenial quarters," and I stepped in to be operated upon. The man of the razor and scissors was quite astonished to find me "Engleese," and knew sufficient about our language to say, after snipping my hair in profound silence for the space of two minutes and a half, "waun frahnc."

There are very few English in Syra. The members of the English Consulate, who occupy a large and pleasant building overlooking the northern side of the harbour, with an extensive marble-paved courtyard at the back, where tropical plants and a few fruit trees flourish; the clergyman of a tiny English church, hidden away behind the market, where the Anglican liturgy is read, and the sacrament of the Lord's Supper administered, and a sermon preached every Sunday morning to a little congregation; one or two clerks in merchants' offices, who bewail the lack of English society, and are glad of the opportunity to see an English face from any steamer that happens to call in port: these constitute the representatives in Syra of our illustrious people. Out of these, and with the addition of a few from English boats in the harbour, we might reasonably expect a larger attendance at the church. But of the twelve present, when I found my way with difficulty along the narrow tortuous streets, and through the door in the wall, two were Swiss, and three or four were Greeks, who had dropped in apparently to gather a little knowledge concerning the English tongue.

An Italian ironclad anchored in the bay while we were there, and the fine brass band came ashore every evening, and courteously played in the public square for the enjoyment of the people. They were well trained, and rendered their pieces with spirit and taste, invariably concluding the evening's performance with the National Anthem of the Greeks, a short and abrupt piece of music, which never failed to elicit shouts of applause. It was very pleasant to see these two new countries, or old countries renewed, fraternizing in a way sure to draw them together, and sure to enlist for each other the kindliest feelings and the deepest sympathy. These Italian sailors shared the proclivities of their seafaring brethren of other nationalities. They came ashore in detachments to enjoy themselves, and one favourite pastime was a gallop on donkey-back into the country. Their equestrianism, if that term may be applied to donkey-riding, was more amusing than graceful, and the faster they could go, and the more violently they were shaken, the greater was their enjoyment of the ride. There is no better fun apparently to those who are tossed upon the sea than to have a tossing upon the land.

Syra is a hilly island. The hills are uncultivated, and there are not many cultivated places in the hollows of the hills. The entrances to some of these hollows are encumbered with massive rocks, clean and bare, as if all the surface soil had been washed from them by a succession of heavy rains; but beyond the entrances, sheltered behind the rocks and between the hills, a few pleasant houses and gardens may be found—houses built centuries ago by Greeks of the Empire, or Genoese, or Turks, and gardens arranged terrace below terrace, and marvellously productive even in their half-neglected state. We drove out one afternoon to a house and garden situated like this, and in this condition, invisible from the main road, and only approachable by dipping into a break-neck hollow, and climbing a rough, steep path, but well worth the trouble, as we speedily proved when there. The house was large and long, with pleasant verandahs. It had been transformed into a semi-café, and two Greek islanders, in their picturesque native costumes, were seated at a small round table, in the shade of a group of olive trees, making a hearty meal of white wine, fruit, and bread. Their asses, fine fleet animals, were waiting patiently for the conclusion of the repast, and, when it was over, carried them away at a quick trot down the rough, steep hill. Confined within a large wire cage, in a kind of outhouse, were a few ringdoves and a number of quails, whether for consumption or to turn into the gardens I could not ascertain. In the gardens were a large number and a great variety of insects. Splendid dragon-flies were darting hither and thither in the hot sunshine in ceaseless quest of prey, and butterflies, sufficiently gorgeous in colouring and peculiar in formation to charm the mind of the most fastidious entomologist, were flitting carelessly among the flowers, and through the orange groves, and between the hanging tendrils of the vines, tempting the hand to capture them; while less brilliant but more homely bees were buzzing their way from flower to flower in that persistent, systematic way which bees have everywhere, collecting their stores of honey for the winter. Hid in the crannies of the rocks and walls, and among the undergrowth, insects without wings might have been found, lizards, scorpions, snakes, centipedes, and others with less than a hundred feet, but very formidable notwithstanding, whose acquaintance very few people desire to cultivate. The precious water from the hills around was carefully collected in stone fountains at the top of the gardens, whence it was carried in little conduits all along the terraces, and down every path, nourishing the roots of the plants and trees—a very necessary precaution, the neglect of which for a single summer would suffice, in this hot climate, to reduce everything to barrenness and desert. In these tiny streams, so well distributed, we have the secret of the luxuriance. Because of these,

> "Here the blue fig with luscious juice o'erflows,
> With deeper red the full pomegranate glows:
> The branch here bends beneath the weighty pear,
> And verdant olives flourish round the year.
>
> * * * * *
>
> Here are the vines in early flower descried,
> Here grapes discolour'd on the sunny side,
> And there in autumn's richest purple dyed."

It was a rare treat to walk through this wild garden. Everything was allowed to grow very much as it liked. Care was bestowed mainly upon the percolating, fertilizing streams, and very little care indeed upon the flowers and plants they nourished; so that terrace after terrace was in a tangle, but such a delicious tangle that it was a pleasure to stride the spaces between the overgrown walks, instead of being confined, as in some gardens, to the trim walks themselves. The smell of the ripening oranges, bending low and tapping the head in passing, and the smell of the clustering grapes, trellissed and covering the long walks, and stretching out to grasp the friendly branches of the trees, and in some places running over the ground, was one to live in the nostrils as a memory for a long time. And to pass through these vineyards and orange groves into spaces where olives, and figs, and pomegranates flourished, threading through them, and up the terraces again to the verandah; and then to partake of the coolest lemonade and the finest coffee, with fruits from this very garden, and sugared gelatines, waited upon all the while with obsequious sedateness by a gentleman in Grecian costume; and afterwards to be driven home by a very brigand of a Greek in personal appearance and violent, erratic horsemanship—all this was strange and exciting, and a true taste of Eastern life.

What a beautiful evening it was as we drove home! That is, to Syra, and our ship's cabin. Any place occupied uninterruptedly for a few weeks becomes very familiar, and its relation to other places briefly visited invests it with the sacred name of home. The moon had hardly attained her full rounded proportions, but she was resplendent, shining gloriously upon the calm sea and the distant islands. The lights of sunset were yet lingering in the mid-sky, and mingling with the tender silvery light of evening. The sea had not lost its blue beneath so clear a firmament. All the islands were as distinctly visible as if it were still afternoon, but darker, with their edges softened in the moon's rays, looking peaceful and asleep upon the quiet tide. As the moon ascended, and the lights of sunset were withdrawn, the scene became lovelier; and I spent an hour, after arriving in Syra, on the mole, gazing across the channel at Deli, between which island and Syra the moon had laid a golden pathway, as if to invite the fancy to wander out to that ancient sanctuary, and look upon the ghosts of heroes assembled before Apollo's mystic shrine.

The shades of evening after the glaring sunshine, and the cooler air after the heated atmosphere of the day, were most enjoyable. We were in no hurry to retire to rest. To look upon the purple waters silvered by the moonlight, and to breathe the sweet, pure, balmy air, was a real pleasure, quite enough for me, but not enough for our crew. They tried to increase the enjoyment by assembling on the forecastle, and singing for two or three hours, without cessation, all the English songs they could remember, to the accompaniment of an old violin. The old violin was a good instrument, and fairly well played; the singers had lusty voices, and could take the different parts moderately, with a decided, but not unpleasant preponderance of bass; and sitting aft, sufficiently far away to lose the grossness, the sound of their mingling voices, and the scraping of the fiddle, were fully appreciated, more so, maybe, because the tones were English, and different from the tones of every one and everything around. But these English tones were not appreciated by several Greeks alongside, who either made their home in the recesses of an old craft, or were employed upon it as night watchmen, for, becoming tired of the incessant singing and scraping, they set up a counter howl, supposed to be an ironical imitation of our serenaders, which had the speedy effect of interrupting their musical flow by causing them to burst into a hearty ringing laugh. But when the laugh was well over, and a few good-humoured spoken salutes in marine English, which is not exactly Queen's English, had been fired at the Greeks, the old fiddle charmed again, and the voices fell in almost automatically with the music of the charmer.

I have had occasion to refer to the unfinished Church of the Resurrection. It crowns the conical north-western hill, and, when completed, will be a fine structure. *When completed:* no one can say how soon, or how late, this will be. It depends upon the offerings of the pious. If the offerings are never made, the church will never be finished, because the ecclesiastical authorities absolutely refuse to go into debt for the erection of any building whatever. No one could persuade them of the wisdom of the course adopted by a certain Christian denomination in England, who are said to build their places of worship by faith, and pay for them by repentance. The Church of the Resurrection has stood many years in this partly finished state, and may stand many more, unless some wealthy man is delivered from serious peril, and completes it as a thankoffering, or becomes alarmed for his soul's salvation, and attempts to unlock the gates of heaven by the old-fashioned and well-worn key of earthly munificence. I suppose it must be finished by such means, if finished at all, because the service of the Greek Church is confined to an ancient liturgy which nowhere rests to permit the word of exhortation, else some modern Chrysostom might cry to the people in the words of Haggai the prophet, and enforce them with thundering anathemas, "Is it time for you, O ye, to dwell in your cieled houses, and this house lie waste?"

The large public buildings of Syra, extending along the entire length of the northern side of the square, are only half completed, if even so much, and have remained in this condition several years. The strong aversion to debt is shared by the civil authorities. They only built while the money lasted, and, when the money was done, stayed the building until funds could accumulate large enough to warrant a recommencement. The accumulation appears to be a very slow process, and apparently the buildings are no nearer completion now than they were ten years ago. It would certainly seem a more sensible plan not to begin building until all the money is ready—a saving in interest on money unexpended, and a further saving in retaining a staff of men, with all their tools and appliances, upon the spot; but there would be the temptation of spending the money in other ways, and the danger of having no large public buildings at all. The custom of never venturing beyond the means actually possessed is, in some ways, highly commendable, and if the custom reaches downward into the private circles of business, and domestic, and personal life, it will effectually prevent much misery, even if it may prevent rapid and extensive acquisition of wealth. Sudden fortunes gained by speculation will be impossible, but so will sudden misfortunes, and life will gain in equableness, in that even play of social forces which are better than upheaval and catastrophe, and in which consists, more largely than we suppose, the happiness of mankind.

The Church of St. Nicholas is completed externally. The internal arrangements are so far completed as to permit of full services being held here. The iconastasis, or screen of images, dividing the holy place from the most holy, with its painted panels and swinging doors, separates the priests from the people, and admits them to their hidden and more sacred functions; a few icons are fastened on the walls, with appropriate lamps, or sockets for candles and tapers, placed before them, although for the most part the walls are uncovered, and, for a Greek church, have a very bare appearance; a beautiful silver candelabra hangs from the centre of the dome, and, upon special occasions, brilliantly illuminates the middle of the church; the choir have their place railed off in the far corner, whence their voices can respond in blending harmonies to the monotonous reading of the priests; everything required for worship, after the form of the orthodox Greek Church, is there, so that services are held every Sunday, and on their numerous feast days, throughout the year. Internally the building has an unfinished appearance nevertheless, a lack of sacred embellishment common to Eastern churches; but it is so constructed as to admit of, and admirably display, embellishment, and in time will make a very fine church indeed. It is a spacious building. It will comfortably accommodate two thousand worshippers. A young priest proudly informed us that it was an exact copy in form of the famous St. Sophia, at Constantinople, but, of course, much smaller. This is not altogether correct. It is, like St. Sophia, an oblong rectangle, and its internal compartments are similarly arranged, but it has no splendid narthex, and it lacks the peculiar dome construction, the central dome supported by semi-domes, which gives to St. Sophia its majestic open space unencumbered by pillars, and which led to the boast of its architect that he had hung its dome in the air. In other respects it is like St. Sophia, but not more like the great Eastern cathedral, which has been degraded into the most famous mosque of the Mohammedans, than many other Grecian churches, for they are nearly all built upon the Byzantine model.

We thought to attend service here on Sunday evening at five o'clock. We found the church empty. A few priests were gathered about the door, who informed us that the public service was held at four o'clock in the morning, and at five o'clock in the evening they met for vespers. They seemed likely to have the vespers entirely to themselves. While we were in the church examining the pictures, a poor and ragged woman entered, carrying a little child about two years old and apparently recovering from a serious illness. She paid a small coin to the doorkeeper, for which she received a thin wax taper, and, approaching a commonplace and badly painted image upon the iconastasis, she lit the taper, fixed it in the socket before the image, crossed herself, bowed, muttered, and then obliged the child to cross itself, not in any way, but in the orthodox way, first touching the forehead, and then the breast, and then from the right to the left shoulder. She afterwards kissed the icon, and put the child forward to kiss it, but the little thing shrank back, and only kissed it under pressure, and very reluctantly. She passed out, leaving the taper burning before the image; and the doorkeeper, as soon as she was gone, took the taper from its socket, and irreverently extinguished the flame. I felt vexed at the man, because I had pitied the woman (she was so poor, and so devout, extracting as much comfort as she could from her religion, and maybe happy in the thought that her piety, represented by that miserable little taper, was acceptable to the blessed Virgin); but I found that not only in Greece, but in Russia, where the religious ceremonial is exactly the same, it was customary for the tapers to be carelessly snuffed out, and carried away, as soon as the worshippers had left the building. In that incident of the mother and child, unnoticed by the priests and the doorkeeper, because quite familiar to them, the mother instructing the child in the forms of devotion, forcing the child to go through the forms of devotion, we have the secret of the strength and continuance of particular types of religious life. Not by those priests, with all their learning, and mysterious functions, and paraphernalia of worship; not by the gorgeously decorated buildings, and burning candles, and painted images, and the observance of saint days, and fastings, and prayers, is the Grecian Church preserved and perpetuated, but by poor mothers like these; and if it were not for their silent and unobtrusive training by which material is ceaselessly provided for the grinding of the vast ecclesiastical machine, that machine would simply grind itself to pieces, and the Greek Church, as any other church in its merely outward organization, would vanish from the face of the earth.

There are much older churches in Syra than the Church of the Resurrection, or the Church of St. Nicholas, and with these older churches, hidden among the houses, I was better pleased than with the two overlooking the houses from the summit of the hills. One of these churches is behind the public buildings, fronting the narrow street that leads to the highest part of the town. It is crammed full of pictures, mostly old and curious paintings of long-forgotten saints, in massive gold and silver-gilt frames. Simply the hands and faces of many of these saints are painted, and the nimbus, the crown, the flowing robes, the sacred books in their hands, and everything else required to complete the picture, are represented by delicately wrought filigree, or thin plates of precious metal richly chased, with an appropriate ornamentation of gems,—as near to a statue, an *idol*, the abomination of the Greek Church, as a picture, an *image* can be, without being an idol altogether. For the world these Greeks would not bow before a carved statue. That would be the height of superstition. That would be gross idolatry. But to bow before a painted picture, attired in a golden filigree cloak, clasped with gems, is worship most acceptable. What a narrow line, a line fine as a hair, is sufficient to divide men into separate religious camps, and make them curse each other! What a thin curtain, thin as a cobweb film, is sufficient to blind men to each other's goodness and sympathy! No wonder if sometimes humanity overtops religion, and strides across the narrow line, and breaks through the thin curtain, and grasps the hand of its fellow in assertion of their common kinship; and what is this but Christianity triumphing over its forms, liberating itself from its fetters, calling men back from their dead images to the real life of Him who not only clearly taught the Fatherhood of God, but the brotherhood of man! From the curious paintings, and silver lamps, and antique furniture, and elaborate decoration of the old church, my mind was called away by the sound of children's voices reading together in an adjoining school (and children's voices everywhere, no matter in what language they speak, sound very much alike); and I could not help thinking that the priests were doing good work, and were rightly employed here, work which would tell better for Greece, and for the world, than the endless genuflections of their worship before bald-headed, meek-eyed, red-faced old saints.

With another old church, near the harbour, I was very much pleased, not so much with the church building as with a set of buildings at the back, forming a quadrangle, and enclosing a grassy courtyard. This quadrangle could be approached either through the church or by a separate entrance of its own. The separate entrance was from the street, up a few steps, and through a large door, admitting to a balcony or raised promenade running on every side of the quadrangle and looking into the courtyard, where the bright green grass, and the dark green leaves of the orange trees, laden with golden fruit, afforded rest to the eyes wearied with the glare of the white streets and the white walls. Opening from the promenade, and on the same level with it, were a variety of rooms appropriated to the uses of an infirmary,—a surgery, a kitchen, a nurses' room, bedrooms for patients, and a large, lofty, well-ventilated room in which the convalescent could assemble for conversation with each other, or reading, or recreation, or rest. This infirmary was part of the ecclesiastical establishment, and maintained by the Church funds—an evidence of practical Christianity all the more pleasing from the fact that poor patients of every faith and nationality are taken in, and carefully and skilfully treated, without any attempt at making proselytes, or even without any unnecessary obtrusion of particular beliefs and modes of worship. A real good Samaritan Church was this, which never passed by on the other side Roman Catholic, Protestant, Mohammedan, Gueber, or any one else requiring medical aid. Within its large room I saw Turks, and Greeks, and Franks, to the number of twenty or more, all recovering from accidents and sicknesses, who had received, and who were then receiving, without distinction, from the young doctor and the white-robed nurses, the most kindly attention, and who would be certain to look back in after years with grateful affection, wherever their home, and whatever their worship, to that little religious hospital behind the old church in Syra.

At least one of our great English medical foundations originated in a similar work to that carried on by this Church in Syra. St. Bartholomew's Hospital, with which was long connected a church and priory, was founded in the reign of Henry I. by a gentleman of the name of Rahere. While on a pilgrimage to Rome, Rahere had a vision in which St. Bartholomew appeared to him, and commanded him to build a church " in the suburbs of London at Smithfield." The bishop favoured his project; the king gave up part of his market, that marshy and least profitable part where it had been customary to gibbet notorious criminals; Rahere gave, and begged, and worked himself, and obtained money and labour from the people, who were willing to help him with both because, as the record quaintly says, "hys lyfe accorded to his tonge, and his dede approved well hys sermon;" and, amid some opposition, the buildings were at length completed. For nearly eight hundred years the art of healing has been benevolently exercised at St. Bartholomew's, which was first an ecclesiastical foundation, and must have carried on, for several centuries, a similar work to that of the old Greek Church at Syra. In Eastern life a few hundred years seem nothing. To look into some out-of-the-way corners of Syra, and other towns on the European and Asiatic borderlands, is like leaping over the centuries, and meeting face to face the customs of mediæval times.

A funeral in Greece is a sadly picturesque sight. My attention was specially arrested by the funeral of a little girl, seven or eight years old, with a most beautiful face, rounded as if in perfect health, but delicately pale,—a white lily plucked suddenly from earth's garden to be added to the living garlands of paradise. It was not a largely attended funeral. First came the coffin lid, upright in order to display its gaudy silver-gilt ornamentation, carried by a boy; then several priests, not in the long dark robes and tall brimless hat which they ordinarily wear outdoors, but in their coloured and bordered service robes, striking and even gorgeous, stepping slowly and solemnly, and chanting in low monotonous tones; then five or six boys carrying tall wax tapers, moulded with floral decorations, on either side of the fair corpse, and the corpse in its coffin, without lid, fully exposed to the gaze of on-lookers, and carried low so as to be more clearly visible, strewn with flowers, and followed by a few mourning relatives. The sweet, silent face of the child was a touching sight, and its deep calm, its intense placidity, its matchless repose profoundly suggestive of many thoughts; but the funeral passed on, not even attracting so much notice as our sombre English funerals, barely looked at by the people in the streets, who stayed not their business or pleasure one moment, or lessen that business or pleasure to any perceptible extent, in the presence of the mystery of death.

Our English Sunday is ridiculed abroad. Our shops are closed, our streets are deserted, what to us appears reverential, to the foreigner appears a foolish and self-imposed melancholy. Their weekly holy-day is a holiday, a time of amusement and pleasure; our weekly holy-day is a day for worship and rest. There must be something very tame to a foreigner about our English Sunday. He cannot appreciate it, because he cannot in imagination occupy our national position, or enter into our more serious religious life. He looks at us, and at our Sunday, from his own standpoint, and his face broadens into a smile at the impenetrable stupidity of Johnny Bull. That substantial gentleman can afford to be smiled at, and I trust will never be smiled into the observance of Sunday after the fashion of Continental Europe. The quiet of an English Sabbath to an Englishman who has experienced the hubbub and gaiety of Sabbaths abroad is worth struggling for, and not only for the sake of the quiet, but for the sake of many other things as well. The way we observe the Sunday has had much to do with the happiness and multiform endearments of our domestic life, and much to do with the formation of the strongest, best, most pronounced types of English character; and it would be a sad change from our sober to the dissipating methods of observance in vogue from the Bay of Biscay to the Black Sea.

On Sundays Syra was like a fair. The square was then more thickly crowded. The streets were then most busily thronged. Business was carried on with an extra zest. The market resounded with the cries of all kinds of salesmen. Smoking, coffee-drinking, card-playing were indulged in at the little round tables, a priest here and there sitting among the company, as ardently engaged as the rest, and dropping beads the while from what appeared to be a rosary, but which some say is only a plaything. Mohammedans carry a string of beads containing ninety-nine in all, representing the ninety-nine attributes of the Deity, and their counting has a religious significance. But they can count, and game, and smoke, and drink coffee all at the same time. The entire population gives itself up to hilarity and merry-making on Sunday. The French and Italian musicians, both men and women, that wander here, and give scenic representations outdoors, realize their largest profits on this day sacred to the worship of Christ, but whose worship has been either forgotten or strangely misunderstood in a so-called Christian country. This noisy play is more akin to the celebration of the old heathen festivals by their idolatrous forefathers than to the celebration of the resurrection of Christ by the disciples who were gathered in these very Eastern cities in early Christian times. Give me the English Sunday, even if it were ten times duller than it is, before this continuous and intensified babel of the week. There is enough clamour and sport from Monday to Saturday. Let the Sunday be peaceful. The world should be hushed for one day.

On St. John's Eve, by the old reckoning, we were startled by fires suddenly leaping up among the houses in every part of the town. As soon as it became dusk these fires were lit, now here, and now there, until a score were blazing at once, and illuminating together the town and harbour; and no sooner did one set of fires die down than others were lit, and others again, mostly in new places, as if every house and almost every person intended to have some share in the conflagration. "What is the meaning of this?" I inquired; and a Greek gentleman replied, "If not burn an old table, chair, basket, something, John send no good luck." Doubtless these Midsummer bonfires are the remnants of an ancient heathenism once prevalent throughout Europe and Western Asia. As in some other instances, the Christian saint has taken the place and appropriated the honours of the mythical deity, and thereby aided in the perpetuation of a custom which might otherwise have been destroyed. Fire must have played a very important part in the idolatrous rites of past ages, and the custom of kindling fires for the various purposes of worship must have spread over wide areas of the earth's surface. But the most curious fact is not the spread of the custom, but the simultaneous practice of the custom in countries separated by thousands of miles, and by people utterly different from each other. In his "Yachting Tour in Norway," Mr. Froude says, "On St. John's Day, by the old reckoning, as we lay at anchor in a gorge, which from the land must have been inaccessible, we saw a large fire blazing, and figures leaping through the flame. It was the relic of a custom, once wide as the Northern hemisphere, on the festival of the summer solstice, old as the Israelitish prophet who saw the children passed through the fire to Moloch. I observed the same thing forty-three years ago in the market-place at Killarney. Thousands of years it has survived, down to these late times of ours, in which, like much besides, it will now end—dissolved in the revolutionary acids of scientific civilization." These revolutionary acids are dissolving the custom but slowly. It must live in the East for a long time yet. And in Cornwall, where, from distant ages, the custom has prevailed, and prevailed too on Midsummer Day, it will not easily disappear. Comparatively cut off for a long time from communication with the rest of Britain, and affording an asylum from the conquering Saxon, and Dane, and Norman for the Druid priests and bards, who exercised for centuries here an almost undisturbed influence over a susceptible people when their influence in the rest of the island was gone, and who practised here last of all their mysterious rites in sacred groves, and by holy wells, and on rugged cairns, Cornwall preserves traditions of fires kindled on sacred granite altars, which to-day are called Sacrificing Rocks, and points out hollow stone basins for catching the blood of the victims offered to appease the wrath, and obtain the favour of the great god Baal. There is a marked difference between the basins of the Sacrificing Rocks and the other basins on the Cornish cairns. The other basins are the result of the action of rain and wind, the rain first of all beating out a softer grain in the surface of the granite, and forming a little hollow, in which, beneath the water, small particles of granite are deposited; and then the wind stirring the water into circular eddies, and whirling the small particles round and round, causing them by this regular rotatory motion to grind the sides of the hollow into an even and smoothly rounded basin, wide in proportion to its depth. But the basins of the Sacrificing Rocks are deep in proportion to their width, too deep for the wind to act upon the particles and convert them into a grinding machine, and must have been formed by human hands.[1] On Midsummer Day the Druids celebrated an important festival, lit their altar fires, and implored the blessing of Heaven upon their lands, and maybe upon the contiguous waters; and the tourist now sheltering in the tiny coves of the picturesque peninsula would very likely behold the Midsummer fires, and the figures leaping through them, as Mr. Froude beheld in Norway. The cry, "O Baal, hear us!" has gone up from many English hills as well as from Mount Carmel. In Penzance the Midsummer fires are kindled in the middle of the streets; torches steeped in tar are swung round the heads of young men who pass up and down on either side of the fires, and fill the street with blazing circles; young lads leap through the flames in quick succession, and enjoy the exciting, but somewhat dangerous, fun; and next day the people assemble for picnics on the water, as if, now Midsummer had come, they might venture on the treacherous element without fear. Years ago, the shores of Mount's Bay, from the Lizard to the Land's End, used to be dotted

---

[1] A good example of these hewn basins may be seen on Carn Brae, near Camborne; and a good example of the worn basins on the Clapper Rocks, St. Mary's, Scilly Islands.

with Midsummer fires; but these revolutionary acids are at work, the custom is dissolving, the fires are mostly extinguished along this coast, and will be in Penzance, at any rate in the public streets, within a comparatively short time. Old customs die hard, however, and, if driven out of the towns, will take refuge in the villages and hamlets, and live on under the kindly fostering of a more simple-minded people.

Syra, unlike many of the islands of the Ægean, has very few historical associations. It must have possessed a considerable city in ancient times. The architectural remains which may yet be traced near the site of the present town prove this, as well as references to the prosperity of the island in the Odyssey. The only eminent person born in Syra was Pherecydes. He was one of the earliest prose writers of Greece, and became a great and much respected philosopher. He is said to have been a disciple of Pittacus, the Lesbian sage; and there is reason to believe he was the master of Pythagoras, and that this learned and ingenious man received from him the doctrine of metempsychosis, and was grounded by him in the knowledge of the movement of the heavenly bodies. Apart from the birth and teaching of Pherecydes Syra has hardly any mention in the history of Greece.

In the Odyssey, however, Syra has an important place. One of the most charming parts of that immortal poem is connected with this little island. Eumæus, the faithful swineherd of Ulysses, every line of whose noble character is drawn with the most delicate precision, was a Syran, and son to Ctesius, the monarch of the two cities which then divided the island between them. Of this Eumæus, who sheltered and entertained both Ulysses and Telemachus previous to the slaying of the suitors, and who himself took part in that terrible fray, Coleridge has left us a very interesting criticism. He considers him to be "a character less within the reach of modern imitation than any other in the

Odyssey. He is a genuine country gentleman of the age of Homer, living at a distance from the town, having servants or labourers under him, but being at the same time the principal herdsman and superintendent of the swine belonging to Ulysses, which of course constituted an important article of the hero's property. . . . The scenes in his house are unequalled in their way. . . . The character of Eumæus is a very complete conception, and a remarkably interesting specimen of rural life and its habits in the very remote age in which it was produced." For the comfort of his master, and in sympathy with his suffering, Eumæus relates his own life's story. In describing his own land, he says—

> "Above Ortygia lies an isle of fame,
> Far hence remote, and Syria is the name
> (There curious eyes inscribed with wonder trace
> The sun's diurnal, and his annual race);
> Not large, but fruitful; stored with grass to keep
> The bellowing oxen and the bleating sheep;
> Her sloping hills the mantling vines adorn,
> And her rich valleys wave with golden corn.
> No want, no famine, the glad natives know,
> Nor sink by sickness to the shades below;
> But when a length of years unnerves the strong,
> Apollo comes, and Cynthia comes along.
> They bend the silver bow with tender skill,
> And, void of pain, the silent arrows kill."

Here we have a very pleasant picture, and save the discharging of Apollo and Cynthia's arrows, a veritable island of the blessed; and, to some people, the exception would be no exception at all, but an increase of the blessedness, for they would prefer the contemplation of a painless and quiet death to the surfeited happiness of a life of hundreds of years. This description agrees well, both in the fertility of the island, its immunity from plague, and the study of its people of the movements of the heavenly bodies, with what we gather of Syra from the later Grecian writers. Then follows the touching and beautiful story of Eumæus. When a very little child at home, a ship of Sidon entered the port of Syra, bringing many curious things from the East, with which the sailors traded, receiving in return whatever the island had to bestow. A Sidonian woman was then residing in the court of Ctesius. She had been captured by pirates, and conveyed to Syra, and there sold to Ctesius; and, because of her skilful fingers, held an honourable and trusted place in the king's household. This woman came down to the shore, where the Phœnician vessel was anchored, to wash her robes, and one of the sailors flattered and won her for himself. She told him she was one of his own countrywomen. A plan of escape was decided upon, and an intention formed of secretly spoiling the king of part of his riches, and kidnapping his child. The sailors took an oath at the woman's request, too glibly, that they would convey her in safety to her native land. A year passed away, during which all conversation with her was scrupulously and purposely avoided, lest it should arouse the suspicion of the king and the people. Their vessel was laden, and they were ready to depart; one of the crew went to the palace, exhibited some elaborately wrought gold and amber chains, and, while the other women were bargaining for the trinkets, gave the sign previously agreed upon to the Sidonian. She passed into the large feasting-room, where the feast was already spread, but the guests not yet assembled, hid three golden goblets in her bosom, laid hold of the child who followed her in innocent glee to the seashore, was lifted with her human treasure, as well as the less costly spoil, to the deck of the vessel, and swiftly borne away.

> "Six calmy days and six smooth nights we sail,
> And constant Jove supplied the gentle gale.
> The seventh, the fraudful wretch (no cause descried),
> Touched by Diana's vengeful arrow, died.
> Down dropp'd the caitiff-corse, a worthless load,
> Down to the deep; there roll'd the future food
> Of fierce sea-wolves, and monsters of the flood."

Here is the bitter feeling of Eumæus towards the fair robber who had deprived him of a father's training, a life of affluence and power, and a lovely island kingdom. The Sidonian vessel was steered to Ithaca, and there, by command of the gods, the little child was sold to Laërtes, the father of Ulysses, the King of Ithaca, with whom he found a happy and comfortable home.

CHAPTER IV.

THE WATERWAYS OF CONSTANTINOPLE.

The two waterways—Railway system—Isolation of Constantinople—Scenery of the Dardanelles—Sea-fowl—Chanak—Sestos and Abydos—Leander—Byron—The army of Xerxes, and its passage across the Hellespont—Alexander—Julius Cæsar—The Turkish invasion—Bride of Abydos—Fortifications—Damage to an English fleet—Turkish boatmen—Ægospotami—The River Granicus—Gallipoli—Origin of the Janizaries—Boulair—Sea of Marmora: its shores and islands—Scenery of the Bosphorus—The Symplegades—The Giant's grave—The Genoese castles—Therapia—Deep waters—The castles of Asia and Europe—Cemeteries—Suburbs of Constantinople.

THERE are two ways to Constantinople, both waterways, one by Varna, across a corner of the Black Sea, and through the Bosphorus, the other by the Grecian Islands, and through the Dardanelles. Constantinople is not yet connected by railway with the continent of Europe. There is a single line to Adrianople. A train runs over this line in each direction once a day, accomplishing the journey of two hundred miles in fourteen hours. Adrianople is also connected by railway with Dede Agatch on the Ægean, and Philippopolis and Sarembey in Eastern Roumelia. We may therefore consider Adrianople as the centre of the scanty European railway system of the Turks. What is wanted is the extension of the Continental line from Pirot, the present terminus, through Sophia to Sarembey; but even then, unless the Turks could be persuaded to accelerate their trains, the present mail route, *viâ* Pesth, Rustchuk, and Varna, notwithstanding the occasional discomfort of crossing the south-west corner of the stormy Euxine, would be better than the slowness, closeness, and monotony of Turkish railway cars. "Hurry is of the devil," say the Turks, and we do not entertain the shadow of a doubt concerning the Turkish belief in the truth of the proverb.

By the want of this railway connection between Pirot and Sarembey Constantinople is isolated from Western Europe. Its inhabitants scarcely regard themselves as resident in Europe. In defiance of geographical boundaries they think and speak of Europe as beyond the Balkans. And not only is Constantinople isolated by the want of railway communication, but its waterways intensify the isolation. The Bosphorus and the Dardanelles are so narrow, and so easily defended, as to shut up Constantinople within herself, and to shut out the rest of the world. Her strength mainly consists in her isolation. This may account for the refusal of the suspicious Turk to extend the railway system. To block the passes of the Balkans, and to close the gates of the Bosphorus and the Hellespont, is to effectually protect Constantinople. If the fortifications of the waterways are well manned the gates cannot be forced. The finest navy in the world could be annihilated in those narrow channels. The real danger to Constantinople is by way of the Balkans, and to successfully defend them is to maintain the crescent on St. Sophia and the sacred banner of Mohammed in the East of Europe.

The Hellespont opens tamely from the magnificent northern Ægean. The swift current rolls between the low, marshy, Asiatic shore, where the classic waters of ancient Simöis and Scamander unite to pour their wealth into the sea, and the sloping and marly European cliffs, scantily clad with brushwood and small trees, rising barely one hundred feet above the tide. The scenery improves very much upon approaching the elbow of the channel. The passage narrows down to a mile in width. The waters sweep round the sharp Asiatic elbow, and form, on the European shore, a pleasant, semicircular bay. The hills are finer and more fertile, rising rapidly from the European shore into high grassy slopes, and gradually stretching away from the shores of Asia into park-like wooded uplands, the spaces between the woods flourishing with vines and olives, and dotted with the picturesque farmsteads of industrious Greeks and Turks. When round the elbow, the channel widens by slow degrees until it is lost in the broad, shining mirror of the lovely Sea of Marmora. From the narrowest part of the Hellespont northward to the Sea of Marmora the scenery reminds one of Windermere in its best summer attire. Of course, the scenery is on a larger scale; the views are ampler; the woods are more extensive. But there is a striking similarity, nevertheless, until Gallipoli is approached, and then the slender, white minarets; the brown-walled, red-tiled houses, with large overhanging eaves, like Swiss chalêts; the expanding Propontis; the magnificent white marble heights of Marmora Island, rising in almost spiritual beauty above the sapphire sea, altogether dispel the similarity to Windermere and assert the peculiarities of the East.

A flock of sea-fowl were skimming along the surface of the Dardanelles: they were small-sized, brown-backed birds, with long-pointed wings, and displayed as they swayed and turned in their flight the under white part of their wings. They fly restlessly backwards and forwards along the course of the Bosphorus and Dardanelles, but never enter the Ægean or the Black Sea. By some these birds are known as "the damned lovers," and are supposed to be animated by the souls of the numerous victims who have been silently sunk in the Bosphorus from the palaces that line the banks, when Sultan, Vizier, or Pacha found this the only resource left them of ending unpleasant domestic broils—a fanciful interpretation of their restless movements, close upon, and backwards and forwards over the same waters, and an unmistakably suggestive name; but imagination is stimulated beyond the bounds of reason when dealing with what is jealously secreted, and the harem must be generally a duller place, and wanting in the exciting and dreadful incidents with which poetry delights to invest it, notwithstanding the refined cruelties to which a Turk will sometimes resort either for policy or revenge.

Near the elbow of the Dardanelles, in its narrowest part, stands the modern fortified Turkish town of Chanak. Here all vessels going up or down must stay for the examination of papers, and to obtain *pratique;* and no vessel can proceed either way in the night, but must wait for the daylight, and the pleasure of the Turkish authorities, before going through the gates. The Turks are very strict in the maintenance of these regulations, and quite prepared to enforce them by cannon mounted and charged on both sides of the straits, between the two fires of which no ship could escape.

That this elbow is the most important part of the Dardanelles may be seen at a glance. Here stood the ancient castles of Sestos and Abydos, and now there are interesting remains of fortresses strongly built centuries ago by the Ottomans when first they ventured into Europe. The masonry of the castle at Sestos is perfect. It is a peculiar structure—huge circular walls, defended by towers, and enclosing a triangular fortress—a formidable place preparatory to the discovery of gunpowder, but upon that discovery, like many other structures, rendered suddenly obsolete. Abydos was a commanding situation for controlling the surrounding country, and, in the early times, the seat of empire. We read of—

> "Asias the great, who held his wealthy reign
> In fair Abydos, by the rolling main,"

and whose name, perhaps, transferred to the region of Ephesus, afterwards spread over an entire continent, and now denotes one quarter of the globe. Here Dardanus, when he brought his household gods from Samothracia, fixed his seat, and allied his arms with Troy. Between Sestos and Abydos is that famous passage of the Hellespont, which, in mythology and history, has played a most important part, and become one of the best known and most interesting places in the world.

The most pathetic and frequently told story is that of Hero and Leander. Hero was the beautiful priestess of Venus at Sestos. Leander, of Abydos, after meeting her at the festival of Venus and Adonis, and falling in love with her, secretly declared his passion in defiance of the vows of perpetual virginity under which the priestess maiden was bound; and she too, in defiance of her vows, returned his love. Night after night he swam the channel, and, to guide him in his dangerous passage across the water, she hung a lantern in the top of a tower by the sea. One stormy night the rain fell in torrents, the heaving billows resounded upon the shore, the swollen waters swept more rapidly by, all warning him of the great risk he ran, but

> "He could not see, he would not hear,
> Or sound or sign foreboding fear;
> His eye but saw that light of love,
> The only star it hail'd above;
> His ear but rang with Hero's song,
> 'Ye waves, divide not lovers long!'"

The blustering winds extinguished the light of Hero's lantern, and, unguided by the accustomed beacon, and whelmed beneath the tossing wave, the lifeless form of Leander was cast upon the further shore. The lovely priestess died disconsolate for the loss of her lover. An old, old story, told in many ways, and always attractive to the fond human heart; and, after all, it is the old, old story of which every human heart knows something, and can respond to, because it is connected with and touches the strings of our purest and deepest human life.

Byron swam the Hellespont from the European to the Asiatic shore. It is not an easy feat. Only a strong swimmer can do it. The current is so rapid that a boat cannot row directly across, and therefore a swimmer would certainly be carried down the stream some distance before reaching the opposite shore. He was not much enamoured of the feat if we may judge from his humorously doleful poem. He says, comparing himself and Leander, who

"Swam for love, and I for glory;

'Twere hard to say who fared the best :
  Sad mortals ! thus the gods still plague you !
He lost his labour, I my jest ;
  For he was drown'd, and I've the ague."

The most numerous and magnificent army the world has ever seen crossed the Hellespont from Abydos to Sestos in the year 480 B.C. The Persians under Darius had crossed before, and conquered Thrace, and carried their arms beyond the Balkans and the Danube in a vain attempt to subdue the savage myriads of Scythia, and then turned southward toward Greece only to be scattered by Miltiades on the memorable plain of Marathon. The Persian power was humbled. Darius made more extensive preparations to chastise and enslave the Greeks, and, in the midst of these preparations, was touched by the inexorable finger of death. Xerxes, his son and successor, was persuaded, almost against his will, to continue the preparations, and avenge the honour of his country. He was not contented with his father's plans. His army and navy must be so large as to be irresistible by the mere weight of numbers, and so splendidly appointed as to gratify the pride of the most powerful monarch upon the face of the earth. Four years were spent in gathering forces from all parts of his vast dominions,—painted negroes from Ethiopia, clad in panther's skins, and carrying bows and flint-tipped arrows; wild and almost naked hordes from the Libyan deserts, armed with hard and sharp wooden lances equally adapted for thrusting or throwing at the foe; agile horsemen from Central Asian steppes, ready to fling the winding lasso, and despatch the entangled enemy with the dagger; fair-skinned men from the mountains of Iberia, and olive-coloured men from the banks of the Indus, and Medes and Persians on richly-caparisoned horses, and in gorgeous chariots, with all their numerous attendants in care of the camp and its luxuries—a representative gathering of the widespread rule of the great king, who could not brook to be insulted by a refusal of submission from a few tribes dwelling in a little rocky peninsula not half the size of the poorest satrapy of his empire.

The rendezvous was Sardis in Lydia. Thence they moved toward Abydos. The army was divided into two parts, and between the two parts rode the king in the midst of the choice troops of the empire. First went the baggage, and then one half the army, a motley mass of every colour, and armed in every way. After a respectful interval came the king's equipage, a splendid chariot drawn by the spirited horses of Nisæa, in which sat the stately monarch, the tallest and most handsome man in the army, but whose height and appearance belied the weakness of his character. His chariot was preceded by another, a more splendid chariot still, for the appropriation of the invisible deity who might attend him, and give him success in his enterprise, to which eight beautiful white steeds were yoked, while other ten steeds of the sacred breed of Nisæa were led before by grooms in royal apparel. A thousand spearmen marched in front of the ten steeds, with the butt end of their spears, wrought in the shape of pomegranates and glittering with gold, held in the air; and in front of them rode a thousand horsemen. The king was followed by two similar companies. Then came the *Immortals*, the ten thousand infantry whose number was always maintained, armed with spears, those of the outer lines adorned with golden pomegranates, and those of the inner ranks with pomegranates of silver. Behind them rode the ten thousand horsemen who completed the magnificent retinue of this luxurious king. After another respectful interval came the rest of the army, the multitude of barbarians who paid tribute, and made war so long as the king had power to hold them in awe; and the camp followers, who always gather in the wake of an army like jackals prowling after their prey.

This numerous army, which has been computed at 1,800,000 fighting men, in addition to at least an equal number of attendants, was assisted by a fleet of over 4,000 vessels, great and small, containing oarsmen and troops to the number of 500,000. Afterwards, in Thrace, 300,000 were added to the army and 24,000 to the navy. One chief danger to such an armament was its own bulk. Only a man of rare military genius could handle it effectively. The provisioning of such a vast host taxed the resources of every country through which it passed. But Xerxes was anxious to frighten the Greeks by a display of unparalleled power, and at the same time flatter his own vanity by the greatness and splendour of a gathering such as had never been beheld before by the eyes of men. A bridge was constructed across the Hellespont, which the stormy winds and waves, caring no more for Xerxes than for the most obscure painted barbarian in the troops, smashed in pieces and carried away; and the angry monarch beheaded his engineers, and, in his impotent rage, lashed the unheeding waters, and flung a set of iron fetters into the tide. Other two bridges were made of boats moored and anchored side by side, over which planks were laid, one bridge for the baggage, the other for the troops. Frankincense was burned upon them, myrtle was strewn over them. The king himself consecrated them by prayers to the rising sun, whom he implored to help him to carry his victorious arms to the extremities of the West; then, after propitiating the previously scourged Hellespont by pouring libations into its waters from a golden bowl, and flinging the bowl, with a golden censor and a richly-engraven and gem-bespangled sword, into the sea, the passage commenced. From a marble throne on a neighbouring eminence Xerxes had surveyed his great army, and he had been moved to tears by the thought that in a hundred years they would all be gone. Now he watched them file over the two bridges. For seven days the long procession crossed, confident in its conquering power. But the stand at Thermoplyé deceived them. The fight at Salamis convinced them otherwise; and before many months they were back again, reduced by the slaughter of the Greeks, but more terribly reduced by famine and pestilence, to find the bridges washed away, and only the shattered remnant of a fleet gathered to convey their emaciated and dispirited companies to the Asiatic shore.

One hundred and fifty years later a conqueror passed from Europe to Asia. Alexander the Great believed in the possibility—and gathered an army for the purpose—of penetrating the Persian Empire, and subduing that Empire to his sway. He was confident in his own military skill and in the unconquerable phalanx of his Macedonian troops. He knew that what the ten thousand Greeks had accomplished under Cyrus, and by the successful retreat of the ten thousand Greeks through the fastnesses of Armenia upon the unexpected death of their leader under his command, Greeks could accomplish again, and much more, and would have no need to retreat, should his life be spared, until the Persian power was thoroughly broken, and the Persian crown upon his brow. Not with an imposing and ostentatious display of forces did Alexander cross the Hellespont. He had an army of 35,000. Of these only 5,000 were cavalry. He embarked at Sestos for the opposite shore. His own vessel he steered himself, and in midstream offered a bull in sacrifice to Neptune, and poured libations from a golden cup into the rolling tide. Alexander was proud of his pretended descent from Achilles. He had a passion for everything associated with the glory of Greece. Homer was his constant companion. And when his vessel came within distance of the famous Asiatic shore, where his ancestor had

"drunk delight of battle with his peers,"

he hurled his spear over the waters and into the land to claim it again as a conqueror for Greece. A tumulus rose on Cape Sigæum, supposed to be the same of which Agamemnon says—

"High on the shore the growing hill we raise,
That wide the extended Hellespont surveys;
Where all, from age to age, who pass the coast,
May point Achilles' tomb, and hail the mighty ghost."

On the tumulus was a marble pillar, and this pillar Alexander adorned with flowers, and paid honour to the great Achilles by running naked round the tomb. Southward went the Macedonian into the wealthy Persian satrapies and toward the heart of the Persian Empire, not to speedily return to the Hellespont with a broken army like the proud Xerxes, but to chase the armies of Asia across their plains and rivers, until the boasted infallible sceptre of the splendid Eastern monarchy was within his grasp. Alas! for Alexander, however, and all such as he. The glory hardly won is soon lost. In the midst of his triumphs death sought him out and summoned him away; and other inferior men broke the sceptre in pieces, and ruled each one with his own part, only to be subdued each one by the invincible power of imperial Rome.

Not on his way to conquer, but as a conqueror, Julius Cæsar crossed the Hellespont, anxiously desirous to terminate his splendid victory by the capture of his opponent. Pompey had fled to Lesbos and thence to Egypt, where the vengeance of Cæsar was forestalled by the treachery of the Egyptians; and the renowned general who won the memorable field of Pharsalia, thereby practically terminated the existence of the Republic, and obtained for himself the supreme position in the Roman world.

The Turks first found their way into Europe across the narrow channel of the Dardanelles. They gradually made themselves masters of Anatolia. They wrested city after city from the hands of the careless and supine Greeks. They swarmed along the Asiatic shores of the Dardanelles and the Sea of Marmora and the Bosphorus, and looked longingly across the waters to the well-cultivated fields of Europe. The Greek governor of the castle of Abydos held out against their arms; but his daughter became enamoured of a young Turk, and surrendered both herself and her home to the Ottomans for the sake of winning her lover. Sulieman, the son of Orchan, who was then Bey or Sultan of the Turks, conceived the bold design of crossing the Hellespont on a raft in the night. The water was a new and untried element to the Turks. They had no boats, and they did not understand the building or the handling of them. But the young prince made his raft, embarked with two courageous companions and eighty followers, landed safely on the European side, and surprised a small fortress near Sestos which was known as the Hog's Castle. The foolish Byzantians, lost in luxury and selfishness, and weakened and blinded by division, smiled at this Turkish invasion, and said the enemy had captured a hog sty; but, once master of the hog sty, they brought across their fierce troops, and marched northward, and invested and took Gallipoli. This important town they were able to fortify. At that time it was the key to the Hellespont. It gave them security in their European possessions. And yet the Greeks affected still to smile, and said, "The Turks had now taken from them a pottle of wine." The Turks were wise enough to know the value of their conquests, and from that time they have remained complete masters of the European shores.

The castle at Abydos brings to mind Byron's charming poem. A white marble pillar, one of many strewn about here, lies on the shore, and has become known as the "Pirate Phantom's Pillow." On the pillar, as on a pillow, so the Turkish legend-says, a turbaned head may be sometimes seen reclining, the phantom-head of a young pirate who was slain here by his foster-father, the pacha of the castle, for daring to make love to, and attempting to carry off, his only daughter. The daughter died broken-hearted, and, to mark her tomb, the pillar was placed above it, but in the night it was mysteriously carried away by invisible hands, and laid upon the shore where the young pirate fell. Probably the pillar is an ordinary Turkish grave-stone, and its sculptured turban (for very few Turkish gravestones are without) has been seen gleaming in the moonlight by superstitious pedestrians whose fertile fancy has gathered about it the incidents of an Oriental romance. In Byron's hands, with such congenial characters, and in such lovely scenes, it has become a very tender and beautiful English poem, free from Byron's objectionable references, and written in his most charming style. Wherever Byron is read, "The Bride of Abydos" is sure to be a favourite. With what sweetly-flowing English does he describe the shores of the Dardanelles!—

> "Know ye the land where the cypress and myrtle
> Are emblems of deeds that are done in their clime,
> Where the rage of the vulture, the love of the turtle,
> Now melt into sorrow, now madden to crime?
> Know ye the land of the cedar and vine,
> Where the flowers ever blossom, the beams ever shine;
> Where the light wings of Zephyr, oppress'd with perfume,
> Wax faint o'er the gardens of Gúl in her bloom;
> Where the citron and olive are fairest of fruit,
> And the voice of the nightingale never is mute;

> Where the tints of the earth, and the hues of the sky,
> In colour though varied, in beauty may vie,
> And the purple of Ocean is deepest in dye;
> Where the virgins are soft as the roses they twine,
> And all, save the spirit of man, is divine?"

And with how much artistic grace does he introduce the Oriental belief already referred to concerning the sea-fowl of the Dardanelles, that departed souls inhabit the bodies of birds, especially, as it would seem, the souls of those whose innocent loves have pierced them through with many sorrows:—

> "the livelong night there sings
> A bird unseen—but not remote:
> Invisible his airy wings,
> But soft as harp that Houri strings
> His long, entrancing note!
>
> * * * *
>
> They scarce can bear the morn to break
> That melancholy spell,
> And longer yet would weep and wake,
> He sings so wild and well!
>
> * * * *
>
> That note so piercing and profound
> Will shape and syllable its sound
> Into Zuleika's name."

The Turks have made the most of the natural advantages given them by the bend in the Dardanelles between Sestos and Abydos. The place bristles with guns. Most of them are guns of heavy calibre, and, properly manned, quite sufficiently heavy to successfully defend that way to Constantinople. From the Asiatic side one monster of eighty tons points its muzzle across the straits. This gun alone could do irreparable damage to vessels obliged to pass within half a mile of it, no matter how admirably constructed the vessels might be. Ever since the invention of gunpowder, or rather the introduction of gunpowder into Europe, this has been a formidable place; and before the art of destruction was developed on scientific lines to anything like its modern precision and thoroughness, a British fleet was once severely handled in forcing its way through to the Ægean Sea.

This fleet consisted of eight ships of the line, two frigates, a sloop, and two bomb boats. One of these ships of the line was the fated *Royal George*. In 1807, in obedience to Government orders, they assembled in Besika Bay for the purpose of enforcing the extraordinary demand of a surrender of the Turkish fleet and arsenal. It was feared that Napoleon might obtain possession of them, and employ them against us. A secondary purpose was the prevention of war, if possible, between Turkey and Russia. While waiting in Besika Bay, the *Ajax*, a fine ship of seventy-four guns, accidentally took fire, and, despite all efforts to save her, was completely destroyed. The fire commenced in the night. The crew tried to save themselves by leaping overboard, and 250 of them were drowned. In the morning the burning ship drifted on the rocky coast of Tenedos. Her magazine exploded, and her charred timbers were strewn far and wide along the coast and over the waters. This sad fatality depressed the spirits of the squadron, and, in olden times, would have been regarded as a certain omen of the ill-success of the mission, and the havoc wrought among the ships by the deadly fire of the Turkish guns when re-passing the Dardanelles.

As now so then, no war vessel was permitted to proceed beyond the bend of the straits without the special warrant of the Sultan. Therefore, when the squadron attempted to pass this point, the Turkish guns opened fire, but, without sustaining much damage, the ships went forward, and suddenly came within sight of a Turkish squadron, apparently prepared to dispute the passage at all hazards. An engagement began. Very soon the Turkish vessels were in flames and driven ashore, and the British entered the Sea of Marmora, and hove to off Constantinople. The Sublime Porte was in no wise intimidated by the presence of the British ships. They treated this display of naval power with their characteristic sublime indifference. The squadron was not sufficiently strong to attempt the bombardment of the city. There were then 200,000 troops in Constantinople. And the Turkish navy was not to be despised. Therefore, after a short indecisive engagement on Proti, one of the beautiful Princes' Islands, the squadron again crossed the Sea of Marmora and entered the Dardanelles. The Turks had been very actively preparing for their return. The fortifications of Sestos and Abydos were speedily manned; the guns were increased; a large brass cannon, which may yet be seen, was ready for action; huge granite balls, and rounded blocks of marble, the remnants of Roman and Grecian architecture, and some of them remnants of an architecture still more ancient, having once adorned the temples of the famous plains of Troy, were fired from this cannon—stones weighing eight and nine hundredweight apiece, and requiring a charge of 330 pounds of powder. The guns were not mounted on wheels, but fixed in the masonry, and the gunners waited the approach of the vessels, and, when the guns covered them, fired as they passed. One after another the ships received these ponderous stones. The *Royal George* was nearly sunk; the *Windsor Castle* had her mainmast cut in two; the wheel of the *Repulse* was swept into the sea, and, by the same shot, twenty-four of her men were killed and wounded. Almost every ship was injured, and yet no ship was taken, and no ship drifted ashore, but, through the brave and skilful exertions of their crews, one by one they sailed gallantly forward until they had all passed beyond the range of the terrible Turkish guns.

When we left Chanak, two Turkish boatmen, wishing to

escape the necessity of rowing against a strong current and an adverse wind, fastened their boat to the stern of the *Treloske*, and were towed along nearly to Gallipoli, and then pulled quietly ashore. Their rope was rather short, and the *Treloske* was steaming at full speed, so that the fore-part of their boat was constantly out of the water, and the after-part nearly buried in the tide. The water flew away from her in two diverging streams, the spray danced about her like feathers, the current, stirred by our propeller, surged beneath her as if the sea were a boiling pot, but the two Moslems reclined in their boat, calmly smoking and gravely conversing, as if it were the most comfortable place in the world. Apparently their equanimity would hardly have been disturbed even by the upsetting of the boat, and, perhaps, if the boat had been upset, it would have righted itself, and revealed these imperturbable Turks smoking as calmly and conversing as gravely as ever.

Near Gallipoli is the ancient Ægospotami, where the Athenian naval supremacy was broken by the Spartan *navarchus* Lysander at the close of the Peloponnesian War. He lay across the straits at Lampsacus, and refused to be tempted out of his advantageous position by the manœuvres of the Athenian ships ; but, watchful all the while of the neglect of the Athenians to protect their own fleet, their foolish choice of an open beach to which to moor their vessels, the necessity they were under of fetching their provisions from so distant a place as Sestos, and even eating upon the shore, he crossed the straits when a favourable opportunity offered, captured nearly the whole of the ships, and made prisoners 4,000 men. This was the last and fatal blow for Athens, and the blow might have been averted if they had exercised common prudence, or listened to the advice of the exiled Alcibiades, who then dwelt upon these shores.

Between the wooded hills that stretch away behind Lampsacus the river Granicus rolls its waters toward the Sea of

Marmora. In crossing this river Alexander was first opposed by Persian troops. The stream was deep; the opposite bank was difficult to climb; the passage was fiercely disputed. Alexander proved himself equal to the occasion. At the risk of his own life, which was nearly lost several times, he personally led the charge of his cavalry, and obtained his first, and perhaps most hardly won victory, upon Asiatic soil.

Gallipoli is a pleasant Turkish town at the head of the Dardanelles. It was more important in the days of Ottoman conquest than now. Here were first formed the terrible regiments by which that conquest was carried forward to its most successful issues. The Spahis, who early became the most renowned corps of Ottoman cavalry, had been already formed. They were originally the children of Christian parents, captured by the Turks, educated in Mohammedanism and to the use of arms, and in time became fiercer missionary soldiers of Islam than the Turks themselves. Perhaps the satisfactory result following upon the formation of the Spahis led to the formation of the Janizaries. By the Mohammedan law a fifth part of the captives, as well as the spoil, belonged to the Kalif, the prophet's successor, and Amurath, ambitious of this high distinction, claimed for himself at Gallipoli the fifth part of the healthy Christian male children who had been taken captive in the European wars. These children became Mohammedans. They were trained for military service; they were endowed with special privileges; the highest places in the State were thrown open to them; they were constantly employed about the person of the sovereign; and Hadji Bektash, who consecrated and blessed them at Gallipoli, by stretching the sleeve of his garment over the head of the foremost soldiers, according to the fashion of the Mohammedans, said, "Let them be called Janizaries;[1] may their countenance be ever bright! their hand victorious!

[1] *Yengi cheri*, meaning new soldiers.

their sword keen! may their spear always hang over the heads of their enemies! and wheresoever they go, may they return with a *white face!*" With a white face, a fair reputation, a good character, these Janizaries did almost always return. Their very name became synonymous with impetuous and irresistible bravery. They were long the terror of Eastern Europe. But, in after days, they assumed and exercised a power which it was never intended they should possess, tyrannized over and made and unmade sultans as they pleased, until they drew on themselves a fearful revenge, and were utterly exterminated in 1823 in the Atmeidan of Constantinople. To educate the children of their vanquished enemies in a religion obnoxious to their parents, and to train them as soldiers for the bloody prosecution of that religion, was reserved for the genius of Mohammedanism. The very currents of nature were not merely turned aside, but dammed up, and made to flow back in devastating floods upon their source. The Christian children of Eastern Europe, ignorant or forgetful of their origin, dead to all feelings of kinship and patriotism, attached by the strong ties of self-interest and personal ambition to the very people who had made them orphans, became a terrible engine of destruction in the hands of these people, and while they settled down in affluence and luxury, over-ran their own countries, massacred their own relatives, fought against the religion in which they were born, and put their masters in possession of some of the fairest provinces upon the face of the earth. Policy so cruelly cunning as this is unknown among Christian people, and has only been approached, not equalled, by the Mohammedans of Egypt in the creation of the famous Mamelukes, who were not captives of war, but slaves purchased from Syrian traders, and obtained by them from the high-lands adjacent to the Caspian Sea. Both the Mamelukes and the Janizaries gained the upper hand in their respective empires, which may be regarded as a proof of the inability of men to foresee the consequences of their creations, and of the power of the hidden laws that regulate human life to produce that perfect balance of evil for evil—to mete out, sooner or later, the exact measure of punishment for men's misdeeds.

Above Gallipoli, where the tongue of land forming the peninsula is narrowest, are the heights of Boulair, looking across the peninsula into the two seas of Marmora and the Ægean. This was the last standing ground of the Turkish army in the late Russo-Turkish War. They lined these grassy heights under the protection of English gun-boats then anchored at the northern mouth of the Dardanelles. The Russian camp was visible in the plains of Thrace. But the English guns were not needed. The Turks did not fly precipitately across the Dardanelles into Asia Minor as it was expected they would do. The paw of the bear was not permitted to rest on Constantinople. And the treaty of San Stefano secured the retreat of the Russians, and prolonged the decline of the Ottoman Empire.

The Sea of Marmora is a beautiful expanse of water, one hundred miles long, and seventy miles wide, the graceful curve of its northern shore almost unbroken, and its southern shore varied by two deep inlets, the Gulf of Isnik and the Bay of Ismid or Nicomedia. The northern shore is not very picturesque. The characteristics of the scenery of the European side of the Hellespont prevail to the walls of Constantinople. There is little or no woodland, but high grassy slopes, fresh and green, pleasant to look upon, but apt to grow monotonous when sailing near the shore. Silivria, overlooked by its ancient fortified castle, is a pretty town, full of interest to the antiquary, being as old as Byzantium itself, and important as one of the last outposts of the tottering Greek Empire; and so is the smaller town of San Stefano, preserving in its name the religious foundation to which it owes its origin, and a testimony to the veneration cherished by the Eastern Church for the first Christian martyr. But these two towns, with their white houses, and domes, and minarets, however picturesque, do not compensate for the lack of natural beauty. On the Asiatic side the scenery is of the richest and most varied description. The coast line is broken; the high lands are splendidly wooded; the deep inlets, especially the Bay of Ismid, presents a series of lovely views. One mountain rears itself behind another, and great Olympus behind and above them all. Beneath an unclouded sky, and reflected in a deep, pure, sleeping sea, the incomparable beauty of the views entitles the southern shores of the Propontis to the name of an earthly paradise.

Marmora Island, from which the sea takes its name, the ancient Proconnessus, is a lofty white marble mountain, rising abruptly out of the sea to the height of two thousand three hundred feet, broken into glittering peaks, and scored by ravines, but devoid of wood—a majestic object presenting itself directly ahead of the vessel immediately upon entering the Sea of Marmora from the Dardanelles. The marble is a durable, close-grained, almost pure white stone, sometimes called alabaster, but not the half pellucid stone of that name, and was found very suitable, and therefore freely used, for the erection of the large buildings of Constantinople. There are smaller islands a little to the southwest of the island of Marmora, of a similar character, but not near so lofty; and directly to the south, larger and loftier than all, the Artaki peninsula, once known as the island of Cyzicus, the headquarters of the Arabs, who, in the earlier days of Mohammedan conquest, twice besieged the city of Constantinople.[1] At the opposite end of the Sea of Marmora, near the mouth of the Bosphorus, various other

> "Isles that gem
> Old Ocean's purple diadem,"

---

[1] Here, too, centuries before the Arabs appeared on the Propontis the brave monarch Mithridates suffered a severe defeat during his long and gallant struggle with the Roman arms.

enhance the view, and attract the vision. Small, but very beautiful, islands are these, forming together one of the most charming suburbs of Constantinople. There are four of them, Proti, Antigoné, Khalki, and Prinkipo, on which last and largest of these islands is the only remaining tomb of the ancient reigning race of the great city, all the others having been destroyed by the Turks, the tomb of the Empress Irene, who, after a cruel, ambitious, and eventful career, ended her life in exile within sight of the palace where she had worn the purple, and ruled the Eastern world.

The Bosphorus differs very largely from the Dardanelles. It is deeper and narrower; the hills on both sides are loftier and more picturesque; the bends in the current afford continual surprises to the eye, and the scenery is enhanced by the cypress groves that run down to the water's edge, and the beautiful white marble kiosks of Europe and Asia that dot the margin of the stream, and prepare the imagination for the magnificent view of Stamboul. The Genoese castles opposite each other at Kavak, immediately upon entering the Bosphorus from the Black Sea; and the two castles of Europe and Asia nearer the city, supply the antique element which adds greatly to the beauty and interest of a picture, and quicken the memory to preserve events which have largely influenced the history of the world. The waterway, sixteen miles long and less than a mile wide, with its high hills lifting themselves one after another along both sides of the stream, is to Constantinople what the long drive through a splendid winding avenue is to a noble mansion; and as the expectation of the grandeur of the mansion is enlarged by the length and splendour of the drive, so the expectation of the magnificence of Constantinople is enlarged by the passage between the hills, and the groves, and ancient castles, and beautiful marble palaces that lie along the deep and narrow channel of the Bosphorus. Nor is the expectation disappointed; for no city has a finer situation, and a more royal appearance than the city which Constantine designed to be the metropolis of the world.

At the northern end of the Bosphorus, on each side of the channel, are "the blue Symplegades," the two rocks that were once supposed to be endowed with the power of motion. Between them nothing could pass.

> " No bird of air, no dove of swiftest wing,
> That bears ambrosia to the ethereal king,
> Shuns the dire rocks: in vain she cuts the skies;
> The dire rocks meet, and crush her as she flies:
> Not the fleet bark, when prosperous breezes play,
> Ploughs o'er that roaring surge its desperate way;
> O'erwhelm'd it sinks: while round a smoke expires,
> And the waves flashing seem to burn with fires."

Vindictive rocks they must have been, delighting to destroy life of every kind, but their own destruction was accomplished by the successful passage of the *Argo* between them, assisted and guided by the Queen of Heaven. Since then they have remained stationary, and although many ships, driven toward the Bosphorus by the stormy Euxine, have failed to make the entrance, and been wrecked upon these rocks, they have never united to crush the ships, and glut their vindictive rage. In this old myth we may trace the belief that, as the pillars of Hercules were one, so the Cyanean rocks were the other extremity of the earth. And we may observe the fact that the Black Sea was then as treacherous and dangerous as now. Often do the stormy winds sweep across it, and roll its dark tumultuous waves towards the Bosphorus, increasing the impetuosity of the southward current, and ruffling the surface of the waters at the mouth of the Golden Horn.

> " 'Tis a grand sight, from off 'the Giant's Grave,'
> To watch the progress of those rolling seas
> Between the Bosphorus, as they lash and lave
> Europe and Asia;"

but not so grand to be on "those rolling seas," for, as Byron continues,

> "There's not a sea the passenger e'er pukes in
> Turns up more dangerous breakers than the Euxine."

"The Giant's Grave" is a high hill, on the Asiatic shore, overlooking the town of Kavak, and supposed to have been the residence of Amycus, the king of the Bebryces. Kavak is the fortified station of the Turks, corresponding with Chanak on the Dardanelles, where all vessels must stay for examination, and permission to proceed toward the city. It is the strong point of the Bosphorus. The channel is very narrow here, and the guns from the fortifications on both sides would make it extremely dangerous for any vessel to force its way. The Genoese castles, erected by the enterprising commercial Genoese colony who were permitted to settle on the northern side of the Golden Horn, still bear testimony to their audacious conduct in the very midst of the Greek Empire, and within sight of the palace of the Cæsars. They dominated the Bosphorus, monopolized the trade, levied tolls upon the shipping, built these castles that they might effectually command the straits, as if they were entirely independent of the empire, and, notwithstanding imperial orders, could do what they pleased.

One of the homeliest houses on the Bosphorus, the first large modern building visible on the way down, is the summer residence of the English Ambassador at Therapia. The house stands exactly on the Point, where the cool breezes from the Black Sea directly strike, and is therefore much to be preferred to any residence in or about the city. Within Therapia Point, the Bosphorus opens into a fine bay, surrounded by high hills, at the foot of which, lying back from the far corner of the bay, an old plane tree still flourishes, said to be the very same under whose branches Godfrey of Bouillon rested when on his way to fight the

Saracens, and rescue the Holy Sepulchre from the defiling hands of the Moslem. This is the only extensive bay along the whole course of the Bosphorus, with the exception of the narrow inlet of the Golden Horn, which cannot be called a bay. Here and there, however, the shores curve and twine, and the openings between the hills exhibit entrancing vistas. Across one valley, above Therapia, on the European side, the remains of a gigantic aqueduct are visible, giving to the view a distinctive character, and awakening reflections concerning the greatness of the city in olden times.

So deep are the waters of the Bosphorus that large vessels may not only proceed in the middle of the stream, but in almost any part of it, without fear. The sides dip many fathoms within a few yards from the shore. For ten miles above Constantinople, and for five or six miles above Scutari, good roads have been constructed along the very margin of the water. People may walk or drive on these roads, and, in any place, call a caique, step directly in, and finish the journey by water. Two English vessels were once steaming up the Bosphorus, endeavouring to outstrip each other, and one of them, near the Asiatic shore, to lessen the distance, ran finely round one of the bends of the stream. The master had correctly calculated the movement of the ship, but not the consequences of that movement to a pacha's harem that stood directly over the tide. The projecting yardarm entered the window of the harem, and the force of the moving vessel tore out the intervening masonry between one window and another, and then another, and then another—revealing the luxurious apartment, and the flying figures of several females who had been terrified by the unwonted and dangerous intrusion. The ship freed herself, and hove to in deep water altogether undamaged, although she had steamed so close to the brink as to nearly destroy the residence of a pacha, and almost kill his wives. Of course, the race proved rather an expensive one, for the harem had to be repaired at the cost of the owners of the vessels.

The Anatoli Hissar, or Castle of Asia, and the more curiously built, and larger, Roumeli Hissar, or Castle of Europe, about five miles from Constantinople, are certain to attract the attention of any visitor to the Bosphorus. The Castle of Asia was built by the Ottoman Sultan, Mohammed I., after he had won the Asiatic lands as far as the Bosphorus; and the Castle of Europe was built by his grandson, Mohammed II., surnamed the Great, the conqueror of the royal city. Amurath, the father of Mohammed the Great, was a man of deep religious convictions. He had a sound sense of honour. He fought bravely when he had to fight, and he faithfully observed his treaties when the fighting was over. But not so Mohammed. Without consulting the Greeks, and in defiance of a well-known understanding, and against all protestations, he gathered a thousand masons at Asomaton, opposite the Anatoli Hissar, and two thousand labourers to assist them, and commenced the erection of the fortress, which was so direct a menace to Constantinople as to be in itself a declaration of war. By fortifying the two castles, he could close the Bosphorus, and starve the city. Ambassadors from the Imperial Court waited upon the inexorable sultan, to try to persuade him from the execution of his designs. He threatened to flay alive the next who should come, and sent these back with the insolent message that "the Empire of Constantinople is measured by her walls. . . . Return, and inform your king that the present Ottoman is far different from his predecessors: that *his* resolutions surpass their wishes; and that *he* performs more than *they* could resolve." The work proceeded. The walls of the fortress, built in curious angles, were twenty-two feet thick, and the walls of the three towers thirty feet thick; and when the fortress was finished, he mounted heavy cannon on the walls and towers nearest the sea, similar to the cannon mounted on the fortress opposite, and levied taxes on all vessels passing to and from the Euxine. The first vessel that refused to obey the mandate of these new masters of the Bosphorus, a Venetian, was sunk by a cannon ball, and her crew were only rescued from drowning to be barbarously slain. The fierce Ottoman sultan had fully made up his mind to capture Constantinople, and remove thither the seat of his empire; and the building of Roumeli Hissar was one important step toward the accomplishment of his design, and neither by persuasion nor threats could he be dissuaded from taking that step, and afterwards investing with his troops and fleet the city of the Cæsars.

On the shores of the Bosphorus there are numerous cemeteries, crowded with gravestones in every state of neglect and decay. Cypress groves are planted in and about these burial places. Mile after mile these groves clothe the hill-sides with their dark green spires, and invest some of the views with a quiet and almost sombre look which is only partially relieved by the white-domed mosque, and the column-like minaret tapering toward the sky. The cemeteries are much more extensive on the Asiatic than on the European side. The cemetery at Scutari is one of the largest in the world. The Turks prefer to be buried in Asia. They belong to Asia. They never forget the fact that they obtained their European possessions by conquest, and that the Giaours may unite to drive them again across the Bosphorus, whence they came. There is a prevailing impression in the Turkish mind that they will have to quit Europe some day, and this impression determines their wishes to be laid at rest in their mother-soil beyond the waters, where there is less likelihood of their graves being trodden upon, and desecrated, by the feet of the infidels.

The Princes' Islands already mentioned, and Scutari, and the long line of kiosks and palaces, with the smaller clustering dwellings, that lie along both sides of the Bosphorus, are suburbs of Constantinople. They are all intimately connected with the city. Many steamers, and launches, and caiques converge from all quarters toward the mouth of the Golden Horn. From this centre Constantinople stretches out its arms in all directions. The centre is crowded, congested, unhealthy; and it must be a pleasant escape, for those who can afford it, to get away, when business is over, to the cool breezes of Therapia, or the quiet shores of Vanikeui, or the lovely islands of Antigoné and Prinkipo. Nothing is more striking, perhaps, than to see—

> "The European and the Asian shore
> Sprinkled with palaces."

The smaller houses are built of wood, with red tiles, and verandahs, and large overhanging eaves, in the midst of luxuriant gardens, where roses grow to perfection, and the air is laden with their delicate perfume. But the palaces are of gleaming white marble, most elegant in their architectural construction, ornamented not with sculptured representation of animal life—for that a strict Mohammedanism will not concede—but with the graceful and involved tracery which, from its Mohammedan source, has become known as arabesque. Mohammedanism could not subdue the fertile fancy of the Arabian mind. It found a substitute for the animal face and form in the endless curves of the plant and flower. Some of these palaces are visions of beauty. The Sultan's kiosk, near the "sweet waters of Asia," for elegance of design, structural compactness, and harmonious ornamentation, cannot be surpassed. The effect of these palaces is doubtless heightened by their surroundings. Pure white marbles, built into splendid architectural forms, and embellished with delicate tracery, would look beautiful anywhere; and the beauty must be enhanced by the lovely flowers around them, and the transparent waters beneath them, and the dark green wooded hills behind them, and a sky above them of the deepest azure and without a cloud.

CHAPTER V.

THE CITY OF CONSTANTINOPLE.

Moonlight view—Suggestions—Morning—Origin—Situation—General description—Population—Old seraglio—Armoury and Museum—St. Sophia: its construction—Byzantine model—Ecclesiastical furniture and service—Mosque—The bloody hand—External appearance—The Achmedie—The Suliemanie—The Pigeon Mosque—Mosque of Ortakeui—Palace of Dolma Bagtché—The Sultan's life—Church of the Fountain—Pera—Galata—Hamals—Old round tower—Genoese—Fires—Atmeidan: its obelisk—Meta—Twisted serpents—The Nika sedition—Triumph of Belisarius—Revolutions, and destruction of the Janizaries—Burnt column—Galata bridge—Mosque of the Sultana Validé—Women—Dogs—Beggars—Bazaars—Walls—Latin siege—Arab sieges—Turkish designs—Bajazet and Tamerlane—Turkish siege—Golden Horn—Caiques—Story of an English seaman—Leander's tower—Scutari—Selimie barracks and English cemetery.

AT midnight, beneath a full moon, we let go the anchor off Scutari. Constantinople lay before us, solemn and quiet; the ample domes and slender minarets of its numberless mosques standing forth with almost supernatural clearness; the Golden Horn, like a polished silver mirror, running far between, and separating the solid mass of buildings into two parts; the gleaming water of the Bosphorus stretching away as far as the eye could see, with a long succession of marble palaces rising upon its shores, and bearing on its bosom the anchored and sleeping ships of all nations; the picturesque Seraglio Point, its old crumbling walls, its clustering cypress groves, its almost prison-like, many-windowed, lofty buildings, overlooked by the weird magnificence of St Sophia; the four minarets of St. Sophia, hung round with lanterns, and, farther back, the six taller and more tapering minarets of the beautiful Achmedie mosque engirdled with lights— and lights gleaming like stars away and away over the endless habitations of glorious Stamboul. The dreamy splendour of the moonlight enveloping the whole city, shimmering on its waters, toning the dazzling white marbles of its towers, and mosques, and palaces, and giving them definite outline against the silvery blue of the sky, and, above all, the silence into which the great city had sunk in this midnight hour, left a deep impression upon the mind,— an impression like that made by a solemn and mysterious vision, distinct in its main features, but filled with a meaning almost too profound for the human mind to fathom and comprehend.

There stood the city, once Christian, now Mohammedan; there rose the huge pile of St. Sophia, once a temple surmounted by the cross, now a mosque surmounted by the crescent; there stretched away, on every hand, an interminable labyrinth of streets, deserted except by the watchmen who walked to and fro, and marked the progress of the night; there lay the myriads of sleeping people, unconscious of the night's progress and the approaching dawn, and yet, at the muezzin's call, ready to rise, and turn toward Mecca, and go through the customary postures, and offer the usual prayers. Will the Christian religion never again assert its ascendency? Will the crescent for ever gleam from the dome of St. Sophia? Will the night of Mohammedanism always prevail? The watchmen know that "the morning cometh." The people may be unconscious of the fact, but the fact is there, nevertheless, and more certainly impressing itself upon the horizon. And the people will wake to another call than that of the muezzin, from another place than the gallery of a minaret, and turn, not to the Arabian prophet's earthly home, but to another and more spiritual *kebla*, and offer their heart's adoration to Him who conquers men by the simple force of His compassionate and redeeming love. Very suggestive was everything upon which my eyes rested, and very helpful to calm reflection was the stillness and beauty of the night; but all suggestions were lost, and my thoughts disturbed by the noises of Scutari. Men began to shout and sing, and beat their tiny Turkish drums, which, if jubilant, were certainly not musical; and the dogs took up the chorus, and barked away to their hearts' content. The spell was effectually broken, and I sought quietude and repose, after a long day's enjoyment, in the dim, noise-impervious, comfortable cabin.

The morning changed the whole scene. The sun rose in a cloudless sky. The waters danced and sparkled beneath the brilliancy of the firmament. Steamers, elaborately fitted, and with awnings stretched over, and sheltering, the decks, were passing up and down the Bosphorus, and to and from the Princes' Islands; painted and gilded caiques, cushioned with purple velvet, and manned by gaily-attired oarsmen, bending the whole weight of their bodies to the sweeping strokes, shot across the water, with incredible speed, in all directions. The streets filled with multitudes in every conceivable garb and colour, and the hum of their moving feet came faintly floating over the tide. The scene was full of animation. The city became a seething mass of human life. The palaces, and domes, and minarets, and innumerable buildings were all aglow in the warm rays of the sun; and it was a relief to turn from their glistering, smooth, white surfaces to the darker shade of the old walls of the seraglio, and the welcome green of the cypresses clustering there, and spreading along the shores of the Bosphorus. The entrance to the Golden Horn was choked with every kind of craft. Collision seemed inevitable. Boats and people appeared to become hopelessly confused. But ten minutes' quiet watching was sufficient to show that collision was easily avoided, and that out of the confusion order was being evolved, simply because every one was intent upon his own business, and going his own way. It was the common sight of all large mercantile centres intensified, for although the trade of Constantinople is not to be compared with that of London, or Liverpool, or Marseilles, the city is apparently busier than any of these places, because its trading thoroughfares are so few and narrow, and all meet at the entrance to the Golden Horn.

Byzantium, by which name, among others, Constantinople still continues to be known, and which was the name of the original city, dates back twenty-five hundred years. It was a Megarian colony. This Grecian tribe, confined within the narrow isthmus between Athens and Corinth, was obliged to find an outlet for its surplus population. Necessity became the mother of invention. The Megarians crossed the seas, and dotted other shores with little enterprising colonies, which, as the world widened, became important centres of industry and wealth. Tradition informs us that a company of emigrants, trading from Megara, founded the city of Chalcedon. Seven years later another company, feeling cramped at home, longing for expansion in a larger and freer soil, consulted the oracle at Delphi, and were told to settle opposite a colony of blind men. Good fortune carried their bark through the Hellespont, and across the Propontis, until they came to the tongue of land running out toward the mouth of the Bosphorus, and separated from the main shore by the deep and narrow inlet of the Golden Horn. This tongue of land was splendidly situated both for commercial and military purposes. Nature had done her utmost to induce men to settle here, but her inducements had hitherto been overlooked and neglected. On the opposite side of the Bosphorus, in a position altogether inferior, was the colony of Chalcedon; and, coming to the conclusion that the oracle at Delphi, with its customary ambiguity, had meant that their kindred were blind men, blind to the plainest natural advantages, they immediately disembarked, and founded the city of Byzantium.

Upon viewing Constantinople one's first thought is its magnificent situation. The men of Chalcedon must indeed have been blind to settle on the opposite shore. Constantine the Great was quick to perceive the advantages of this site, and wise to select it in preference to others which had occupied his attention; and, the first Christian monarch though he was, and designed to made this city the new capital of a Christian world, so much of the influence of the old Grecian mythology remained with him as to lead him to construe the flight of an eagle from the Asiatic shore to Byzantium into an assurance of Divine favour, and a presage of the future greatness of Constantinople. Dean Stanley says, "Of all the events of Constantine's life, this choice is the most convincing and enduring proof of his real genius. No city, chosen by the art of man, has been so well chosen, and so permanent. Alexandria is the nearest approach. All the others erected by the fancy or policy of individual sovereigns are miserably inferior, Berlin, Madrid, and even Petersburg. . . . The situation is, indeed, unrivalled. It stands, alone of the cities of the world, actually on two continents. It has the advantages of the confluence as of two rivers, and of a splendid maritime situation besides; for such is the effect, both in appearance and reality, of the Bosphorus and the Golden Horn, and the deep waters of the Propontis. As in the combination of these advantages, narrow straits, deep inlets, numerous islands, prolonged promontories, Europe is the miniature of the civilized world; and Greece, with its Ægean Sea, is the miniature of the geography of Europe; so the local peculiarities both of Greece and Europe are concentrated and developed to the highest degree in Constantinople. It is impossible to look down from the Galata Tower, on the complication of sea and land, island and mainland, peninsula and promontory, strait and continent, and not feel that the spot is destined to be, what it seems more and more likely to be both historically and politically, the Gordian knot of the world." [1]

Another writer, Mr. Edward Upham, says, "The appearance of this city from the harbour fills the beholder with wonder and surprise; its situation is the most agreeable and most advantageous of the whole universe. Its stately mosques and minarets shining in the sun, together with the adjoining suburbs of Pera, Chalcedon, and Scutari, form a prospect of unrivalled grandeur; and combining these in one view, Constantinople is assuredly one of the largest cities of Europe." [2]

Stamboul, or *the city*, occupies almost the entire length of the narrow peninsula. The peninsula is triangular in shape, the point of the triangle running seaward, and its base stretching from the extremity of the Golden Horn to the Sea of Marmora, and marked by the ancient massive walls and towers, and the deep fosses, that yet exist as memorials of the sieges of olden times, picturesque in their ruin and decay. The extreme point of the triangle is occupied by the buildings of the old seraglio. Behind the old seraglio, one after another, stretching far back, are the seven hills, not high, but distinct, each one crowned with a stately mosque, around which the slender minarets shoot from the midst of luxuriant gardens, towards the clear sky. In the far distance, bordering upon the walls, is the faubourg of Fanar, where the Turks condescend to allow the Greeks to live, and where is situated the poor palace of the Patriarch of the Orthodox Greek Church. The very position is indicative of servitude. The power of the Ottoman conqueror is emphasized by the banishment to these quarters of the successor of the Patriarchs who, amid the splendours of a ritual to which that at St. Peter's is an ordinary show, ministered to imperial penitents within the walls of St. Sophia. Round

---

[1] " The Eastern Church," lect. vi. p. 207.
[2] "The Ottoman Empire," vol. i. chap. viii. p. 175.

the head of the Golden Horn is the cemetery of Eyoub. The Ottoman Sultans, since the capture of Constantinople, have been invested with the Sword of State in the mosque of Eyoub, which was built over the grave of Eyoub, who fell fighting in the first Mohammedan siege of Constantinople by the Arabs, not long after the Prophet's death. This venerable Arab was one of the *ansars* or companions of the Prophet, who protected the Prophet when he fled to Medina, and fought under the green banner at Beder and Ohud, and was therefore held in the highest esteem by all the professors of Islam. Upon the capture of Constantinople by the Turks, the place of his burial is said to have been revealed in a dream to the Sheik Schems-eddin, and the victorious Sultan erected a mosque over his grave, in which, from that time, the successors of Othman have girded on the sword in token of their assumption of the sovereignty. The pretty faubourg of Kassim-Pacha lies between the cemetery of Eyoub and the arsenal; and from the arsenal, on hills rising rapidly above the Golden Horn, and running parallel with Stamboul, are the Frankish quarters of Galata and Pera, rounding off, opposite Seraglio Point, through Tophané, towards the Bosphorus. The Golden Horn is spanned by two long, low bridges, one at Galata, always crowded, and one near the arsenal, generally quiet. The Turk has shown his characteristic impenetrable indifference to the convenience and welfare of the people by providing the strongest bridge near the arsenal where scarcely any one goes. The bridge at Galata is a standing disgrace to the Turkish authorities. From Tophané, up the European side of the Bosphorus, the lovely suburbs of the city run for many miles. On the Asiatic side also, from Scutari, which itself is one of the faubourgs of Constantinople, the gardens and palaces of numerous pachas are reflected in the deep, blue waters, while southward, along the strip of land that forms the opening of the Bay of Ismid, run the suburbs of Haider-Pacha and Kadi-Keui.

Constantinople covers an immense area, and in the city, and in Scutari, Pera, and Galata, the streets are very narrow, and the houses crowded together. Its population must be very large, but, on account of the objection of the Sublime Porte to a census of the city, the number can only be approximately ascertained. The estimates of authorities differ, but we may safely conclude, however, that there are at least eight hundred thousand people in Constantinople, and we may as safely conclude that the Turks divide this number about equally with all other races. Mohammedanism is dominant in Constantinople because its professors are the dominant race, and not because they outnumber those who profess another faith. The mosques are very numerous. They occupy all the advantageous positions. Christian churches are few, and, for the most part, in obscure places, lest the sight of them should offend the prejudices of the Moslem, and raise an outcry against the presence of the infidel.

The old Seraglio, whose buildings cover the extreme corner of Stamboul seaward, is the place where the women, who composed at one time the harem of the Sultan, are banished upon the accession of his successor to the throne. As soon as their lord and master expires, they are driven off to the confinement and solitude of this ancient and prison-like fortress, amid its groves of cypress, and almost surrounded by the sea, in order that their places in the seraglios of the occupied palaces might be taken by the women of the new Sultan's harem. An exception is made in the case of those women who have become mothers. For State reasons they are provided for in the imperial palaces. The rest are watched for years in the old Seraglio, and only permitted to leave it upon attaining an age when they may be safely allowed to settle in one of the numerous royal residences without any special supervision of the Sultan's slave.[1]

[1] For the condition of women in Constantinople, and Mohammedan countries generally, see the following chapter on Islam.

Other buildings stand near the old Seraglio. In the corner of a courtyard, an ancient church, probably the church in which met the one hundred and fifty bishops of the second General Council, has been turned into an armoury. The nave is desecrated by the array—rather a poor array—of swords, axes, coats of mail, and other offensive and defensive weapons of days long gone by. Various sculptured marbles have also been collected in a museum, without any classification, or attempt to ascertain their comparative value. The severe iconoclasticism of the believers in the Koran has thrown them confusedly together, and would probably treat an offer to sort them out, and arrange them, as a connivance at idolatry. There are several sarcophagi, said to have once contained the bodies of Constantine the Great, Justinian, Theodora, Julian the Apostle, but all are now empty. The Imperial Treasury stands on this ground, the gate of which, as the *Sublime Porte*, has become the official designation of the Turkish Empire. In the Treasury are stored an extensive collection of antique objects, but here there is the same lack of order as in the museum, and the same indifference to comparative value, golden vessels of rare beauty, adorned with priceless gems, in the midst of a mass of mere tinsel worth nothing at all. The entire space covered by these buildings was originally occupied by the magnificent palace of the Cæsars. The situation is superb. A palace, overlooking the Bosphorus, and in the midst of luxuriant gardens, spreading themselves over a sea-washed peninsula, was worthy of the name Imperial; but the Ottoman Sultan destroyed it, and built for himself, out of its ruins, the Seraskierat, which itself has been abandoned for quieter and more favourable places, and converted into the offices of the Ministry of War.

The most interesting object in Constantinople is the great mosque of St. Sophia. For four hundred years it has been *the* mosque of Constantinople, and for nine hundred years previously it was *the* cathedral of Eastern Christendom. It is supposed that on this site originally stood a heathen temple dedicated to Wisdom, and when Constantine built the city he selected the site for the erection of a Christian church which should be worthy of the city, and worthy to be associated with his own name. He retained the heathen appellation with a Christian significance. St. Sophia the church was called in memory of the Eternal Wisdom. But the building of Constantine was burnt down in the riots following upon the banishment of Chrysostom, and the building that rose on its ashes was consumed during the wild contentions of the different coloured factions of the Circus. The Emperor Justinian, however, determined to erect another and a grander church. Wood was to be precluded from its construction as a safeguard against any attempt to burn it down. The plan of the work was entrusted to Anthemius, the most distinguished architect of the empire, and the wonderful building stands to-day as a proof of his real genius, and a testimony of the age to the zeal and devotion with which it regarded our Lord Jesus Christ.

Ten thousand workmen were employed upon the building. The emperor himself overlooked the growing work, and stimulated the endeavours of the workmen by special rewards. Every workman was paid each night in new silver coin of the realm. A few days less than six years sufficed to complete the building, and at the dedication service, so resplendent was its internal appearance, that Justinian rapturously exclaimed, "I have vanquished thee, O Solomon!" The peculiarity of the building, and that which contributed more than anything else to its majesty and grandeur, was the height and area of the dome, supported by semi-domes, and giving the roof of the building that aërial appearance which led to the boast of its architect that he had hung the dome in the air. But alas! for the boast of an architect and the pride of an emperor. Hardly twenty years had passed before an earthquake shattered the eastern side of the dome. The damage was repaired, the ornamentation restored, and after thirteen hundred years the fabric remains substantially the same as the chief adornment of one of the greatest cities in the world.

The more solid parts, upon which the weight of the fabric mainly rests, are composed of freestone cut into squares and triangles, fastened together by iron clamps, and further strengthened by having the interstices filled up with quicklime and lead. The other parts of the building are composed of brick covered with slabs of marble. The dome and semi-domes, in order to lessen their weight, are constructed of pumice-stone and light bricks from the island of Rhodes. The pavement was furnished by the pure white marble of Marmora, and eleven other precious marbles from various countries, and all differently and richly veined, adorn the interior. Massive granite columns on the northern and southern sides help to support the circle of the dome and semi-domes. Eight windows let in the light from above, and a large west window floods the nave with light, and reveals the beauty of the fine marbles that everywhere meet the eye. The centre of the dome is one hundred and eighty-two feet above the pavement, and one hundred and fifteen feet in diameter. The two semi-domes are of the same diameter. Each of these semi-domes is again divided into three other semi-domes, and the wide and lofty space, unencumbered by pillars, thereby obtained, impresses the worshipper with a sense of majesty unequalled by any other building in the world. Altogether there are one hundred and twenty-four columns supporting the different galleries and ceilings, eight of which are of porphyry from the temple of the sun at Baalbek, and another eight of fine green marble from Ephesus, and many of the columns are adorned with capitals, wrought in the form of interlacing foliage, and, therefore, escaped the hands of the destructive Mohammedans. The church was once filled with splendid mosaics, and even now, through the whitewash and paint with which the zealous Turks have tried to hide the figures, the mosaics reveal their outlines, and attest the original uses of this magnificent sanctuary. The building is in the form of a Greek cross inscribed within a parallelogram, and with its narthex, or large exterior portico, has formed the Byzantine model. Many Eastern churches are built upon this model, with greater or less modification, but not many in the West. St. Vitale, at Ravenna, is Byzantine; but the most conspicuous Western example is St. Mark's, at Venice, whose present splendour gives one some idea of what St. Sophia must have been in the best of its days. Since the capture of Constantinople by the Turks, St. Sophia has become a pattern for the construction of Mohammedan mosques. As the religion itself borrowed largely from Christian sources, and as it owes its purest and soundest maxims, and especially its central idea of the unity of God to the Holy Scriptures, so its architecture is indebted for its most worthy features to the cathedral of St. Sophia.

The ecclesiastical furniture of St. Sophia necessary for the elaborate ritual of the Oriental Church was of the most gorgeous description. The dome and semi-domes, the choir, the galleries, the capitals of the pillars, the folding doors, were lavishly ornamented with glittering gold; the five hundred ecclesiastics employed about the church in the ministration of its services were clad in vestments of the richest material and finest texture; the crucifixes, and censors, and candelabra were of the purest gold, and adorned, as well as the altar covering, with rare and precious stones. Amid the pomp of religious ceremonial the emperors of Constantinople were crowned in St. Sophia. The impressiveness of its ordinary services was assisted by a dramatic effect unequalled among the services of Christendom. Now the cathedral services of Russia outshine in the splendour of their scenic representations the services of St. Peter's at Rome, and these Russian services are the perpetuation on a smaller scale of the services of St. Sophia.

What the effect of these services were may be gathered from the account of the visit of the Russian ambassadors sent by Vladimir to inquire into the merits of the different religions that were then bidding for his conversion. When the Russians beheld the illuminations, and heard the music, and saw the deacons passing in and out of the holy places with torches in their hands and white linen wings on their shoulders, we are told that they "took their guides by the hand, and said, 'All that we have seen is awful and majestic, but this is supernatural. We have seen young men with wings, in dazzling robes, who, without touching the ground, chanted in the air, Holy! holy! holy! and this is what has most surprised us.'" The guides replied, "What! do you not know that angels come down from heaven to mingle in our services?" "You are right," said the simple-minded Russians; "we want no further proof; send us home again." When they arrived home they said to Vladimir, "We knew not whether we were not in heaven; in truth, it would be impossible on earth to find such riches and magnificence. We cannot describe to you all that we have seen. We can only believe that there in all likelihood one is in the presence of God, and that the worship of other countries is there entirely eclipsed."

All this was changed after the Turks broke into the city. St. Sophia was plundered by the Janizaries. The Sultan had given the wealth of the city to his soldiers, but the buildings he had reserved for himself, and therefore, after the movable treasure had been appropriated by whoever could first secure it, the sacred edifice fell into the hands of Mohammed. The affrighted people had sought refuge in their sanctuary. The fierce troops burst in upon them, and commenced the inevitable massacre. The work of death was stayed by the appearance of the Sultan in the portico, who, without dismounting from his steed, rode up the nave to the altar. Leaping from his horse, and standing on the altar, he proclaimed the simple confession of faith which transformed the

Christian temple into a Mohammedan mosque—" There is no God but God, and Mohammed is His prophet." Thenceforward Islam was the religion of St. Sophia. The Christian symbols were obliterated. The names of the Prophet and his four successors, in very large characters, were hung round the circle of the domes. Innumerable lamps were suspended by small cords from the ceiling. Four minarets were erected outside whence the muezzins might call the faithful to prayers. The Mihrab was fixed, directing the faces of the worshippers toward Mecca; and to this day the curious sight may be witnessed of thousands of Mohammedans kneeling in long rows upon the pavement of the mosque, not parallel with its eastern and western ends, but at an acute angle, required by the fact that Mecca is neither directly east nor west of this originally Christian cathedral.

On one of the pillars of St. Sophia, about fifteen feet from the pavement, is the mark of a bloody hand. Two stories account for this, both sufficiently horrible, and such as we may credit from a knowlege of the fierceness and barbarity of the early Ottomans. One story says it is the imprint of a soldier's hand. He put his hand against the pillar to steady himself in stepping over the bodies of the slain. The other story informs us that the Sultan, upon entering the building, saw one of his soldiers wantonly hacking the pillar with his sword. He called to him to desist, and reminded him that the buildings of the city belonged to the Sultan, and, as a warning to others who might be tempted to the same destructive work, he caused the man's hand to be struck off and fastened to the pillar. Such stories are memories of the sacking of Constantinople, but whether they truly account for the bloody hand mark or not it is impossible to say. It may be that the mark is a peculiar grain in the marble itself, an erratic flecking of colour not unusual in some marbles, and no memento whatever of the terrible carnage that took place four hundred years ago in St. Sophia.

The external appearance of St. Sophia is rather disappointing. Its external appearance was sacrificed for the sake of internal effect. The loftiness and vast, unencumbered area produced by resting the dome on semidomes has broken the altitude and majesty of its outward form. There are other mosques in Constantinople more pleasing to the eye externally, but none internally so impressive as the mosque of St. Sophia.

The Achmedie mosque is near St. Sophia. It is a graceful building. The Sultan Achmet I., a feeble monarch, engrossed in the luxuries of the harem, incapable of governing with a firm hand, distinguished himself by the erection of this mosque, and by no other solitary deed. Upon the mosque, however, which was to bear his name, and keep his memory fresh among the people, he lavished riches incomputable. It is said that he secretly picked out the gems from their settings in the imperial throne, and replaced them with coloured glasses, that he might raise money for the accomplishment of his favourite task. The high dome is supported by fluted columns thirty-six feet in diameter. All the details of the building, the necessary accompaniments to Mohammedan worship, are of the most elaborate description. The lamps are ornamented with emeralds; the gates are of burnished brass; the pulpit is beautifully carved; the copies of the Koran are studded with jewels. Achmet went as far as the Koran would allow in placing on each side of the Mihrab nine magnificent golden candelabra. Six graceful minarets were erected round the mosque, equal in number to the minarets of the sacred mosque at Mecca, and the Ulemas would only permit that number on condition that Achmet should add a seventh to those of the Holy Shrine. Within the Achmedie, every seventh year, are displayed the sacred carpets annually sent by the Sultan to cover the Caaba. This man, who succeeded in nothing else, certainly succeeded in adding to the beauty of Constantinople.

Behind the Seraskierat is another famous mosque, built

fifty years before the Achmedie, and not quite so large as the Achmedie, nor so elaborately furnished, but more pleasing, because all its windows are of glass stained in the form of intertwined foliage and flowers—the mosque built by Sulieman the Magnificent. This monarch is to Constantinople what Haroun Al Raschid is to Bagdad. Under his long and able reign the Ottoman power reached its climax. It was the Ottoman golden age. He conquered the knights of Rhodes. He carried his victorious arms under the walls of Vienna. He successfully waged war with the Shah. He employed Barbarossa as Capitan Pacha of the Turkish navy, and gave him an honourable burial on the shores of the Bosphorus. His reign was full of activity. He was magnanimous to his foes, and beloved by his people, both of which are very exceptional statements to make of an Ottoman Sultan, but both true, nevertheless, of Sulieman the Magnificent. The charm of romance is not wanting in his eventful life. He cherished a deep and tender affection for Roxalana. She became his favourite queen. She obtained absolute ascendency over his heart, and, of course, the domestic troubles of the harem followed when the question of successor to the throne forced itself upon the women's attention. The Suliemanie mosque occupies perhaps the finest site in Stamboul. It crowns the highest of the seven hills. Its splendid dome, and four graceful minarets, two of them loftier even than those of the Achmedie, rise from the midst of a mass of dark green cypresses, that add very much, by their contrast of colour, to the harmonious and glittering pile of white marble.

There are hundreds of mosques in Constantinople. But to describe one is almost to describe them all. St. Sophia, the Achmedie, and the Suliemanie are quite special. Other mosques have interesting associations. The mosque of the Sultan Bajazet is known as the pigeon mosque, because Bajazet commanded that the pigeons settled there should not be disturbed, and left a provision in his will for their perpetual maintenance. The result may be imagined in the innumerable flocks that gather about the dome and minarets and courtyard of the mosque of the Sultan Bajazet. On the Galata side of the Golden Horn, a little beyond Tophané, is the more modern mosque of Ortakeui, —a small, pure white marble structure, the very acme of elegance in design and execution, most elaborately carved, and overlooked by two high, fluted column-like minarets,— where the Selamlik, or public devotional visit of the Sultan, is sometimes observed, when the visit is made by water. This mosque stands on the very edge of the Bosphorus, and is one of the conspicuous objects in passing up and down the waterway. The Selamlik is one of the sights of Constantinople. Every Friday the Sultan visits one of the mosques, chosen by himself an hour or two before, and therefore not generally known to the people, for prayer. The gay procession, with all its military accompaniments, may pass through the narrow streets, or the Sultan may prefer the caique to the carriage, and, all glittering with green and gold, and shaded astern by a tasselled canopy, the royal boat, manned by silk-clad rowers, will shoot over the blue waters quicker than the quickest steamer, attended by several others of similar build and speed, while the men-of-war *en route* salute their sovereign, every sailor averting his eyes, in accordance with the etiquette of the Turkish Court, from the face of his august presence.

The Imperial Palace of Dolma Bagtché is on the shores of the Bosphorus above the mosque of Ortakeui. This is the largest and most ornamental palace among the many palaces of the Turkish Sultans. Its elaborate white marble façades—for there are several detached buildings included in the one palace—are directly above, and reflected in, the crystal tide. The present Sultan, Abdul Hamid II., because of the troubles immediately preceding his reign, and associated with the Dolma Bagtché palace, has taken a dislike to it, and lives elsewhere. The Tcharagan, a large square palace, on the brow of the hill behind, is oftener favoured by his presence; but he makes his home mostly at the Yildiz Kiosk, where, surrounded by a faithful regiment of Nubians, men black as ebony, and tall and strong as giants, he feels comparatively safe. The present Sultan has had by no means a pleasant reign. The deposition of Murad, who was invested with the Imperial Scymitar upon the death of his uncle Abdul Aziz, was an unhappy termination of a short reign, and an unhappy inauguration of a troublesome reign for the present Sultan. More than one conspiracy for the restoration of Murad has been discovered and suppressed, but his lunacy places him beyond restoration, and takes from him the power of personally injuring his brother. Abdul Hamid's attempts at reform roused the fanaticism of the Ulemas, although he is a devout Mussulman, and probably cares more for his position as Caliph of Islam than Sultan of the Turks. His sovereignty is not to be envied. His comfort cannot be increased by standing between the two fires of European demands and Mohammedan bigotry. But the comfort of a devout believer in Islam is less likely to be disturbed, and more certain to bow to the inevitable, than the comfort of any other person in the world.

Beyond Fanar, the Greek quarter of the city, and near the walls, is a church called sometimes the Church of the Fountain, sometimes the Church of the Fishes, a favourite resort of pious Greeks who have unbounded faith in all kinds of ecclesiastical miracles. In this church is a standing miracle of living fish, swimming about in a fountain, whose ancestors were cooked on one side, and yet survived the operation, transmitting the marks of their wonderful experience to their sanctified posterity. On the site of the church a monastery stood during the siege of Constantinople by the Turks, and, within this monastery, on the day of the last assault, a monk was calmly frying fish for his brethren's delectation, when a messenger burst upon his culinary superintendence with the disturbing and exciting news that the Turks had carried the city. He replied that as soon as give credit to such an impossible story he would believe that the objects of his artistic attentions, the trout upon the fire, would come to life again. Whereupon, says the record, the good man was astonished to see the fish revive, notwithstanding the perfect cooking to which they had been subjected on one side, and, to preserve the permanence of the miracle, he sacrificed his dinner and the dinner of his brethren by placing the trout in a tank of fresh water, and allowing them the benefit of a cooler environment. Their children still live, and are well cared for, in the Balukli of Fanar, and no doubt appreciate the unremitting attentions of the Greek *papas*, and hope always to enjoy this solicitous concern for their welfare.

Pera, meaning the place *beyond*, occupies the high plateau on the opposite side of the Golden Horn from Stamboul. The people of Western Europe—the Europeans properly so called—are congregated here. Most of the foreign Consulates are in Pera, and the Grand Rue de Pera is the most fashionable and representative street in Constantinople. It it very narrow and ill paved, but it can boast a few good shops, and more than a few itinerant venders, and opens out, in one part, for a few hundred yards, into a wide and respectable-looking boulevard. It has a thoroughly cosmopolitan character. All nations may be met with here. The far East and the far West, with all the graduating connective links, are to be seen in the Grand Rue de Pera, and the picturesque sight is only equalled, if indeed equalled, by the sight of the human streams that flow incessantly over the Bridge at Galata.

Galata, so named from the Gauls who founded a colony here previous to its occupation by the Genoese, stands below Pera, on the steep hillside that rises from the Golden Horn. Its narrow streets are broken by steps here and there. The

British Consulate, which is built about halfway up the hill, is approached by a long flight of steps. To save the difficult ascent of this stiff hill, those who care may be lifted by a tramway, and, if they have no objection, one of the *hamals* of Constantinople, generally met with in or near Galata, will be quite willing to put them on his saddle, and carry them to the top. The *hamals* are the porters of Constantinople. There are eight thousand of them, and they are united in a Guild under a Grand Master. They do all the carrying work of the city. Where the streets are so straight and rugged, the conveyance of goods by a waggon or dray would be very inconvenient and well-nigh impossible. These *hamals* are a necessary body of men, therefore, and get a good living, and they certainly earn all they get, for five of them will carry a ton weight if suspended on a pole so as to equally rest upon their shoulders, and a single *hamal* may not unfrequently be seen staggering through Galata beneath a burden of five hundred pounds. The porters on the Liverpool docks carry immense packages, but even they are outstripped by the *hamals* of Constantinople.

The old round tower of Galata, on the top of the hill, and overlooking the whole city, reminds one of the enterprizing Genoese who built it, and who were so long a thorn in the side, nay, pricking the very heart, of the Byzantine Empire. Upon the re-taking of Constantinople by the Greeks, who had been exiled for a time from the city and sovereignty by a Latin occupation, the Genoese were permitted to settle as *liegemen* in the faubourg of Galata. They were governed by their own laws, and subject to their own *podesta*, but required to acknowledge the over-lordship of the Emperor of Constantinople. The spirited Genoese, however, encroached upon the clemency of their over-lord, and aimed at the mastery of the Bosphorus, and a monopoly of the trade of the Black Sea. An attack upon Galata by the Venetians, and the destruction of the suburb, caused the Emperor to give them liberty to surround the suburb with walls and towers, not suspecting that these Genoese would employ their stronger vantage ground against himself, and in furtherance of their own ambitious designs. When the fortifications were completed the Genoese unmasked themselves. The city of Constantinople was at their mercy. The provisioning of the city was in their hands. They defied the Emperor, and showed him how able they were to damage his people and property by flinging huge stones, from the military engines on their ramparts, clear across the Golden Horn, and into the midst of the city. The Emperor, in his weakness, played the part of Hezekiah, who called in Egypt to fight Assyria—a very foolish thing to do. He called in the Venetians to fight the Genoese. The Venetians, nothing loth, ready for any opportunity to carry war into an enterprizing colony of their enemies and rivals, sailed into the Bosphorus and gave battle, but the Genoese, after a fierce combat in which the odds were against them, obliged the Venetians to retire with heavy loss, and were able to enforce their own terms on the Greek Emperor. They had what they wanted, a monopoly of trade, and what they hardly expected to have, a very liberal extension of power; and, in the last days of its feebleness, for some little time between the Latin expulsion and the Turkish domination, the Greek Empire was not much better than a dependency of the Genoese Republic.

The tower of Galata, a massive round building, with an external gallery, and a summit like the lantern of a lighthouse, remains as a memorial of these troublesome Genoese merchants and sailors. It is now used as a watch-tower, like the tower of the Seraskierat in Stamboul, for the detection of the first outbreak of fire in any part of the city. Fires in Constantinople are very common. The houses are mostly wooden, old and dried, badly constructed and built close together, and the pipes of the heated stoves, and the open braziers of glowing charcoal, easily ignite the timber near them, and the sparks rapidly spring into fierce flames.

One house after another is devoured, one street after another is obliterated, and sometimes a whole quarter is burnt down before the fire can be subdued. When a fire occurs the whole city is roused. News is sent into every suburb, from Fanar to Prinkipo, that they who have property in the neighbourhood of the fire may come and look after it. The firemen rush along the streets, and work away at their pumps with a hearty good will, sparing no efforts to stay the ravages of the destructive element, but very seldom succeeding in checking it until several hundred houses have been consumed. Standing one on each side of the Golden Horn, and both on high hills, the towers of Galata and the Seraskierat are well adapted for the important uses of watch-towers, and some one is always posted there to give the alarm at once upon any outbreak of fire.

The Atmeidan of Constantinople is a large open space near to the Achmedie mosque, and originally formed the public Circus or Hippodrome of the city. It was constructed in the days of Constantine the Great, surrounded by marble seats, and splendidly adorned with statuary choicely selected from the examples of Grecian art then scattered throughout many Eastern cities. Here the chariot races were held, and the entertainment was generally graced by the presence of the Emperor and Empress; and here the people gathered in orderly or tumultuous assemblies to discuss or enforce their rights as citizens of the new Rome. During long years the Atmeidan has become closely associated with the pageantry of paraded conquests, and the misery of awful massacres. This large, silent, and almost deserted area, as it now sometimes is, if it were gifted with language, could tell unparalleled secrets in illustration of the pride and cruelties of the human heart. Every foot of the ground, every object left from the desolating hand of the Ottoman, is invested with the interest of striking historical memories.

A huge granite obelisk stands in the centre of the Atmeidan, inscribed with Egyptian hieroglyphics, which tell of its origin in the days when Moses must have been residing at the Egyptian Court as the foster-child of the Princess Thermuthis. This must be, therefore, one of the oldest inscribed records in the world. Not of Moses, however, does it speak, but of the Pharaoh who then sat upon the throne. The marble *meta* of the Hippodrome, the goal toward which the horses strained, amid the plaudits of the people and the lash of the charioteer, is still there, stripped of its ornaments, defaced and wearing away; but the most interesting relic of the past is what remains of the three brazen serpents, twisted into one column, and on whose heads is said to have reposed the golden bowl of Mardonius, the Persian general, who was defeated at the battle of Platæa. If tradition is correct, and in this case it may be, these serpents, with their bowl, formed the welcome tripod, presented by the warriors of Greece to the pythoness at Delphi, in devout and grateful recognition of their splendid victory. It was brought from Delphi by Constantine the Great, who rifled Greece to adorn his capital, and was converted into a spouting fountain perhaps to cool and refresh the contending steeds of the Hippodrome. In the museum of the old seraglio the Turks show a brazen serpent's head, which, they say, belonged to this column, and was struck off by the powerful axe of the Sultan Mohammed as he rode through the Atmeidan on his way to St. Sophia in the first flush of his conquering pride. The column is now broken and dilapidated, filled with stones which have been apparently pelted at it by the mischievous children of Stamboul; and, unless the Turkish authorities will exercise a little more care in its preservation, which is not likely, this interesting relic will vanish very soon from the eyes, and maybe from the memory, of man.

One of the most remarkable riots that ever disturbed Constantinople had its origin and termination in the Hippodrome. The drivers in the chariot races were attired in four different colours, white, red, green, and blue. The white and red, the two colours first worn, afterwards fell into comparative disuse, but the more recently introduced green and blue became identified with the opposing political parties of the city and empire. The green faction was attached to the memory of Anastasius, and was supposed to have espoused his heretical views; the blues were strictly orthodox. Thus to these opposing colours was added a religious meaning and bitterness as well as a political; and these factions, on the occasion of the public games, and on every other convenient occasion, persecuted each other, and often broke out into open riot and slaughter. So predominant did they become, that all candidates for political and religious offices were obliged to obtain the favour of one or the other, because only by the help of one or the other, whichever happened to be the stronger at the time, could any office be procured. The factions made havoc among families, and friends, and communities of all kinds, dividing them, estranging them, embittering them, kindling hatred in bosoms where beforetime dwelt affection and peace. A very sad result truly, and not without its lessons, but mankind is slow to learn, and will repeat what has led, and what can only lead, to disaster and misery.

Justinian favoured the blues, as the monarchical and orthodox party, and freely expressed his favour during the chariot races celebrating the ides of January, 532, A.D. The greens were discontented with the result of the races, and incessantly murmured at the apparent partiality, until the Emperor was provoked to remonstrate with them by the voice of his herald, upon which the blues rose from their seats, drew their swords, and drove their opponents from the Hippodrome. Tumult ensued, and, unfortunately, during the tumult, an execution of seven men, assassins, belonging to both parties, was carried out in Pera. Five were hung; the last two, however, one a green, the other a blue, escaped on account of the breaking of the rope, and were mercifully rescued by a few monks, who carried them away to a safe asylum in their monastery. This event united the two factions, who cried out against the authorities, burnt the palace of the prefect, massacred his guards, burst open the prisons and let out the prisoners to follow their own bent in the wild excitement of sudden liberty, and spread themselves on every hand for a work of general destruction. The priests interfered for the protection of the people, by marching in procession, under sacred banners, and carrying with them the precious relics of their faith, thinking thereby to awe the rioters, and disperse them; but a company of fierce Heruli, whose barbarous minds were untouched by shaven crowns and ecclesiastical wonders, broke into the procession, scattered the relics, tore down the banners, and sent the priests flying back to their sanctuaries glad of their lives. This sacrilege inflamed the people, who fought with desperation from the roofs and windows of their dwellings, even women joining in the fray. To plunder and massacre the terror of fire was added, and street after street was wrapped in flames, which, spreading rapidly, caught the sacred pile of St. Sophia, and burnt the cathedral to the ground. For five days the city was abandoned to the maddened factions, who adopted the cry, *Nika*, meaning vanquish or victory. Justinian made concessions in order to quell the tumult. Obnoxious authorities were removed, and new men put in their places; and the Emperor repaired to the Hippodrome to meet the citizens, and assure them of his anxiety for the public welfare. He was sullenly and mistrustfully received. He became fearful of a conspiracy to dethrone him, and bestow the purple buskins upon one of the nephews of Anastasius, the favourite of the green faction, and not only retired to his strongly fortified palace, but cowardly premeditated a secret flight from the capital. His wife, Theodora, and his great general, Belisarius, saved him. She spoke with the Imperial haughtiness as of one born to the purple, notwithstanding her obscure origin, and the despised calling of an actress from which she had been raised to the throne, and affirmed herself prepared rather to die an Empress than to live a cowardly, self-condemned, disappointed exile. She asked if there were not yet troops left to quell this sedition,—if it were not yet possible to revive the old enmity, and turn the blues against the greens. Belisarius was ready. Three thousand veterans were quietly brought to the gates of the Hippodrome, where the rioters were still assembled, and bursting in, slaughtered them *en masse*. The blues were roused to vengeance, and turned their hands against their green brethren of the riot, and thirty thousand people fell in the fearful massacre that ended one of the most memorable tumults that ever afflicted the capital of the East.

Two years after this the Hippodrome witnessed a very different sight, in which the chief actor was Belisarius, who, to prove his fidelity to the Emperor, and to confound the schemes of his enemies, had suddenly returned to Constantinople from his victorious campaign in Africa, bringing with him costly spoils, and noble captives, among whom was Gelimir, the Vandal king. So rapid and successful had been the conquest of Africa, so transparently true the loyalty of Belisarius, and so unexpected his return amid the splendid proofs of his military genius, that he was honoured with a public triumph in the Hippodrome, after the fashion of the triumphs of the old Roman generals—an honour which had never yet been conferred upon any one in the city of Constantinople. The Emperor and Empress sat in state; the people assembled in vast multitudes; the long procession traversed the streets, and filed into the large area; the spoils were displayed, ivory, gold, gems, statuary, vases, all the wealth of a conquered people who in their turn had conquered a wealthier people than themselves, and conspicuous among them the vessels of the Jewish temple, which, after long and varied wanderings, were at length sent back to their sacred home; the captive Vandals walked behind their lost treasures, and their brave king, Gelimir, with haughty step, and clad in purple, still a monarch even if a captive, murmured to himself, "Vanity! vanity! all is vanity!" a significant comment on the pomp and pageantry of which he himself was a reluctant part; and then came Belisarius, on foot, marching in front of his veterans, and cheered by the loud acclamation of the great gathering. The captive monarch and the victorious general prostrated themselves before Justinian in acknowledgment of his Imperial sovereignty; and the procession passed on, and became a memory, an historical record, which will never fade.

Very different from this, and more akin to the scene terminating the *Nika* sedition, was that which men now living can well remember. The terrors of Constantinople in the beginning of this century were only exceeded by those of Paris in the end of last century. In Constantinople it was not an oppressed people rising like the bursted fountains of the great deep, devastating, overwhelming, submerging every surface object, and then indulging in the passionate expression of their own wild will, but it was a fanatical soldiery, who, because of their religious alliance with the most renowned of the dervish sectaries, and because of their victories for Islam and the Turk, had been privileged beyond other troops, and had encroached on their privileges until they were absolute masters of the Ottoman power. When the Janizaries were first formed from the bands of captive Christian children at Gallipoli, Amuruth little thought that they would cause such trouble to his successors, and so frequently disturb the peace of the future empire. The wars of the early part of this century tried the courage of the Janizaries to the utmost. They persisted in the use of their obsolete weapons, and antiquated tactics, and consequently were not able to cope with the artillery, or outmatch the modern manœuvres of the regiments of Austria and Russia. The Sultan Selim III. saw the necessity of introducing reforms into the army, if the empire was to be maintained, and attempted this, notwithstanding the fanatical resistance of the Janizaries. He had unfortunately, however, the traitorous Musa for his Grand Vizier, a man outwardly attached to his sovereign, and willing to aid him in his reforms, but inwardly hating his sovereign, and determined to resist reforms. Through his machinations the Janizaries were provoked to fury, and admitted into Constantinople. They gathered in the Atmeidan. They protested against the new institutions, and demanded the death of those ministers of the Sultan who were favourable to them. Musa had everything in his own hands, and compelled his reluctant sovereign to behead those ministers, and present their heads, with his *hatt-sheriff* abolishing the new institutions, to the Janizaries assembled in the Atmeidan, in order to pacify and disperse them. But this was only one step in the progress, one link in the chain. The Janizaries were neither pacified nor dispersed. They demanded the deposition of the sovereign. Selim was calmly informed that he was no longer Sultan, and the poor, weak, dissolute Mustapha, a mere puppet of the Grand Vizier, and therefore altogether to his mind, was invested with the Imperial sword.

The necessary counter revolution soon came. Biaractar, the Pacha of Rustchuk, who owed his elevation to Selim, and who cherished a sincere affection for the unfortunate Sultan, gathered his troops in Adrianople, marched upon Stamboul, unfurled the *sanjak-sheriff* or green banner of the Prophet and thereby enlisted the sympathy and help of the people, thundered at the gates of the Seraglio, and demanded admittance. He was told that admittance could only be given by command of the Sultan Mustapha. He passionately exclaimed, "Speak no more of the Sultan Mustapha: it is the Sultan Selim, vile slave! thou must address, whom we are come to rescue from his enemies, and to replace on his throne." Mustapha himself, who had been away at a kiosk on the Bosphorus, now appeared, and told them to say that the Sultan Selim should be there in a few minutes. The Pacha, fearing foul play, broke down the gates, and entered; and the eunuchs of Mustapha flung the newly strangled body of Selim at his feet, and said, "Behold the Sultan whom ye seek!" Biaractar was filled with distress. He fell on the body of his master, and reproached himself with having sought to prolong his life, and really caused his death. From his grief he was aroused by his friend Seyd Ali, the Capitan Pacha, instantly arrested the Sultan Mustapha, and at once proclaimed the new Sultan Mahmoud in his place. Mahmoud was the only surviving member of the royal house. Search was carefully made for him. For a long time he could not be found. He had been designed for the bow-string by his weak and cruel brother Mustapha, and had prevailed on a slave to hide him in the furnace of a bath; and at last, from this cramped and grimy retreat, he was extracted to be elevated to the throne of the Ottoman Empire.

This counter revolution was effected by the help of Albanian troops against the wishes of the Ulema, the Mufti, and the Janizaries. It was necessary both for the Sultan and his maker, the Pacha of Rustchuk, to act cautiously. Biaractar declared himself a Janizary, and was ultimately regarded as the liberator of the people. Mahmoud was a wise monarch, and refrained at first from offending their prejudices. But he had secretly resolved upon the extermination of the janizaries. These passionate, fanatical troops had been so insubordinate that, although it would greatly diminish the army when all the soldiers he could muster were wanted for foreign service, he saw their extermination was necessary for the welfare of the empire and the stability of his own throne. The new institution was revived under a changed name. For some time the Janizaries were ignorant of the fact, and only discovered it on carrying out the arrangements for a grand review in the Atmeidan, on the 15th June, 1823. During the evolutions one of the standard-bearers cried out, "This is very like Russian manœuvring!" and immediately the troops broke their ranks, forced the dwelling of their Aga, murdered his servant, scattered his harem, and, rousing their companions in every quarter of Constantinople, proceeded to the Sublime Porte, plundered the palace, and destroyed the archives of the city. Then they gathered in the Atmeidan, to the number of twenty thousand, and were ready for any kind of mischief whatever. But their time had come, the time which Mahmoud expected, and had long prepared for. They were secretly surrounded by troops upon whom the Sultan could depend. He took the *sanjak-sheriff* from the Imperial treasury, and, accompanied by the Ulemas and Softas, proceeded to the Achmedie mosque. Thence he sent four superior officers to the Atmeidan to inform the Janizaries that, if they would immediately and quietly disperse, they should be pardoned. They answered him by murdering the officers. He then asked the Mufti for a *fetva*, or religious mandate, to suppress by force the rebellion of the Janizaries. The *fetva* was given. He issued his command for the massacre. And the first intimation the Janizaries had of their peril was the rattling of grape shot from every opening into the Atmeidan, riddling their ranks through and through; but, in the face of it all, they fought their way to the adjoining barracks, only, however, to meet with a more terrible death. The barracks were first fired and then surrounded by cannon, and the fire raged, and the cannon roared, until the awful work was done. The gates of Constantinople were shut for two days, and diligent search made everywhere for the Janizaries. Public executioners were fixed in certain places, and the victims inhumanly dragged before them for decapitation. Thousands were beheaded. The streets and squares were everywhere encumbered with the severed heads and bleeding trunks of the hapless soldiers. The *fetva* was proclaimed in the provinces. Wherever the Janizaries were the deed of death was carried out. And so thoroughly was the massacre planned and executed, that only one attempt at revenge was ever discovered, and that not until five years later, when a few of the remaining troops, who had secretly entered Constantinople, conspired against the Sultan and his empire, and were promptly put to death, and no more has been heard of them to this day.

Near to the Atmeidan is a cracked, blackened, broken pillar, resting on a heavy square pedestal, which is known as "the burnt column." It was once an ornamental part of the Forum. It stood 120 feet high, and is supposed to have been surmounted by a splendid statue of Apollo, with a sceptre in his right hand, a globe in his left, and a coronet of rays about his head, executed by the marvellous chisel of Phidias. But now hardly any traces of its former glory remain. The fires of Constantinople have nearly destroyed it. Like other relics of an artistic past in the Mohammedan city, it is now in the last stage of decay.

The Galata Bridge is an interesting sight, because of the continual ebb and flow of a cosmopolitan tide over its uneven surface. At each end of the bridge men stand, in white cotton smocks and turbans, collecting toll from all who pass over it. There are no gates, no turnstile. The men keep a sharp eye on the people, and no one has a chance of crossing the bridge without the customary fee. Money-changers are seated not far from the collectors, with their notes and coin on small tables, protected by a wire and glass covering, ready to pay Turkish money for the money of any other nation, glad especially of English gold, and charging a trifling commission for the transaction. Passing over this bridge you may see all sorts of people, Persians, Egyptians, Arabs, Armenians, Jews, Greeks, Albanians, Circassians, Negroes, Maltese, Russians, Germans, Italians, French, English, Americans, turbaned Turks, and closely-veiled women from the harems, dressed in their different national garbs, and presenting a picturesque and animated appearance, almost like a fancy fair, except that every one is too serious and quiet—for quietude is one of the peculiarities of the busy Constantinopolitan life—and too much intent upon his or her own concerns.

At the Stamboul end of the bridge you suddenly come upon the mosque of the Sultana Validé, almost lost among the crowd of buildings when viewed from across the Golden Horn, but a really beautiful structure when close to, with its many fountains for the ablutions of the faithful, its wide marble steps, its ample dome, its triple galleried minarets, and, beneath a quaint postern, and beyond a cool corridor, in a courtyard at the back, its busy little market, where venders of fruit and delicacies in gelatine drive a thriving trade.

All the streets in Constantinople are very narrow. The paving, if it can be so called, is simply barbarous. The wooden houses, with their latticed windows and overhanging eaves, lean towards each other, and nearly meet at the top. A tramway has been laid for a short distance in Stamboul. The car is divided into two compartments, in order that the women might be alone; otherwise the car would not be tolerated. It is a sufficiently obnoxious innovation to some of the stricter Mohammedans as it is. All the women of Constantinople are veiled. None are ever seen in the streets unveiled, nor even anywhere else unveiled, except in the harem, and there only by their nearest relatives. And a woman in Constantinople is never accompanied by her father, brother, or husband. She is either alone, or with members of her own sex, generally of her own harem, and possibly with one or two children. The *yashmack*, or veil, consists of two pieces of white muslin, one covering the face from the bridge of the nose downwards, the other covering the head and eyebrows. Only the eyes are visible. The veil is mostly close enough to completely hide the contour of the face. Sometimes you may meet with an old and ugly negress with the veil carelessly put on, and nearly the whole face visible, but never a maiden or young wife. With the *yashmack* is worn a mantle called the *ferigee*, a very loose garment, which altogether hides the outline of the figure. It is often made of rich silk, and beautifully coloured, partiality for violet shades prevailing. The *ferigee* falls below the knees, and below that, tied across and dropping over the ankles, are the *shalwars*, what I suppose may be properly called "the divided skirt." As an artist has remarked, Turkish ladies in a crowd are simply "blots of colour;" there is no shapeliness, no pleasing outline of figure, no interesting contour of face; and yet the *blots* do not spoil the picture. The pure white muslin veils and the violet silk mantles give contrast and variety of colour to the crowd, which, after all, would be rather too sober a picture if the veils and mantles were not there.

To say that there are no sanitary regulations in Constantinople is to express the truth in one way and not in another, for the sanitary regulations are superseded, in the usual Turkish manner, by permitting thousands of dogs to infest the city, and act as scavengers, by devouring whatever may be thrown into the streets. These dogs are very numerous in Pera, more numerous in Stamboul, and more numerous still in Scutari. The Turks are a kind and hospitable people, and the dogs fare better among them than among the Franks. The dogs are of one breed, in size a little less than a colley, in colour of that brownish yellow called tawny, thickly built, with short hair, small rounded ears, and a sharp muzzle. They lie about in the streets anywhere, and the people have to pick their way among them, or step over them, unless they are provoked enough to kick them aside. A Turk will seldom do this. They sleep much, and therefore need little food, and they get little, so little in the keen competition of many mouths that one might reasonably expect them to be nearly skin and bone. They appear to have tribal distinctions, each tribe having its own quarter, and fiercely resenting the encroachment of any member of another tribe upon that quarter. Fights are common, and therefore most of them exhibit the scars received in many a howling, tearing conflict. Man they seldom attack. They gather suspiciously about him when he ventures through a lonely street in the evening, but they have a wholesome dread of a walking-stick, and generally keep well out of reach. The evening is their time for exercise and diversion, and there are very few nights when the sleeper is not awakened once or twice by the long howl or sharp yelp of some unfortunate dog beneath his window. Notwithstanding their number, cases of hydrophobia are very uncommon, accounted for by the ample supply of fresh water, and an unrestricted, unmolested freedom. During a visitation of the plague, at the beginning of the seventeenth century, the Sultan Achmed I., fearing that these dogs carried about the infection, would have had them all destroyed; but the Ulema declared that each dog had a soul, and to destroy them, therefore, was against the teaching of the Koran. They were simply sent into a temporary exile on one of the islands of the Sea of Marmora, and, when the plague disappeared, were all brought safely back again into the city.

Another nuisance of Constantinople, at any rate to the English visitor, is the incessant importunity of the beggars. There are as many beggars as dogs. To sit an hour in any merchant's office in Galata, where the office is on the ground floor, and watch the poor human objects that come one after another, ragged, dirty, diseased, lame, blind, incarnations of every kind and stage of earthly misery, with extended palms, pleading in plaintive muttering monotones until they are served, is a sight indeed; and to see the pile of tiny Turkish coin, smoother and thinner than the most well-worn English sixpence, without a particle of the Sultan's signature left on it to show that it is a coin at all, and made of metal compared with which German silver is valuable, on the merchant's desk, if the merchant is a Mohammedan, ready to supply the wants of all who come, is a significant comment on Islam and that state of society in which beggary so largely prevails. To give to a beggar is one of the religious duties of Islam. No devout Mohammedan will refuse alms. And so the beggars increase, make a trade of it, grow not only persistent but insolent, obtruding themselves on the foreigner, bitterly resenting his denials, and doubtless cursing him as a dog of an infidel. Some of these beggars belong to the Koreish; they have descended from the Prophet, and may wear the green turban; they feel not the disgrace of their beggary, and sponge upon the veneration of the faithful in that calm, deliberate way which only arises from a settled conviction of the respectability of their calling. While we were in a café in Galata, a blind and lame beggar, led by a boy, presented himself just within the doorway, and began his doleful plaint. He was an obstacle to the people passing out and in, and three times the attendants in the café forcibly turned him away, but all to no purpose. He was back again in a moment, muttering, and muttering, and muttering; and when the attendants attempted to remove him the fourth time, he swung his crutch round his head, showing that he was not so lame as he looked, and, with a contorted furious face, threatened to strike any one who came near. Eventually, however, he saw the uselessness of continuing his requests in a Frankish café, and retired to carry on business in a more favourable quarter.

The bazaars of Stamboul are full of interest. They are simply the narrow streets covered in with a rounded roof of masonry, along which are galleries in some places, and windows to let in the light. They look like the old corridors of some immense mediæval castle or monastery, converted into a market, and run in every direction, crossing and recrossing each other, until a stranger is as much lost in them as if he were in the catacombs at Rome. There are different quarters in the bazaars appropriated to the sale of different articles, and here meet all the materials of the world—the watches of America, the silks of China, the furs of Siberia, the ivory of Central Africa; whatever you want you may have in the bazaars at Stamboul. But you can only have after long and leisurely bargaining. No business is done in a hurry; every transaction is lingered over with that refinement of sale and purchase only understood by a Turk, a Persian, an Armenian. The world is not going to end yet, and even about the mere buying and selling of a fez, or a pair of embroidered slippers, or a phial of otto of roses, one might as well extract as much quiet enjoyment as possible. The price first mentioned is always many times in excess of the value of the article, and it may generally be bought for a quarter, or less than a quarter, of what it was said to be worth. As in the days of the Jewish king, so now in the East, "It is nought, it is nought, saith the buyer; but when he is gone his way, then he boasteth." The Armenians are the closest hands at a bargain; even a Jew has no chance when an Armenian steps in. The most interesting part of the bazaars is the part in which are displayed the Oriental manufactures. Weapons, perfumes, pottery, carpets, embroidered curtains and covers—articles distinctively Oriental, these are most attractive to a foreigner; and, projecting from a recess in the long corridor, the low stalls or platform, raised about two feet from the ground, on which the articles are displayed, and the merchant sits cross-legged, calmly smoking his narghilé, and sipping his coffee, recalls the pictures of one's imagination, and associated not merely with Constantinople, but with the really Asiatic Damascus and Bagdad. A group of ladies from some Pasha's harem may be met with in the bazaars, sitting near each other on the platform, or on the ground, chatting in undertones, and darting quick glances from their fine black eyes—the only part of their faces visible—at the passers-by, while bargaining themselves, or superintending the bargaining of an attendant for articles of domestic use or personal luxury. Even a group may be met with sometimes busily stitching coverlets with white and yellow silks into a variety of arabesque designs, names of the caliphs, passages from the Koran, to sell to the wealthy gaiours as memorials of their visits to Stamboul. The little that may be seen of these women is enough to prove that they are not all of the same race. Beside Turkish women, there are Georgians, Circassians, Slavs who have been converted to Islam, Egyptians, Nubians —not with low brows and thick lips, but beautiful, like the woman of Solomon's Song, upon whom the sun had looked;[1] some of them purchased with gold, really slaves, and the rest married after the loose fashion of Mohammedan law. There is a startling array of armour on some of these platforms, old guns and pistols, with carved handles and barrels damascened in every Oriental pattern; swords short and long, straight and crooked, with passages from the Koran inscribed upon the blades, and gems studded in the hilts; scymitars sharp as razors on one side, and on the other thick and heavy, to aid the force of the swinging stroke, and, that the stroke might gain still further impetus, grooved, and charged with running quicksilver. Surely war was a refined calling—*the* calling of a people who ornamented and perfected their weapons in this way. It was their business to kill, and they followed their business at one time most ardently, not only because of its large profits here, but because of its sensuous rewards hereafter.

Constantinople was once surrounded by walls and towers. The most extensive remains of these ancient fortifications are along the landward side of the city, from the Sea of Marmora to the head of the Golden Horn. Some parts of the old walls remain, however, near Seraglio Point, and give the Point, from a distance, that worn and antiquated look which adds not a little to its charm. The walls were twelve miles in circuit, and on the landward side a double wall ran, of great breadth and strength, fortified by ramparts, and defended by a deep fosse fifty yards wide, lined with masonry, and so constructed as to admit the sea. By this fosse, Constantinople was converted into an island. It would appear almost impossible, with the artillery of four hundred years ago, to capture the city. It had been often besieged and

[1] Song of Solomon, chap. i., vers. 5 and 6.

taken, and re-taken in the Grecian wars. Philip of Macedon had won it. The ten thousand, provoked by the falsity of Anaxibius, the Lacedemonian navarchus, then in possession of the city, threatened to sack it, and were scarcely prevented by the persuasions of Xenophon. They forcibly kept open the city gates, and spread terror for awhile among the people. But the gates and walls of those days would be nothing like the gates and walls of mediæval times; and, if a sufficient force had occupied the city, and a spark of patriotism had existed in the hearts of her people, neither the Franks nor the Turks would have succeeded in their sieges, notwithstanding the persistent character of their courage, and the efficiency of their arms.

The French and Venetians took up the quarrel of the Emperor Isaac Angelus and his son Alexius. They fought desperately, and gained their ends; only to be soon defeated, however, by the "perfidious Mourzonfle," who murdered the son, and hastened the death of the father, and himself usurped the throne of the Angeli. The French and Venetians, who had been dissatisfied with the ungenerous conduct of Alexius after his restoration, resolved nevertheless to avenge his death. They commenced a second siege. But this time the Greeks fought more valiantly. Mourzonfle encouraged them by his presence and help, and after three months' terrible conflict the Latins saw the impossibility of taking the city on the landward side. They prevailed very little also on the side of the Sea of Marmora. The city must be taken, if taken at all, from the side of the Golden Horn. The Venetians were ready; the natural harbour was entered. The Greek fire-ships were repulsed and sunk, by men who were more at home on the sea than the Greeks themselves. "Blind old Dandalo," the doge of Venice, was there to share in the conflict and the spoil, and to find a last resting-place, when fast approaching his hundredth year, in conquered Byzantium. The Bishops of Troyes and Soissons fought with the foremost, for it was regarded as a holy war against the heretical Eastern Church, and an acceptable diversion on their way to fight the Saracens in Palestine. The Venetian ships ran under the walls and grappled them, and laid bridges across the space between the walls and the ships. On these bridges the conflict was terrible. The Greeks gave way; the French knights were landed. To cope with them in open street and square was impossible. And Constantinople was won by the crusaders, who basely signalized their victory by plunder, and rapine, and fires, and the wanton destruction of religious relics, and matchless antique statuary, and the accumulated literature of ages.

Fifty years sufficed to exhaust the Latin occupation of Constantinople. Then the Greeks retook it, and held it feebly for another two hundred years, when it finally fell before a mightier and more inexorable foe, who have had the genius to keep it (how much longer will they keep it?) to the present day. Nearly eight centuries before the Ottoman gathered about Constantinople, and when his fathers were only wandering shepherds of the Caspian, it had successfully resisted two terrible Mohammedan sieges, and had formed the boundary of the Mohammedan conquests to the north-west. In the forty-sixth year of the Hejira, the Arabs attempted to subdue Constantinople. They wintered in Cyzicus, and for six summers in succession invested the city, and patiently fought, confident in the triumph of Islam, and then retired with the loss of thirty thousand men. In another forty years they were back again, this time with larger forces, and a splendid navy of the combined fleets of Egypt and Syria. But the Greeks launched their fire-ships among them. That burning liquid, the composition of which was scrupulously kept as the special secret of Byzantium, did its deadly work. The navy was destroyed; the Arabs were confounded and repulsed with the feeling that if God had given the land to them, He had given the sea to the infidel. But later on the Ottoman came. Greek fire had been superseded by gunpowder; and the Greeks had no gunpowder monopoly. Their walls were less vulnerable against the huge brass cannon of Mohammed than they were against the old battering-rams of the Arabs. The Byzantians were weakened by long divisions and individual selfishness. They had estranged the people of Western Europe, who could have helped them, or who might, if they had not been too busy fighting among themselves. And the inflexible purpose of Mohammed was accomplished in the downfall of the city.

The Turks had long cherished designs for the capture of Constantinople. Since their formation as a separate power, their eyes have always been westward. They conquered Phrygia and Bithynia, from Antioch looking towards Brusa, and from Brusa towards Nice, and from Nice towards Byzantium. They were possessed with all the fiery ardour of Islam. The doctrine of the prophet was like honey to their lips, and unction to their souls. War was their element; the battle-field was their home. As soon as ever Constantinople came within the sphere of their vision, it was coveted as a supreme prize, not only because of its commanding position, and as the natural seat of extensive empire, but because the prophet had said that the sins should be forgiven of the first army that captured the city of the Cæsars. They widened their borders slowly, but surely, until they were only separated from their prize by the gleaming waters of the Bosphorus. They crossed the Dardanelles, established themselves at Adrianople, and gradually worked their way round to Byzantium on the landward side, until the city was completely closed in, and Mohammed, upon the remonstrance of the Greek Emperor at the building of the Roumeli Hissar, was able to return the insolent message, "The Empire of Constantinople is measured by her walls."

The Ottomans were prepared for the siege years before they actually commenced it. Constantinople would have fallen sooner if it had not been for the menace of the

Ottoman Eastern frontier, and the defeat of the Ottoman forces, by Tamerlane of Samarcand. This military genius, who combined the vast hordes of Central Asia, and led them in battle against China, India, Persia, Syria, the peoples of the Caspian, the Scythians of the Russian steppes, Mohammedan as he was, demanded submission from the house of Othman, but found in Bajazet, surnamed Ilderim, or the lightning, a spirit almost as proud as his own. Their messages one to another have the true barbaric assumption of superiority and contempt. "Thou art no more than a pismire," said Tamerlane; "why wilt thou seek to provoke the elephants?" at the same time telling him it was only out of consideration for the fact that he was a Mohammedan, and his country the frontier and bulwark of the Mohammedan world, that he was prevented from destroying him utterly. "What is the foundation of thy insolence and thy folly? Thou hast fought some battles in the woods of Anatolia; contemptible trophies! Thou hast obtained some victories over the Christians of Europe. . . . Be wise in time; reflect, repent; and avert the thunder of our vengeance, which is yet suspended over thy head." Bajazet was ready with his reply: "What are the arrows of the flying Tartar against the scymitars and battle-axes of my firm and invincible Janizaries?" he asked; and insulted his foe by a reference to his harem—a mortal offence to a Mohammedan, and one which could only be avenged by the sword. They met on a large plain near Angora, Bajazet with four hundred thousand, Tamerlane with eight hundred thousand men, and fought from daybreak till sunset. But the Turkish Sultan was no match for the great Khan. He had not the foresight, the tact, the manœuvring genius of his terrible adversary. His men were as brave, but they were worn out with the fighting, and Tamerlane had men in reserve. The day ended in a complete victory for the Tartars. An equal number of men—four hundred thousand in all—fell on both sides. Bajazet was taken captive, and, because of his own haughty demeanour, was imprisoned in an iron cage, and carried about as a public spectacle, until death mercifully ended his shame. Tamerlane, satisfied with this chastisement, and abandoning the country to its fate,—a proceeding characteristic of Tamerlane, who seldom made any provision for the consolidation of conquered countries, and their attachment to his Empire, as if fighting were the first, and government the second, consideration of a monarch,—withdrew into Central Asia, and prepared for his campaign against the Chinese.

The Turks soon recovered themselves, and in fifty years were quite ready for the final attempt upon the city of their desire. Mohammed the Great, the opener, or vanquisher, as his people call him, because of his successful siege, was a patient, determined, courageous monarch. He studied economy in his own household that he might have the means to accomplish his favourite design. On the 6th of April, 1453, he invested Constantinople with more than two hundred thousand men, and a fleet of three hundred ships. Constantine Palæologus, the Emperor, the last of his race, and a braver man than many who had preceded him, defended the city with his eight thousand troops in a manner which compels admiration, and anxiously looked for succour to his Christian brethren of the West. Five ships came, four of which were Genoese, laden with provisions and soldiers, and they gallantly fought their way through the Turkish lines extended in the form of a crescent at the mouth of the Bosphorus to intercept them, anxiously and excitedly watched by thousands of people on the European and Asiatic shores. They came safely to anchor in the Golden Horn. They were the beginning and end of his succour from the West. For several weeks he hurled back the foe from his ramparts into the deep fosses, and fairly held his own. His troops were thinned and weakened. His walls were battered and broken by the cannon of Mohammed. Nevertheless, by the help of Justiniani, the Genoese, he continued the contest, and scorned to accept the terms offered him by Mohammed if he would capitulate, namely, the sovereignty of a portion of the Morea. The Turks could see that, nothwithstanding their superior forces and huge brass cannon, the city would never be carried unless a simultaneous assault could be made from the landward side and from the side of the Golden Horn. The defenders would not be sufficiently numerous to successfully repel both assaults. But how were they to get into the Golden Horn? A clever stratagem was hit upon. Eighty ships were run ashore near to where now stands the Dolma Bagtché Palace, and, during the night, by the aid of rollers, carried over the low-lying land into the centre of the Golden Horn. Of course the ships were not very large. Still, the feat was not only clever, but arduous; and sufficient were conveyed into the harbour to assault the city on that side. It is supposed that the Turks were assisted and directed in this effort by the Genoese of Galata; and it is certain that a treacherous Genoese of Stamboul revealed to the enemy the design of the Byzantians to destroy the eighty ships by the terrible Greek fire, and, consequently, the few brave men who attempted to carry out this enterprize were entrapped and beheaded within sight of, and for the purpose of striking terror into, their fellow-citizens. On the morning of the 29th of May, without any noise of drums or musical instruments, quietly, but with deadly fanaticism, having been prepared the previous night, amid their blazing camp fires, by the preaching dervishes, the double assault began. Mohammed personally superintended the assault on the landward side, surrounded by ten thousand Janizaries, and supported by one hundred thousand cavalry, in addition to the troops spread before the walls from sea to sea. The worst troops were forced on first, and as fast as they approached they were thrown into the ditches, until their dead bodies became a bridge for the passage of braver men. Then came the Janizaries. In one long linked line they commenced the attack. The Sultan had promised the government of his largest and fairest province to the man who should first mount the ramparts, and Hassan, a Janizary of gigantic stature, was the man to claim the reward. With thirty companions he scaled the walls; eighteen were killed, and he was hurled wounded to the ground. But he mounted again. The Genoese leader, Justiniani, who had fought bravely during the whole siege, received a wound in his hand at this critical juncture, and sullied his fame by retiring from the conflict. It was the last fatal act. Constantine met him and reproached him, but he would go. Soon the walls were carried. The Emperor removed the emblems of his sovereignty, fought to the last, and was afterwards found beneath a heap of slain; the citizens fled to St. Sophia, under the belief in a prophecy that, upon the Turkish approach to the sacred edifice, a miracle would be wrought, and the foe beaten back by the interposition and assistance of heavenly power. A poor man was to be seated at the foot of the column of Constantine. To him, upon the approach of the Turks, an angel was to appear, and handing him a sword, say, "Take this sword, and avenge the people of the Lord!" But the poor man was not there. The angel never came. And the tremblingly expectant multitude in St. Sophia was deceived by the Janizaries thundering at the doors and exultantly entering the building. The city was pillaged in the night. Sixty thousand people were sold into slavery. The crescent replaced the cross on the dome of St. Sophia. Constantinople became the greatest Mohammedan city in the world.

The Golden Horn is a poetical name for the long, narrow, deep, curved inlet that separates Stamboul from Galata. It affords excellent natural harbourage for the Turkish fleet. It is certainly not unlike a horn in shape, and the reflection within its waters of "glorious Stamboul" may entitle it, in the opinion of the Turks, to the name golden. It catches the beams of the rising and setting sun, and the reflected golden glory of the sunrise and the sunset may further entitle it, in the opinion of all people, to its poetical name. But we must not take Turkish names to mean all they seem to mean. They borrow them from paradise. We have to beware the suggested heavenly character of the scenes. There are many places more beautiful than the Golden Horn. The Valley of the Sweet Waters of Asia implies, to a Western mind, a delightfully romantic place. Imagination fills in the details suggested by the poetical outline far otherwise than what they really are. We have gone to the other extreme in naming our fashionable resort Rotten Row. This Valley of the Sweet Waters of Asia is the Rotten Row of Constantinople. Very frequently the loveliest scenes, the places most like a terrestrial paradise, have no name, and are altogether unknown. The wooded slopes beyond the Bay of Buyukdere are far lovelier than the level meadow and narrow stream, called by its highly poetical name, on the opposite shore.

Among all the shipping of the Golden Horn and the Bosphorus the most noticeable are the caiques. What the gondolas are to Venice the caiques are to Constantinople. They are lightly built, very buoyant, and without keel; both the prow and stern curve out of the water, and terminate in long points; they have no rudder, the direction, as well as propulsion, being managed by the oars, which are fastened by cords to the gunwale, and are thick and heavy toward the top, thereby securing balance and ease of movement; they are gaily painted and comfortably cushioned, although the seats, on account of their shallowness, are only a few inches from the bottom; and they shoot through the water with a speed unequalled by any other craft in the world. Some of them are large, and well adapted for sailing; but they are mostly handled, whether large or small, by a set of rowers who are adepts in management, and can calculate all their movements to a nicety

The large caiques have many rowers, and their method of rowing is peculiar. They sit in pairs along the middle of the boat, the passengers sitting astern, and the pairs rise from their seats simultaneously, stand on the seats of the pairs before them, lay the weight of their bodies to the stroke, and gradually pull themselves back into their places. Their motions are as exact as the motions of a machine, and the caique cuts the water as a bird the air, skimming swiftly along with all the grace and swiftness imaginable. The caique is the ordinary passenger boat. Steamers ply across the Bosphorus to stated places and at stated times, but if you want to take a special journey, at your own time, you must hire a caique.

An amusing story is told of an English seaman, who obtained leave to go ashore, found his way into some drinking saloon in Galata, became intoxicated, and remained beyond the allotted time. He ransacked his brains for some plan of return, which should be gratifying to his own vanity as well as striking and laughable enough to put his superior in a good humour, and, counting his money, found that he had just sufficient left to pay for the hire of five caiques. These caiques, under his direction, were roped together; he seated himself in the stern of the last one, a solitary passenger, inflated with his own importance, and told the rowers to "fire away." Out they went into the Bosphorus, one after another, quite a procession of them, attracting the attention of every one within sight, and, as they bent their way toward the English vessel, drew to the bulwarks the inquisitive eyes of all her crew. Whoever was coming? Some Pacha, the Sheik-ul-Islam, or the Sultan himself? Surely a big dignitary he must be to require five caiques to bring him! But when the fifth drew near, and they recognized the form of their shipmate reclining among the cushions with all the complacency of intoxication, and affecting the air of a lord, they greeted him with loud laughter, and generously helped him aboard. It is a pity that a man with so much ingenuity, and characteristic English humour, should have to exercise it for the covering of his own faults, and the saving of himself from the disgrace of deserved punishment.

On the Scutari side of the Bosphorus, built upon a rock about half a mile from the shore, is a square tower, ninety feet high, with an external gallery, and surmounted by a flagstaff. It is now used as a lighthouse. Sometimes it is called Leander's tower, sometimes the Maiden's tower. Its latter name is supposed to have arisen from the imprisonment of a lady within its narrow walls by the Sultan Mohammed. This may be so, but an event occurred in the troubles of the early part of this century, the troubles which were terminated by the destruction of the Janizaries, sufficient to stamp it for ever with the name of the Maiden's tower. Upon the successful counter revolution of Biaractar, which placed Mahmoud II. upon the throne, wholesale executions followed as a matter of course; and among the unfortunate sufferers were the Odalisks of the Seraglio. As I have already described, Biaractar demanded the restoration of Selim III., and the body of that monarch, newly strangled, was thrown at his feet. The Odalisks, or favoured maidens of the Seraglio, were imprudent enough, not knowing how affairs were likely to turn, to express satisfaction at Selim's death; and their imprudence was punished in a shockingly barbarous way. They were carried to the tower in the Bosphorus, sewn up in sacks, and flung from the summit into the sea—a public execution which, in the less important and unknown domestic revolutions of many a Pacha's palace, has had doubtless its private parallels, even if imagination based upon rumour is only approximately correct. What can be said for that state of society, created largely by its professed religion, which tolerates deeds like these? nay, which leads up to deeds like these as to results expected and inevitable?

Scutari is more Turkish than Stamboul. There you touch

Asiatic soil. There you come completely into contact with Asiatic life. There Mohammedanism is in its own home. There caravans are seen from the interior,—long strings of camels, and ragged, olive-coloured camel-drivers, with all the equipment of Oriental life not seen in Stamboul. That strip of water, narrow as it is, makes a difference to the feelings; when you have crossed it, and landed at Scutari, you have left Europe behind. You are on a new continent, and in the midst of a new life. The life of Stamboul is too near Pera, too permeated by Western influences, to be new. Scutari is beyond the reach of Pera. Western influences do not prevail there. The Turks look across the water fondly. It is the place whence they came, and whither they *must* return. They are not of Europe, but only sojourners on European soil, and, by the burial of their dead in Scutari, confess the feeling that sometime their sojourning will cease.

There are two places in Scutari dear to all Englishmen. One is the English cemetery, neat and trim, and presenting a decided contrast to the neglected cemeteries of the Turks. Here lie the soldiers, who were wounded beyond recovery in the Crimean War. The Selimie barracks is the other, overlooking the cemetery, the building placed by the Sultan at the disposal of Florence Nightingale and her companions, who nobly devoted themselves to the tender Christian work of nursing the wounded men. These two places must have many memories, both sorrowful and joyful, for the English people, sorrowful because of their countrymen who lie there, joyful because of their countrywomen who endeavoured to save them, and, when they could not save them, who ministered to their comfort and peace in their dying hours. The English traveller, entering or leaving Constantinople, as he looks upon the grey barracks and the flower-decked "God's acre," must often have his mind drawn away from the surrounding splendours of Europe and Asia to his own people and his own home.

CHAPTER VI.

ISLAM.

Origin—Knowledge of Islam important—Condition of the Christian Church—Condition of Arabia—Birth of Mohammed—Personal appearance and character—Hanyfism—Mecca and Medina—Rapid spread of Islam under the perfect Caliphate—A localized religion—National embodiments—Claim of the Sultan to the Caliphate, and to the title of Imaum-ul-Islam—Its influence upon the foreign and domestic policy of the Sublime Porte—The Mahdi—God—The Koran—Prayer—Almsgiving—Fast of Ramadan—Pilgrimage to Mecca—Disallowance of gambling, usury, and the use of wine—War—Slavery—Woman—The royal Seraglio—Paradise—Ulema—Imaums—Preaching—Muezzins—Mysticism—Dancing dervishes—Howling dervishes—Influence of Islam upon Turkish life and character.

ISLAM originated in the seventh century of the Christian era. It dates from the Hejira, corresponding with 622, A.D., in which year Mohammed fled from Mecca to Medina. No religion can compare with Mohammedanism in the rapidity of its extension, and in the suddenness of its arrest and decline. Its adherents now number two hundred millions. Of these, forty-five millions are Hindoos, subject to our own Queen-Empress Victoria, able to exert a mighty influence upon the course of events in our Indian Empire, and, therefore likely to affect, for good or evil, the future welfare and destiny of the English race. To no nation is a knowledge of Islam, and, based upon that knowledge, the necessity of a prudent attitude toward the Moslem, more important than to the English, **not only** because of the **forty-five** millions of Moslems **in Hindostan,** but because of **another** forty-five millions living between Hindostan and the Eastern **borderland of** Europe. The Eastern Question, which **is ever recurring,** in many forms, as the Gordian knot of European politics, cannot be comprehended and dealt with, **except by** men who understand the Mohammedan **religion.** A knowledge of Islam will **explain the apparent incapacity of the Turk, and** the real retrogression **of the Ottoman Empire.** The study of Mohammedanism **is as interesting and essential to the statesman as to the missionary,—to the statesman if** he would **know how to guide events for the benefit of mankind, to the missionary if he would know how to deal with men possibly as intelligent as, and even more outwardly religious than, himself; and by the working of these** two, in unconscious unity, each one from his own standpoint, each one with the advantage of **a clear** understanding, very much would be done to purify the atmosphere, drive away the mists, bring **the East and** West nearer together, **and** solve some of those **difficult problems that now appear, to** many people, **incapable of any solution whatever.**

Islam sprang from the teaching of one man in a very degenerate period of Christian history. The Church was rent by controversies. Nice theological distinctions engaged the attention of the learned, divided them into hostile camps, drew from them mutual anathemas, and not unfrequently caused them to rouse against each other the passions of the willing mob in their contentions for powerful vacant ecclesiastical sees. The original simple services of the Church had been superseded by gorgeous and elaborate rituals. The people were practically excluded from all participation in the services. Their attention was diverted from the real object of worship **to certain** media, such as sacred pictures and the relics **of saints, and to** these media **were** attributed mystic virtues which led the worshipper to pay obeisance to them for their own sake. They became as gods, and the people were ignorant idolaters. It was a barefaced compromise with heathenism. Hermits and Cœnobites multiplied greatly, and endeavoured, by the vagaries of religious fanaticism, to lift themselves into a state of spiritual rapture. They retired from their fellows, many of them to lead indolent and selfish lives, and nearly all, by ingenious methods of self-mortification, to obtain a reputation for special sanctity, and thereby impose upon the credulous, and feed the vanity of their own morbid minds.

Arabia was not Christianized. The Arabs were polytheistic idolaters. The different tribes into which they were divided worshipped their own particular deities. The heavenly bodies were regarded by them all with excessive veneration. The brilliant constellations of an Oriental midnight sky impressed the Arabs deeply. In their wanderings over the sandy wastes they depended as much for guidance upon the positions and movement of the stars as the mariners in their wanderings over the watery wastes. The firmament was as familiar to them as the desert. The signs of heaven, indicating the times and seasons, were matters of common knowledge. Although divided into independent tribes, each tribe under its own patriarchal government, and sometimes in deadly feud with one another, they all met in peace to worship in the temple at Mecca, and in this temple, known as the Caaba, their domestic gods found a common resting-place. All kinds of images, to the number of three hundred and sixty, were placed here, and, with various ceremonies, more or less repulsive, these images were worshipped. Human sacrifices were specially acceptable. Strong inducements were presented to offer a favourite child, and, should the vow be made, the child barely escaped by the substituted sacrifice of a hundred camels.[1] The Caaba was under the care of the tribe of the Koreish.

---

[1] The father of Mohammed was dedicated for sacrifice, and ransomed by the hundred camels. (Gibbon, chap. 50.)

They had special privileges. They obtained great influence. They were strong in the sanctity of their religious office.

Into a world like this Mohammed was born. He was of the tribe of the Koreish, and of the family of Hashem. This family was numerous, wealthy, and powerful. The grandfather of Mohammed was the patriarch of the family, and his father the favourite of nineteen children. But his father, and mother too, through whom he was related to the illustrious tribe of the Zahrites, died while he was an infant, leaving him to the mercy of his uncles, who, with the right of might, the only right recognized in a society like theirs, appropriated all his fortune, with the exception of five camels and a black slave. One of these uncles, Abu Taleb, took charge of him, until he reached his twenty-fifth year. Then he became the servant, or steward, of Cadijah, a wealthy widow of Mecca, whom he afterwards married, and, by this alliance, was able to take his place again among the affluent members of his own family.

Mohammed was a great man. That no one can doubt. Only a great man could have done the work he did—a work, in its earlier stages, quite commendable, and in its effects, especially considering his ignorance, truly marvellous. His personal appearance was very striking. Even after making the necessary deductions from the warm descriptions of his contemporary admirers, we have the portrait left of a man of splendid physique. His walk was commanding. His head was finely poised, his eyes were black and sparkling, his eyebrows long and curved, his mouth was large and well formed, covering teeth "like hailstones," the Arabs say, beautifully clean and white. He was of the most highly developed Arab type. Men like him may yet be met with among the Bedouins of the wilderness. He was singularly gifted in many ways. He was a man of strong will, penetration, foresight, statesmanship; his nature was fervent, expressing itself in eloquent discourse, and magnetic, attaching people to his person as well as to his cause; his disposition was open, gentle, gracious, generous; he loved those about him, and died, poisoned, as he believed, by a Jewess, four years before, since which his health had gradually declined, manumitting his slaves, and distributing the scanty remains of the wealth left him after the continual replenishings, and as continual hospitalities, of twenty years. His faults were great, and were especially manifest in the second half of his life, the half which commences with the Hejira, when, having fled from Mecca, he unfurled in Medina the standard of Islam, and commenced his missionary warfare, not only as a prophet, but as a king. He had deceived others already with the pretended revelations from heaven embodied in the Koran, and his military successes may possibly have helped him to deceive himself. There was no basis of truth in his character at any time, so far as his religious teaching was concerned. He was densely ignorant, accepting mythical accounts as genuine, confounding persons and historical events separated by centuries, and yet locking up all these incongruities along and mixed with his own ideas, in a book deemed infallible, and which the Moslem unquestioningly accepts, and lives by, as unchangeable and Divine. Success weakened his character, confirmed him in his purpose of propagating Islam by the sword, and led him into sensual indulgences in contravention of his own precepts,—an example which his disciples have not been slow to follow, and which has contributed more than any other single thing to shatter Mohammedan States, and hasten the ruin of the Mohammedan religion.

His life at Mecca was that of a prophet, a teacher, one who wished to convert his countrymen from their idolatrous practices to the worship of the one God. There had been a few before him, and there were a few among his contemporaries, who knew how foolish and ridiculous and pitiable it was to worship idols. They called themselves Hanyfs, or Puritans, and endeavoured to restore the original faith of their great ancestor, Abraham. Mohammed was a Hanyf.

The genius of his character, as well as his illustrious birth, marked him out as the natural leader of these men. His mercantile journeys to Damascus as Cadijah's steward, and the contact with Jews and Christians into which he was brought thereby, widened the horizon of his mind, and furnished him with materials for his pretended prophetic revelations. Neither Judaism nor Christianity met with his approval. The narrowness of the one, and the grossness of the other, as represented in his day, repelled him; and, true to his profession as a Hanyf, he called Islam a restoration of the pure faith of Abraham, and, true to his own ambitious nature, he proclaimed himself as the last and most glorious Prophet of God. He met with very little success in Mecca. Thirteen years were spent in gathering two or three hundred disciples. Then, because of the persecutions of his own tribe of the Koreish, whose calling as keepers of the Caaba was at stake, and the income of whose priestly offices was threatened, by the success of Islam, he fled to Medina. He was accompanied by some of his disciples, joined by others who had previously sought refuge in the Abyssinian court, and welcomed by those residents of Medina who had already been converted to his cause. Now he had might on his side, the might of armed men, and now he assumed the character of a monarch as well as a teacher, and enforced his government and doctrine upon the Jews of the neighbourhood at the edge of the sword. The caravans of the Koreish passed by Medina, and, with the true Arabian instinct, he retaliated their persecution by plunder; and in eight years after fleeing from Mecca, entered it again as a sovereign-prophet at the head of ten thousand men. The tribes gathered about him. Islam did what all else had failed to do, bound the tribes together into one people, under one monarch, and Mohammed reigned from the Red Sea to the Persian Gulf, from the Indian Ocean to the borders of Palestine.

Mohammed was succeeded by men braver and fiercer

than himself. He had thoroughly roused the martial spirit of the Arabs, he had given them the fanatical war cry, "There is no God but God, and Mohammed is His Prophet," and he had inspired them to make to all people the threefold offer of Islam, the Tribute, or the Sword. Upon the Prophet's death the Arab tribes revolted, but, by the vigour of Abu-bekr, and the terrible sword of Caled, they were brought into submission to the Prophet's chosen successor. Under the first four Caliphs, Abu-bekr, Omar, Othman, and Ali, generally regarded by Mohammedans as the perfect Caliphate, Islam spread very rapidly. The succession of the perfect Caliphate was not without its troubles. Ali, the husband of Fatima, the Prophet's favourite daughter, was regarded by an influential section of Islam as entitled to the Caliphate first of all. His claims were overruled, however, and three Caliphs preceded him; but, by the sect of the *Shi-ites*, who are predominant in Persia, his memory is cherished with peculiar veneration. By the *Sonnites*, who are predominant in Turkey, and who are considered the orthodox of Islam, equal veneration is paid to all the four. They trod faithfully in the Prophet's footsteps. They fired the Arab hosts with fanatical enthusiasm; they sent them forth against Syria, and Persia, and Egypt, and everywhere success crowned their arms. Riches untold were suddenly poured into their treasuries. The fair women of many nations filled their harems. Thousands, to escape the sword, consented to pay the tribute, and tens of thousands, seduced by the certainty of wealth in this world, and the promise of sensual pleasures in the world to come, pronounced the prescribed formula, and were enrolled among the believers of Islam. In a single century from the Prophet's death the green banner was waving over the Straits of Gibraltar, and on the banks of the Oxus, and the millions that dwelt along this immense territory were offering the prayers, and keeping the fasts, and observing the laws, and believing in the precepts of Islam.

Along this immense territory, but neither then nor afterwards very far to the North or the South of it. Mohammed was a real Arab, and Islam was primarily for Arabia He was ignorant of the differences of climate in the far North and the far South, and he prescribed forms of religion impossible to be kept except where the nights and days are much the same in length and mildness as the nights and days of Arabia. Beyond forty-five degrees North and South latitude, Mohammedanism cannot exist. Natural conditions are against it; and among Northern peoples it finds no favour. Its home is Asia. It is simply suited to the Asiatic mind. Mohammedanism is therefore essentially a localized religion, and never can become anything more. It contradicts its own claim to universal dominion. It gives the lie to the assumption of its founder as the final and perfect Prophet of God.

The national embodiments of Islam have been shortlived. They have made little, if any, progress. They have contributed very slightly to the world's growth in arts, sciences, laws, literature, or any other mark of advanced civilization. Islam seeks national embodiment. Its highest expression, like that of Judaism, is through the State. In Mohammedan countries the religion is the law, the body politic is the body ecclesiastic. Islam is not a Church in a State, but the State itself churchified (if such a word may be allowed). The highest ecclesiastical authorities are the acknowledged lawyers of the land, and they rule both the people and the court. They are supreme. The Ottoman Empire is a religio-political organization. It is governed by the Sublime Porte, and the Sublime Porte is governed by the Ulema.

Islam has passed through several national embodiments since the termination of the perfect Caliphate. In Damascus, in Bagdad, in Cordova, in Samarcand, in Constantinople, the seat of Mohammedan government has been fixed, and empires of greater or less extent have been swayed in the name of the Prophet, and for the glory of Islam. They have been illustrious for a short time, and have then rapidly sunk into decay. The Ottoman Empire is the last creation of Islam. Whether we shall have another or not, when the Ottoman Empire vanishes, it is impossible to say; but all the probabilities are in favour of the opinion that Islam has run its course. Persia is Mohammedan, but heterodox, and of small importance compared with Turkey. Other Mohammedan States are smaller than Persia. The Padishah of Constantinople is the head of the Mohammedan world in power, and he claims to be head of the Mohammedan world by right. He regards himself as the Caliph, the Prophet's successor, the custodian of the green banner, the guardian of the faithful, the defender of Islam.

This assumption of the Caliphate by the Sultan of Turkey, this belief that the Caliphate of right belongs to the Sultan of Turkey, must materially influence the foreign and domestic policy of the Sublime Porte. But the Caliphate of the Sultan is not universally acknowledged by the Mohammedan world. It may be acknowledged by the Ottomans, and that portion of the Slavs and Circassians who have been converted to Islam, and who are under Turkish rule; but the great bulk of the Mohammedan peoples would repudiate the Caliphate of the Sultan, and refuse to obey his commands. The last of the real Caliphs, Mohammed XII., died in Egypt in 1538, A.D. It was through the enforced cession of the Caliphate by Mohammed XII., to the Sultan Selim I., that the rulers of the Ottoman Empire have styled themselves the Caliphs of Islam. But Mohammed could not cede the title and authority of the Caliphate to an alien. The Prophet had declared that the Caliphate should be kept in his own family. The Ottoman Sultans are not of the family of the Prophet: they are not even of the race of the Prophet. The blood of the Arab does not run in the veins of the house of Othman. They are aliens, and their foreign source is an insurmountable objection to their claim to the Caliphate. The Moslems, beyond the confines of the Turkish Empire, are more inclined to accept the Sheriff of Mecca as the true Caliph, because he is of the Prophet's family, and he dwells within the sacred walls. The Sheriff of Mecca does homage to the Sultan, and graciously accepts from him every year the *kiswah*, or holy carpet, for the covering of the sacred shrine. The Sultan is sovereign; he has the power on his side. He can demand submission, and he can enforce the demand. But if ever the Sultan's sovereignty is overthrown, his power paralysed, his demands unenforceable, then the Caliphate will drop from his grasp, and he will become as any other ordinary Moslem. This is implied in the independent argument of the Ulema in favour of the Caliphate of the Sultan. They say, "The rights of the house of Othman are based upon its power and success, for one of the most ancient canonical books declares that the authority of a prince who has usurped the Caliphate by force and violence, ought not the less to be considered legitimate, because, since the end of the perfect Caliphate, the sovereign power is held to reside in the person of him who is the strongest, who is the actual ruler, and whose right to command rests upon the power of his armies."

To the title of *Imaum-ul-Islam*, in the absence of any one else sufficiently strong to fulfil the duties of the office, among which are not only the recital of public prayers on a Friday, known in Stamboul as the Selamlik, but also the defence of the frontiers, the raising of armies, the administration of the law,—to this title the Sultan may have a stronger claim. It rests, nevertheless, upon the same basis as the more important claim to the Caliphate, because the Prophet restricted the office of *Imaum-ul-Islam* to the members of his own family.

The foreign and domestic policy of the Sublime Porte is largely influenced by the religious offices of the Sultan. If the Sultan cherish strong religious convictions, and pride himself upon his position as successor of the Prophet, and defender of Islam, the policy of his government must be influenced so much the more strongly in resisting the pressure of the infidel upon the confines of his dominion, and the interference of the infidel in the management of the affairs of his realm. He has a reputation to maintain among the Mohammedan peoples which can only be maintained by resisting the infidel, and proclaiming the supremacy of Islam; and in order to maintain this reputation, no wonder if the Sultan is tempted sometimes to dream of a Pan-Islamic movement for the purpose of welding into one Empire the Moslems of Asia, Africa, and Europe, and presenting an unbroken front to the infidel world. *To dream* simply, for to realize this truly grand purpose is an utter impossibility. The division between the two sections of Mohammedanism is too deep for this to be ever realized, and the orthodox section is too much disagreed concerning the real Caliph even to realize it to any appreciable extent. To the real Caliph alone they will render implicit obedience, and the Ottoman Sultans do not fulfil the primary conditions. Nevertheless, the Ottoman Sultans believe in their right to the Caliphate, and when a Sultan ascends the throne, who has been reared in privacy, and under the direction and beneath the influence of the Ulema, like Abdul Hamid II., and who may think more of his religious supremacy than of his kingly power, there is not much hope of internal reform, and there is not much likelihood of concession to the Christian peoples either within or upon the frontiers of his realm. The Ottoman Empire is endangered not by the inherent incapacity of the Turk to govern, and not by the want of forces and courage to maintain and defend the Empire, but by the religion which called it into being, like the others before it, only to stay its growth beyond the limits of its own inexorable system, and cripple it incurably and fatally. The Turks are a modern people. It is not many centuries since they emerged from the obscurity of the desert. They ought yet to have been in possession of the vigour and elasticity of national youth. But everywhere they exhibit signs of a premature old age. They cannot grow; they are cramped, bound everywhere by the strong cords of Islam, and they must either burst the cords and live on, or the cords, which have hindered their development, will hasten their decay.

For several years the Mohammedan world has been agitated by the expectancy of the Mahdi. The Prophet, following the example of Moses, and perhaps influenced by Christian views concerning the coming of the Christ, declared that twelve centuries after his death another prophet should arise, and obtain for Islam a complete triumph in every part of the world. The real Mahdi has not yet appeared. There have been cries of Lo, here! and Lo, there! but the anxious expectations of the Moslems have been so far disappointed. And will be. For a Mahdi, such as they expect, whether they be *Shi-ites* or *Sonnites*, will never come. The *Shi-ites* are looking for the reappearance of the twelfth Imaum of the race of Ali, a little lad who disappeared at the age of twelve, and who, according to their traditions, lies hid in a cave somewhere, awaiting the appointed time; but the *Sonnites* are looking for a celestial warrior, surrounded by 360 companions, who shall finish the work of the Prophet by accomplishing the universal victory of Islam. The hopes of the Mohammedan world are centred in the fulfilment of this prophecy. The perfect Caliphate is to be restored, and should any impostor ingenious enough, and with sufficient forces, arise, and seemingly fulfil the conditions to almost any, even the most limited, degree, then woe betide the Caliphate of the Sultan! Beyond his own borders it will vanish like smoke, and within his own borders it will receive so rude a shock as, maybe, never to recover.

What is Islam? What are its doctrines? What is its practice? The meaning of the word *Islam* is *resignation* —a meek submission to the will of God. The name is appropriate. The Divine will, as revealed in the Koran, is supreme in the individual and in the State, theoretically supreme, and practically supreme to a very high degree. The freedom of the human will is unhinged by Islam. The State is plunged into an abyss of apathy. The individual is confirmed in ultra-predestination, if not quite fatalistic, beliefs. For Islam is not resignation as understood by Christian peoples, not the blending of the human will with the Divine, but the mastery of the human will by the Divine. This is inherent in the Mohammedan conception of God, which is truly Semitic, a return to the primitive monotheistic idea of the early Hebrews—a God of terrible majesty and awful purity, alone, eternal.

This belief in the one God is the strong point of Mohammedanism. Its assertion had an electric effect upon the Arabs, rousing them, knitting them together, enrolling them under one banner beneath one prophet and king. "There is no God but God, and Mohammed is His Prophet!" This was their war-cry, and the repetition of this short formula was sufficient to transform enemies into friends, and to bind them under the strictest mutual obligations of brotherhood. Now, when the Arabs swarm about the Upper Nile, and when the Turks dash into the Russian trenches, the cry oftenest upon their lips is "Allah!" But the God of Mohammed and the Moslems has no identification with human life. He is altogether apart. The Living, the Self-Subsisting, the High, the Great, the Mighty—these are the terms employed to describe Him. He is also called the Merciful, the Compassionate, but in a very different sense from that of the Christian, not in His mercy and compassion entering into our human lot that He might lift us above our weaknesses and sins, but in His mercy and compassion looking upon our human lot and indulging us in our weaknesses and sins. The Mohammedan creed knows nothing of the God who is not far from every one of us; in whom we live, and move, and have our being; whose heart throbs with a father's tenderness, and yearns with a mother's love; who cannot rest apart, but who must go forth to seek and to save that which was lost. The idea of incarnation is utterly foreign to the Mohammedan mind. And so is the idea of a Divine, suffering Saviour.

God has revealed His truth through the prophets, say the believers in Islam, and finally through the last of the prophets, Mohammed. The Koran is the very word of God. Not only its teaching, but its form, is Divine. It is a sin to translate it. It is the embodiment of absolute wisdom. Beyond it there is no appeal. In the Koran, not only the unity of God and the authority of the Prophet are taught, but also certain supposed truths concerning angelic beings, the final judgment, and the decrees of Allah, mostly fanciful, sometimes sensual, and mixed with a mass of incongruous incidents from Mosaic and Christian sources. The book is the compilation of a clever man, who could have done better had he been better informed, but who, even with the materials available, succeeded in binding men and nations by a mere letter—a dead letter—and enforcing obedience to his commands.

Mohammed enjoined upon all believers in Islam the duty of reciting the prescribed formula, praying five times a day, almsgiving, observing the fast of Ramadan, and performing the pilgrimage to Mecca. The service of prayer, called the Namaz, consists of a series of genuflections, and the repetition of certain words, always the same, and always with the face toward Mecca. This is the only devotional exercise of the Mohammedan. But he observes it everywhere, and in all kinds of company. He is never ashamed of his religion. When the time for prayer arrives, whether in the crowded city or the lonely desert, he performs the ablutions, with sand if water is not nigh, removes his slippers, spreads his carpet, and, oblivious to his surroundings, goes through his prayer. Doubtless there are many to whom the Namaz is a piece of officious formalism, but there are also many who are perfectly sincere in their genuflections and repetitions, and cherish the satisfaction arising from the performance of a religious duty.

Almsgiving is regarded as an obligation binding upon the faithful. A niggardly Mohammedan cannot hope for Paradise. He must give ten per cent. of his grain and fruit, two and a half per cent. of his income from business, and one per cent. of his property in camels, and he is at liberty to give as much more as he likes—the more the better. It is wonderful how freely the early Mohammedans distributed their wealth. They received it rapidly, and in very great abundance, but they never grew avaricious. Their hospitality knew no bounds. Every application was liberally met. The swarms of beggars in Constantinople, and every Mohammedan town, are proof of the continuance of the practice. They need no poorhouses. Perhaps they escape the grinding poverty too plainly visible in many Christian cities. But surely indolence is indulged by this indiscriminate bestowal of alms, and a mass of floating fanaticism maintained upon the surface of society, ready to be turned in any direction to the danger of the common weal.

Mohammed laid a heavy burden upon believers by the institution of the annual fast of Ramadan. For a whole month, sometimes a hot month in summer, neither food nor drink is allowed to pass the lips of a Mohammedan from the sunrise till the sunset of every day. No matter where he may be, the fast must be observed. Traversing the sandy wilderness, floating on the lonely Nile, busy in the streets of Damascus, faint beneath the hot Indian sun, nothing may be taken to relieve him; he may not smoke tobacco, he may not smell any reviving perfume, he may not chew any hunger-killing, thirst-allaying herb; he must simply endure his misery till sunset. Then he may eat and drink his fill. The next day brings a repetition of his misery, and the next, and the next, for a whole lunar month. He must abide by the infallible teaching of the Koran. He must obey the word of God and the Prophet. He cannot be numbered among the faithful of Islam unless he strictly keep the fast of Ramadan. It is a divinely-appointed spiritual discipline to which he must meekly submit. A good Moslem would never think of disobeying the injunction of the Prophet, and breaking his fast during Ramadan; because to disobey, and eat between the rising and setting of the sun, would be to imperil the future welfare of his soul, and bar against him the gates of Paradise. But how they rejoice when *Ramadan is dead*, as the children cry, when the fast is over, when they enter upon the feast of Bairam, and make up for Ramadan by a real good time!

A burden not much less heavy is the required pilgrimage to Mecca. Every Mohammedan is bound to visit the sacred shrine at least once during his lifetime. Wherever he may live, however long and toilsome the journey may be, he must come. Of course every Mohammedan does not come. Some neglect the duty. Some pay for a substitute. But all are expected to come, and are under spiritual penalties if they do not come; indeed, the Prophet declared that a man might as well die an infidel as a Moslem, if he had not once been to the house of the Lord. The numbers visiting Mecca fluctuate according to the strength or weakness of the common spiritual impulses, the waves of religious feeling that pass over the Mohammedan world as over every other, sometimes sinking to fifty thousand, sometimes rising to two hundred thousand annually. The pilgrims have the privilege of trading by the way, and some of them make good use of it, and are not averse to repeating the pilgrimage, especially when they can lay up a substantial spiritual balance against the time to come while providing for their earthly welfare. That Mohammedans are any the better for the pilgrimage is an open question, but that Mohammedanism is the better is no question at all. The individual advantage depends upon the individual intelligence. There are very few who see the truth which Goethe has expressed quaintly in the lines—

> "If the Ass whose back did carry,
> 'Mid pomp of palms, the Son of Mary,
> To Mecca should devoutly fare,
> And worship with the pilgrims there,
> He would go, and back return,
> An Ass—the Ass that he was born!"

The advantage to Mohammedanism in the enforced pilgrimage to Mecca was foreseen by the Prophet. By the selection of Mecca as the holy place of Islam he enlisted the sympathy of the Arabs. It was already a holy place, consecrated by their idols, a centre for the gathering of their tribes; and Mohammed met their heathenism half-way by adopting the Caaba as the temple of Islam, and more than half-way by permitting the superstitious veneration of the mystic "black stone." From Morocco and from Malay, from the banks of the Congo and from the shores of the Dardanelles, the Moslems meet in Mecca; it is the centre, the local habitation of their faith; they behold each other's faces, and have before them an evidence of the wide area over which the faith is spread, and their unity is accentuated, their brotherhood definitely set forth, by the gathering of Islam within the walls of a single sanctuary. Mecca to the Mohammedans is what Jerusalem was to the Jews. Islam professes to reach back over the centuries beyond Judaism, and claims as the builder of the Caaba, Abraham himself. Within the precincts of the temple is the well Zemzem, from which Hagar obtained water to quench the thirst of her dying son, and which is therefore regarded as a second giver of life to the Arabs. To drink of this water, to walk round the temple, to kiss the "black stone," to press his form against the sacred structure, to run between the mountains, to stone the devil, to offer his sacrifice—these are the ambition of a Moslem's heart, and by the help of these he hopes to walk over the path, finer than a hair, and sharper than the edge of a sword, into the delights of Paradise.

Islam lays other restrictions upon its adherents. Games

of chance are not permitted. The loan of money for the sake of gain is forbidden. Wine-drinking is disallowed. So that Mohammedan countries are comparatively free from vices which sometimes threaten the happiness and prosperity of Christian countries. These commands are not universally kept. Various excuses are resorted to by a lax minority to whom present gain is better than future reward, who would rather make sure of the pleasurable excitement of the vinous nectar of these earthly gardens than wait for the doubtful joys of Paradise. Still usury and gambling and drunkenness are strangers to Islam. Those who indulge in them are false to Islam. An interdict is placed upon them, and when the Moslem is tempted to tamper with these evils, so common in Christian lands, the temptation is from the devil, and to the peril of his soul.

But Islam permits indulgences which much more than counterbalance these restrictions. It is essentially a fighting religion, martial in every tone of it; and the fierce spirit of the Arabs, of the Tartars, of the Turks, of all its devotees, it not only freely indulges, but sanctifies. The spirit is not only allowed to burn, but to burn upon an altar. To serve Islam faithfully is to fight for Islam to the end. Her saints are warriors. The scene of their exploits is the battle-field. Those who die sword in hand are martyrs. And a sufficient *casus belli* is a difference in faith. Islam proclaims war against the world. The world must either accept Islam as its faith, or pay tribute to Islam as its master. When any Mohammedan nation sheathes the sword, it falls below its religion. It fails to fulfil the mission for which it was called into being. And, as a matter of fact, as soon as any Mohammedan nation ceases to fight, it ceases to grow. The period of decline commences exactly where the period of aggression ends. Wherever the flow of Mohammedan conquest has been checked, the ebb has set in. A Mohammedan country cannot develop on peaceful lines. It is against its very nature. In a peaceful Mohammedan country growth would be miraculous. Decay is inevitable. The short history of the Ottoman Empire is the last and most illustrious example. That short history is a series of brilliant conquests until the repulse from the walls of Vienna. The limits of their Empire were set. They had acquired dominion over earth's fairest provinces. They were masters of a city incomparable as a seat of government and commerce. The means of consolidation were within their grasp. They had wealth without end. Everything was favourable to their future prosperity, everything *but their religion*. They were the people of the Koran. They had to conform to the Letter. And

> "While the world rolls on from change to change,
>   And realms of thought expand,
> The letter stands without expanse or range,
>   Stiff as a dead man's hand;"

and the dead man's hand held them in its inexorable grip. They could not grow. Exactly at the point where Christian nations have shot forth with renewed vitality, Mohammedan nations have shrunk into helplessness and decay.

But what a gospel was this to give to the wild children of Ishmael! To put them under a religious obligation to fight, to preach to them the sacred privileges of plunder, to bless them in their divisions of the spoil, to promise them the crown of martial martyrdom, was an indulgence which they could appreciate to the full. It was whetting their natural appetites. It was quickening their inbred desires. It was fanning their favourite calling into a fanatical flame. No wonder that Islam spread rapidly. The wonder would have been if it had not spread rapidly. But "they that take the sword shall perish with the sword." A religion whose success depends upon the battle-field, must be contented with a very brief existence. It will run a rapid course to a violent end.

Not only the property, but the persons, of the vanquished,

passed into the hands of the victors. The general plan was to massacre the males, and enslave the females. The males who were saved were sold, traded with, offered for ransom, made money of somehow; the females were distributed in the harems. Slavery is an inevitable part of Mohammedan social life. While Mohammedanism exists there must be a demand for slaves. In the palmy days of Mohammedanism the demand was met, and more than met, by hosts of female captives. Now it has to be met in other ways. The slave-hunters of the world are the Arabs of Africa. The slave markets of Islam are yet open to the nefarious traffic in human blood. Some Roman Catholic countries allow the traffic, and maybe the majority of negro slaves find their way into the fields of so-called Christian lands. But there is this difference. Slaves are demanded in these lands for the tilling of the soil, notwithstanding the silent protest of Christianity, whereas, in Mohammedan countries, slaves are demanded for the maintenance of the domestic life peculiar to Mohammedanism, and with the full sanction of the Koran. The slavery of Turkey is by no means confined to African blood. There are many white slaves in the harems of Constantinople. With the system of concubinage expressly sanctioned in the Koran, inevitably bound up with Mohammedan social life, necessarily consequent upon the Semitic idea of womanhood, slavery must exist, and must be perpetuated. The abolition of slavery would be the destruction of Islam.

Mohammed adopted the Semitic idea of womanhood. Woman is a secondary creature, a mere servant, and less than a servant, a mere article, dealt with by man according to his pleasure or fancy. The sacredness of the marriage tie is unknown. Polygamy existed in Arabia previous to the rise of Islam, and it would have been disastrous to Islam to have forbidden polygamy. Mohammed never thought of forbidding it. But he attempted its restriction. He set the limit at four wives. This limit he transgressed himself, for his own household consisted of nine wives and two slave-girls; and, having his example as an excuse, his early disciples multiplied their wives without end, and purchased as many concubines as they could well support. An attempt was made by some to obey the Koran, notwithstanding the Prophet's example, by never exceeding four wives *at a time*, and the extreme facility of divorce enabled them to do this. Hassan, the grandson of the Prophet, exercised the privilege of divorce seventy times, and generally kept within the letter of the law. In all parts of the Mohammedan world, in Penang, Zanzibar, Stamboul, Cairo, Morocco, wherever Mohammedanism exists, men in middle life may be met with who have had twenty, thirty, as many as fifty wives, changing them as often as they pleased. There are certain classes in Hindostan who confine themselves to one wife, not because they are Mohammedan in religion, but because they are Aryan in race. The conjugal rights of the wife are very limited. The slave has no conjugal rights at all.

This degradation of woman to a mere article is the darkest blot upon Islam, and the fruitful source of evil and decay. The veil, the harem, the strict seclusion of woman, the impossibility of conversational intercourse between the sexes, the deprivation of woman's refining and ennobling influence in the home and in society, the abandonment of the sanctities of wifehood and motherhood—these lie at the very centre of Islamic life. The fountain is impure, and what can the streams be? The roots are evil, and what can the fruit be? As Dr. Fairbairn has well said, "A religion that does not purify the home cannot regenerate the race; one that depraves the home is certain to deprave humanity. Motherhood must be sacred if manhood is to be honourable. Spoil the wife of sanctity, and for the man the sanctities of life have perished. And so has it been with Islam. It has reformed and lifted the savage tribes; it has depraved and barbarized civilized nations. At the root of its fairest culture a worm has ever lived that has caused its blossoms soon to wither and die. Were Mohammed the hope of man, then his state were hopeless; before him could only lie retrogression, tyranny and despair."[1]

The Ottomans are truly Mohammedan. The wealthy among them maintain immense harems filled with Circassian slaves. The system reaches its height in the household of the Sultan. He is separated from his people by an impassable chasm; he cannot marry as they can. All the inmates of his harem are slaves. The penetralia of the Seraglio is crowded with women purchased for him from among the fairest of his people. Not one among them is associated with him on the throne. The Sultana Validé is not his wife, but his mother; she is at the head of the Seraglio. Beneath her are many ranks—wives, favourites, aspirants, to the number of four hundred, each with their separate households, and groups of female attendants, from which menial position any one of these attendants may be raised to honour by the slightest wish of the Sultan. One day may find her a servant-maid, the next a queen. The mother of the Sultan, Abdul Medjid, was once a menial in one of the minor households of the Seraglio. By the sudden caprice of the Sultan she became the head of a household of her own, and, several years afterwards, having given birth to a son, was proclaimed the Sultana Validé. The expense of the Sultan's harem must be enormous. But oh! the sadness of it all; the pernicious influence, the degradation, the misery! How terrible its effects! and how far-reaching! Beneath the incubus of a system like this no State could rise into eminence, and prosperously perpetuate itself. The State, most favourably situated in every other respect, would succumb beneath the stifling pressure of this gigantic evil. It might fight for life a long time, but the fight could only end in defeat and death.

[1] "The City of God," Part i. p. 97.

The paradise of Islam is in harmony with its earthly indulgences. Immortal youth, gardens of delight, black-eyed virgin houris to consort with, everything to gratify a refined Oriental sensualism—these are what the Prophet promises to the disciples of Islam. With such a heaven before them the crown of martyrdom was eagerly desired by the warriors of Islam. They boasted in the fact that they loved death more than their enemies loved life. Their ardour was fired by the visions of paradise. Beneath the excitement of the battle-field their fervid imaginations beheld the joys of the blessed, and they fought with terrible earnestness, as if cutting their way to them through the ranks of their foes. The cry "Paradise!" rung from their lips as they flung themselves into the thickest of the fray. "Under the walls of Emesa," says Gibbon, "an Arabian youth, the cousin of Caled, was heard aloud to exclaim—'Methinks I see the black-eyed girls looking upon me; one of whom, should she appear in this world, all mankind would die for love of her. And I see in the hand of one of them an handkerchief of green silk, and a cap of precious stones; and she beckons me and calls out, Come hither quickly, for I love thee!' With these words, charging the Christians, he made havoc wherever he went, till, observed at length by the governor of Hems, he was struck through with a javelin."[1] An aged Moslem, upon the fall of his comrade, said: "O Paradise! how close art thou beneath the arrow's point and the falchion's flash! O Hashim! even now I see heaven opened, and black-eyed maidens all bridally attired, clasping thee in their fond embrace." Notwithstanding the restrictions of Mohammedanism, its numerous indulgences and its promise of the future won the attachment of the wild Asiatic races. It became known to the Saracens themselves as *the easy way*, and the end of it was all that their earthly natures could desire.

The administration of Islam is in the hands of the Ulema.

[1] Gibbon, chap. 51.

They are predominant in Turkey; they stand in the way of all reform. To offend them in the prosecution of any enterprise is most disastrous. They are zealous for the law, because by the law they live and prosper. The Ulema are not a priesthood; there is no priesthood in Islam. Every man is a priest for himself. All Moslems are equal. The Ulema are the interpreters of the Koran, and the Koran is the law, civil and ecclesiastical. They are the men of the book, learned in its precepts, the unfolders of its meaning; and they are deeply venerated, because of their distinguished office, by all the faithful.

Next to the Ulema are the Imaums, or readers, who read the Koran in the mosques for the edification of the faithful. In the more frequented mosques of Constantinople several Imaums may be seen reading the Koran, each with an intently listening little group about him. To listen to the reading of the law, and to duly perform the daily Namaz, almost covers the entire ordinary religious worship of the Moslem. Much importance is attached to preaching; and the preaching is sometimes very effective. The preacher begins by reciting the formula, "Peace be with you, and the mercy of God, and His blessings," after which the Muezzin, standing at the foot of the pulpit, utters the call for the sermon. Burton, describing a service in the great court of the Caaba, says: "The old man stood up and began to preach. As the majestic figure began to exert itself there was a deep silence. Presently a general 'Amin' was intoned by the crowd at the conclusion of some long sentence; and at last, towards the end of the sermon, every third or fourth word was followed by the simultaneous rise and fall of thousands of voices. I have seen the religious ceremonies of many lands, but never—nowhere—aught so solemn, so impressive as this spectacle."

The Muezzin is the religious crier of Islam. Five times a day he climbs the minaret to summon the faithful to their devotions. Placing his thumbs beneath his ears, extending his palms, and closing his eyes—the first position of the Namaz—he cries, "O God most high, I say there is no God but one, and Mohammed is His Prophet. Come to prayer! Come to the temple of salvation! God is great! There is no God but God! Prayer is better than sleep! Prayer is better than sleep!" Mohammed was puzzled how to call the faithful to prayers. Flags were not dignified enough, torches were the signals of the Guebers, bells were appropriated by the Christians, and trumpets by the Jews. In his perplexity Abdallah came to his relief. He had been favoured by a vision, in which an angel had revealed to him the call of the Muezzin, and, mounting to the roof of the mosque, he repeated the formula. The difficulty was solved. The result was the building of minarets, and the institution of a new ecclesiastical order.

The baldness of Mohammedanism compared with the decorative profusion of Eastern Christianity, in the religions themselves, and in all their expressions, is very conspicuous. The severe simplicity of the Mohammedan mosque rebukes the ornate embellishment of the Christian temple. The almost entire want of ritual in the individual worship of the Mohammedan is in direct contrast with the elaborate ceremonies of the priesthood of the Greek Church. The doctrines of Islam are few and clear; the doctrines of the Eastern Church are numerous and cloudy. And yet Islam has its mystics. The stiff, repressive character of the Mohammedan religion may have succeeded in checking the spiritual exuberance of the Asiatic nature, but it has by no means destroyed it. Mohammed detested the Christian monks. He had no patience with the ecstatic vagaries of the eremites. There were to be none in Islam, so he said. But to prevent the cultivation of the inner mystic life was beyond the power of the Prophet. Many in Islam have devoted themselves to a solitary life, frequent fasting, severe self-mortification, meditation, and prayer, in order to lift themselves nearer God and become partakers of the Divine nature. Their experiences are very like the experiences of the so-called Christian saints who have endeavoured by the same means to reach the same end. They have generally been persecuted by their brethren. They have mostly been in ill-favour with the Ulema. But the people have believed in them. In Turkey alone there are now thirty-two separate communities of such men, commonly known as Dervishes, sometimes called Fakirs, living according to certain prescribed rules, worshipping after certain defined forms, more tolerant towards other religions than the ordinary Moslems, a people who are feeling, in many strange ways, after the spiritual and Divine.[1]

The dancing dervishes of Pera were founded about 1226, A.D., and are held in high reputation by the Turks. It was among these people that the candid, generous-hearted, truce-keeping Sultan Amarath twice retired to enjoy the quietude of a religious life. The dancing is a quick, balanced, whirling motion, begun and finished suddenly, and repeated three times, each time more rapid than before. The eyes are closed, the arms extended, the open palms pointing one to the heavens, the other to the earth. No signs of giddiness are apparent either during the dancing or at its close. There is a seeming absorption of all the faculties in the even gyrations, as if the purpose of the dancing were to forget themselves, and everything about them. The turning from the chief dervish, which forms the first motion of the dance, is said to be a symbol of humility. It represents the averting of the eyes from the presence of God. Their circular movements signify God's omnipresence, and their desire to seek Him wherever they may be. The dance itself, with its increasing rapidity, sets forth the course of human life; the uplifted palm the receiving of God's blessing, and the down-pointing palm the bestowal of the blessing on others.

[1] In the *Contemporary Review* for August, 1883, there is a very interesting article by W. S. Lilly, on "The Saints of Islam."

The howling dervishes reside in Scutari. Their services are much more exciting and difficult to understand than the services of the dancing dervishes of Pera. After the recital of the preliminary prayers during a long prostration toward Mecca, the dervishes rise, range themselves in a row, and at a signal from one of the company seated in the middle of the floor, begin swaying their bodies violently backwards and forwards, to the right hand and to the left, their heads swinging loosely, and their lips ejaculating, "Allah-how! Allah-how!" The swaying increases in rapidity and violence the longer the service continues. The ejaculations grow louder and fiercer until they become like the howlings of wild beasts. For more than an hour they will continue, until their faces are livid, and the sweat pours down them in streams. They lose themselves in the ecstasy of the rhythmic motion, and the regularly repeated deafening sound. Peculiar smiles appear upon their countenances; they are in a blissful frenzy. Their movements still increase in rapidity, their voices are hoarse with howling; the wondering spectator expects to see them fall in sheer exhaustion, but, sustained by their excitement, on they go. And in the midst of it all their chief sits calm, impassive, unmoved. Sick people are brought in, laid upon the floor, and he walks over them, and even over tender babies, only to relieve the pressure upon them he is supported on either side; and when that curative ceremony is over, in obedience to a sign from him, the howling ceases, the swaying stops, and, with the recital of a final prayer, the service is over. Round about this meeting-place are hung instruments of torture once employed by these dervishes in the self-infliction of pain. Their use is now forbidden. But surely they need no torture beyond that to which they now subject themselves in order to induce the pleasurable ecstasy! The service is repulsive in its barbarity. How horrible it must have been, when, in addition to the howlings and the shakings, their bodies were lashed into pain and disfigured with blood!

These are abnormal developments of Islam. They have their influence upon individual character, and to some extent mould the national life. The vulgar believe in the dervishes, and are as ready to obey them as to obey the Ulema; but it is to the interest of the dervishes not to provoke the Ulema too much, because they are the guardians of Islam, and can set in motion the civil power. The life of the people is interwoven with the religion of Islam. Mohammedanism explains many of the idiosyncrasies of Turkish character. Their apathy, their want of business tact, their lofty demeanour toward all foreigners, their benevolence, their general regard for honesty both in their dealings with each other and with the stranger in their midst, and many other conspicuous traits of Turkish character, are largely due to their religion. Upon an attempt to cheapen the wares of a Greek huckster on board the steamer in the Bosphorus, by a comparison between his prices and the prices of a Turk, he said: "Greek no like Turk. Turk head like this," significantly tapping the iron sides of the chart room, "but Greek head no like this." It is quite certain that the Turks do not make the money in Constantinople, but the Greeks and Jews and Armenians. The Turks are fairer to deal with; they are not cheats. You may trust them. Whatever may be the faults of Islam, one of its leading virtues is the inculcation of veracity. A Moslem seldom breaks his word. A typical story is that of Hormuzan, the Persian Prince, who, after a severe struggle, was at length captured and conveyed to Medina. There, in the Great Mosque, stripped for the humiliation of the scourge, he begged for a drink of water. "Give it him," said Omar, "and let him drink in peace." "Nay," answered the Prince, "I fear to drink, lest some one slay me unawares." "Thy life is safe," the Caliph said, "until thou hast drunk the water up." No sooner had the promise been given than the cunning Persian poured the water on the ground. Omar was angry. He was tempted to punish the deceiver; but his word had been given, and his word was kept. Hormuzan repeated the formula of Islam, and was immediately raised from his captivity to one of the first nobles of the realm.

CHAPTER VII.

THE BLACK SEA AND THE SEA OF AZOV.

The Black Sea—Name—Sunset—The hoopoe—Eastern legend—Acalephæ—Porpoises—Rapidity of motion—Crimea—St. Vladimir—His baptism—Massacre of the Tartars—British bravery—Fortifications—Russian officials—Kertch—Green waters—Straits of Yenikalé—Sea of Azov—Sturgeon—Smaller fish—Pelican—Mosquitoes—Robins—Russian fowls—Dragon-fly—Locusts—Lightning—Mirage.

WHY should that vast expanse of water beyond the Bosphorus, receiving into its bosom the wealth of the Danube, the Don, the Dnieper, and other smaller rivers, and laving the coasts of Europe and Asia, be called the *Black* Sea? The White Sea, at the northern extremity of Russia, is fringed with snow, and, for the greater part of the year, frozen over and covered with snow, and therefore named appropriately; and it may be in contrast with it that the great South Russian waters are called the Black Sea. Beneath the clear waters of the Red Sea the coral reefs are distinctly seen, and on its eastern shore lies ancient Edom. Here are two reasons why that sea should be called *Red*—a physical reason in the colour of the wonderful insect architecture of its rocky bed, an ethnographical reason in the presence of the descendants of him who came in faint and weary from the hunting field, and said to his brother, "Feed me, I pray thee, with that same red pottage; for I am faint: therefore was his name called Edom." The shallowness and muddy appearance of the Yellow Sea sufficiently account for its name. But there is no discoverable reason for the name of the Black Sea. Its waters are not black; they are a deep blue. This blue is not the ultramarine of the Mediterranean, but the blue that shades away to purple seen in sunny weather on the south-western shores of our own land. When the Greeks first made the acquaintance of the Black Sea they called it αξινος, *inhospitable*, but afterwards they found it a friendly element, and changed its name to ευξινος, *hospitable*—and by the name of *The Euxine* it is generally known to this day.

My experience was like that of the Greeks. As we left behind us the Turkish forts, and came from between the hills into the open waters, we were met by a northerly wind, a smart shower of rain, and a lumpy sea; and I found it impossible to retain my equilibrium. I was anxious to do so. The clifts running on either hand, artificially whitened, to assist mariners making in the night the northern entrance of the Bosphorus, if not picturesque, were interesting. The sun was going down blood-red, and the flying, broken clouds were tinged with pale greens and sickly yellows. I struggled for awhile to preserve a dignified perpendicular position, and then honourably succumbed, seeking a refuge for my dignity in a fairly comfortable horizontal position in the recesses of my berth. There sweet sleep came to my assistance, and I became oblivious to the inhospitable seas.

Next morning they were still inhospitable. The sky was clear, with a fresh wind: all day we were rolling and pitching northwards, and I managed before evening to accommodate myself to the motion of the vessel. We had an *édition de luxe* of the previous evening's sunset—the sun a deeper blood-red, and the clearer sky suffused with peculiar greens and yellows toned down near the horizon into a long strip of light grey.

While re-passing these waters two visitors came aboard— one, a small bird with silvery grey throat and breast, and light brown back and wings, uttering a plaintive *too-wheet* as it flitted fore and aft, sometimes perching in the rigging, and sometimes venturing on deck; the other, a beautiful hoopoe. With his light golden crest thrown back, and his white and buff wings spread in the sunshine to great advantage, he flew aboard; and, when settled comfortably on a rope above the well deck, he straightened his feathers, and erected his crest, and made himself quite at home. But he was too attractive a visitor to be left quietly in possession of his resting-place. Soon the eyes of one, and then another, were directed towards him, and sundry attempts were made to capture him. These attempts he eluded, and, discovering his perilous position, he flew away westward, and doubtless safely joined his kindred on the low marshy plains at the mouth of the Danube.

Hoopoes are sociable birds, living in flocks; and yet, strange to say, it is not unusual for them to migrate separately. This was crossing the Euxine all alone, and making use of our vessel as a half-way house, a resting-place in its long flight of probably four or five hundred miles. They visit England in the autumn but rarely, and may be more frequently seen in the environs of Paris: their home, however, is the East. Asia Minor and the Grecian Archipelago are favourite resorts of the hoopoe. They are somewhat less in build than the Cornish chough, but not otherwise unlike that cunning, mischievous bird. They belong, indeed, to the same family, notwithstanding their brighter dress, and the softer note, *hoop*, from which they derive their name.

A pretty Eastern legend accounts for the crest of the hoopoe. Solomon was once on a journey, his ivory throne resting upon an enchanted carpet, whose corners were held by four genii. The sun was intolerably hot, and the king became faint and ill. A flock of vultures were met with, and were requested by Solomon to spread their wings between himself and the sun, and thereby afford him shelter. This they refused to do. They were going the other way, and would not alter their plans to please him. In his anger, Solomon decreed that they should be divested of their neck feathers, and continue ever afterwards exposed to the burning sun. He next met with a flock of hoopoes, and requested them to screen him. They said, "We are a little people, but we will all assemble and make up for our size by our numbers." And, flying in multitudes immediately above the king, he was effectually sheltered during the rest of the journey. Desirous to recompense them for their kindness, Solomon sent for the chief of the hoopoes, and asked him to prefer for his people whatsoever request he liked, and it should be granted. Time was given him to consult his people. The consultation was long and garrulous. At last his own vain little wife and queen made herself heard above the rest, and insisted upon her husband asking for a golden crown. When Solomon heard the request he was sad, knowing the possession of golden crowns would be fraught with danger to the hoopoes; therefore he told the chief that if they should ever regret the choice, and desire his help in difficulty, he would most willingly render it. The chief flew away with his golden crown. All his people were decked with golden crowns. They became vain. They spake to none of their old acquaintances. They strutted before pools of water constantly admiring the reflection. But dangers came. Soon it was known that the hoopoes wore golden crowns. Bird-catchers increased. The resorts of the hoopoes bristled with gins, and were swept by arrows; and it became evident that without some speedy alteration their days were numbered, and their race would soon become extinct. The chief hastened back to Solomon, and begged him to remove the golden crown. This he compassionately consented to do; but he gratefully supplied its place with a crest of feathers. When no more gold was to be had, the work of extermination ceased; and the little hoopoes were left in unmolested possession of the modest but appropriate reward for their kindly service.

Some people cannot read between the lines of a legend. They miss the gem in an over-close scrutiny of its fantastic setting. Those who have the power to read between the lines—who can see the gem, and obtain by its fantastic setting a better knowledge of its purity and worth—will appreciate and profit by this legend of the hoopoes.

Looking over the bows of the vessel as we re-crossed the Black Sea, an interesting form of marine life presented itself in numerous specimens of Acalephæ—a radiate, gelatinous creature, with soft tentacles gently swaying in the current, and an almost transparent body floating near the surface of the water. As their name indicates,[1] they have a stinging property, one family being called the *sea-nettle*. I have seen them in abundance after the spring tides upon the Lancashire coast, without tentacles, however, and larger and less rotund than those of the Black Sea. They mostly frequent the warmer latitudes, and may be seen in immense numbers off the Azores. The stinging property consists in a secretion, which, upon irritation, or even when the creature is brought into contact with foreign matter, is exuded through the tentacles; and bathers have found that, when the tentacles have been cut off, the power to sting remains for a considerable time. The creature itself may be so long irritated as to exude all its poison, and then it can be handled with impunity. Whales feed upon them; through the narrow gullet of that mammoth of the seas they slip much more readily than the smallest mackerel. The poet Crabbe speaks of them as—

> "Those living jellies which the flesh inflame,
> Fierce as a nettle, and from that its name;
> Some in huge masses, some that you may bring
> In the small compass of a lady's ring."

The playfulness and agility of the porpoise in these seas were very conspicuous. A shoal tumbling in the distance to

---

[1] ἀκαλήφη, a nettle.

port or starboard, and sometimes far astern, would become aware of the presence of a vessel, and, skimming alongside with incredible speed, dart one over another, and finally reach the bows; then a marine game would begin, beautiful and exciting to behold. The seas, broken in upon by the plunging bows of the vessel, seethed deeply, and the blue was changed into a superb green, through which floated upward, like pearls in liquid malachite, the innumerable air bubbles that burst into white foam upon the surface; and across this, turning from side to side, and sometimes completely over, their white bellies a silvery gleam, the porpoises would dart, now rising above the wave to take in a fresh stock of air, and then diving completely under the bows and appearing on the other side apparently as full of frolic as fish could be. With delicate precision they would regulate their speed to that of the vessel, allowing the vessel sometimes to touch the tips of their tails, and then, as if their joy was exuberant, too much to contain, dart away at five times the speed of the vessel, and come skimming back again to meet her. When the porpoise is seen breaking the water from a distance it has all the appearance of a very lazy creature. But when seen in clear seas, completely under water, the gracefulness and velocity of its motion, explained partly by the perfect curve of its body either way to the tapering nose and tail, cannot be surpassed. It reminds one of the sweep of a gannet when it sights the prey. The power of motion, and the gracefulness and graduated velocity of motion, in many birds and fishes, surrounded the one by the yielding air, the other by the yielding water, present a curious problem. We go from step to step, slowly and awkwardly; they, without any apparent movement of wing or fin, simply with wing or fin spread, perhaps vibrating, but, if so, vibrating so rapidly as not to be perceived, float, wheel, curve, and dart away at any angle at a speed which cannot be measured in some instances at less than seventy miles an hour. Mechanism, the adjusted parts of their several frames to their environment and mode of life, and the acknowledgment of the vital principle operating within the mechanism, do not entirely account for this, unless we likewise acknowledge that this vital principle possesses properties other and beyond those discovered by the most advanced modern science. The phenomena of life, even in the lower ranges of being, baffle the comprehension of man; how much more, therefore, in the higher ranges of the human mind and spirit!

The Crimea! How I strained my eyes to catch the heights of Balaklava as they rose next day from the now still waters, and watched the changing contour of the land as we drew nearer and nearer the memorable shores! This peninsula, so important to the Russian Empire as the dominant position of the Euxine, links itself with the mythological past. Agamemnon's daughter, Iphigenia, was carried hither by the offended goddess, to appease whose wrath the warrior was ready to offer her in sacrifice. Long before the peninsula obtained from the settlement of the Crim Tartars the name Crimea, it was known as the Taurian Chersonesus, a name revived by the Russians in their province of Tauris, or the Taurida. The Taurians, a family of the Scythian race, were very cruel. Plunder by sea and land was their customary occupation, and their ordinary means of livelihood. All sailors wrecked upon their shores were sacrificed to a virgin deity in a shockingly barbarous manner. Their bodies were buried, the head alone reserved for exposure in the temple; or, they were brained, and hurled from the summit of the hill upon which their temple was built. Better the orderly tyranny of Russia than the wild excesses of a brutal and savage people.

Vladimir, canonized by the Russo-Greek Church and known as Saint Vladimir, but whose character was as far removed from saintliness as a torturing iron fetter is removed in nature and design from a richly jewelled bracelet of the purest gold—*Saint* Vladimir, the rough instrument employed for the introduction of Christianity into Russia, *fought for baptism* in the Crimea, near the place where now stands the modern fortified town of Sebastopol. The rich, commercial Grecian city of Kherson then stood there, a city which has given its name to another city at the mouth of the Dnieper, built and peopled by Prince Potemkin to flatter the vanity of Catherine the Great. This latter city was built by forced labour, and not by a pretended rapidly developing commerce to meet commercial needs; it was peopled by serfs driven in from the country for the time, and not by a pretended mercantile community reaping the profits of an extended marine trade: for the sake of theatrical effect the pretence was well kept up; and that nothing might be wanting to indulge the dreams of an ambitious, dissolute woman, over the entrance to the city was inscribed that sentence which gave such mortal offence to the Ottoman Power, "The road to Byzantium." The Kherson besieged by Vladimir, for the express purpose of *demanding* baptism as one of the conditions of peace when the city should surrender, was the older Kherson, whose ruins may still be seen in the immediate vicinity of Sebastopol. A city was never besieged under such circumstances before. It is a unique event in history, and an example and proof of the rugged haughtiness of this early Russian autocrat, and the rude, uncivilized condition of the country over which he ruled.

The fame of Vladimir had spread to other lands, and the religious chiefs of other lands were bidding for his conversion. Although he had been zealous in his heathenism, he was now disposed to part with it. But what should take its place? There were Judaism, Mohammedanism, and Christianity represented by the Roman Catholic and the Greek churches, and they were all wishful to obtain so illustrious a convert as himself: which of them would suit him best, and by which would his interests be most surely advanced. A deputation of boyars was sent to the various countries to witness the different religious ceremonies, and inquire into their fitness and worth. They returned. Judaism was out of the question. It had been precluded, because its adherents had no country, and a mere name. Mohammedanism was tempting, especially its prospect of a voluptuous paradise, and might have been accepted had the boyars visited Bagdad, and witnessed its splendour there, and had it not demanded circumcision and interdicted the use of wine. The Roman Catholic form of Christianity lost this illustrious convert partly because of the power of its Pope. But the magnificent ritual of the Greek Church, beheld in Byzantium, captivated the imagination of the Russian nobles; and upon their recommendation, strengthened by the fact that Olga, his ancestress, had been baptized already, and by the desire to ally himself with the Cæsars, Vladimir resolved to embrace the Christianity of the Eastern Church.

Now a difficulty arose. He could not humble himself to ask for religious teachers from Constantinople. He would go to war and demand them. And in this way came about the siege of Kherson. The city was invested. Through the treachery of one of its inhabitants the water supply was cut off, and the horrors of thirst compelled the city to surrender. Vladimir dictated the conditions of peace. He was to be baptized, and the hand of the sister of the Cæsars was to be given him in marriage, under the threatened penalty, in case of refusal, of the conquest of Constantinople. The conditions were accepted. Kherson was restored. Vladimir received the name Basil in baptism, and the Princess Anna became his wife. He carried home, as the result of his conquest, a few popes, and icons, and sacred relics; Perune, the heathen god, was dragged at the horse's tail, well cudgelled, and pitched into the river; the inhabitants of Kief, by a royal mandate, appeared at the river-side and were all baptized; and Russia has been Holy Russia from that day to this.

The Tartars of the Crimea were the last independent

survivors of that great Asiatic invasion of Eastern Europe under Ghengis Khan. When the power of the Golden Horde, so long dominant in Russia, and at whose pleasure the Russian Czars held their sovereignty, was completely broken by Ivan III., the Tartars of the Crimea maintained their independence, and afterwards, by an alliance with the Turks, were able successfully to withstand the armies of Peter the Great. Their subjugation was effected in 1783, partly by stratagem, and partly by a bloody massacre, than which there is nothing more treacherous and cruel in human history. Dowlet Gherai was elected Khan of the Crimea in 1774, and, because of his friendly feeling towards Turkey, the Russians, by intrigue and money, raised against him a pretender in the person of Sahim Gherai. Then, they said, an armed mediation was necessary, and proceeded at once to occupy territory in the Crimea. Dowlet Gherai fled to Constantinople. Sahim Gherai was elected Khan, and became a mere creature of the Russians. The Sultan was obliged to acknowledge him. He was flattered and cajoled by the Russians, made a lieutenant-general of the Russian army, appeared before his people in Russian uniform, was decorated with the order of St. Anne, and, finally, gave up his title to the Khanate for an annual consideration of one hundred thousand roubles, the payment of which, however, being left to the avaricious Prince Potemkin, he never received, and, neglected at last by his flatterers, ended his days in starvation and beggary. The brave Tartars were not willing to submit to the supremacy of the Russians. A struggle for liberty was in process of organization, when Prince Potemkin, through his cousin Paul, put to the sword 30,000 Tartars—an indiscriminate butchery of men, women, and children which was called the conquest of the Crimea. And where are the Tartars to-day? "That numerous, free, and rich race of people, clothed in silks, and of noble appearance, has now dwindled into a crowd of starving beggars; their magnificent tented cities are become gipsy encampments, and their houses and palaces exhibit mere masses of ruin and decay."[1]

Steaming along the eastern shores of the Crimea, my mind was filled with thoughts of the Englishmen who had fought and fallen there, as it had been only a few days before when we lay close by the barracks at Scutari, where the wounded were nursed by Florence Nightingale. Alma, and Balaklava, and Inkerman, and Sebastopol will never be forgotten, and especially the memorable execution of the mistaken order immortalized by the Poet Laureate in " The Charge of the Light Brigade." The sacrifice of brave men must be regretted, nevertheless it affords a wonderful example of the obedient spirit and matchless courage of our race. Not many are capable, like these men, of

> " Charging an army, while
> All the world wonder'd :
> Plunged in the battery smoke,
> Right thro' the line they broke ;
> Cossack and Russian
> Reel'd from the sabre-stroke
> Shatter'd and sunder'd.
> Then they rode back, but not
> The six hundred."

It was not against a few detached regiments of the Russian army that Lord Cardigan led his men, but against the army itself, charging their centre, and,

> " Storm'd at with shot and shell,"

in twenty minutes, 335 saddles were bare, and the remnant ploughing its way back under cover of the Chasseurs d'Afrique and the heavy dragoons.

The fortifications along the shores of the Crimea are much more efficient now than they were thirty years ago. At the north-eastern extremity of the peninsula the foot of the low cliffs bristles with guns of large calibre, and so covers

[1] " Russia," by W. H. Kelly.

the entrance to the Sea of Azov as to make that sea with its towns and villages almost impregnable. The town and bay of Kertch lie behind these fortifications. We dropped anchor in the bay in the evening with the sun dipping behind the hills from a clear sky. The watchful Russian officials sent two soldiers aboard to see that, under cover of the night, we attempted nothing detrimental to the august authority of the white Czar. They were weak and rather dilapidated representatives of that authority. They wrapped themselves in their great cloaks, inhaled the fragrant clouds from several cigarettes, and ejected these clouds in two streams through the nostrils; and then, these sentinels of Russian honour, these defenders of the two-headed eagle glancing imperiously over and governing by the brands in its claws the people of the East and the West, curled themselves up behind the binnacle, and, for anything I know to the contrary, fell fast asleep. With the morning light the boat was lowered, and the captain pulled ashore to obtain *pratique.* In a few hours a medical officer came alongside, and desired to see all hands; we were mustered aft near the cabin and leisurely looked at for a minute or two, and then, without a single inquiry, told to disperse. Our faces were a sufficient indication of general healthiness, and we were, therefore, not subjected to a useless and impatient quarantine. After the doctor came the custom-house officials, tall, well-dressed, good-looking men, who overhauled the ship's papers, and overhauled the ship too, peering everywhere and into everything from the chart-room to the fire-hole. All drawers were opened, and all doors unlocked; even my portmanteau did not escape their scrutiny. Tape, and wax, and seals were all in readiness to put under official ban anything objectionable; but everything being found satisfactory, they politely disappeared over the ship's side, and we immediately weighed anchor, swung about, and steamed through the barely navigable straits of Yenikalé into the Sea of Azov.

The town of Kertch is a long, straggling place, built on the further shores of an expansive, semi-circular bay. It is flanked by low, rounded hills, which run along the northern shores of the bay, covered with the greenest pasturage, and affording sustenance to large herds of cattle. It is an official town, the residence of soldiers, custom-house officers, pilots; and the inhabitants are doubtless well used to the booming of cannon, and the presence within the bay of the ships of all nations. While we lay here, the soldiers at the fortifications below were engaged in marine target practice; and the puff and bang, with the leaping waters and spray where the balls fell, were welcome breaks in the monotony of waiting the pleasure of the Russian officials.

The waters near the Crimea assume a greenish hue, and they deepen in colour farther north and nearer the land, until, in the bay of Kertch, they are a vivid green, and with the corresponding colour of the pasturage ashore make up a peculiar picture. It is a cold, clear picture, a monochrome; and in direct contrast with the rich and varied colouring of the seas and shores of Greece, where vivid green is never looked upon, except when near enough to catch a sight of the fresh vines in the hollows; and even in contrast with the Dardanelles and Bosphorus, where green is plentiful, but in every conceivable variety of hue.

Advancing through the straits towards the Sea of Azov, the vividness of the green is lost in muddy yellow, an indication that the shallow waters become shallower still. The straits are four miles wide, but the navigable channel is very narrow, its course marked on either side by floating poles, affording sufficient space, but not more than sufficient, for two vessels of 1,000 tons register to pass each other. Once free from the channel, and properly within the Sea of Azov, the navigable waters open out to a considerable breadth, but are nowhere deeper than five or six fathoms. The waters gradually become still shallower further north, and the anchorage ground for ordinary steamers connected with the South

Russian trade in grain and wool is a full twenty miles distant from Taganrog. The Sea of Azov is little more than a wide estuary of the river Don. Its waters are fresh; and, being so shallow, they are easily ruffled. Beneath a south-western gale very troublesome seas arise. A lady, wife of a sea captain, informed me that once she was there in the late autumn, and, while they were anxiously waiting for a cargo, a gale sprung up, and blew so violently that sometimes the bed of the sea was actually laid bare. To a vessel with only a few feet of water under her keel, even should her anchors hold, and her cables stand the heavy strain, a gale like that must be fraught with very great danger.

Sturgeon, the royal fish, is found in abundance in the river Don and in the Sea of Azov. It may be caught occasionally in the North Sea and in the Mediterranean, but the finest and the greatest variety of sturgeon (for there are several species) are to be found in the Caspian and in the Sea of Azov. To attain full size it requires both fresh and salt water, living in the salt water frequently, but swimming up the deep, wide fresh-water rivers in the spawning season, and thereby offering greater facilities to the fishermen in their efforts to take it. The spawning season is the time when the fish is most valuable, because from the full-charged ovary is made that delicacy of Russia, universally esteemed, called *caviare*. The sturgeon, under favourable conditions, will grow to an immense size, weighing sometimes twelve hundredweight, and when it is considered that the contents of an ovary are often equal in weight to a quarter part of the fish, some estimate may be formed of its value. Not only, however, does the sturgeon supply *caviare*, but isinglass; and, carefully cooked, the common sturgeon is pleasant eating, and some species are a rare delicacy. In the Volga, above Astrakhan, piles are driven into the bed of the river, sufficiently apart to permit the fish to pass through in their upward passage, the piles curving about the middle of the river toward the shores again. Cords are connected with these piles, by the agitation of which the presence of fish is known. The agitation is sufficient to close a wicker door upon the fish, and also, in the night, to ring an alarm bell, rousing the sleeping fisherman on the platform raised above the piles, and calling him to active and lucrative employment. Within the piles a false bottom covers the bed of the river, and upon this being raised the sturgeon becomes an easy prey. Another method of capture is sometimes adopted. A number of fishermen, knowing the haunts of the sturgeon, will assemble and enclose the haunts with nets, then, crying out together, startle the fish, which, rushing from their quiet habitations, become entangled in the nets, and are dragged ashore. I saw two fishermen pull a sturgeon, caught a few miles away, up the embankment at Taganrog. It was five feet long, and weighed about four hundred pounds: unwieldy enough to require their combined efforts to land it safely on the low vehicle waiting to carry it away. At the hotel in Taganrog, sturgeon was among the ordinary viands at our dinner table.

Fish, not unlike the herring in size and appearance, is very plentiful in these waters. It was interesting to watch them playing about the stern of the vessel as we lay at anchor, and with the break of the waves, sometimes right upon a small shoal, dart from the water like hundreds of polished silver arrows. They would suck an insect, especially the smaller moths, from the hook, but seldom bite keen enough to be caught. A few were secured, but they were found so bony and tasteless as not to be worth the trouble for food; and they were certainly only an apology for sport, a very indifferent enjoyment indeed. These and other small fish are caught at Taganrog in a dredge net, flung with the arm far into the water, and then slowly drawn ashore, similar to the dredge nets at present in use by the fishermen of the Sea of Galilee.

The common pelican is a regular visitor to this shallow, fresh-water sea. My attention was drawn to it the first day

I spent there. A flock of them were flying to the south of the vessel in that peculiar oblique line, that segment of a circle, which is one of the unfailing features of their flight. Visitors to zoological gardens will have observed these birds: their almost white feathers, altogether white but for the rose-colour tint tipping the edges of their feathers, and barely showing itself; their strong, short legs and immense wings, stretching sometimes twelve feet across; their deep, fleshy pouch hanging from the lower mandible, capable of holding twelve quarts of water, and in which they store the fish caught until the time arrives for the gorging process so common among many sea-birds; and their sluggish, side action, shovelling the fish into the pouch during feeding time. This last feature is peculiar to their state of confinement. When at liberty the pelican is quick, seizing the fish with adroit, unerring aim; and, after filling his pouch, will raise himself upon his wide wings, and sail away to some desolate and lonely place that he may eat and sleep in peace. The tradition that the female pelican feeds her young with her blood, piercing her breast for the purpose, is owing to the fact that, in order to dislodge the fish from her pouch into that of her offspring, she presses her pouch firmly against her breast; and may be the tradition has held its ground longer than it would have done had not the feathers of the pelican been tinted red, thereby appearing as if they had been covered with blood, and then insufficiently washed during the process of fishing. The pelican is a picture of perfect melancholy. It is a confirmed hypochondriac—the most lugubrious object in creation. David said, "I am like a pelican of the wilderness." Dr. Thompson informs us in "The Land and the Book" that he first met with it at Hûleh, and he tells us "it was certainly the most sombre, austere bird I ever saw. It gave one the blues merely to look at it. David could find no more expressive type of solitude and melancholy by which to illustrate his own sad state."

The wind setting in from the shore brought many winged insects to the vessel, and the wool and linseed with which we were loading helped to swell the number, by an introduction of insects without wings, not quite so interesting and much more troublesome, except, of course, mosquitoes. They claimed relationship by their little insinuating song of *cousin, cou-sin, c-o-u-sin*, and a share in our domestic arrangements of cabin and berth; and they would not be turned out. Relations ought not to be turned out. They have the privilege of consanguinity. There is so much of human blood in the whole mosquito tribe, because their fathers and forefathers for many generations have fattened upon it, that what wonder is it to hear them sing *cou-sin !* Their fondness, their unwavering attachment, is amazing; like that of some in human shape, with human hands and feet, and what should be human hearts, who come tenderly buzzing about you, whispering delicious flatteries into your ear, singing *cousin* and meaning *cozen*, as you find out when once they have fairly settled where your blood is richest : human mosquitos, more to be dreaded a million times than the tiny creatures of the Azov and the Danube.

The creeping things were slaughtered on the deck by a pair of robins. They remained with us many days, and we were grateful for their timely service. Three chickens, of most comical aspect, and with a preposterously conceited manner of walking up and down the deck, designed for the dinner of the Greek foreman, a confirmed dyspeptic and consumer of *Vichy*, did handsome work also in keeping down the wingless insects, and deserved a much better fate than awaited them. While one was admiring the sea-view through a hole astern, his brother commenced energetically to trim the feathers of his stumpy tail for him, and the consequence was that the little fellow popped through the hole into the waters below. A second, under fright, flew overboard, and eluded all efforts at rescue. The sole survivor of the noble triad, the most preposterously conceited of them all, who trod the deck as if within his expanded bosom dwelt the spirit of a skipper, lived to see the anchor weighed and to begin his first voyage; but ere many days he found his way into the cook's relentless fingers, and was converted into soup: the dyspeptic Greek missing them all three.

During the hot, still days we were much pestered with a fly a little larger than the mosquito, with a bright yellow body, and so soft that a very gentle touch would kill it. This fly persisted in crawling over the hands and face, and produced a strange and most uncomfortable tickling sensation, by which, I presume, it must have some peculiar formation of what entomologists call the *calcares* and *taurus*. A delicately shaped bronze-blue dragon-fly danced in the sunlight, and clung, with its little feet, to the rods of the awning, and on every narrow ledge and projection; while a more magnificent specimen, three inches long, with a large, greyish, velvety head, and a body somewhat brighter but very much like the variegated body of an adder, was darting hither and thither with great rapidity. The power of flight of the dragon-fly is marvellous, being able, in a chase for life, to outstrip the swallow; and no less remarkable is its voracity. Little hope of escape has any other insect if once the dragon-fly sets upon it: quickly is it caught, and quickly does it disappear. Considering its size, it is the most voracious of all living creatures. It *must* eat or die, and, as a matter of fact, when the summer is passing, and insects are few, its unerring instinct leads it to the surface of the water whence it emerged, there to deposit its eggs and quietly expire. So voracious is it, that it has been known to eat its own body. In its preparatory aquatic life, as well as in its aerial, this voracity is remarkable; and we see in it a provision of nature for ridding both the water and the air from that superabundance of insect existence which, otherwise, would become a nuisance, and might become a plague.

The largest and most interesting of all insects blown from the shore were the locusts—stragglers, and then finally separated from some great army; or, the remnants of an egg deposit only partially destroyed, but intended to be destroyed altogether. One very large locust I failed to capture. I was fortunate in securing four, a little less in size, and yet full grown, by stealing behind them, and very quickly seizing them. They struggled powerfully within the palm, scraping the palm with the spurs of their hard, horny legs, and causing a very disagreeable sensation. I placed them beneath an inverted tumbler, with a little wadding soaked in spirits of camphor, by which they were speedily suffocated; and then kept them in a perfectly dry place, until all the moisture was gone out of them. The bodies were shrunken, but not decayed, and only a very little discoloured; and I have my four specimens in excellent preservation, even to the antennæ, with the head, and mailed neck, and spotted wings, and every part of the insect except the abdomen, as bright as when alive. The strength of the insect may be gathered from the fact that a Russian boy, in a lighter alongside the vessel, tied a string to the leg of a locust, and amused himself by flying it along the deck, pulling it in at pleasure. The engineer placed one under a large glass with a sufficient allowance of air, fed it every day, and, in his warm cabin, kept it alive until we reached England. It was quite at home, moving its small antennæ in front of its horny-looking eyes in its endeavour to understand such a peculiar prison house, and contentedly munching its three grains a day, whoever was by. The cooler atmosphere, when the fires were gone, and the engines at rest, reduced it to somnolence, the preparatory stage to a painless death. Locusts vary in colour. Most we saw were of a brownish grey, some had a greenish hue, and several were so brightly green as to suggest in colour, as well as form, their kinship with the grasshopper.

The locust is an insect of Eastern and Southern climes. Occasionally a scourge of locusts will visit Spain and Italy from the African shores. Italy, in the sixth century, was visited by an enormous swarm, which, after devouring the vegetation over a large part of that beautiful and productive peninsula, caused a deadly pestilence, by its intolerable stench, to spread among the inhabitants and their cattle. In 1748 a considerable number visited England. But, in northern latitudes, locusts have no chance. Even in warmer climes a colder night than usual will benumb them and impede their movements. The hotter the weather and the livelier they are. Their devastations are terrible. St. Augustine informs us that an army of locusts once caused the death of 800,000 men. They leave behind them famine, eating up every green thing, and pestilence, because when there is nothing more to eat they die, and, in their countless myriads, poison the air for miles around. When they visited Egypt, in obedience to God's command by Moses, "they did eat every herb of the land, and all the fruit of the trees which the hail had left: and there remained not any green thing in the trees, or in the herbs of the field, through all the land of Egypt."[1] Speaking of them as God's army, "a great people and a strong," the prophet Joel says their coming shall be "a day of clouds and of thick darkness, as the morning spread upon the mountains," and that, in their march, "the land is as the garden of Eden before them, and behind them a desolate wilderness. . . . Like the noise of chariots on the tops of the mountains shall they leap, like the noise of a flame of fire that devoureth the stubble, as a strong people set in battle array. . . . They shall run like mighty men; they shall climb the wall like men of war; and they shall march every one on his ways, and they shall not break their ranks: neither shall one thrust another; they shall walk every one in his path: and when they fall upon the sword they shall not be wounded."[2] This is not the fanciful tracery of oriental imagination, but a sober statement, a circumstantially correct record of the movements of this terrible insect scourge. They darken the sun by

[1] Exodus x. 15.   [2] Joel ii. 1-11.

their numbers. The rushing of their wings is as the rattle of chariots, or the roaring of a mighty flame, and may be heard six miles away. When they alight they march straight before them in an unbroken, irresistible phalanx: as Solomon says, they " have no king, yet go they forth all of them by bands.[1] So dreaded are they, that taxes of locusts, destroyed in the egg, larva, and adult stages, have sometimes been imposed upon people in the East. After they have marched over a land all vegetation vanishes, even the bark of the trees is eaten off, and the land has the appearance of having been scorched with fire. Their numbers are almost incredible, millions upon millions defying all efforts at extermination. Trenches are dug, but the trenches are filled up, and the innumerable lines that follow march on over the bodies of their companions. Large fires are lit, but into and over the fires they go, perishing apparently without fear, until the fires are died out, and the pressing ranks behind roll forward over the embers. When Charles XII., in 1709, led his defeated army from the fatal field of Pultowa over the South Russian wastes, he encountered a swarm of locusts; and, exactly a century later, another and a larger swarm alighted in South Russia, and commenced their devastating march. Serfs were brought down from the interior to arrest and destroy them, but the army of insects conquered the army of man. So has it been many times in different parts of Africa and Asia. Surely Joel was right when he said, "His camp is very great."

In the Jewish law, regulating the diet of the people, an exception was made in flying creeping things of those "which have legs above their feet, to leap withal upon the earth."[2] The locust, the bald locust, the beetle, and the grasshopper were declared clean, and of them the people might eat freely; but "all other flying creeping things, which have four feet," were an abomination, and could, under no circumstances, be partaken of. The food of John the Bap-

[1] Prov. xxx. 27. [2] Lev. xi. 22-24.

tist was locusts and wild honey; and locusts are now eaten by the Bedouin Arabs, the poor people of Egypt and the Soudan, and also by the people of Madagascar. The head, wings, and legs are plucked off, and the body eaten with salt; or, the whole insect is dried, and dipped in oil before eaten, the flavour not being unlike that of a crab. Camels will eat locusts with avidity; and the beautiful, spare-living Arabian steed will not turn away from such fare. An almost exclusive locust diet is said to shorten life very considerably by breeding a fearful worm disease within men whereby they are gradually consumed. In Eastern Arabia a tribe lived whose food consisted mainly of locusts. They caught them by kindling large fires, and suffocating them when the swarms passed by. Notwithstanding their agility and hardihood in youth, and the apparent promise of long life, these men never exceeded forty years of age.

The locust is very irregular and uncertain in its movements on the wing. This must arise from a keen susceptibility to currents of air, or from the construction and habit of the insect itself. Possibly it arises from both, for a wind will soon clear away a swarm of locusts;[1] and, although the wings are long and powerful, the head and thorax are thicker and heavier than the abdomen, and apparently cause the insect to incline that way in its flight, and frequently to fall after the manner of a tumbler pigeon. David said, "I am tossed up and down as a locust,"[2] and, to any one who has observed the flight of a locust, the figure will be a most appropriate one of uncertainty, unrest. From the movements of some creatures we obtain a sense of deep repose. There is a most delicate equipoise in their swiftest motions. But not so is it with the locust. Its flight is always at irregular angles, as if it lacked power to control and guide itself; it is tossed up and down like the heart of man in the day of trouble.

The Mohammedans have a superstitious veneration for

[1] Exodus x. 13 and 19. [2] Psalm cix. 23.

the locust. The great prophet himself caught a locust, and examined its wings, and professed to find written thereon, in the Hebrew tongue, "We are the troops of the Most High God; we each one lay ninety-nine eggs. If we were to lay a hundred, we should devastate the world." He prayed to God to deliver the faithful from such a dire calamity, and God mercifully granted the prayer; and the Mohammedans, to avert a plague of locusts, write an invocation to the prophet, place it in a reed, and put the reed in the middle of their crops; or, and as some think a more effectual plan, they catch four locusts, write a verse of the Koran, specially provided for the purpose, on the wings of each, and then set them at liberty. These four are supposed to join the swarm with the sacred message and lead their companions another way. There is a long-standing and popular tradition among the people of the East that the locust carries on its back a Hebrew letter signifying God's wrath, and doubtless this tradition may be traced to Mohammed, and through him to the Hebrew Scriptures from which he borrowed so largely. The tradition must have been strengthened, however, by the ravages of the locust, regarded by Eastern peoples, like all other calamities, as a special visitation from God.

At one time there was a great scarcity of locusts. The Caliph Omar-ben-el-Khottal was in deep distress, and sent searching parties throughout his dominions to find one, and when, at last, a few were brought him, he exclaimed, "Allah is great!" and revived. Why? Because the locust was formed from the surplus dust out of which man was created, and it was Allah's decree that when locusts die man must quake: he too will soon follow so near a relation. At least the Mohammedan will, for the Christian is not so anxious to claim the relationship. In the sixteenth century the monk Alvarez, in Ethiopia, exorcised the locusts. His people were threatened by a plague of them, and he caught a few, and read them a long and carefully composed sermon by way of adjuration, and commanded them to fly to the sea, or to the land of the Moors. What wonder is it that, after such an infliction, they should speedily obey him, and betake themselves to the Moors, their own relations ! and maybe they told them of the monk's largeness of heart in sending them to plague their kindred dust.

Sheet lightning is very beautiful when seen to advantage, and nowhere may it be seen to greater advantage than from the bosom of a large lake, or inland sea. Late one night, in the southern heavens, quickly succeeding illuminations spread themselves east and west, until half the horizon and a third part of the sky were bathed in the soft, bluish flame: then would it suddenly disappear, and leave us in total darkness, only to be renewed again and again in ever-changing forms. Sometimes it would appear as a quivering light behind a mass of fleecy cloud, doubtful whether to die away in fitfulness, or burst forth into glory ; and, as if deciding upon a middle course, it would shoot out from all round the cloud, and shoot again and again over all the southern heavens, and be at once extinguished. And sometimes in one sudden outburst the heavens would be a mass of splendour, which, in a moment, while you looked, would be gone. Shakespeare, speaking of the course of true love, by the mouth of Lysander, in "A Midsummer Night's Dream," says :

> "Brief as the lightning in the collied night,
> That, in a spleen, unfolds both heaven and earth,
> And ere a man hath power to say,—Behold !
> The jaws of darkness do devour it up ;
> So quick bright things come to confusion."

The clouds were thrown into fine relief; and the broad expanse of water, even to the low cliffs far away on either shore, with the many steamers riding at anchor in the still, deep, solemn eventide, made a fine picture, seen momentarily, but so vividly as never to be forgotten.

In Taganrog, one very sultry evening after an intolerably

hot day, the day of our return from Rostoff, the company at the hotel sat under the verandah smoking and chatting. From my quiet corner I was half listening to the conversation, and, at the same time, carefully observant of a huge mass of dark cloud slowly gathering in the south-east. Presently a flash of vivid lightning, not sheet lightning but forked, leaped from the cloud, and revealed, for an instant, the bay beneath us, and the further shore. Breaking the sultry silence we heard the soft rushing of the wings of innumerable insects, and immediately felt little taps upon the face and hands, and the creeping sensation produced by insect feet upon the human skin. Hundreds of half-grown beetles were pouring in through the open windows, and flying round the swinging lamp. Then commenced a slaughter of the innocents, but every one had many relatives to his funeral. We were fain to give up the fight, and with the one exception of not allowing them upon the hands and face, let them have their way. They were doubtless attracted by the light, while fleeing before the onsweep of the pelting rain; for, by and by, it rained, and heavily. Before the rain came, we had flashes of lightning in quick and ever quickening succession, with the rumble of distant thunder. The lightning was most intense. To watch it caused me pain as if a needle had been suddenly darted in the eyeball, and I was obliged and glad to seek shelter indoors. Statistics prove that nine times as many people annually suffer death from lightning in Russia as in the British Isles, a fact easily understood by the prevalence of electric storms like these. If, when the summit of Olympus is black with gathering clouds, lightnings like these leap forth, accompanied by thunders so loud and terrible as are not unfrequently heard in Greece, I wonder not that the Greeks should have called it the home of the gods, and hid their faces from the blinding gleam of these darts hurled by Jove's mighty hand; and I can see new force and beauty in the Lord's question to Job, when, comparing His Divine Majesty with Job's weakness, He said,

"Canst thou send lightnings, that they may go, and say unto thee, Here we are!"

No sea affords such fine examples of marine mirage as the Sea of Azov. In these regions mirage is a common phenomena ashore. A Russian scientist, commissioned by the Czar Nicholas to examine the topography of his southern provinces, informs us that in the vicinity of the Azov, between the Crimea and Taganrog, "when the sun rises amid damp vapours, and gradually ascends over the plain, the deceptive phenomena of mirage frequently occurs, painting lakes, rivers and meadows on the refracting morning mists, transforming the smallest stem rising above the ground into a magnificent tree, converting a man into a tower, and a baggage-waggon into a gigantic palace." In the Ægean mirage may occur. Standing on the mole at Syra, and looking out towards Delos, that island once appeared to me completely out of the water; I could clearly see beneath it. But for mirage the Ægean cannot compare with the Azov. Taganrog is not visible from the anchorage ground. It lies below the horizon; and the tugs plying between the town and the vessel drop below the horizon, and entirely disappear from view. Watching a tug one day on its way to town, I every moment expected to see it dip and vanish; but no! apparently it left the horizon, and continued its course in mid-air. I could hardly trust my vision. I took the glasses and examined it. But on it went, like a tiny fairy steamer, becoming less and less palpable, and gradually fading away into the heavens, as if bravely bent on some voyage of celestial discovery. I had only one proof, so far as my vision was concerned, that what I saw was mirage, a deception. There were two lines of smoke from the reflected funnel, which, the air being perfectly still, were straight and undisturbed; one line from the funnel upwards into the air, the other from the funnel downwards to the place where the tug left the horizon, the two lines forming an angle of about 45 degrees.

Since then, when I have thought of this, I have found myself deriving comfort from it, as illustrative of the passing away of our loved ones, the dropping below the horizon that marks off, and shuts out our world from the world beyond, of those whom God is calling into the eternal rest. We watch them. We expect to see them pass, and vanish from our earthly vision; but no! apparently no! Their eyes open. Their faces become suffused with a marvellous sweetness. They speak of things unfamiliar to us. Scenes are open to them which we have never looked upon. Blessed spirits are present with them whom we have never seen. They are already below the horizon. They are gone from us into the eternal world. And God is giving us this beautiful reflection, this spiritual mirage, to prove to us that they are really continuing the journey. Let not the lesson be lost upon us. Let us receive the proof in all its power to comfort us. Very soon the reflection itself passes, the spiritual mirage is gone, and our loved ones are beyond the veil of blue in the eternal heavens.

CHAPTER VIII.

TOWN AND COUNTRY SCENES IN SOUTH RUSSIA.

The great plain—Flat land around the Sea of Azov—Taganrog—Shallow water—An ice accident—Streets and buildings—Public gardens—The Czar's palace—Death of Alexander—Visit to the palace—Journey to Rostoff—Tumuli-Grain track—Sunflowers—Hamlets—Kingfishers—The delta of the Don—Horses—The city of Azov—Tamerlane—Turks and Russians—Peter the Great—Rostoff—Circus—Wool-washing—Central Asian route—Selim's attempt to open it—Napoleon and Paul—House of Romanoff.

THE scenery of South Russia is far from picturesque. All round the Azov there are nothing but low cliffs, and behind them a vast, undulating plain country, part of the great plain of Central Europe, stretching from the German Ocean to the Oural mountains, and from the Crimea to the White Sea. European Russia lies mostly within this great plain, and the water-shed of its mighty rivers is formed by the insignificant group of hills known as the Valdai Hills, only 1,200 feet high. What this plain loses in picturesqueness it gains in utility. Nature's inevitable law of compensation steps in, and gives to Russia rivers finer than any in Europe, broad, deep, slow, and navigable almost throughout their entire length; and these rivers, with the canals which everywhere intersect the country, afford means of communication and transfer both cheap and sure. The Russians say a boat may pass through rivers and canals from the Baltic to the Sea of

Okotsk, across the two continents of Europe and Asia ; and, as a matter of fact, tea is conveyed by river and canal boats from Western China to Moscow and St. Petersburg.

The plain country in the vicinity of the Azov is very monotonous. Demidoff, the Russian scientist, travelling overland from the Crimea to Rostoff, by way of Taganrog, says, "Still the same endless plain lay before us, the same tedious and flat horizon vanishing in the distance, in the midst of which how delightful a relief it was to chance upon a human being." The utter absence of wood increases the monotony of the view ; and what must be the view on the eastern side, between the Azov and the Caspian, where the uncultivated and almost uninhabited steppes stretch their cheerless wastes before the wearied eyes? The northern and western plains are cultivated, and to some extent inhabited, presenting no variety of propect certainly, covered in spring with the same interminable lengths of green springing corn, and in autumn with the same yellow harvests, but this monotony is pleasanter than that of arid wastes of coarse grass and sand. These steppes, and the cultivated lands, which may easily be laid waste, speedily stripped of their fertile grain, form an effectual barrier to any army aiming a blow at the centre of the Russian Empire. Only two men have tried it since Russia became a consolidated power, and one, Charles XII. of Sweden, found but the remnant of an army left him to fight at Pultowa, and, assisted by Mazeppa, the Hetman of the Cossacks, escaped in ruin across the Ukraine, destined to wear away a great part of his life in fretful exile among the Turks, whom he stirred up again and again to revenge him ; the other, the first Napoleon, after a terrible sacrifice of life, entered Moscow, only to behold it burst all around him into flames ! and forced to retreat across the now snow-covered plains, the fearful and most memorable retreat ever recorded, left behind him, some of them shot and sabred, but far more dead and dying through fatigue and cold and hunger, 420,000 men. It may be thought that the vast area and sparse population of Russia is a source of weakness, but it gives her the advantage of being able to withdraw herself, to gather herself in, to retreat upon her own centre, and destroy before her all means of sustenance ; and although to do this requires the sacrifice of immense wealth, and the infliction of untold misery, it renders the citadel of her national existence almost impregnable.

Taganrog cathedral stands on high ground in the centre of the town, and lifts itself above all the other buildings ; and the first object visible, when approaching the town from the sea, is the large gilded cap of the dome glittering in the sun. It is no mere tinsel covering that burns and gleams over the whole town, but real beaten gold bestowed in a moment of pious gratitude by one whose son was saved from an impending calamity. His devotional zeal outran his wealth. He paid for his pious munificence by living afterwards almost in beggary. The dome itself next appears, and the towers with their sets of bells ; then, rising in quick succession, the towers of other churches, the larger public buildings, the tops of the gravel cliffs, and the peasants' huts that fringe their base, until the whole town stands revealed a pleasant little picture. The tug turns right about, and steams stern afore in four feet of water to the edge of the wooden landing-stage ; and, standing under an arch, beneath which is the way to the town, an officer demands an examination of boxes, portmanteaus, luggage of every kind, glancing at and occasionally fingering the contents, if with suspicion, certainly with bashfulness and timidity. Once passed him, the dhrosky drivers beset you with the clamour of their class everywhere, expressing their willingness, for a few *kopecks*, to drive you wherever you wish to go.

The sea of Azov is becoming shallower. When Taganrog was founded by Peter the Great, nearly two hundred years ago, he intended it to be a deep sea port, not only for the defence of the southern part of his Empire against the

Turks and Crim Tartars, but also for the development of trade with Central Asia and the Black Sea. In his gigantic enterprises, this marvellous monarch spared neither money nor men. Natural obstacles were struggled with and overcome. Cities rose in the most unlikely places. Ports were opened where he thought fit. But had he known what immense quantities of sandy gravel were yearly rolled down the river Don and deposited in even layers over the bed of the Azov, slowly but surely filling it up, and throwing its waters into the Euxine, he would never have built Taganrog. There it stands, however, with its long embankment of masonry standing out from the crumbling cliffs, a monument to the tireless energy of the greatest Russian autocrat. The waters stretch from this embankment to the opposite shore, a distance of several miles, and, running to the north inland, form an expansive semicircular bay, but so shallow and so firm in its bottom, that a horse and cart may drive clean across, and bathers disport themselves fearlessly in any part of it. Fifty years ago vessels were discharged three miles from shore into carts brought for the purpose, but now vessels are of much larger burthen, and steam lighters of shallow draught pass between them and the shore. Even these very seldom visit Taganrog, but proceed up the Don to Rostoff, which stands in a similar relation to Taganrog as a warehouse to the office where the books are kept and the business is done.

For three or four months during the winter the Sea of Azov is blocked with ice. The bay at Taganrog becomes a fine skating-ground. An elaborate religious ceremony, in which the cutting out of an immense cross of ice forms a conspicuous part, is gone through by the priests amid the jubilations of the people. The fishermen drive out their rough, wiry horses and low carts to the deeper water, and, piercing the ice, capture the unwary fish, attracted by the light and the bait, and sell them at a handsome profit. The ice is not always safe. Should the winter be mild, there is a danger of the ice breaking loose from the land, and floating southwards, cracking and dissolving in the deeper and warmer waters. On the 28th of January, 1886, while a thousand fishermen, with their horses and carts, were on the ice, it broke loose, and away went the treacherous raft with its precious burthen, to the horror of those, who could render at the time little or no assistance, standing upon the shore. Boats were got out and the raft followed, and hundreds rescued next day, but a great many were beyond rescue: they felt the ice crash around and beneath them, and went down to a watery grave.

The streets of Taganrog, like all the streets in the smaller Russian towns, are very wide and mostly unpaved; dusty enough to choke you in summer, muddy enough to bury you in winter. This is no imaginative statement. The streets are covered in summer with dust as fine as flour, and when a strong wind blows, it rises in great clouds most distressing to encounter. In winter this dust is turned into mud, and the ruts and holes of the streets are quagmires. If some poor fellow crossing in the night should tumble into one of these holes, he might easily be buried, lost sight of, indistinguishable in the smudge all about him. The streets must be in their most satisfactory condition during the time of frost and snow. The main street in Taganrog was being paved while I was there, and if the whole town is to be paved it will be a wonderful improvement. The streets are not only wide, but almost invariably run at right angles. The buildings are low, and frequently liberal spaces are left between one building and another. What the buildings lose in height they gain in area. Some of them are built of stone, in a heavy and depressed style of architecture, of not more than one, or at the most two low storeys—an external exhibition of defiant solidity, not incompatible with internal comfort and careless ease. There are one or two houses of brick, lighter in construction, and several coated with cement; but throughout the whole town there is no attempt whatever at uniformity. The whole town is a medley—a spacious hotel, and by the side of it a long row of poor-looking shops; a prince's palace, and next door, or round the corner, a shed-like drinking saloon; a splendid church, where lies the heart of Alexander I., the whitest Czar that ever wore the crown of Muscovy, in the midst of a common dotted with labourers' huts and a miserable-looking railway station. The large open spaces between the buildings, and the huts, tiny wooden or earthen tenements, standing off from the streets and hidden sometimes in little hollows, give to the whole town the general appearance of a tract of land laid out in allotments, half of which have been taken, while the other half still wait for purchasers.

There are pleasant public gardens in Taganrog, where, in the cool eventide, hundreds of people resort, and promenade round and round the music-stand. Sometimes an efficient string band will play, and sometimes a military band of Cossacks, whose martial music is full of fire and splendidly rendered. Here and there seats are placed beneath the shady trees, where lemonade, and Turkish coffee, and cigarettes are provided from booths hard by; while, from these booths, the sound of singing French girls mingles softly with the louder music outside. The people are sober, orderly, and well-dressed, chatting pleasantly together, and keenly appreciating the music. Notwithstanding the balminess of the summer evening air, they leave the gardens early, as soon indeed as the band retires; a proof that the music is the chief attraction. The national anthem is the signal not only to rise, but to uncover, and if you should neglect to pay this tribute of respect, even though you are a foreigner, a man accoutred in military dress, with sword and revolvers complete, would politely remind you of your duty, and, upon a refusal to conform, forcibly remove your hat, and oblige you on Russian soil, outwardly at least, to acknowledge the authority of Russia and her Czar.

Entering Taganrog by the cliff road, one of the first

objects to attract attention is a long, low, substantial stone building, with an extensive court-yard and out-offices, known throughout the town as the Czar's palace. This palace is intimately connected with several important events in modern Russian history. To the Russian people it must ever be a memento of that far-reaching political conspiracy, shared in by so many nobles of the Empire, and crushed by the Czar Nicholas, in the beginning of his reign, with the iron heel of despotism; and to the house of Romanoff it must ever have tender associations, as the place where Alexander I., by his pathetic devotion to his wife during his last few months, tried to atone for the wrongs of years he had done her, and where, amid the gloom of a known conspiracy closing in and threatening his life, he breathed his last on December 1st, 1825.

The Russian officers and soldiers engaged in the continental wars at the beginning of the present century, and becoming acquainted thereby with the political constitution of the different European states, returned home averse to the continuance of the Russian autocracy. They desired some form of representative government, and some amount of political freedom. Up to the year 1815, Alexander had been liberal in his political opinions. Until then some hope of concession might have been reasonably indulged in, but after then the spirit of his predecessors, in his public life, largely possessed him, and there was no hope whatever of his willingness to forego the least particle of despotic power. The failure of his plans in Poland confirmed him in his autocracy. Madame de Staël said to him, in his earlier days, that his people, having no constitution, were happy in the possession of so liberally-minded a monarch; and he replied, regretfully, "I am but a lucky accident." He must have been thoroughly sincere in his liberalism, and, had he not changed his views and policy, in all probability the conspiracy in the later years of his reign would never have been thought of, and could never have enlisted the sympathies of so many of the best men of the realm.

The conspirators of the north and south were not in full agreement. The societies to which they belonged were both known as the Society of Public Welfare, and professed to be one, not only in name, but in principle and design; nevertheless, a different spirit animated the two branches, and they were practically two societies. Pestel, the chief southern conspirator, attempted to reconcile their differences in conference at Moscow, but failed. The society of the south aimed at the emancipation of the serfs with a free grant of land, and were persuaded that one inevitable step to success was regicide. The society of the north, governed and influenced by men of aristocratic birth and fortune, among whom were princes of the royal blood of the ancient house of Rurik, shrank from such extreme measures. They dreaded Republicanism. They desired a limited monarchy. Both in the north and the south the conspiracy spread widely, and men of high position in the army gave in their adherence to the scheme. Alexander was at Taganrog. The plot ripened. Men were willing to assassinate him. He was secretly made aware of it, and yet feared to take vigorous measures of arrest and suppression. And, while the conspirators were waiting for a favourable opportunity in his visit to the military manœuvres, bodily disease, aggravated by nervous anxiety and domestic sorrow, was working to prevent them. Suddenly, so suddenly as to arouse suspicion of assassination, and suspicion which was not easily quieted, it was announced that the Czar was dead. The conspirators' plans were thrown into confusion. They knew not what to do. And, depending upon the action of the society of the north, the usual end to a Russian conspiracy soon came in torture, and hanging, and exposure to the horrors of continual hardships and warfare on the frontiers, and banishment to Siberia.

The Czarevitch was Constantine. He, however, by a

secret document, and because of his *second* marriage with Jane Grudzinska, daughter of a *Polish* Count, and a *Roman Catholic*, all barriers in the way of her exaltation to the high position of Czarina, had for some time renounced his hereditary rights in favour of his brother Nicholas. Three weeks of an interregnum were spent in messages between Constantine and Nicholas, and if the society of the north had acted with promptitude and decision, they might at least have succeeded in obtaining concessions in favour of a constitutional Government. They waited. Nicholas accepted the crown on December 24th. Despatches were received from Taganrog concerning the discovery of the conspiracy, and the arrest of the ringleaders. The northern band marched into the great square of St. Isaac, and posted itself behind the statue of Peter the Great. A few hours' parley ensued; then the grape-shot rattled over the square, and riddled the ranks of the insurgents; and Nicholas baptized his newborn sovereignty in the blood of his people. It was one of the darkest days in Russian history. The shadow of it was thrown into the future. Some of the bravest and noblest men of Russia lay for months in the dungeons of St. Petersburg; and when sent to the intolerable wretchedness of an exiled life amid the mines and among the snows of Siberia, the wives of these men, ladies of high birth, voluntarily, in the grandeur of womanly heroism, went with them and shared their toil and sorrow, with the full knowledge that every unborn babe of their exile would come into the world a slave. And there they remained, and there they have died. The shadow of December, 1825, is upon Russia to-day.

Alexander I. was married when only sixteen years old to the Princess Maria, of Baden, who, upon her marriage, took the Russian name of Elizabeth Alexeiovna. She was only fifteen years old, a sweet-natured, beautiful girl; and the promise of her girlhood was fulfilled in a womanhood amiable, accomplished, virtuous, a wife fit for a monarch, and in every way likely to make him happy. The marriage was arranged by Alexander's grandmother, Catherine the Great, who had a special liking for the young grand-duke, and whose intention it was to proclaim him her successor in place of his father, the Czarevitch, afterwards the eccentric Emperor Paul. Before this intention took effect she was stricken with unexpected paralysis, followed by a speedy dissolution. It was no honour to be liked by so bad a woman, a woman who treated his father so harshly as to almost make him an imbecile, and who tried to find in himself a fitting tool to serve her unholy ambition. It was an honour, under her influence, to escape, to so large an extent, the pernicious effects thereof; but she spoiled his domestic life, and greatly increased the sorrow of his later years. The marriage was arranged and celebrated, young as they were, and unacquainted with each other (acquaintance should have ripened into intimacy in the few years they might have reasonably waited): notwithstanding this, the marriage would doubtless have been a happy one if Catherine had left the young people alone. She intermeddled, kept them apart, put them under restrictions. The two girls who were born in the first two years, the only two children they ever had, died in infancy, and a natural tie was severed thereby which might have held them together in the years to come. He forsook her, and sought other favourites. The beautiful Countess Narishkin bore him three children. Only one lived, and she, though very handsome, was weakly in health. He clung to her tenderly, fondly; she became his sole domestic joy; and the wife of his early years, Elizabeth Alexeiovna, knew it. The rigorous climate of North Russia, however, after a long residence in the South, broke down the feeble health of Sophia Narishkin, and in her eighteenth year she passed away. Alexander's heart was nearly broken. He bitterly exclaimed, "I receive the reward of my deeds." And who was it that soothed him? Who was it that shared the burden and made it lighter? Who was it that shed tears because he was so deeply wounded? The wife whom he had slighted, and who had been true to him all through the weary years, Elizabeth Alexeiovna; and when her constant womanly heart stood thus revealed, the memories of his life rushed in upon him with overwhelming reproaches. He took her back to her rightful place, and loved her as he had never loved her before, and in pathetic concern for her welfare endeavoured to wipe out the grievous past, a sadder and a wiser man.

The Czarina's health was so unsatisfactory that her physicians advised a return to her native air. She refused to take this advice. Her husband had need of her, and she would remain with him. It was then thought the next best step would be a prolonged residence in the southern part of Empire. Alexander, anxiously solicitous for her recovery, selected Taganrog, and the house in Taganrog which has since been known as the Czar's palace. The selection was a wise one. Elizabeth recovered quickly, and was soon sufficiently well to permit of the Czar's absence on a tour in the Crimea; and so favourably did this tour impress him, that he expressed an intention, maybe a long cherished intention, of vacating the throne, building a palace at Orianda, and, with his wife and nearest friends, spending in private the remainder of his days. Those who heard him were taken by surprise. They need not have been, for they could see how changed he was, and how sad he looked. With his haughty spirit broken, with the spring of his nature gone, what could they expect? He was haunted by those premonitions of coming misfortune, those indefinable and baseless fears with which men are troubled sometimes near their approaching end. A comet nightly visited the heavens. "Ilya," said he, to his aged, trusty coachman, "have you seen the new star? Do you know that a comet always presages misfortune? But God's will be done." We call this superstition. But we do not cover everything and solve everything by the word superstition in cases like this. Is there not in the realm of the inner human life, when that life is threatened by unforeseen trouble and death, something answering to the stillness, the hushed and quivering expectancy in nature, preceding the sudden outburst of storm? We cannot explain it. We cannot tell why the spirit should be so wide-awake, so keenly sensitive, so vital with fear, possessed with one absolute feeling of the dread of approaching calamity unknown and undiscoverable. Yet so it is. Alexander returned to Taganrog. Fever set in. His nervousness increased. His physicians were useless. And a fortnight served to close his reign. He had many faults. He did many wrongs. And yet if any Russian autocrat merit the name of the white Czar, we may give it with the least compunction to him. The Czarina Elizabeth mourned his death, and in five months followed him to where the misunderstandings of earth are remedied, and the cares and fears of earth are no more.

Before the entrance to the Czar's palace at Taganrog, a sentinel, with drawn sword, is continually pacing. I was anxious to obtain admittance, and, through an interpreter, ventured to ask the sentinel if it would be possible to see the interior of the building. The man looked at me dubiously, with a half-smile upon his face, as if I were not altogether to be trusted, and as if he declined to take the responsibility of any attempt I might make to damage Imperial property. My foreign face may have been a reasonable excuse for the man's fears. I looked straight into his eyes, however, and smiled his fears away; for, presently, he said he would inquire. Stepping within the large doors, he called an elderly man across the enclosure, and mentioned my request to him—somewhat doubtfully, I should imagine, by his looks and gestures; but the elderly man beckoned me forward, and motioned me to the right hand into a square hall, from which a flight of stone stairs ascended to the leading suite of rooms once occupied by the Czar's household.

Here I waited a minute, until I was joined by the elderly man—a man of the real Russian type, an undoubted *moujik*—reinforced by three young soldiers, with their swords drawn, who took their places, mechanically, one on either side and the other directly behind me. These young fellows glanced at me with the same uncertain, dubious air I had previously noticed in the sentinel outside, and appeared rather timidly to fulfil their appointed office, an air altogether absent from the face of my *moujik* friend, the conductor, who was attentive and deferential, without being obsequious, and took everything as a matter of course. I had not reckoned upon so honourable an escort through the rooms of the palace, and certainly I had not reckoned upon so faithful an escort, for wherever I moved, there to right and left and immediately behind were my three men, apparently ready to do, not my bidding, but the bidding of my elderly and mannerly friend, the conductor; and I never remember a time, in my whole life, when I was more carefully attentive to the details of correct behaviour. During that half-hour I was a pattern man.

We ascended the stairs to a short corridor, and from that entered a large, lofty room, running the whole breadth of the building, with windows at either end. It was barely furnished, in part carpeted, and chairs evenly arranged down the sides. It would make, if necessary, and no doubt had been, a splendid reception-room. From that we passed to smaller rooms on the left, in which were tapestry wrought by the Czarina Elizabeth, a heavy mahogany writing-table used by the Czar, an engraved portrait of the Czarina, and a marble bust of the Czar, and sundry other things carefully treasured because of their associations with royalty. The Czarina's portrait revealed a lady of slender figure, and gentle countenance; with features decidedly Teutonic, and what must have been, in the flesh, a strong contrast to the Slav beauties of the Russian court; a lady of sweet, winsome looks, with the soul of goodness beaming in her eyes and breathing from her lips: and the conductor called my attention to the portrait with evident pride. Her memory is still fragrant to the Russian people, for they had discovered in her what her husband for many years had failed to see. While examining a corner room at the extremity of the suite, a small secluded room, whose one window overlooked the courtyard, I was informed that here the Czar was seized with the paroxysm, or fatal stage of his malady, and was carried hence to a room at the opposite end of the building, where he expired. We proceeded to this other room, which, in memory of his decease, was converted into a chapel. The folding-doors were there, hiding from vision the holy place of the priests; the painted icons, or sacred pictures, with their lamps burning before them; the candelabra, ready for an extraordinary display of piety, and all the paraphernalia of a well-appointed Russian place of worship. Upon inquiring if service were ever held here, my elderly friend solemnly and seriously said that, once a year, the schoolboys of the town came to this chapel to have their sins forgiven. I had no desire to enter into religious controversy with the sincere and probably good man, or explain to him nice theological distinctions; therefore I smiled, and kept my thoughts within my own mind. It would have been casting pearls before swine, and not indifferent swine either, but such as might turn again and rend me; for in Russia, where the church is the reflection of the state, theological and political heterodoxy are so closely connected as to be confounded, and if a heretic is not a political offender—well! he ought to be, to keep his character at all. Otherwise he becomes an anomaly. But is there not deep political wisdom in bringing the schoolboys of Taganrog to have their sins forgiven in the chapel where the Czar died, and thereby associating in their minds God's most gracious act with the solemn departure of him who, in some real sense, like every Czar, stood to the Russian people in the place of God, and was regarded by the Russian people as little less than divine.

Attachment to the autocracy is incalculably increased when the autocratic power becomes associated with the dispensations of grace. And this is truer in proportion to the deeper ignorance of the people. From the chapel we passed below, where the cooking of the establishment is done, and where, in winter, the heat is generated and sent along the passage ramifications I had observed throughout the whole building. Lastly, we entered a low room, in the centre of which was a heavy square vault, with a bronze representation on one side of Alexander's last moments. Here are buried the clothes, towels, nursing appliances, and what else were employed about the dying person of the Czar, too sacred to share the ordinary fate of such things, and yet the mute memorials of the common misery of kings and slaves in the last extremity of their earthly life. I thanked my conductor, bestowed on him a gratuity which he did not expect, and which I regarded as an evidence that not many people are shown round the palace, and was glad to breathe again the freer atmosphere beyond the gates unaccompanied by the shadow of the triple sword.

Taganrog and Rostoff are connected by a railway line, over which express trains, at the rate of fifteen miles an hour, pass backwards and forwards about four times a day. The trains are composed of cars, the little platforms at either end of which are joined together, affording first-class passengers the privilege of traversing the entire length of the train, from the engine to the conductor's seat—a privilege more appreciated according to the slowness of speed and the length of the journey. Second-class passengers have the privilege of passing through the second-class compartments, and the compartments of their humbler brethren in the thirds; and these latter have to be content with their own restricted domain. To business men the express trains must be the very abode of Tantalus. To me they were quite enjoyable. It was pleasant to step out upon the platform and look over the surrounding country, not generalized by the quickness of the motion, but detailed, picked out vividly here and there, as we passed leisurely along.

Some distance from the railway, and upon the direct high road from Taganrog to Rostoff, there are many conical mounds, from twenty-five to thirty feet high, and called by the people of the neighbourhood "Khourgans." These mounds, or tumuli, have been the subject of much speculation. They run straightly, from north-east to south-west, beyond Rostoff into the steppes, and beyond Taganrog into the Crimea. Near Taganrog they are surmounted by a piece of granite roughly chiselled into the head of a sphinx. There is no bed of granite in the locality; the stones must have been brought from a distance. The earth, of which the mounds are constructed, has been thrown up from all around, leaving a hollow place about the bases of the mounds. By whom, or for what purpose, they were erected, it is impossible to say with absolute certainty. In all probability they were erected by those early wandering tribes whose power culminated in the Golden Horde. They may have served more than one purpose. Their line of march may have been indicated thereby. A mound may have been thrown up at every encampment, for present protection against storm or the attack of enemies, and for future guidance as to convenient stages in their long journey. And they may have been the burial-places of the dead, especially if these Tartar tribes regarded the sphinx head, with which several are surmounted, as the memorial of the impenetrable calm and mystery of death. These mounds are landmarks in human history, telling us of a people whose home was in any place upon the vast steppes where a tent could stand and a horse could feed. These people rejoiced in the wild freedom of a wandering life, unmolested by the state craft of an ambitious power. But now the vast steppes are measured; taxes are demanded by the Czar's official, and the soldier stands by ready to pitilessly enforce the demand by the muzzle of the rifle and at the point of the sword; even the iron road is laid, and the Imperial messages are carried to yet more distant peoples; and beneath the pressure of Imperial power these more distant peoples, as well as the ancient wanderers of the Ukraine and the Kuban, are fast becoming centralized and crystalized, dwellers in towns, and amenable to civic law.

Between Taganrog and Rostoff, the train skirts the immense grain tract whence comes the bread of thousands in our own and other lands. This grain tract covers an area of 450,000 square miles, and is composed of decayed vegetable matter varying from three to six feet deep—the remnants of a forest more gigantic even than the forest of Volkonskoi, between St. Petersburg and Moscow, and said to be the largest in Europe. Nowhere else in the world is there a similar extensive vegetable soil, except in the North of Hindostan. The growth and exportation of grain is a source of great wealth and power to Russia, and were she so careful for the development of her commerce as the largeness of her Empire, her wealth and power from this source might yet be much increased. From the platform, and through the windows of the train, I beheld an undulating country covered with yellow harvests, short in the straw, but heavy in the ear. Roughly clad men were busy reaping with the sickle, and short-skirted, small-sized, broad-set women were binding the sheaves; while over ill-made roads, rickety and laden carts were being slowly drawn homewards by lazy bullocks, as if time were of no importance, and the very acme of life a chronic condition of falling asleep.

Here and there, amid the yellow harvests, and near the homesteads, were garden patches of sunflowers all in bloom. Sunflower seeds not only yield a plentiful supply of oil, but the seeds themselves are a delicacy with the lower order of Russians. Every street, and square, and railway station has its vender, and the husks, plentifully scattered in places of public resort, are evidence of the taste of the people for the seeds of this remarkable plant.

Hamlets are thinly scattered on the edges of the grain tract: low wooden houses, with overhanging eaves, and small doors and tiny windows, looking almost like dolls' houses, and so fragile that a strong wind might carry them away; and mud huts, like inferior cattle-sheds, and totally unfit for human habitation. These hamlets are mostly built on sloping ground, having the appearance of cliffs from which the water has receded; and in the sides of the cliffs are rudely built ovens of brick and clay, surrounded by charred embers, which answer the purpose of public bake-houses, and are considered general property.

Where these cliffs were parted and broken, and a stream ran down the opening into the flat land below, brilliantly plumaged kingfishers sat upon the bushes and boulders intently watching for their prey; and scores of them, satisfied with their day's fishing, were quietly perched upon the telegraph wires, and in no way disconcerted by the passing train. It was a wonder to me to see them in such numbers, and so familiar with the hissing steam and rumble of the railway vehicles as to pursue their occupation with all the calmness and regularity observable hardly anywhere but in undisturbed solitude. Their awkward gait, the rapid action of their little wings, the dexterity with which they seize the unwary fish and strike it senseless upon a stone with their firm, strong mandibles, are all interesting, and here quite easily noticeable. To behold them sitting upon the telegraph wires, like priests in gorgeous vestments, their eyes half closed, their heads thrown back, their long beaks pointing heavenwards, as if complacently calling down upon civilization in general, represented by the Russian railway, the choicest benedictions, was enough to provoke a smile; and especially in connection with the thought that could some old heathen mystic, skilled in halcyonic prognostications, return, and trace out the entrails of the most solemnly wise among them all, he might a tale unfold concerning the results of advancing civilization to the haunts and existence of the kingfisher tribe, as to cause them to refrain from their blessings to the end of their days.

From the base of these cliffs a strip of flat land runs out to the edge of the sea. Near the mouth of the Don this flat land becomes extensive—stretches for miles on every side into a luxurious delta, covered in parts with rushes, and in parts drained and yielding splendid pasturage to large herds of horses and cattle. In winter the delta of the Don is infested with wolves; bears also are not unfrequently seen, and occasionally the wild ox. But in summer the horses and cattle peaceably feed, and the bees, from innumerable hives, hum through the sunshine, and carry home heavily laden bags of honey. Not only are bees found wild in Russia, but the culture of domesticated bees is perhaps better understood by the Russians than by any people in Europe. Horse-rearing is also largely indulged in, and has been a lucrative employment; but the Russian Government, becoming alarmed at the increased export of horses, very greatly restricted the export, and in some localities forbade it altogether. The Ukraine, and the country to the east of the Ukraine, has been a recruiting-ground for horses, vast herds of them roaming wild over the steppes; and the Cossack's horse is almost as famous as his more beautiful, but not more sagacious, relative, the Arab. Byron has made us familiar with the Cossack's horse in his poem "Mazeppa."

> "Shaggy and swift, and strong of limb,
> All Tartar-like he carried him;
> Obeyed his voice, and came to call,
> And knew him in the midst of all:
> Though thousands were around—and night
> Without a star pursued her flight—
> That steed from sunset until dawn
> His chief would follow like a fawn."

And, also, in the more spirited passage, descriptive of the horse in his wild state :

> "'Bring forth the horse!' The horse was brought;
>   In truth, he was a noble steed,
>   A Tartar of the Ukraine breed,
>   Who looked as though the speed of thought
>   Were in his limbs; but he was wild,
>   Wild as the wild deer, and untaught,
>   With spur and bridle undefiled—
>   'Twas but a day he had been caught;
>   And snorting with erected mane,
>   And struggling fiercely, but in vain,
>   In the full foam of wrath and dread
>   To me the forest-born was led:
>   They bound me on, that menial throng,
>   Upon his back with many a thong;
>   Then loosed him with a sudden lash—
>   Away! Away! and on we dash!
>   Torrents less rapid and less rash."

Across the delta of the Don, lifting itself above level land and silvery sea, its antique embattled walls, and domes, and towers showing through the haze like the grey ghost of a city long since forgotten, is the place which gave a new name to the sea. Its old classical name, Palus Mœotis, was lost with the loss of Byzantium, and then it became known by the name of this city, the city of Azov. Here stood once a more ancient city still, which gave its name to the river, now the river Don, that swept under its walls—the city of Tanais. Many fierce struggles have taken place here. It has become a memorable place in the world's history, but it is never likely to become memorable again. Men's knowledge of the world has widened, the seat of empire has moved westward; what were once splendid Eastern monarchies have dwindled into insignificance, or become dependencies of younger and stronger powers, and other places, as Azov once was, have become crucial geographical points where the destinies of empires must sooner or later be decided.

The dreaded Tamerlane of Samarcand, who carried his victorious arms to the Ganges; who almost broke the

power of the Osmanlis, and thereby delayed for many years
the capture of Constantinople, and who would have broken
their power completely had they not been, like himself,
followers of the great prophet, and fighting for the faith
against the Christians; who contemplated the conquest of
China, and aspired to the empire of the world—Tamerlane
swept his troops into Azov, sacked the city, and, in search
of richer plunder, appeared to the affrighted Russians
beneath the walls of Moscow.

Once and again the Janizaries of Turkey have fought under
the walls of Azov. They thought to penetrate the northern
frontier of the Persian Empire, and it was necessary to
capture and retain Azov as a fortress by the way. Their
attempts failed. Seeking the Persian foe, they unexpectedly
found another and more formidable. For the first time the
Russian flung himself upon the Ottoman, and drove the
startled Janizaries down the Don. When the Russian
retired, the Cossack came, and settled on the banks of the
noble river, and occupied Azov; and when, years after, the
Sultan sought to recover the fortress, and strike another
blow at Persia's northern frontier, he was met by men equal
in dash and daring to his Janizaries, and more than equal in
their powers of resistance and endurance. Fifty-five thousand Turkish troops invested Azov, breaking through intrenchment after intrenchment, until at last the Cossacks
were shut up within the city walls. There, at bay, they
maintained the unequal contest—repairing the breaches,
counter-working the mines, dealing reprisals with a quick
and heavy hand, until the Turks were forced away by the
approach of winter. During winter the fortifications were
strengthened. In the following spring the Turks returned.
The siege was recommenced with redoubled energy. The
Cossacks fought like tigers, but they were very few, and
daily becoming fewer. Scorning defeat, and yet persuaded
that if they continued the struggle in the city defeat was
inevitable, they blew up the fortifications, and gallantly

dashed out at the foe, breaking through their lines, and retreating to the safe shelter of the steppes and marshes that lay between the Azov and the Caspian.

The Turks held Azov nearly a century. Then arose Peter the Great, who, among his other gigantic schemes, determined to obtain the mastery of the Black Sea. Azov had been very strongly fortified by the Turks, and was splendidly garrisoned; and the Turks were much better sailors than the Russians, and likely to be able successfully to defend the fortress by sea. But Peter, nothing daunted, employed Venetians to build boats, that he might cope with the enemy on the water as well as on the land. Through mistaken management these boats failed to enter the Sea of Azov. Nevertheless, he commenced the siege, but, for lack of boats, and because of the desertion of the German director of his artillery—who, bitterly resenting the corporeal punishment to which he had been subjected, went over to the enemy, and skilfully defended Azov against the Russians—he lost many of his men, and did not take the city after all. The next spring, however, saw a small Russian fleet in the Azov, which attacked and captured several boats of a Turkish fleet sent to reinforce and victual the Azov garrison. The siege was renewed under more advantageous circumstances, and the city fell in July, 1696. With his customary vigour, Peter at once began to strengthen this important place. A harbour was dug out; ship-building was commenced. The intention was formed of making it a base for maritime operations against the Crimea. Already the supremacy of the Azov was in his hands, and, with the acquisition of the Crimea, he would be master of the Black Sea.

Two important events followed the capture of the city of Azov: the striking of the first Russian medal, upon which Peter is styled "the august Emperor of Muscovy," and said to be "victorious by fire and water;" and the first public triumphal entry of Russian troops into Moscow, amid many decorations, and the general rejoicing of the people.

Thirty miles above the city of Azov, the more modern city of Rostoff stretches itself on both banks of the Don; and thirty miles above Rostoff, of less commercial, but greater political importance, lies the capital of the country of the Don Cossacks, Novo Tcherchask. Rostoff is one of the finest cities in South Russia, not to be compared with Odessa, but a fine city nevertheless, and likely to become an increasingly flourishing commercial centre. The streets are wide, but ill-paved; the buildings lofty and imposing in the main streets, and not so heavy and depressed in architectural style as the buildings in Taganrog; many churches lift their gilded domes above the houses, and innumerable bells clang out their calls to religious devotions; a spacious hotel, with an ample, well-furnished, tastily decorated dining-hall, ferns and flowers on every table, and a cool glass tank in the centre in which gold fish are gliding, provides French fare of five courses for the small charge of a single rouble; a large and well-kept pleasure-ground is frequented by crowds in the summer eventide; places of amusement cater for the public taste, conspicuous among which, and more harmless than any, is Salamansky's Circus, one of the best of its kind, and said to contain some of the most beautiful, carefully trained horses in the world.

On the journey to Rostoff, seated in the opposite compartment of the railway carriage, I observed a fairly tall, compactly built gentleman, well dressed, with dark hair and moustache, and a pleasing rounded countenance, who, upon inquiry concerning the time of the train's arrival, volunteered an answer in good English; and I was somewhat surprised to find this gentleman in the evening in the ring of the circus, greeted by the audience as the proprietor, and, with conscious and pardonable pride, putting the horses through their various evolutions in the most skilful way. The entertainment consisted almost exclusively in exhibiting the cleverness of the horses. There was hardly any sensational and dangerous display of human strength and agility, so common in the English circus. The clown appeared twice, and jested in French, and went through the customary grotesque antics; but the main feature of the entertainment was the cantering, and wheeling, and leaping, and regular movements of the horses themselves. Several were valuable English animals, others were Russian, and Arab; and, in the interval of the entertainment, the stables were thrown open to inspection, that the beasts might be more critically and leisurely examined by those versed in equine lore.

The Don at Rostoff is from three to four hundred yards wide, deep in the centre of the stream, and flowing slowly. On the right bank of the river are storehouses for wool and grain. The storehouses for wool are connected with portions of the shallow margin of the river, staked off, and forming enclosures, within which the wool is washed by being trodden in the slowly flowing water under the naked feet of women. Thousands of women are so employed during the greater part of the summer, while men are constantly going to and from the storehouses, carrying thither the washed wool, and returning with fresh supplies. The wool and grain trades of Rostoff give to the river a very animated appearance. It is an immense busy hive. The surrounding people flock into the town in summer to reap the benefit of these profitable and well-prosecuted industries, returning to their homes on the approach of winter to enjoy their hard-earned and scanty gains. Therefore Rostoff has a large fluctuating population, and in winter, apart from its religious festivals, must be a comparatively quiet place.

A splendid bridge, not unlike Brünel's famous structure across the Tamar, spans the Don at Rostoff, and carries over the river the Caucasian Railway. Through Rostoff, therefore, lies the direct and quickest route to Central Asia; and with the completion of the Trans-Caspian Railway, and the consequently rapid development of Russian trade with Central Asia—a development detrimental already to British commercial interests beyond the mountainous northern frontier of Hindostan—Rostoff must become a town increasingly important to the commerce of the world. On the 12th of May, 1885, Mr. Condie Stephen, the second secretary of the British Legation at Teheran, arrived in London from Afghanistan with despatches from Sir Peter Lumsden, having accomplished the journey from Meshed to London in nineteen days. He came across the Caspian Sea, and the Caucasian mountains, and by railway through Rostoff and Kharkoff, joining the St. Petersburg and Berlin express at Dünuburg;—a wonderfully quick journey, and yet to be still further accelerated by the engineering enterprise of the Russians beyond the Caspian. This is the natural route from the heart of Europe to the heart of Asia, and, in opening up this route, the Russians are only following geographical indications long ago perceived by restless and ambitious men who have dreamed of uniting in one vast unbroken empire the far East and the far West.

The Turks attempted to open up this route under Selim II., in the sixteenth century. Their intention was, primarily, to drop down the Caspian, and unexpectedly strike the Persian foe in his northern province of Shirwan. Two hundred miles above Rostoff the Don forms an elbow, the point of which is only thirty miles distant from the point of a similar elbow of the Volga, and Selim's intention was to cut a navigable canal from one point to the other, and thereby transport his troops, without any fatiguing marches, directly into Persian territory. It was a splendid design, and might have been successful, notwithstanding the resistance of the Russians, but for the requirement by the Koran of a prayer from the faithful in the third watch of the night. So far north, in summer, there is no third watch *of the night*, for before the third watch it is already morning; therefore the prayer could not be said. Nature was against the Koran, and mightier than the Koran. The Janizaries were startled to find themselves outside the geographical sphere of Mohammedanism, and, against nature, still believing in the Koran, they came to the conclusion that they had no business there, that they would not stay there, and that no Sultan should oblige them to make the attempt again. It is now believed by the ordinary Mohammedan that there is an interdict upon the land of the North, and that it can never be possessed by a Mohammedan power. Lord Beaconsfield, in his "Endymion," has told us how the very trifling circumstance of the disease of a root—the potato—in Ireland, altered the course of the world's history; and the historical current of the world was here turned aside by the impossibility of scrupulously observing a minor religious ceremony of no importance to any one but a devout Mussulman, and, if he had been intent upon the spirit instead of upon the letter of the ceremony, of very little importance even to him.

Another, and more remarkable man than any Turkish Sultan, designed the ruin of the British Empire by striking at her famous Eastern possession, and intended moving his troops along the very route chosen by Selim three hundred years ago. Napoleon negotiated an alliance between France and Russia, the Russian Czar then being the capricious, if not insane, Paul; and one purpose of this alliance was to permanently cripple England by the conquest of India. Paul was murdered, Nelson obtained his brilliant victory at Copenhagen, and the alliance vanished like a dream. But Napoleon actually arranged for 35,000 French troops to descend the Danube, and be transported from the mouth of the Danube in Russian boats to that very elbow of the Don where Selim commenced to cut his canal; thence to march the thirty miles to the elbow of the Volga, and drop down this river to Astrakhan; and, joined in Astrakhan by 50,000 Cossacks, and 25,000 Russian cavalry and infantry, cross the Caspian to Astrabad, making Astrabad the military depôt for the expedition, and pushing forward to India by way of Herat and Candahar. A most startling project, and, considering the means of transport then available, apparently ridiculous! But the project was entertained, and there was wisdom in the selection of the route, if in nothing else.

Rostoff gave the Russian Empire its present illustrious reigning house, the House of Romanoff. The ancient dynasty of Rurik, whose Grand-Princes captured first Novgorod, and then Kief, and then Vladimir, and then Moscow, successively uniting these, until in Moscow they became Czars, reigned 736 years. Ivan the Terrible, a monster of cruelty, dealt blow upon blow at the representatives of his own house, making exile welcome, and leaving the throne a lonely terror; so that, upon the death of his weak-minded eldest son, who reigned after him for a very brief period, and the murder of his youngest, a little child, with whom the direct line became extinct, no distant connection of the Rurik dynasty cared or dared to occupy a throne defiled with so much blood. The country was plunged into helpless anarchy. Boris Godunoff, the murderer of the royal child Dmitri, reigned six years; then his son; then pretender after pretender arose calling himself by the name of the murdered child, and contending with ambitious successors of the tyrant Boris, until Russia was torn and bleeding in every province, and at the mercy of every external foe. The Swedes in the North, the Poles in the West, the Cossacks and Tartars in the South, afflicted the Empire, and national sentiment almost died out, until the preposterous claims of the Poles, and their subsequent defeat in Moscow, revived the national sentiment, and resulted in the assembly of a national council for the purpose of ending the stormiest period in Russian history by the election of a new Czar and a new dynasty.

Philareto, the head of the House of Romanoff, which house was distantly allied on the female side to the dynasty of Rurik, in order to escape the savage fury of Ivan the Terrible, had become a priest, and risen to the bishopric of Rostoff. When the election of the new Czar was about to take place, he was a captive among the Poles, having formed one of an embassy to treat with Sigismond at Smolensk, and, with the rest of the embassy, having been siezed by Sigismond because he would not favour his personal claims. Philareto was held in the highest esteem by the Russians, on account of his gentleness, ability, and devotion to the welfare of the state; and, upon the refusal of two princes to accept the crown, and the unsuccessful candidature of others, the choice of the council, strengthened by the recommendation of Hermogenes, the patriarch of Moscow, and possibly by a letter to the council from Philareto himself, fell upon Michael, the son of Philareto, and till then unknown among all classes of his countrymen. A young man of sixteen years, unused to power, inexperienced in statecraft, supposed to inherit the virtues of his father but having had no opportunity himself of showing these virtues to the people, Michael Romanoff ascended the Russian throne, at a period when Russia was smarting under long years of anarchy, and sore bewildered as to her rightful king; and he proved himself the worthy head of a new dynasty by steering the vessel through the rocky, intricate channel into deeper and clearer seas. Upon his coronation he swore to observe conditions which limited the power of the crown. He associated with himself his venerated father Philareto, and the *ukases* were issued in his father's name, as "the mighty Lord and most holy Patriarch of all the Russias," as well as his own. The magnificence and power of the Patriarchate continued until the greatest Romanoff, a century later, Peter, roused by jealousy, struck it so crushing a blow as to make it reel to its ruin; and in him appeared again, to the full, that hydra-headed despotism apparently indigenous to Russia, and which, while it has contributed largely to Russia's barbaric splendour, will prove in the end Russia's heaviest curse and surest ruin.

CHAPTER IX.

THE RUSSIAN PEOPLES.

Different races—Muscovy and the Muscovites—House of Rurik—Cossacks and Tartars—Cossack troops—Music—No middle class—Artificial government—The *tchin*—Its effect—Personal appearance of the State officials—Lower orders—Contrast between the Russians and the Greeks — Dress — Dhrosky drivers — Recreation — Tea-drinking—*Vatké*—Domestic life—Marriage customs—Woman—Women's rights—Education of women—Development of trade—Jews and Greeks—Russian labourers—Development of particular industries—Cotton—Woollen, silk, iron, oil, &c.—Repressive power of the Government—Domestic policy—Foreign aggression.

WITHIN the far-reaching confines of the Russian Empire we might reasonably expect to find many different races. But we might not expect to find that the Czar of all the Russias autocratically governs a hundred different peoples —many of them allied in race, it is true, nevertheless so different as to speak originally a hundred different tongues, and to possess, at one time or another, independent national existences. That is a marvellous fact, and more marvellous still when we consider the increasingly rapid advancement of this enveloping process during the last two hundred years. A map of Russia, showing the acquisitions of the Empire since the accession of Peter the Great, is an interesting study, and, in connection with Russia's favourite idea of Pan-Slavism, a significant indication of her future history, if she be wise enough to suppress internal revolution, and strong enough to overcome external foes.

The true Russians live in the heart of the Empire. The fortress of Russia is Muscovy, and the central citadel of the fortress is Moscow; and, to true Russians, in whom the national sentiment is deeply rooted, from whom the Czar receives the most implicit obedience, by whom the very name of Russia is revered as holy, Moscow, and not St. Petersburg, is still the metropolis, the mother city. Thither the monarchs of Russia must repair to receive the iron crown, and put on the robes of royalty; and, sanctified by the oil of God's grace, be made meet to rule over Holy Russia in God's name, and as God's representative. In Muscovy serfdom had its seat; in Muscovy absolutism was developed; in Muscovy first arose those institutions introduced into, and then securely fastened upon, one conquered province after another : and the vast dominions of the Czar are more surely becoming every year reflections of the original Empire, which included very little more than that central region of forests and rivers, long cut off from the influences of European civilization, and known by the name of Muscovy.

The true Russians are Slavs. And yet the ancient founder of this greatest of the Slav powers was a Teuton. A thousand years ago, when there was so much agitation among the free, brave, hardy peoples of the North; when they went forth to fight for, and win, richer lands than their own, and, in the providence of God, sow the seeds of future empire, and hasten on the accomplishment of God's "increasing purpose,"— a thousand years ago Rurik, and his Varangian warriors, went eastwards, and became first protectors and then possessors of the populous, peaceful, wealthy mercantile city of Novgorod. These Varangians were few. They were soon swallowed up and forgotten in the surrounding Slav myriads; their language was lost in the Slav tongue; but the descendants of Rurik were able and brave men, commanding respect, compelling acknowledgment, until, themselves more Slav than the Slavs, they became the Grand-Princes of the Slav cities, and the rightful inheritors of the Russian throne.

The predominant element in the population of that part of Southern Russia bordering upon the Sea of Azov is not Slav, but Cossack and Tartar. The province of South Russia is divided into five governments. Of these, the one embracing the towns of Taganrog and Rostoff, and having for its capital Novo-Tcherkask, is called "The country of the Don Cossacks." The origin of the Cossacks is obscure. Several authorities think them to be the descendants of Nomadic tribes who were attracted by the rich pasture-lands on the banks of the South Russian rivers, and finally settled there under the government of separate military chiefs. Others, however, are of opinion that the Cossacks came from Central Russia; that they found unbearable the autocratic yoke of the Muscovite princes of the thirteenth and fourteenth centuries, and fled southwards, beyond their reach; and that, in their newly formed political constitutions, they retained a considerable measure of the individual freedom and privilege which was a chief characteristic of the republicanism of the ancient Russian cities. The Tartars are near relatives of the Turks, and the remnants of the last mighty invasion of South-Eastern Europe by the hordes of Central Asia. Mingled with the Tartars are many Slavs, but because of the gradual intermixture of races, and the influences of climate, food, labour, and common religious and social customs, the distinguishing facial features of these two peoples are not generally well marked. Cossacks are easily noticeable, but it would puzzle an ethnologist to say whether many of the rest are Slavs or Tartars.

The finest troops in the Russian army, the wildest, bravest, and most tenacious, are the Cossacks. They are a fairly tall, muscular, bony race; with dark-skinned oval countenances, full foreheads, noses depressed between the eyes, but large about the nostrils, firm and closely drawn lips, and quick bright eyes; easily roused to vigorous passion, and ready to obey all orders unquestioningly, pitilessly, and without remorse; strong in their attachment to each other, and very loyal to the Russian throne. They have political privileges above many. They have been conciliated, and an important and distinguished position in the Empire secured for them, by appointing the Czarevitch their Hetman, or acknowledged chief; and it was partly for the purpose of presenting the Czarevitch to them in this capacity that the Emperor undertook his journey to the South in April, 1886. This purpose, however, was partially defeated by the activity of the Nihilists. After many years of singular freedom from political agitation, the country of the Don Cossacks even has been sown with revolutionary literature, yielding the usual results in plots to assassinate the Czar.

The Cossacks have a passion for music. This passion is fostered in the army by the formation of military bands. To sit and listen to their correct and spirited rendering of martial airs, accoutred in a pleasing dark and crimson-embroidered uniform, their figures erect, their long hair nearly falling upon their shoulders, their fine eyes all aglow with musical sympathy, is a favourite evening recreation; and, to a foreigner, the scene gathers additional interest from the curiously attired groups, moving round and round, unconsciously stepping to the music, and engaged in animated conversation. A goodly proportion of these crowds are women, whose appreciation of the music is keener than that of the men.

There are only two classes in Russia, the high and the low. The great want of Russia is a middle class. This would give the Empire security and stability, cohesion and firmness; and it would suggest a different way out of the slavery of absolutism into the freedom of constitutional government than that advocated in the secret revolutionary press, and attempted by desperate and mistaken men. But how to create a middle class, under the present conditions of Russian political life, is the grand difficulty! Nevertheless, should no middle class arise, the absolutism of Russia must hold on its perilous course, until some fearful cataclysm, or mighty upheaval, rend the Empire, and engulf it; and what will take its place no one can tell.

If Russia had been allowed to grow like other nations, she might have had a middle class; but Peter the Great, in his anxiety to place Russia alongside the other European nations, was not content to let her grow. She must be forced into a certain mould. She must be hammered into a certain pattern. She must be made to take a certain shape. And the consequence is the most artificial and anomalous political production of modern times. If he had been wise enough to frame laws regulating the natural growth of the Empire; if he had permitted the Empire gradually to develop herself along her own lines; if he had been more of a nursing father to his people, and less of a revolutionary autocrat, forcing upon his people customs obnoxious to them, secretly resented by them, and yet which they were obliged to observe, Russia might have been smaller in size, weaker in external influence, but she would have been happier, more compact, and likelier to live long and illustriously among her sister communities in Europe.

Peter the Great found himself impeded in his policy by the nobility of Russia, and therefore determined to supplant the old aristocratic families by a new aristocracy, not of families, but of men, who, by long service to the state, in a military or civil capacity, should rise to the highest distinctions the state could confer. The boyars, the titled Muscovite princes who had stood near the throne, and counselled their Grand-Prince and Autocrat, were thrust aside, and the aristocratic ranks were thrown open to the host of foreigners whom Peter had gathered about him to assist him in his ship-building, and city-rearing, and wars by land and sea, and also thrown open to any freeborn Russian who was willing to enter into the service of the state. This institution is yet intact. It has been very slightly modified since Peter's death, and the modifications have been in the civil rather than the military ranks; and the effect of this institution has been to sharply divide the whole nation into two classes—the government class, and the lower orders. In Russia, a man who is not in the service of the Government, who does not hold some civil or military position, of which in each there are no less than fourteen different grades, is a nobody, one of the unclassed, one of the lower orders; and however wise a man he may be, in commercial pursuits, in literature, in science, in any walk of life which in every other country in Europe would secure for him respect and honour, in this country, Russia, he is liable to be snubbed, and badgered, and oppressed by the *tchinovniks*, the bureaucracy, those subordinate officials of the Government who increase their poor pay by peculation, extortion, and bribery. The desire of every freeborn Russian is to enter into the *tchin*, the privileged orders. And every freeborn Russian may. A commoner, a man whose father before him was not an aristocrat, has certainly a long and laborious service before him, especially in the army, preparatory to his first advancement, a service of twelve years, if he cannot by money or favour procure a shortening of the term, whereas a born aristocrat obtains his first advancement almost immediately; but this long and laborious service for the commoner does not deter him from entering the service. He must enter it to escape oppression. He must enter it to be anybody at all. Consequently the lowest rank in the Government service is crowded with men whose interest it is to maintain the Government, to fall in automatically with that administrative machine which manufactures link after link of the heavy chain of slavery binding the millions of Russia, and increasing, at the same time, the weight and stability of the Russian throne.

This establishment of the *tchin*, this creation of a new aristocracy, has made modern Russia, and unmade Muscovy.

Peter the Great may be regarded as the famous founder of a mighty empire, but he is certainly the ruthless destroyer of a nation which might have been mighty if its national aspirations had been developed along natural lines. The *tchin* is an artificial institution, appealing to personal ambition, carefully fostering self-interest, and yet skilfully subordinating personal ambition and self-interest to the highest power in the state, the autocratic Czar. May not this prove to be a pyramid standing on its apex, and sure sooner or later to fall over, and break into a thousand pieces? No country can be long governed artificially. There are unknown forces in national life that some time will have way. The living power in an acorn, buried beneath the foundation of a prison or a palace, would rend the foundation, and shake to ruin prison or palace in its effort to get free. So is the living power of a nation. No prison, no palace can crush it. Russia will rise, and the despotism beneath which it is now buried will be broken and disappear.

The sharp distinction between the government class and the lower orders is noticeable in the facial expression and general appearance of the people. The officials of the Government are intelligent-looking men, with well-developed foreheads, close and firm mouths, and eyes cool and steady; and the ideas you obtain in looking at them are reticence, determination, courage—at least these are the ideas revealed in their faces to a foreigner. There is a singular lack of vivacity: no humorous light, no merry twinkle in the eye. They are courteous, but coldly courteous; obliging, but severely obliging; appearing as if their inner life were suppressed, confined, and only so much allowed to escape at a time as was really required for the automatic movement of their gentlemanly bodies. When the foreigner has become familiar, or when with themselves, this peculiarity departs to some extent; smiles are more frequently seen, and the eyes become a little brighter, but even then they are never vivacious. They are capable, however, of strong family affection, and their words at home to their wives and children are full of fond phrases, each of their children having a pet name, a peculiar Russian ending to the christened name converting it into a term of endearment; and there are numerous instances of long and faithful service on the part of servants to their masters, which prove that beneath the stolid exterior there is deep, if not fervent, attachment—an admirable quality in any people. An English lady in Taganrog praised her Russian servants as I have heard very few ladies praise their English servants at home.

The general facial expression of the lower orders is not different in kind, but only in degree, from that of the Government officials. The intelligence is feeble. The reticence becomes sullenness, the determination stubbornness, the courage patient animal force. There is not only a lack of vivacity, but a positive deadness. They are with difficulty roused to passion of any kind. They will bear oppression without resentment; they will look upon self-sacrifice without enthusiasm. If goaded to rebellion, as sometimes they are, they strike blindly, and then endure punishment as a matter of course. They expect it. They even seem contented with it. Jacob said of one of his children, " Issachar is a strong ass couching down between two burdens," and that might be said of the Russians. No people were ever so plastic in the hands of an autocracy. No people were ever so satisfied with an autocracy. Their dull, patient, immobile faces seem to imply impossibility of struggling against their lot. They must take it, such as it is; and do with it, what they are allowed. Education, of course, alters all this, but very few of the common people are educated; and, therefore, social and political revolutionary movements in Russia must be directed by, and can only spread among, the educated classes. The ranks of the Nihilists—understanding by that term members of secret societies whose object is the delivery of the people by the overthrow of the autocracy—are not reinforced from among the common people, but from among the educated classes; and the common people will not be with them until they are sent to school.

There is the greatest possible contrast between the facial expression and temperament of the Russians, and the facial expression and temperament of the Greeks; and yet both peoples believe in the same form of Christianity. In the Churches of Greek and Russian alike there is substantially the same splendid ritual. They are united in religion, but divided in everything else. They stand at exactly opposite poles of human nature. The Grecian features are regular and well-defined; the eyes full of light, and ready to flash fire upon the slightest provocation, revealing the quick, passionate, revengeful spirit within; a wonderful animation playing all over the face, especially during conversation; and a readiness to comprehend words and signs very different from the dulness of the Russians. In the Grecian Archipelago it is not difficult to make a man understand what you want, but in Russia! On one occasion I spent an hour in a vain attempt to convey my meaning to three obtuse waiters in the hotel at Rostoff. They looked at me in mild amazement, and tried again and again apathetically to solve the enigma presented to them, until, mutually confounded, we were fain to retire to rest.

The Government officials dress well, at least those of the higher grades, in a close-fitting dark-coloured uniform; and wear the round cap, with inclined brim in front, common in Russia, and not unfrequently worn by English sailors. Some of them carry dirks in ornamental sheaths, and others swords and revolvers. The private soldier is shabbily dressed in a grey material, which, with his dull face, makes him a very sombre individual indeed. There is nothing striking in the dress of the ordinary people. You may meet women, young women, who retain the costume of the Cossack, notwithstanding the Parisian influence generally observable in the dress of the great majority. They look very well in it. It becomes them better than the mysterious arrangement honoured with the name of *dress* sometimes imported from the centre of fashion, in which the human frame does penance for an hour or two, and serves to publicly exhibit the amazing ingenuity of the Parisian mind. This Cossack costume consists of a simple skirt of one deep colour reaching to the ankles, round the bottom of which runs a broad band of prettily designed crewel-work in very many colours, with a many-coloured ornamental border. Over this, fitting close to the waist, and secured round it by a coloured ribbon, is a bodice of alternate strips of crewel-work, corresponding with the broad band round the skirt, and lace; and from the waist falls down in front of the skirt a similarly designed apron. The bodice is tied round the throat by another ribbon, and from the waist, and from the back of the neck, a variety of ribbons are left loose, each ribbon having its corresponding colour among the silks of the crewel-work of the dress proper. Neither hat nor bonnet is worn. The hair is brushed back, and plaited behind, and into the plaiting flowers are fastened; and in the cool summer evenings a lace shawl is thrown over the head after the manner worn by Spanish ladies. The whole makes a very picturesque costume, in no way impeding the movement of the body; and many Russian ladies, whose countenances are generally very pleasing, and sometimes beautiful, look remarkably well in this ancient costume, which, however, beneath the influences of Western fashion is certain speedily to disappear.

The dress of the Russian dhrosky driver is comparatively well known. The dhrosky is by no means a comfortable conveyance for long distances, but very handy for short runs through the town. It it a low four-wheeled carriage, with a seat for the driver, and a seat directly behind for his fare. The seat behind will only accommodate two persons. These seats have no back rest, and the dhrosky is generally driven through the uneven streets at a furious pace, slackening very little even when turning the corners; therefore one has to be very careful to prevent being pitched out. The horse is mostly a rough, wiry brute, miserably caparisoned, and fastened about the collar to a kind of bridge going from shaft to shaft directly over the horse's withers. The dhrosky driver wears a caftan, a garment worn also in Persia and Turkey, and having in both these countries a similar name; in all probability, therefore, it is of Asiatic origin, and was introduced into Russia by the Tartar invasion. The Russian dhrosky driver's caftan is made of heavy dark-brown material, and reaches from the throat to the ankles. It is belted round the middle, and padded and quilted from the middle downwards—a very wise provision for securing the warmth and comfort doubly necessary when exposed to all kinds of weather, and seated on a smooth, hard, leather seat the whole day long. The dhroskies are all labelled, after the manner of our English cabs, and the drivers are by no means exorbitant in their charges. Some of them are men of fair intelligence. One I met with could speak a little English, but like most of his fellows he was given to drinking *vatké*, a vile spirit which rendered him altogether incapable of driving straight, and which almost led at one time to a serious upset by going clean over a large mound in the street; and, therefore, our English-speaking friend had to be carefully watched afterwards, lest, with broken limbs, we should have been obliged to taste the joys of a Russian hospital.

The habits of the Russian peoples are simple. They have very few amusements. That intense love of sport which appears to be ingrained in the nature of Englishmen, is almost unknown in Russia. Theatres are not very numerous. Promenading in the gardens in summer, skating and sleighing in winter, are the favourite modes of recreation. The food of the poor is rough, and far from cleanly, and, indeed, they are far from cleanly in person; but the rich have good fare, and whiter and sweeter bread than any in Europe. Tea is a common beverage, obtained overland by the slow canal routes, and therefore necessarily expensive, but as delicious as you can drink in China itself. They do not spoil it by adding milk or cream, and they drink it from glasses, and flavour it with the juice of a lemon. The price varies even more than in England. For a pound you can give any price between two roubles and twenty. The uniform excellence of Russian tea, however, is threatened with extinction. International intercourse is producing its inevitable commercial results. Russian tea merchants attempt extensive purchases in England, and introduce inferior tea for the sake of larger profits; and you cannot now depend so much upon the rich aroma as when the chests were slowly transmitted from the north-western provinces of China across two continents, not unfrequently reaching their destination in the Russian capital after two years.

The Russians are not only addicted to tea drinking, and by this custom suggest comparison with the English, but they suggest still closer comparison by their habits of intemperance. They are a drunken people. The Greeks are sober compared with them. And the Turks, fortified by the provisions of the Koran, are very sober. But the English are more drunken still, and more dangerous in their drunkenness. *Vatké* does not infuriate a man. It makes him physically powerless and mentally imbecile. Two drunken Russians, crooning unintelligible gibberish, would crouch in the same doorway, and look with their blear eyes and nod with their helpless heads one at another like good-natured, if bestial, lunatics. Two drunken Englishmen would indulge in a free fight. And only being partially robbed of their bodily strength, and sometimes not robbed at all, a free fight in England too often means serious injury and death. And an Englishman, for want of a companion to fight, will batter his wife and children at home. When shall we wipe away this reproach from our nation? When will English legislators see that drink is our curse, and may be our ruin ? When will our statesmen hear the loud cries of the complicated miseries that flow from this terribly fruitful source ? We blazon our reproach abroad, and let every nation see it. Not many drunken Russians came under my notice; but one evening, in the public gardens, I was startled to behold four English sailors, arm in arm, all intoxicated, stumbling along the main path, and bawling loudly an old English ditty, and I thought at the time it was a piece of reckless conduct only possible to the Anglo-Saxon.

The family life of the Russians will compare very favourably with that of any people in Europe. Doubtless, among the ignorant, in out-of-the-way districts, the family life is far from pure; and in places where the sons bring their wives home to dwell under the father's roof, and the father exercises for his own bad ends the ancient patriarchal authority, stories of licentiousness and cruelty are not to be altogether set aside as malicious fabrications. There is some truth in these stories. Overcrowding everywhere will produce the same results, and what wonder if we find the results aggravated in regions utterly secluded from the rest of the world, and where the one visible pattern of morality and religion, the priest, is of low character and loose life ! But in the towns and their immediate neighbourhood, and among what we should call respectable people, the families of Russia stand high among the families of Europe, and command the unstinted praise of all acquainted with them. There are several causes for this. There is a very great difference between the town and country clergy in Russia. The town clergy are patterns of virtue, and not only in their individual, but in their family life—for the Greek Church is no advocate for the celibacy of the priesthood—influence aright those to whom they minister. This is one indirect cause, but a cause more direct is the disfavour with which second marriages are regarded in Russia, and the entire disapproval of third marriages—a disfavour and disapproval arising from their idealistic views of matrimony. The sanctity of marriage is deeply felt in Russia. Devotion to one woman, contentment with one wedded life, is the ideal set before men by the Church, and in the spiritual significance of marriage it is the Scriptural ideal; and the consequence is purity in the family life, and loving relationship between the different members. I do not mean that second and third marriages lead to impurity, or destroy loving relationship, though sometimes the latter consequence follows; but I mean that the one marriage preserves the family unity, and lifts the family idea into a higher atmosphere, with the result to the nation at large of a purer and happier domestic life.

Another cause is the custom which obtains in all respectable families in Russia of the brothers endeavouring to secure suitable husbands for their sisters, and refraining themselves from marriage until their sisters have been provided for. Where the families consist of several brothers and sisters, each brother will take under his wing the sister or sisters between himself and the next brother younger, and, if the father be too poor to dower his daughter, he will work for a dowry himself, and send her away from the father's roof with becoming honour and joy. This custom is scrupulously regarded by the young men of South Russia. To disregard it would be a serious breach of etiquette. It reveals an acknowledgment of woman's claim, a solicitude for woman's welfare—a deference to woman's *womanliness*, shall I call it? the spirit of chivalry finding tender expression in the daily life. Such a custom has the double tendency of hastening the marriage of women while still young, and deferring the marriage of men until the approach of middle life. There is generally a disparity in age between the husband and wife in Russia, but the disparity is seldom so great as to interfere with their domestic happiness. Nevertheless the disparity tends to support the ideal of one marriage, because the wife will not unfrequently outlive the husband, and the husband, upon the death of his wife, will be too old to think of marrying again.

A still further cause for the excellence of family life in Russia, and one which underlies the preceding cause, is the position of woman, the rights and privileges of woman, exceeding those of her sex in every other country in the world. The time was when women were kept in the same seclusion, and guarded with the same jealousy, in Russia as in Turkey— nay, even more strictly kept and guarded than in Turkey, because a Russian woman was only permitted to behold the faces of her father and brothers, and, when she was married, of her husband and sons, beside the faces of her own sex. Her liberty was sadly restricted, her education utterly neglected, her life at the mercy of her lord—a position more intolerable than that in the zenanas of Benares or the harems of Stamboul. But Peter the Great altered this. He shocked his people by the publication of a *ukase* abolishing these restrictions, and permitting women to mingle freely in society, thereby creating society, for without the presence of women society is impossible. Men may be the framework of society, but women are certainly the muscles, the nerves, the blood, the life of society, and without them it is a mere skeleton. To see a woman walking through the street was as awful in the eyes of a Russian, as to see a man with a shaven face; the autocrat willed it, however, and off the long beards came, and out the women walked, shattering in a week the prejudices of centuries. Peter the Great was succeeded by his wife, Catherine, the first Empress of Russia; and since her, three women have occupied the Russian throne—Anne reigning ten, Elizabeth twenty-one, and Catherine II. twenty-four years, a considerable period of the whole time from the death of Peter the Great until now; and these women have not been slow to follow up the *ukase* abolishing the restrictions placed upon their sex by securing for them solid and permanent advantages.

The women of Russia are under no civil disabilities whatever, but, in the eyes of the law, are equal with the men. This equality of the sexes was recognized and established under the reign of Elizabeth Petrovna, the grand-daughter of Peter the Great. A woman retains her own property after marriage, and manages her own affairs altogether apart from her husband. Her position is one of entire legal independence. She can sell or mortgage her property without her husband's consent, and in all matters of property between herself and her husband the law deals with them as if they were strangers. Upon her death, only the seventh part of her estates passes to her husband, and the fourth of her personal possessions; that being her share of his estates and personal possessions should he die before her. In certain rare instances a titled lady might marry a commoner, and, before the emancipation of the serfs, she might marry her own bondman without even setting him free; and, in such instances, the husband and children would remain commoners, or serfs, and have no right of association in the management of the estates of the wife and mother. If the husband were a serf, and she were dissatisfied with him, she might even place him in the army, or send him to Siberia; and as a serf, his position as husband of a titled lady giving him no legal right above that of a serf, he must submit. Of course, this freedom of the woman, this right to manage her own property, this absolute control of her own fortune, has developed in woman a capacity for business unequalled by the women of any other country; and many of the landed estates in Russia, and some of the few manufactories, are in the hands of women, and so successfully conducted by them as to place them in possession of immense wealth. Tupizyn's large phosphorus factory at Perm, under the skilful management of the widow of the late founder and proprietor, has been developed into a splendid establishment, turning out annually no less than 156,000 lbs. avoirdupois, and supplying almost all the match works in European Russia. And this is only one case among many.

The education of women is carefully attended to, and not only the elementary but the advanced education of women. In the Russian Government there is a special department of female education, the outgrowth of solicitude for the welfare of her sex on the part of Catherine the Great. She established the first school for girls, and since then the state organization for the education of women has assumed magnificent proportions. The late Empress helped on the movement by introducing into Russia the day schools of Germany; and gradually the objections arising from class distinctions were broken down, and girls of high and low, rich and poor families, met together in public schools, and pursued their studies side by side. An outlet had to be found for the mental activity of women, and especially those dependent upon their brains for a living, beside the outlet of teaching in public and private schools; and many of them gave themselves to the study of medicine, and became qualified practitioners, rendering acceptable service under the *Red Cross*, during the war between Russia and Turkey, and engaging themselves to the village authorities as public doctors in out-of-the-way places where doctors are very much needed. One-fifth of the entire medical faculty of Russia reside in St. Petersburg and Moscow, and even including these there are only fifteen doctors to every 100,000 people, a fact which reveals how utterly neglected medically millions of Russian peasants remain. The Government have hampered the women somewhat in their attempts to obtain diplomas, and the unrestricted right to practise, not, however, because they were women, but because of the influence of the Nihilists over some of them, and the courageous activity of Nihilist women in carrying out revolutionary propaganda. Nevertheless, the path is clear before them. Medical women will win their way into the rural districts of Russia, and meet a deeply felt want in their mission of skilful mercy.

Russia is not a mercantile nation. The spirit of her

government is opposed to commercial development and
prosperity. Where everything is under secret *surveillance*,
and liable to be disturbed by the exactions, and destroyed
by the tyranny, of state officials, business cannot take root ;
the confidence born of certainty, the successful manipulation
resulting from a private knowledge of details, are almost
impossible, and unless the state pursues a policy of non-
interference, altogether impossible. The genius for trade is
not in the nature of the Russians; if it is, it either lies
dormant beneath the soporific effect of the autocracy, or
crushed beneath the weight of that autocracy into an un-
consciousness very like death. Comparatively few Russians
engage in trade. Commercial men are despised by the
tchinovniks and disliked by the labouring classes. The Jews
are numerous in South Russia. Their commercial operations
are restricted in the capital, but in South Russia they have
freer scope ; and it has been said, upon good grounds, that
four-fifths of the trade, both home and foreign, in Odessa,
and throughout South Russia generally, is in the hands of
the Jews. The cargo of wool and grain shipped in our
vessel was from an English firm, and the man responsible for
the stowing of the cargo a Greek ; and only the poor fellows
shooting the grain, and pressing the wool, doing the hard,
laborious, mechanical service, were Russians.

This Greek was a native of Cephalonia. For many years
he had spent his summers in the Sea of Azov, as a ship-
chandler and contractor for the loading of cargoes, returning every winter to the salubrious climate of his sunny island
in the south ; and, by the careful exercise of that business
tact which the Greeks possess in no unusual degree, he had
made for himself, while yet in middle life, a fair fortune.
And his is not a solitary case. Others take advantage of
Russian commerce to line their pockets well, and afterwards
spend their money, not in Russia, but at home. Under
better political and social conditions, Russia herself might
receive the benefit, and keep the money in her own land,

and evidences are not wanting that, in the future, she will endeavour to do this. She may not be able to do it successfully without some sacrifice of her despotic system, and, in her shortsightedness, she may consider this too dear a price to pay.

Eighty-five Russian labourers were at work on board the steamer, mostly engaged in stowing and pressing the wool in the main holds. They were all meanly clad and dirty looking. An awning was stretched for them amidships, beneath which they took their meals in the daytime, and slept at night; in every conceivable posture they slept, twisting their bodies into the shapes most comfortable for repose upon the iron decks, and those averse to so hard a bed curled themselves between the bales of wool in the close, warm holds. Their fare was of the roughest kind. Two of the company acted as cooks. Fires were built in the well deck, over which huge crocks were hung, and in these crocks soup was made every day for the entire company. The soup was served to each man in a wooden porringer. The fresh water of the Azov, drawn over the ship's side, muddy and filthy, was used for the soup, which was made mostly of leek and other strong vegetables, with now and again a morsel of meat; and into the hot liquid they sopped the dark brown bread, dried and cracked by exposure in the sun, and looking like chips of mahogany. The faces of these men were invariably of the sullen, stolid cast, sometimes broken during work hours with a grim merriment arising from the ribald jests of their ordinary conversation, and ever settling again into dulness, heaviness, almost despair. Many of them indulged in smoking cigarettes, a cheap luxury in Russia, inhaling the fumes until their lungs were filled, and then slowly driving them thence in two streams down the nostrils. Some few were superstitiously devout, turning their faces toward the cathedral at Taganrog before retiring to rest, crossing themselves, and muttering prayers; others were careless and abandoned, sneering at these expressions of religious zeal; while nearly all wore around the neck, in common with others of their class I had seen ashore, a small cross, to which they attributed the mystic virtues of a talisman. They were not hard workers, but they were very patient workers, accompanying their labours with a species of melancholy chant, pulling altogether with the last note, and minding not to let the last note come too frequently. With the rope in their hands they would start singing in unison, finishing with a weird harmonious refrain, the last note of which was the signal for the pull. It was varied occasionally by a solo from one of the company, a twisting and sliding up and down the scale from one note to another, like the motion of a snake in a thicket, ended by a repeated chorus in which were two signals for the pull, making four pulls altogether. The solo, however, was so long that no harder work was done under its inspiration than under the inspiration of the singing in unison. They worked long hours, from dawn to twilight, resting two hours in the middle of the day; and, when the cargo was all in, and stowed away, returned ashore, the majority of them to spend their scanty earnings on a poisonous intoxicant, and turn themselves for awhile into maudlin and helpless imbeciles, until poverty led them again to engage themselves to sing and work in the hold of another steamer.

During the last few years Russia has paid special attention to her commerce. She has encouraged to her utmost various industries which, under the fostering care of her autocracy, have marvellously increased; and, in the future, Russia may become one of the great commercial nations of the world. A change is taking place in the attitude of the Russian Government toward trade. For some time she has not only pursued a policy of non-interference, but thrown over trade her all-powerful ægis, and, although the spirit of her government may be against commercial development and prosperity, by a prudent exercise of its absolute power, the Government may foster commerce to some considerable extent. Already Russia is entering into serious competition with England in several industries that have been considered peculiarly English, and in one great market at least—the Central Asian—has almost succeeded in supplanting England, and attracting business exclusively to herself.

The cotton industry of Russia is increasing at a very rapid rate. In nine years, from 1877 to 1886, the number of spindles has increased 38 per cent., and the number of looms 51 per cent., old machinery being rapidly replaced by the most recent inventions. When we remember the much longer hours of the workpeople in Russia, and the less remuneration, we can see how keen the competition must be between English and Russian cotton goods in those markets more readily open to Russia, and where she can forward her goods with the greatest facility. A Russian weaver attends to two looms, works eighty hours per week, and receives about 7s. 6d.; a minder of the spinning-mule receives 11s. 6d. Contrast with this the fifty-six hours per week of Lancashire operatives, and their double wages, and say whether in the Central Asian market Lancashire will not have a difficulty to hold her own? Cotton of excellent quality is being grown in South Russia, and, in time, the country may raise its own supplies. The location of the Russian cotton factories is determined by the nearness of fuel. There are several in the vicinity of St. Petersburg, obtaining their supplies of fuel partly from the North of England coal-fields and partly from the wooded land of the lakes; there are more in Central Russia, gradually diminishing for fuel the immense forests of the interior; but the largest number, and the most rapidly increasing centre of the cotton industry in Russia, are in the western provinces, on the borders of the German Empire, and along the South Baltic seaboard, where the presence of large coal deposits naturally attracts an industry so dependent upon the production of steam power. There are two hundred spinning and weaving factories in Russia, many owned by English firms, and superintended by English skill, but many also owned by Russians—a small number for so vast an Empire, and yet a large number considering how recently that Empire has turned its attention to trade, and the commercially depressing conditions of its social and political life.

Woollen and silk industries, as well as cotton, are being fostered; large iron and steel works are springing up in the south, supplying the Government with girders for bridges and rails for extensive lines; engineering establishments are providing machinery; petroleum wells in Batoum are yielding enormous supplies, and giving employment to thousands of people. All these comparatively new branches of commercial enterprise are being successfully worked, some by English firms and capital, others by Russian, in addition to her old trade in furs, and her increased activity in the mines of stern Siberia, where lie incalculable stores of precious metal. The torpor of the country is being disturbed by the activities of trade, and Russia is waking up to take her part in the world's commerce—a part which, if she be careful to develop her immense resources, will necessarily be an increasingly important one. The construction of the Trans-Caspian Railway is evidence of her earnestness to largely secure, if not to monopolize, the trade of Central Asia; and there are rumours of a projected line from Merv to Meshed, which would place at her command the markets of Eastern Persia. Steel, and leather, and sugar, and tea, as well as cotton and woollen goods, are finding their way through Askabad into Khiva, and Bokhara, and even Afghanistan, and there is a considerable diminution in English trade in these articles sent by way of the north-western provinces of Hindostan. A letter from a correspondent in Askabad, published in *The Novœ Vremya* in November, 1885, giving an account of the increase of Russian trade in Central Asia, and the decrease of English trade, was considered of so much importance, that a translated copy of it was forwarded to the Manchester Chamber of Commerce by the Marquis of Salisbury; and, indeed, notwithstanding the fact that the majority of the trading firms in Russia are not Russians, the competition arising from the increase of trade, and especially the gradual monopolizing of the Central Asian markets, are worthy of the serious consideration of English merchants and manufacturers. The foreign trading firms of Russia, the firms worked by foreign capital, are Russian in everything but name, and in course of time must become Russian altogether.

The repressive power of the Russian Government is visible everywhere. Travellers in Russia have been conscious of a stillness in the social atmosphere, a fear to speak freely, to move freely, almost to think freely, as if the whole country were under an incubus from which it could not shake itself, and beneath which it would stifle and die. The armed man walks the streets. The state-paid spy is in every company. It is said that wherever three persons are found, one is sure to be in the secret service of the Government. The home is not inviolate. A man may be startled in the night by the knock of the *gendarme*, and have his house ransacked from top to bottom; his person may be taken possession of, or the person of his wife, or child, upon suspicion of speaking too plainly against the Government. The congregations that gather for worship in the churches and cathedrals become familiar with the sight of the sword. Armed men are there. When the priests leave the holy place to stand among the people, as upon some occasions in a certain part of the service they do, soldiers, with naked weapons, protect them from the people. To my surprise I beheld this in Taganrog, and wondered why, in the house of God, during the performance of a religious ceremony, the Government should thrust in its strong arm, except it might be to proclaim: "These are Government priests. Slight them who dare. This is the religion provided by

Government for the people. Differ from it who dare." Surely this country is Holy Russia! But how deftly the holiness is made to run through Government channels! In comparison with the freedom of England we should call all this a reign of terror, were it not for the fact that this is the normal condition of things. It would be a reign of terror in any country which had tasted the joys of liberty; but where liberty is unknown, where for centuries there has been the most complete and abject submission to the ruling absolute power, terror is hardly possible.

This repressive power is specially marked in the relation of the Government toward literature. Nothing can be printed in Russia, outside St. Petersburg and Moscow, without the special sanction of the Government. Every book, every newspaper, must obtain the consent of the censor for publication. The natural consequence is that no book, except one whose views are approved of by the Government, that no newspaper, except a newspaper whose articles are a glorification of the Government, can possibly live. Every writer must be politically and ecclesiastically orthodox; if not, he must make up his mind to one of two things, either to give up his profession or to suffer inveterate persecution. Writers have been fined, imprisoned, exiled, sent to Siberia; even booksellers have been driven from city to city, their trades ruined, and themselves glad to leave the country. The expression of liberal opinion, the indulgence in adverse but honest criticism, cannot be tolerated in Russia; such opinion and criticism cannot find its way through the public press into the hands of the people, or, if it does find its way, only by inadvertence, and to be speedily suppressed; and, therefore, all dissentients from the present state of things, and who wish to see things altered, are obliged to make their wishes known by the secret presses in cellars and garrets, clandestinely worked in the dead of the night, when the authorities are supposed to be fast asleep. Only supposed to be, for oftentimes secret presses are discovered, followed by the usual arrests, and the consequent imprisonments and exiles. St. Petersburg, the favoured capital, has only one daily paper, and that has been threatened with extinction. This severe censorship is exercised over translations of foreign books, and even the introduction of books and newspapers printed in foreign languages. The newspapers passing through the post are examined. I now have in my possession a copy of *The Daily News*, from which two paragraphs are so completely obliterated that not a single trace of what they contained is visible. My curiosity was excited, and, upon reaching home, I procured a duplicate copy, and found the objectionable paragraphs to be two Vienna telegrams, one concerning the discovery of a dynamite plot against the Czar, and the other concerning the meeting of the Emperors at Ischl. The most reprehensible use the Government makes of the literary censorship is to cover the venality of its own officials. Not long ago a railway accident occurred on one of the Government lines, by which a hundred people were killed and very many injured, through the faulty material of the permanent way, supplied at the instance of the officials, who pocketed the price between that and the good material which should have been supplied ; and a significant refusal was given to the newspapers to publish accounts of the occurrence. A Government so mistrustful of the people as to resort to such wicked and miserable expedients, tacitly confesses that there must be something radically wrong in its relation to the people. The real strength of a Government is in proportion to the enlightened confidence the people have in it ; but the Russian Government reverses this, and places its strength in the people's ignorance. "The people must not know. Throw dust in their eyes. Deceive them." This is its advice to its agents. This is its policy— a policy which, if pursued to the end, will be found to be an insane policy, and an end full of bitterness both to the Government and the people.

The continuance of this repressive policy depends mainly upon the decisions of the Czar. He is absolute. He could change or modify the policy if he found it desirable, but modification and change would have to be wisely and firmly undertaken. The interests of so many are bound up with the continuance of repression that any interference whatever would lead to loud laments, and maybe actual rebellion. On the other hand, the continuance of repression is the excuse for secret conspiracy. In a country like Russia, however, whose traditions are autocratic, whose history is interwoven with the absolutism of the Czar, secret conspiracies are more likely to hinder than help modification or change. Every revolutionary outburst will only tend to confirm the Czar in his iron-handed rule. There is not much hope of a constitutional Government in Russia, and, what would be the necessary consequence of a constitutional Government, not much hope of comparative freedom for the Russian peoples, while the *tchin* remains what it is, and while the conspirators continue secretly to plot against the person of the White Czar.

The attention of the people is diverted from domestic affairs by an aggressive foreign policy. History repeats herself in the behaviour of Russia toward the peoples on her frontiers. Secret interference, armed intervention, open annexation—these are the three successive steps by which her territory has grown to its present immense proportions, and by which it is now growing both toward the East and the West. *Punch* has facetiously said that Russia's motto in Europe is "Bear and for Bear"—a motto not unwarranted by her general attitude toward the European powers, and her recent exploits in Bulgaria. But the motto is truer in Asia than in Europe. There Russia has made her most gigantic strides. There she displays a ceaseless activity. Year after year she presses patiently forward, widening and ever widening her vast dominions, increasing her power and prestige, steadily approaching the confines of empires as mighty as herself. Side by side with China, and side by side with Hindostan, must she surely come, and then her progress will be checked, unless she ventures to cross swords with powers larger, and much more vigorous, than any she has yet met with in her Eastern march. It is very difficult to persuade the English that Russia has no designs upon her Eastern Empire. But we may be too suspicious. We may credit Russia with larger foresight than she deserves. The bear may become a bugbear. We may find ourselves fighting a phantom. It is quite certain that there is a party in Russia who are quite willing to keep alive our fears by their chauvinistic expressions; but they are not the only party in Russia. They have great influence. The press is at their command. Katkoff, the most illustrious journalist ever produced by Russia, during the latter part of his life, was their ablest leader; and his death, at a comparatively early age, must be a severe blow to the party, but a blow which they will certainly survive. The glamour of Pan-Slavism is too enticing to the Russians generally to be destroyed by the death of any single man. A short poem which appeared in Katkoff's paper some years ago, when to the titles of our Queen was added that of Empress of India, is a significant indication of the feelings and wishes of many in Russia. The following translation of the poem is from *Macmillan's Magazine*:—

> "Say that in thee again the Prophet doth arise,
> Say, an thou wilt, thou'rt of the gods elect;
> But, Empress of the East! in native eyes
> No sway imperial shall thy claim reflect.
> There in the Orient, rooted in the soil,
> Live prophecies and very old traditions,
> Which round the hearts of men like serpents coil
> And nestle in the strangest superstitions.
> The Eastern mind has strange prognostic drawn
> Of dark dominion chased by northern star,
> Which, as the herald of a promised dawn,
> Shall signalize the reign of the White Tsar!"

CHAPTER X.

NIHILISM.

> Peculiar to Russia—Origin of the name—Misleading term—Its creed: religious and social—Raskolniks and Jews—Political creed—Moderate and advanced sections—Organization—Subterranean press—Conversations—Official converts—Weapons—Adherents—Students—Women—Disaffected aristocracy—Mercantile classes—Peasantry—Veneration for the Czar—Cossacks—Causes—Characteristics of the Russian peoples—Liberties of Novgorod—Rural Communism—Invasion of Tartars, and rise of absolutism—Introduction of the *tchin*—Political agitation in the early part of the nineteenth century—Peasant revolts—Government interference—The Nihilistic struggle—The Czar—The people—The future of Russia.

THE scourge of modern Russia is Nihilism. By the desperate deeds of its adherents, it has succeeded in attracting the attention, not only of Russia, but of the world. It is the most acute form of that disease of the political body which more or less afflicts every country in Europe. In Russia the disease has reached the stage of madness, and a madness all the more terrible because, while not devoid of method, it is entirely fearless of results. In other countries we have Socialism and Communism, but we have only Nihilism in Russia. The word itself is an immense advance upon the other two. They are constructive; it is destructive. They breathe the atmosphere of hope; it gasps in the gloom of despair.

Nihilism was first accepted as a name and a creed by

Russian secret societies about the year 1859. The students of certain colleges, prominent among which was the Agricultural College of Petrovski, near Moscow, with a curiosity naturally awakened by the refusal of the Russian Government to allow the introduction and dissemination of German Socialistic literature, secretly procured, and circulated among themselves, this literature. The seed found a congenial soil in their dissatisfied hearts, and a favourable atmosphere in the repressive autocracy of the Russian political system. The fruit appeared in hidden and deep-rooted conspiracies which are generally known as Nihilistic. The name Nihilism was given by outsiders to the doctrines and propaganda of these conspirators, and was first intended as a name of reproach, and perhaps of ridicule; but the conspirators accepted the name, and, notwithstanding its only approximate correctness to express their real views, have invested it with a terrible meaning, especially to those against whom their efforts are directed. Their prison-like environment made it no reproach to them. Everything was justifiable, in their opinion, if they could only escape from the intolerable tyranny of irresponsible rulers. They changed the ridicule into grim earnestness, as if they had said, "You call us Nihilists. So we are. Better the chaos of individual license, than the order of absolutism. Better the utter destruction of society, than its continuance as a fettered slave. Better nothing, than *this* we now endure. Nihilists! you are right. So we are."

These words would be spoken by extreme men. For Nihilism has become a general term covering all kinds of social dissatisfaction. In Russia a man of fairly liberal ideas would be suspected of Nihilism. His views might not proceed beyond a constitutional government under a limited monarchy like that of England. His methods of realizing these views might be by slow processes, instituted by the Czar himself, and regulated by the capacity of the people to receive succeeding enlargements of liberty and power. All the safeguards necessary to prevent a too rapid development of the constitution, and the agitation consequent thereon, he might plainly advocate. But he would be classed among the Nihilists, nevertheless. Between him and the incendiary of the agrarian "Reds" there would be a wide gap. The wide gap would be bridged over by many parties, having somewhat in common, and yet differing from each other. But they would all be called Nihilists. The term is therefore misleading. It does not simply represent one organization, and one set of views, but many. Still, there are Nihilists to whom the term is specially applicable, and who acknowledge the term as a fair definition of their views. Their views differ from those of the constitutional liberal on the one hand, and the fiery agrarian on the other. Their chief object is the overthrow of the established order of things, by the destruction of him who is at the head of this established order, and of them who work out his will. There are two sections of these Nihilists, a moderate and an advanced. The moderate section stops short upon the attainment of certain reforms; the advanced only accepts these as instalments towards very much larger changes in the constitution of the Russian realm.

The Nihilistic creed has to be gathered from what its believers have written, from what has been revealed in the examinations of prisoners and witnesses at the state trials, and from what is implied in the actions of the Nihilists themselves. The sources are scanty, and the creed self-contradictory; the latter feature explainable by the fact that the Nihilists do not accept their tenets from a single central fount, as they do not yield obedience to a single central committee. The secrecy of their organization makes this impossible. Of necessity, there must be much individual thinking, and each member will interpret Nihilism for himself, or, at any rate, take his interpretation from the leaders in his own community. Nihilism has been represented on its religious side as atheistic; on its social side as subversive of the family life. Its adherents are supposed to deny the existence of God, and the immortality of the soul of man; to set at nought the sacredness of the marriage tie, and declare not only common rights in property, but the common possession of women. This may be true of a few of the more abandoned spirits of the party, but to say that it is true of the Nihilists as a body is certainly a caricature. If the high social position, and sound moral character, of many who have been arrested, and imprisoned, and banished for Nihilism, are not sufficient to disprove these serious allegations against the movement, the sympathy with which the movement is regarded by the Raskolniks of Russia, the dissenters, whose belief in God is never doubted, and whose views on the sacredness of the marriage tie are stricter even than those of the Orthodox Church, places the movement above suspicion in these particulars. The Raskolniks give the movement a tacit support, because by the destruction of Czardom as it now is, they hope to return to Czardom as it once was, the Holy Russia of those happy days before the seat of government was removed from Moscow, and when the Church rejoiced in her primitive simplicity and purity. But not even for this would they secretly countenance Nihilism if it were generally true that its religious tenets were atheistic, and its views of domestic life lax and immoral. It is well known that many of the young Jews of South Russia are supporters of Nihilism. The Socialistic sentiment finds a ready response in their hearts. They not unfrequently take part in active propagandism, and are willing to do and to dare for the liberation of Russia as much as the Russians themselves. And they would not ally themselves with an organization which undermined the foundations of all moral and religious life. Certainly Nihilism accepted in its bareness, as some accept it, worked out to its legitimate issues, as some are willing to work it out, would destroy religious and family life as among the established order of things, careless concerning what might be evolved in the place of religious and family life from the chaos into which everything had been plunged; but not many so accept it, and are so willing to work it out. They confine their Nihilism to political life, and they aim simply at the annihilation of the present political system. They work for the downfall of the Czar, and the abolition of the *tchin*, believing that whatever may come when they are gone cannot possibly be worse, and will probably be better.

The political doctrines of the moderate section of the Nihilists are by no means startling in a country like ours, but are sufficiently startling in a country like Russia. We are quite familiar with many of them. Some are embodied in our constitution, and others are advocated in our newspapers; and it is difficult for Englishmen to understand why these doctrines should be spoken with bated breath, printed by a clandestine press, and circulated at the risk of liberty and life. The moderate section asks for a representative national assembly; local government in provinces and townships; freedom of speech and freedom of the press; the removal of educational restrictions; the abolition of the secret police; the inviolability of the home; religious equality; the engagement, control, and dismissal of public servants by public bodies; the reduction of the army; the improvement of the economic and social condition of the people; and a new Government department to preside over industrial and agricultural co-operative communities, and direct and assist them in developing the varied resources of the Empire. These demands are a suggestive commentary on Russian life. There is nothing very unreasonable in these demands to a mind familiar with representative institutions, and not only at liberty, but trained, to express its opinions, and to listen calmly to the opinions of others; and what condition must that country be in where such demands are considered revolutionary, Utopian, injurious to the common weal, and punishable by law with stripes, imprisonment, and even death? The advanced section go far ahead of all these by requiring the abolition of the monarchy, the army, the State Church, landlordism, all class distinctions; the complete subversion of everything as it now is, and the introduction of the bare communistic principle to every phase of life throughout that mighty realm. This is more than revolutionary—this is Utopian madness; this is deadly injurious to the common weal: but the way to defeat the purpose of these wild men is not to treat the moderates as if they were wild too, and put the iron heel upon both of them, without distinction, and try to grind both into the dust. That is the way to help the purpose toward fulfilment. The Russian Government itself is doing the work of the advanced section of the Nihilists by its harsh, cruel, repressive measures. These measures only serve to fill the ranks of the revolutionaries with men from the moderate section who have become hopeless and desperate in their struggles with an inexorable, armed foe. The moderate section should be conciliated. Their demands should receive a fair hearing. What might be granted without harm should be granted ungrudgingly. Above all, equal justice should be administered in every station. The official position should not become a covering for crime. That would defeat Nihilism. That would work out the freedom of the Russian peoples. That would satisfy the longings of Russia's best men.

The various Nihilistic communities are not all affiliated with one grand central association. They do not all obey one supreme head. The difference in their views; the enforced secrecy of their work; the wide spaces of the Russian realm, and the difficulty of quickly conveying intelligence from one part to another; the supreme necessity of guarding against detection—all prevent the unity of the organization. If the organization were *one* throughout, and could work from one centre with the inflexible exactness of a machine —to borrow an example from the religious world, an organization like that of the Society of Jesus—it would be much more formidable in its attacks, and much more difficult to overcome. By a succession of rapid and well-connected blows, it would thrill the Russian realm with horror; it would appal the Government, reduce it to helplessness, and speedily obtain its ends. But this is not the case. Its blows are erratic. Its organization is divided. There are many communities grouped around different centres, and each one obedient to its own head. They work as they can, as opportunities present themselves in their own neighbourhoods, and with only a general reference to the work in the neighbourhoods of other communities. Some are directed from abroad by means of secret correspondence. Some are directed from within themselves by signs of their own. Every man is held to his oath of fidelity by the certainty of the terrible consequences that would follow upon betrayal. It is said that if three men meet in Russia one is almost sure to be a State spy. The Nihilists have met this espionage of the Government by a corresponding secret ramification of their own. If one of any three is almost sure to be a State spy, the other two may be Nihilists. For the cancerous roots of the malady have spread everywhere, and are feeding upon every part of the Russian system. And although the knife may go down deep, and cut out a cancer here and there, every separate root will form for itself a centre of putrefaction and decay.

The work of the Nihilists is carried out in various ways. Their methods are partially determined for them by the relentless hostility of the Government. Other methods they adopt as circumstances arise—all secret, however, and all calculated to undermine the foundations of the present political system. The subterranean press is freely employed in printing seditious circulars, and these circulars are distributed through the post and by Jewish pedlars; they are passed from hand to hand in open fields and busy streets, and find their way through mysterious channels into the remotest peasant's hut, and into the very audience-chamber of his

Imperial Majesty. These fly-sheets are ubiquitous. They turn up everywhere, and no one can tell where they come from. Sometimes a printing machine is pounced upon by the secret police, its workmen arrested, its productions destroyed. But, with an unquelled audacity, other machines pour forth their revolutionary matter, and the police are puzzled to find out where they are.

Much work is also done by quiet conversations. The discontented mind is ready to listen. The naturally morose disposition, embittered by the harsh treatment of the *tchinovniks*, and cherishing its bitterness in quietude, is tempted to revenge. The oath is taken, and the name enrolled among the brotherhood. No opportunity is lost of winning members among the servants of the State. A man who has climbed high in civil or military service, who detests the peculation of the officials, who yearns for the liberation of the people, who is nearly stifled by the atmosphere in which he is forced to live, and who feels that he must have breathing room, and must give breathing room to those below him and worse off than himself—a man like this, and there are many, is worth more to Nihilism, if he can only be converted, than a hundred *moujiks*. He has opportunities of service which present themselves to very few. And they do not stop short at the conversion of such men. To obtain for them still higher posts, and thereby secure for them still larger opportunities, is one of the avowed objects of their propaganda.

They shrink not sometimes from the employment of terrible explosives. They tax their ingenuity in the construction of the most deadly machines. They bring them within the smallest possible compass, and give them the most innocent external appearance. To merely arouse suspicion they know is fatal, and therefore they take the most elaborate precautions both in the form and use of their weapons. If the books containing the infernal machines carried by the students on the occasion of the

Czar's visit to the cathedral of the Neva Fortress, in commemoration of the death of his unfortunate father, had been smaller and lighter, they might never have attracted attention, and the terrible deed they had so deliberately planned might have been accomplished. The death of the Czar, not for any fault of his, but because he happens to be the head of the system they are sworn to destroy, is the supreme object of the extreme Nihilists. They resort to any and every other method, however, by which the system may be so violently shaken as to hasten its downfall. The Czar's ministers are sometimes marked out for vengeance. But this is generally in retaliation for some special persecution or gross injustice. They do not strike blindly at the Czar's ministers simply because they are his ministers. There must be some other reason. They cannot be charged with wanton and indiscriminate destruction. There are too many evidences of careful plotting, and often a too sad and terrible precision in their work, to substantiate this charge. They keep their ends in view. They do not unnecessarily take the life of any man, and yet any man's life is not allowed to stand between them and the accomplishment of their designs.

Nihilism has obtained a strong hold upon the educated classes. Very many university students are Nihilists. They bitterly feel and resent the careful, and sometimes senseless, restrictions under which they are placed, both with regard to the books they may read and the classes they may have; and the Government espionage of their private behaviour is most irritating, and likely to spread, instead of cure, the evil to which they are prone. They may not assemble publicly except for the clearly defined lessons of their educational course; and to attend even them they must obtain a passport, renewable at frequent intervals, from a Government official. They may arrange for no lectures, concerts, social gatherings of any kind, either within or without the walls of their colleges. They must furnish information of their whereabouts, and give an account of their doings, should they absent themselves from the classes. They are hedged about with many kinds of galling regulations, so paltry, some of them, as to be impossible of enforcement. The regulations are there, however, and the dreaded Third Section, the secret service of the Government, over which the Czar personally presides, has its agents scattered among them everywhere, to enforce the regulations when they can, or otherwise to report the neglectful and disobedient to their chiefs as suspicious, and maybe dangerous, characters. Young men of spirit and independence, to whom freedom of thought, and liberty of conversational intercourse, are like the vital air, will not submit to this State interference. They will not run themselves into a political mould, and turn themselves out solidified patterns of the most approved Russian type. They hear of other countries where men are not hampered in their studies, where any pursuit may be freely followed without let or hindrance; and they know not why they should be exceptional. And what wonder if they secretly combine to break the iron bands which have been fastened upon them so securely, and emancipate themselves, and the future children of Russia, from this heavy yoke!

The surest evidence that Nihilism has struck its roots deeply into the soil of Russian life is the large number of women connected with its organizations, and actively engaged in its work. These women are mostly well educated, and not a few are connected with the higher social circles; indeed, the names of the Nihilists who have been arrested, both women and men, show that the movement has its adherents among the old aristocratic families, and among families whose heads have risen to places of distinction and influence in the comparatively new aristocracy of the *tchin* introduced by Peter the Great. The perfect equality of the sexes in Russia will account partially for their common association in secret political societies for the attainment of political ends. Where the woman is dealt with as the man, her education cared for, her social rights separately guarded and preserved, her position as man's equal before the law jealously recognized in everything where the claims of the sexes may possibly clash, her interest in political questions must be as deep as that of the man; she has quite as much to lose or to gain by the continuance or alteration of existing institutions; absolutism presses as heavily upon her as upon her brother, and she joins the Nihilists, and enters all the more passionately into the prosecution of the revolutionary propaganda, because, while freeing herself, she also frees him. Her womanly nature can be more deeply moved, and is capable of intenser devotion, than the nature of man. She has the timidity, along with all the gentler qualities of her sex; but when she rises superior to her timidity, she has also all the sublime courage, the pure heroism of her sex, along with its patient endurance. Her influence over man is the same in Russia as elsewhere. She can lift man nearer his ideal, all the more easily because she shares the ideal, of a life consecrated to his country's welfare, and, to the utmost of his power, endeavouring to free his country from the fetters of a system whose iron enters into the soul. As one might expect, Nihilism has its romances, many of them, and most of them, too sad; but there are some of a more joyful course and termination, like that of the student of Moscow, who, by the evidence, reluctantly given, of a young girl who was obliged to appear against him, was sentenced to twenty years' hard labour in the mines of Siberia. The girl sold her jewels, bribed the Cossack guard who had charge of her lover, succeeded in escaping with him across the frontier, and married him in Switzerland; there, doubtless, to help him in the direction of work which nearly cost him his liberty, and maybe his life.

Beside students, both men and women, the ranks of Nihilism are recruited from the men and women of the disaffected aristocracy, and the trading population of the large towns. Landowners, who have suffered from the emancipation of the serfs, who care not to enter into the civil and military services of the State, who have very little to do but brood over the evil times of taxation in which their lot has been cast, who regard the Russian bureaucracy, and all its arrogance and injustice, as a foreign innovation to be resisted in every way possible, are tempted into Nihilism, and commence, in desperation, the struggle for liberty. The severe trade restrictions; the contempt in which mercantile pursuits are held by the officials, and the multitudinous annoyances to which mercantile people are subjected by these officials; the necessary intercourse of a trading population, not only with the Russians themselves, but with the people of other countries, and the influence of this intercourse, incline them toward Nihilism as almost the only form of political agitation whereby they may bring about a desirable change. Sometimes they find life in Russia unbearable, and leave it for a freer home. Not long ago, a hundred Jews, residing in and about Odessa, all young people, combined, and departed from their birthplace for the United States. They could endure no longer the unjust and arbitrary military conscriptions, which, of late years, have severely drained their communities; the by-laws which have injured their trades; the fanaticism which has refused a quiet observance of their religion; and, filled with vague hopes, socialistic, obtained primarily perhaps from their sacred records, and afterwards fed by the literature of the clandestine press, landed in New York, distributed themselves as labourers until they could gather money sufficient to purchase land of their own, came together again, and bought for their common use an estate of eight hundred acres at Glendale, in Southern Oregon, which is now known as the New Odessa Community.

Nihilistic views do not spread much among the peasantry of Russia. They are given to agrarianism in some of its most revolting forms, but Nihilism, as such, they are almost impervious to. The forest of Livadia was set on fire in the spring of 1886, and much valuable timber destroyed. It was reported in our newspapers to be the probable work of Nihilists, but the greater probability is that it was the work of agrarian incendiaries belonging to the community known in South Russia as the "Red Cock." The firing of farmsteads, woodlands, standing corn, anything combustible, is a common mode of the peasant's revenge when he has been more than ordinarily ill-treated; but sometimes, when extremely exasperated, he will proceed beyond this, and inflict the cruellest torture imaginable upon those who directly oppress him. We have heard of instances where the living body of a victim has been rolled over broken glass until the excruciating agony has been ended by death. These, outrages, however, have no political significance. They are local manifestations of a miserable condition, caused, as the peasants think, by the magnates immediately above them.

There is one strong and almost insurmountable barrier to the spread of Nihilism among the *moujik* class in Russia. They cherish the deepest veneration for the White Czar. To them he is not only the fountain of earthly power, but the emblem of immaculate purity. They hate the *tchinovniks*, but the *Czar* they cannot hate. He is enshrined in their hearts. He is the embodiment of all goodness. He is God's representative. They believe him to be kept in ignorance of their condition. His foes, as well as theirs, are the officials who oppress them, and deceive him. He is their *Czar* (which appears to be not a corruption of the word Cæsar, but an Oriental word, received by the Russians through their Sclavonic interpretation of the Bible, signifying supreme authority), their *White Czar;* and they will obey him, not the *tchinovniks*, and fight to deliver him from the influence of the *tchinovniks*, should occasion arise. The tradition has rooted itself deeply in the *moujik* mind, that the day is coming when the White Czar will arise in their behalf, deliver himself and them from their mutual enemies, and confer upon them the soil of Holy Russia, which has been wrested from them by unfair means. This veneration for the White Czar, and this traditional expectation of his appearance as the champion of their rights, and restorer of their privileges, while it presents an almost insuperable barrier to the conversion of the peasantry to Nihilism, gives the Nihilists, as it has given other conspirators before them, a fulcrum for their lever. They are able to move Russia through her peasantry, and because her peasantry believe in the Czar. The literature spread among the peasantry purports to come from the Czar. It calls upon the peasantry, in the Czar's name, to rise and rescue him from his foes and theirs. They feed the veneration, they confirm the tradition, at the same time increasing their animosity to the officials, whom they bitterly hate as well as the peasantry, hoping to attain their ends by means of that which would otherwise defeat them. In a girls' school in Taganrog, a secret printing-press was found during a recent visit of the Czar to South Russia, and seven men and five women, engaged in printing a manifesto for circulation among the peasantry, were arrested. Three thousand copies of the manifesto were seized. They were significantly printed in red ink, and bore the Czar's name. They informed the peasantry that the rich nobles, combined with the high Church dignitaries, had threatened his life because of his intention to bestow all landed property upon the peasants; that, consequently, he had been compelled to seek refuge in his more loyal southern provinces; and he now called upon them to protect and defend him, and gave them liberty to seize the possessions of the wealthy, and appropriate them to their own uses. In addition to these three thousand copies of the manifesto, other Nihilistic literature was found, and a store of fire-arms and dangerous explosives, ready for terrible work when the time came. This discovery at Taganrog defeated the plans of the Nihilists, and ensured the comparative safety of the Czar during his visit to the country of the Don and the Crimea.

One object of this visit of the Czar was the installation of his eldest son as the Hetman of the Cossacks in their capital of Novo-Tcherkask. The Cossacks have always been noted for their loyalty to the Czar's person. Up to that time, they would have repudiated any hint, however slight, of their want of attachment, and would have felt insulted by the charge of treasonable designs. Revolutionary propaganda had been thrown away upon them. They were supposed indefectible. Because of their well-known loyalty, the Cossacks have been treated with singular consideration. Their pride has been gratified by the acceptance of the Czarevitch of the highest honour they could confer, and their pride has not been wounded by a refusal to *confer* that honour, to *elect* the Czarevitch as Hetman according to their free and ancient usage. But the special diligence of the police discovered causes for suspicion, and, carefully following up their clue, traced home to the son of the patriarch of a Cossack village, near the capital, a design upon the Czar's life. Dynamite had been stored for the occasion. The son in the village was found to be acting in conjunction with another son in St. Petersburg. The Cossacks were very much concerned at the loss of character they had sustained by reason of this discovery. The visit was deferred for a year. Then, amid much jubilation and display of military exploits, among which were the remarkable equine feats of two regiments of boys, numbering fourteen hundred, and varying in age from nine to fourteen years, who could ride with all the daring and wield their weapons with all the skill of men, and with nothing to mar the ceremonies, their Hetman was elected, and they were happy once more in the possession of the royal favour.

Nihilism is by no means the result of a single cause. Many causes have combined to produce Nihilism. From many fountains the dark waters have come to mingle in one stream which threatens to inundate and submerge Russian society. In no other country has Socialism taken this complexion, partly because no other countrymen share the characteristics of the Russian peoples. These characteristics have been determined to some degree by the nature of the land in which they live. The scanty seaboard, the interminable steppes, the unbroken monotony, have all tended to give the Russian a gloomy caste of mind. The want of intercourse with other people; the settled, changeless life; the continual views of long stretching dead levels, will largely account for his peculiarities. His dull face; his small perceptive faculties; his heavy, patient, obedient disposition; his proneness to indulge pessimistic ideas of life, and its conditions and possibilities, are the inner reflections of his physical environment. His country, shut off from other countries; swept by tempests that meet with nothing to oppose them, and gather volume as they go; covered with snows throughout the long winters, which the genial sea-breezes never reach and melt away, and oppressed in the short summers with untempered heat, during which the harvest must be hastily gathered; the same colourless life year after year, have all predisposed him to accept a philosophy of despair. The Russians are afflicted with a chronic melancholia, a *can't help it* disposition, a stolid endurance of their hard lot, as if it were by Divine arrangement and never could be other than what it is; and, therefore, when the destructive pessimistic literature of Germany fell into the hands of Russian students, it found them willing disciples of the gloomiest ideas, and ready to carry out these ideas—another peculiarity of the Slav mind—to their ultimate issues. And yet their philosophy of despair is not one of *utter* despair. Hope refuses to be entirely extinguished in the human heart. In the midst of their sternest Nihilism, vague notions of another, juster, purer society palpitate. Despair is only the pathway to a happier state. They must go through the lowest deep only to emerge in a fairer, brighter, truer world.

The historical causes of Nihilism reach back a long time. For many centuries in Russia two opposite streams have been running side by side, but not until recent times have the currents met, and struggled for the mastery. When Rurik and his Varangians entered the great Novgorod, the city was a mercantile republic, and its republican institutions were respected by Rurik and his successors even after their government had been removed further south, and nearer the centre of the future empire of Muscovy. The Novgorodians managed their own affairs. The citizens were summoned by the vetchevoy, or great bell, and could freely deliberate on everything affecting their interests without consulting the Grand Duke, without so much as asking him to be present; and they could decide upon peace or war, elect their own magistrates, impose their own taxes, enter into what commercial treaties they pleased, legislate for their own villages, send their judges on circuit, and empannel their own juries for the trial of all offenders within their own territories. This free constitution became the basis for the constitution of other cities. The rural districts, beyond the reach of the cities, were self-governing, in Central Russia by the *Mir*, in South Russia by the *Gromada*, a village communism in which all the villagers had the right of public assembly and discussion, and the privilege of voting upon any question pertaining to the management of their own affairs.

The development of the Russian Empire on these free lines was checked by the invasion of the Tartars. This invasion hurled back the promising civilization of Russia into the dark abyss of barbarism, from which Russia has painfully climbed into the light again, a lame and distorted image of what she might have been. For two hundred years the Tartar yoke was fastened on the Russian peoples, and when, at last, the Tartar power declined, and the Russian Grand Dukes were able to defy the Khan, and defeat him, they assumed the Khan's autocratic authority, and became, not over-lords of free cities and rural communes, but absolute masters, Asiatic tyrants upon European soil. They encroached upon the liberties of the cities. They enslaved the people of the villages. Nevertheless, the old communal system of the land was allowed to continue side by side with the absolutism of the Czar, and continues to this day. It lived through the Tartar supremacy, and it has lived along with the supremacy of the Emperors of Moscow and St. Petersburg, preserving and deepening the conviction of the Russian people that the land belongs to them, that they have a right to hold and cultivate it for their own benefit, and to assemble and deliberate on matters connected with it and related to the common good. Agrarian revolt has been the natural consequence, and, among the educated classes, whose views have been enlarged, agrarian revolt has merged itself in Nihilism.

The freedom of the old Russian Constitution might have proved itself strong enough to grapple with, and throw, the absolutism of the Czar, if it had not received another check to its development by the violent changes of Peter the Great. These violent changes have been the most fruitful source of Nihilism. The country has outlived and almost forgotten many changes in dress, manners, education, social life, the ways of Western Europe forced upon an extremely conservative people; but the country has not outlived, and never will forget, the changes in the system of government. Foreign favourites introduced to positions of influence and power; the creation of a new aristocracy in the place of the boyars who had been for ages the hereditary counsellors of the king; officialdom, with all its civil and military grades, and its multitudinous candidates and understrappers, developed and perpetuated in the modern *tchin;* the assumption, and contempt, and annoyances, and tyrannies of the *tchin*, have all tended to produce the feeling of dissatisfaction and resentment which finds its expression in Nihilism. There are two Russias: an official Russia created by Peter the Great, and a Russia that existed before the introduction of his innovations, and that exists still beneath the official iron yoke, and hates it, struggles against it, strives to break it; but the man who fastened it was strong in his own genius, and in the absolutism of his throne, and he fastened it so securely that the yoke cannot be broken without breaking the Empire too.

Nihilism has drawn part of its strength from the political agitations of the early part of this century. The enlargement of view consequent upon the movement of Russian troops in Europe, resulted in the conspiracy of 1825. Nicholas inaugurated his reign by the massacre of the Square of St. Isaac. One of the leaders in that extraordinary conspiracy, the poet Ryleief, said, "Patience! In history God is *retribution*: he will take care that the seed of sin shall bear its fruit." His words are true. The fruit of that massacre, of the cruel executions, of the wholesale banishments to Siberia, is seen in the Nihilism of to-day. Nicholas proceeded as he had begun. His nature was stern, relentless, unbending; he ruled the people with the rod; he loaded them with restrictions; he closed against them the avenues of knowledge; he drained their blood and treasure in expensive and disastrous wars; a deathly stillness reigned in his realm, not only the stillness of the great steppes reflected in the spirit of a despairing people, but the stillness of repression, the nightmare of absolutism: and when he died, and a man of milder temperament ascended the throne, the necessary reaction set in, and the struggle for freedom entered upon that phase which has obtained, and justified, the name of Nihilism.

The great peasant revolts of South Russia, in the seventeenth century under Stenka Radzin, and in the eighteenth century under Pugatchef, had very little in common with Nihilism. They were both agrarian. They both succeeded for a time, as the Nihilists now try to succeed, by persuading the peasants that they were fighting for the Czar. Nihilism has been assisted by agrarian disaffection, but Nihilism is a wider and deeper movement than Agrarianism, of more recent development, and aiming at vaster results. These agrarian revolts have their place in the history of Russian conspiracies, but they belong to an essentially different class of conspiracies from those which seek the downfall of the Czar as the head of a hateful political system.

The evil is aggravated by the continuance of the system. The officials are corrupt. Their peculations are enormous. The expenses of the Government are exceedingly heavy, and increasing every year. Financial ruin lies ahead. Taxes are extracted from the people by corporeal punishment. The conscriptions for military service are frequent and arbitrary. No trade is safe from molestation. No home is ensured against the entry and examination of the secret police. On the barest suspicion a man may be roused in the dead of the night by the demand of admittance from an officer af the Third Section, his dwelling searched, his sons or daughters catechized and arrested. They may be detained in prison on suspicion, or released only to be jealously watched by State-paid spies. For an offence involving no moral delinquency—a few words spoken against the Government; a paper read, and passed on to another, condemning the policy of the Government; correspondence with a so-called enemy of the Government—they may be banished to some distant frontier to fight in border raids, or exiled to languish in the wastes of Siberia. Alexander Krapotkine's life and death is not the only sad record of Russian tyranny. In 1858, when a student in St. Petersburg University, a copy of Emerson's essay on "Self-reliance" was lent him by one of the professors, and because the copy was found in his possession, and he would not tell whence he had obtained it, feeling bound, as a gentleman, not to draw the professor into trouble, he was arrested and imprisoned; but the professor hearing of it, confessed himself the owner of the forbidden book, and obtained his release.

He was a marked man, however, and the Government kept its eye on him. He once said to an American friend, "I am not a Nihilist, nor a Revolutionist, and I never have been; I was exiled simply because I dared to think and to say what I thought about things which happened around me, and because I was the brother of a man whom the Russian Government hated." He was sent to Eastern Siberia, then to Western Siberia, and died, in despair, by his own hand. Thus Russia treats her scholars who have courage enough to think for themselves. The press is gagged. Abuses cannot be revealed in the newspapers and remedied by the pressure of public opinion. Men may not assemble for mutual conversation and improvement. The fingers of the Government are on the country's throat, and need we be surprised if the country sometimes endeavours to rid itself from the strong grip in its convulsive struggles for the breath of life?

These convulsive struggles take violent forms. When in convulsions, a person never thinks of appearances. He fights anyhow if he only may get rid of the pain. So with Nihilism. Any weapon that comes first is acceptable. Any mode of warfare possible at the time will do. Hand grenades, clockwork machines, strychnine-coated bullets, dynamite stored in subterranean mines, anything and everything to accomplish regicide and destroy the system under which they live. The mode of warfare is wicked. The weapons are diabolical. But the blame cannot rest exclusively upon these wild and desperate men. The blame partly belongs to the Government which insanely persists in maintaining the system, and provoking an opposition so disastrous and implacable.

The Czar of all the Russias is the least envied man in Europe. He pays a very heavy price for his august position. If all crowned heads are uneasy, then his head only enjoys the minimum of repose. In the midst of such dangers he must be a grave and serious man. He has an objection to being reminded of his dangers. He dislikes to witness the elaborate precautions for his safety. Gatschina is considered to be his most secure residence, but, when at Gatschina, gardens and park are closely guarded by armed men. He must not see them, no matter how many there are; and the problem with the secret police is how to effectually protect him in the least visible way. During his visit to the Crimea in the spring of 1886, one hundred thousand men patrolled the railway lines. Wherever he moves, an army moves with him. He is not terrified by the attempts upon his life. He is a man of strong nerves, and iron will. The day after his narrow escape from assassination, upon the occasion of his visit to the Cathedral of Peter and Paul in commemoration of the sixth anniversary of his father's death, he returned from Gatschina to St. Petersburg to attend a ball given by his brother, the Grand Duke Vladimir; and it was remarked by all how composed he was in his demeanour. Only a brave man would appear in the midst of his people, fresh from deadly perils, unmoved, and calmly determined, in the midst of those perils, not to depart from his accustomed habits of life.

These attempts at regicide must have a very disturbing effect upon the people. They are sudden revelations of national disquietude. The people are carefully kept in ignorance. They know not how political currents are running. Sources of information are cut off. And when any deed is openly attempted so terrible that it cannot be hushed up, it falls upon them with surprising force. They are startled into a knowledge of the restlessness secretly working in the heart of society. Many of them find that they are not alone; that others feel as they feel, and even more deeply; and they are drawn by sympathy toward these men, who, even if mistaken in their actions, are nevertheless yearning like themselves for the liberty of Russia. The vast majority of Russians shrink with horror from the crime of regicide. The Czar, after all, is the *father of the people*, and his death would be regarded as the greatest national calamity. But anything short of regicide designed to deliver the people from the tyranny of the officials would be hailed with satisfaction. In the public trials the Nihilists have met with the support and approbation of the people. During their examinations in court they have taken the opportunity—almost the only opportunity permitted—of explaining their views. And when women have been arraigned, the sympathy has been strongly manifested. Their condemnation has excited pity; their acquittal has called forth applause.

The future of Russia is involved in obscurity. The contention between the Government and the people cannot last for ever. Nihilism may not accomplish its ends. The Government may prove too strong for it, and stamp it out. But if Nihilism is extinguished, the sources which have fed it will feed some other subtle, terrible, and maybe successful revolutionary movement, and the country will be as bad, and even worse than it was before. The only way to effectually defeat Nihilism is to forestall it in its moderate demands. Russia has a basis for liberal legislation in her rural communal system. Her people are not strangers to liberal ideas in their local affairs. With the education and enlightenment of her many millions, and a gradually increasing confidence in them, and the cessation of unnecesary interference with them, and the bestowal of freedom in proportion to their capacity to receive and ability to use it, the rulers of Russia might find a way out of the dark and intricate maze in which they and their people have been wandering for many years. In urgent tones the cry comes to the White Czar from within his own great realm—

> " Preserve thy threaten'd State,
> Or one vast burst of all-involving fate
> Full o'er your towers shall fall, and sweep away
> Sons, sires, and wives, an undistinguish'd prey."

CHAPTER II.

THE RUSSO-GREEK CHURCH.

Introduction of Christianity—The two legends—Olga and Vladimir—Influence upon the nation, and alliance with the Czars—Independence—Michael and Philaret—Splendour of the patriarchate—Nicon—Peter the Great—Suppression of the patriarchate—Synod—Reforms—National Church—Architecture—Cathedral at Taganrog—Clergy—Monks and monasteries—Hermits—Doctrines—Liturgy — Veneration for pictures — Baptism — Confirmation — Chrism: its preparation—Visitation of the sick—Marriage service—Bells—Choirs—Description of a service—Noisy Sabbath—Saints: •catacombs at Kief—Martyrs—The persecution of the Uniates — Raskolniks—Starovers — Safeguards against dissent—Constantinople.

CHRISTIANITY was introduced into Russia in the ninth and tenth centuries. The rough and savage heathenism of the Slavonic tribes prevailed previous to that time, but rapidly gave way before the influences of Christianity after the conversion of the Grand Dukes and the warrior aristocracy, by whom the Slavs were then governed. Legend has been busy with this period, and has furnished us with two separate accounts of the introduction of Christianity, both valuable as indicating the sources whence it came, and the direction of the streams which finally overflowed and covered the Empire. From Italy, a saint of the name of Nicholas, or Anthony, found his way through the Straits of Gibraltar, across the Bay of Biscay, into the Baltic, down the Neva, and by the great Russian lakes to the city of Novgorod, and there planted the standard of the Cross. This legend is superseded by the other and more favourite legend of St. Andrew of Sinope. On his way to Rome, he crossed the Black Sea and entered the Dnieper, the old Borysthenes, and proceeded northwards until he came to the hills of Kief. He prophesied that on these hills a great city should be reared, whence hereafter should shine forth the grace of God. Kief, and not the great Novgorod, has become the holy city of Russia. From Greece, by way of the Dnieper, and not from Italy, by way of the Neva, came the stronger and prevailing current of Christianity. The Russian ecclesiasticism is not Latin, but Grecian; not Occidental, but Oriental, and in some respects the most remarkable development of the great Eastern Church.

After the death of Rurik, Kief became the capital of Russia. This important change was due to Oleg, regent of Russia, and guardian of Igor, the son of Rurik, during his minority. Igor died leaving a young son, Sviatoslaf, and for some years the regency was held, and the State vigorously administered, by the widow and mother, Olga. She was the first Christian princess of Russia, and has been canonized by the Russo-Greek Church. She was baptized in Byzantium, receiving the name of Helena, and being led to the font by the Emperor Constantine Porphyrogenitus. Her influence over her son was not sufficient to induce him to be baptized. Indeed, very few were willing to follow her example. But the son of Sviatoslaf was the famous Vladimir, the conqueror of Kherson, the threatener of Constantinople, the demander of the hand in marriage of Anna, sister to the Cæsars of the New Rome; and by the force of his example, and the terror of his commands, all Russia hastened to be baptized, and Kief became a holy city. Vladimir was most zealous in establishing the new religion. The idols were destroyed. Churches were built and lavishly endowed: and priests and sacred pictures, and the numerous paraphernalia peculiar to Christian worship in the East, introduced from Constantinople. So thoroughly did Vladimir accomplish the work, that he has been ever since regarded as one of the most eminent saints, and allowed to rank with the apostles. The Russians were then as submissive and obedient as they are now. For their king to be a Christian was enough that they should be Christians. There was no trouble in the conversion of Russia. It did not cost the Church a single martyr. The order went forth, and the people flocked to the rivers and were peaceably baptized.

The Russian Church continued for several centuries dependent upon Constantinople, receiving its chief bishop from the Constantinopolitan patriarch, and, in all things doctrinal and ceremonial, acknowledging his supreme authority. It preserved itself, and kept Christianity alive in the hearts of the people, throughout the long and troublesome oppression of the Mohammedan Tartars. Upon the decline of the Tartar power it rose with the rise of Muscovy, linked itself with the absolutism of the Czars, and intertwined its fortunes with theirs and with the fortunes of the realm. The Tartars dealt generously with the Christian priests. They were not the strictest of Mohammedans. They believed in the goodness, and desired the prayers, of all religious men, and, consequently, allowed the priests to live in peace, exonerated them from the payment of taxes, permitted them to acquire lands and build monasteries, and many of them were so impressed by the splendour of the Greek ritual as to become Christians themselves. Therefore, when Muscovy began to lift itself from the incubus of the Tartar oppression, the ecclesiastics were the men best able to help the growing Empire. By espousing the cause of the Grand Dukes of Vladimir, they very largely contributed towards securing the ascendency of that branch of the house of Rurik. The Metropolitan Peter removed the seat of the central ecclesiastical authority to Moscow, and requested Ivan Kalita to build there the national cathedral. This cathedral has gradually grown into the famous Kremlin. The Grand Dukes removed to Moscow. They could not remain in Vladimir after the Metropolitan of the Church had gone. Moscow became the seat of the civil government. Beneath the fostering care of the priests it obtained pre-eminence over the three previous capitals, Vladimir, Kief, and Novgorod; its Grand Dukes became Czars; the absolutism of the Great Khan was conferred upon its monarchs; and, born of the conflicts of many centuries, and nursed into vigorous life by the tender hands of the Church, at last appeared the mighty Empire of Muscovy.

In the latter part of the sixteenth century the Russian Church became independent of Constantinople. The Constantinopolitan see was then disputed by Jeremiah II. and Metrophanes, and, to strengthen his cause, Jeremiah visited Russia. He consented to proclaim the ecclesiastical independence of the Russian Church, and consecrated Job, the Archbishop of Rostoff, the first Patriarch of Russia. He required, however, that all future patriarchs should be approved by the Patriarch of Constantinople, and that a stipulated sum should be paid into the treasury of the mother see. When he obtained the Patriarchate of Constantinople, the ecclesiastical independence of Russia was confirmed by a council of the orthodox Greek Church, and fifty years later the great Eastern Patriarchs of Constantinople, Jerusalem, Alexandria, and Antioch removed all restrictions from the patriarchate of Moscow, absolved it from tribute, and recognized its complete independence. During the next hundred years the Russian Church rose to the height of its power. The splendour of the patriarchate was little inferior to that of the throne. Its influence was both deep and wide. And when Russia was involved in the internecine wars of the pretenders following upon the insane destruction of the royal house by Ivan the Terrible, the Church gave to the nation a new Czar, and a new dynasty, in the person of Michael, the first Romanoff, and son of its most illustrious hierarch, Philaret, the Archbishop of Rostoff. Roman, the name of Michael's grandfather, has become the name of the memorable house reigning in Russia to-day. Rostoff is therefore identified with two of the most important events in Russian history—the consecration of her first patriarch, and the crowning of the first monarch whose family is now seated upon the throne.

When Michael was crowned, he associated his honoured father with him in the government of Russia. At the time of his coronation his father was a captive among the Poles, but the restoration of peace resulted in his liberty. As soon as Philaret appeared in Moscow he was created Patriarch of the Russian Church. The *ukases* were issued in his name as well as in the name of his son, and separate *ukases* were issued sometimes in his name alone. On all State occasions he stood beside his son, received with him the foreign ambassadors, and shared to the full the honours and authority of the sovereign power. This association of the regal with the sacerdotal office, especially under the circumstances—Michael being a young man, and inexperienced: Philaret being an old man, and not only thoroughly acquainted with national affairs, but a warm-hearted patriot—doubtless contributed to the pacification of the realm, and the firm establishment of the dynasty. At the same time it still further strengthened the influence of the patriarchate, clothed it with an unwonted splendour, bestowed upon it a dignity which deeply impressed the minds of the people, and increased toward it a veneration already deep and strong. Powers like these are very dangerous for any ecclesiastic to possess, and, in after years, they roused the jealousy of Peter the Great, who, in his own cunning way, abolished the patriarchate in order the more thoroughly to confirm the absolutism of his own will.

Previous, however, to the appearance of Peter, in the days of Alexis, the second Romanoff, a great reformer had arisen in the Russian Church, whose influence is felt therein to-day. Nicon was created Patriarch in 1652. He rose from the obscure ranks of the peasantry, through the offices of Archimandrite of the Solovetzky monastery, and Metropolitan of Novgorod, to the archiepiscopal throne. He was a man of immense stature, and strong will. While passionately attached to the liturgy and ceremonial of the Oriental Church, he set himself earnestly to the difficult task of rooting out abuses in the behaviour of the priests and mistakes in the Scriptural canon. These abuses had gradually grown, and these mistakes slowly crept in, during the course of ages. Amid the most violent opposition he persevered and succeeded. He caused the classical languages to be taught in the schools. He removed the *icons*, round about which the superstition of the people had gathered, and which they had exalted into miracle-working idols. He supplanted the nasal, dronish recital of the liturgy by the clear, musical voices of trained choristers, and thereby gave additional interest, as well as refinement and beauty, to the services. He thoroughly examined the old Slavonic version of the Scriptures, weeded out the glaring errors in the sacred text, and produced a new and better translation. He reintroduced the printing-presses, whose salutary work had been interfered with by the civil discords of the realm, and scattered his new translation far and wide. He even varied the dulness of the liturgy by the delivery of sermons. He set a worthy example to the clergy by his own benevolent and abstemious life. Many of the priests were avaricious, and many more were drunkards. He punished them with a heavy hand, but he did not himself transgress the rules which he would have them abide by. All this roused against him the enmity of the clergy. He was strong, however, in the close friendship of the Czar, and while that friendship lasted his enemies had no power to hurt him. They plotted for his downfall. The favourable moment arrived. An estrangement parted him from the Czar, and he resigned his holy office. Troubles multiplied, and, at last, he was banished, an old man, to the shores of the White Sea. The Czar died. Further intrigues were entered upon, and succeeded in, for his restoration; and he came back, broken and feeble, only to lay his weary limbs to rest, amid the lamentations of the people, in the chapel of Melchisedek, connected with the Cathedral of the New Jerusalem, which, in his happier days, and upon the model of the Holy Sepulchre, he had built, at the Czar's suggestion, in the neighbourhood of Moscow.

Peter was a man of another type. After removing the capital to St. Petersburg, and radically changing the civil and military constitution of the realm, he conceived the idea of introducing extensive and far-reaching reforms in the ecclesiastical constitution; and, jealous of the influence of the patriarchate, and vexed at the Oriental and barbaric splendour of the court which had grown about and become annexed to the patriarchate, he began the work by its abolition. He could not bear to divide his absolute power with any other man. He could not suffer to exist so formidable a barrier to the introduction of Western fashions as the court of the Patriarch at Moscow. His plans were aided by the Archbishops of Pskoff and Rostoff, the latter town again taking a prominent part in turning the history of the nation, and were afterwards confirmed by all the Eastern patriarchs. The abolition was not brought about suddenly. Peter was too astute a man to rouse unnecessary opposition, and yet too determined a man to fear opposition, however strong it might be. For years he kept the office vacant. He accustomed the clergy and the people to the sight of an empty chair. When asked to appoint another Patriarch, with one of those savage gleams which occasionally flashed from him, notwithstanding his affectation of Western civilized manners, he exclaimed, "I am your patriarch. There is your patriarch," and he flung before the eyes of the astonished assembly, and upon the table about which they were sitting, his large, glittering hunting-knife. For twenty-one years the chair stood empty. Then the abolition of the patriarchate was formally proclaimed, and Peter endeavoured to bring it into contempt by buffoonery of the most barbarous and revolting kind.

In place of the patriarch he established a synod, over which at first presided one or another of the archbishops, but afterwards the presidency was assumed, and has since been retained, by the Czar. Peter practically became the head of the Russian Church, and his successors have been since his time; not that any sacerdotal function pertains to this headship: all strictly religious ceremonies belong to the priests, but in ecclesiastical legislation, and even in the consideration of doctrinal questions, the final appeal is to the Czar—his sanction is necessary, and his decisions are absolute and incontrovertible. The doctrine of a purgatory was discussed by the synod in the days of Nicholas, and the usual document of the discussion, *pro* and *con*, was presented to his Imperial Majesty, and his final judgment sought thereon. He glanced through the document, dipped his pen, and hastily wrote on the margin, "No purgatory!" —a rough and ready way, and truly autocratic, of settling a question about which a synod, with no such power above them, might have squabbled for years.

Peter's changes were not restricted to the abolition of the patriarchate and the formation of a synod presided over by, and responsible to, him. He followed up the work of Nicon in several particulars, and especially in his attempts to secure the dissemination of the Scriptures, and their correct explanation to the people. He was tolerant toward members of other communions. He gathered about him so many foreigners, members many of them of the Lutheran Church, that he could hardly help being tolerant; he would have defeated his own ends if he had been anything else. Nevertheless, he was very careful to keep Roman Catholicism without the Empire. The synod was particularly to guard against the propagation of Romish doctrines, and the Jesuits were forbidden to teach among the Russian peoples under any pretext whatsoever. The customs of the people were interwoven with religious prejudices. These prejudices had to be broken through in forcing upon them the customs of the West. His reforms met with the most violent opposition. That schism of the Church, which has been perpetuated in the existence of the Starovers, was caused thereby. The Muscovites had many peculiar notions which they clung to as indisputable marks of their orthodoxy. One was the wearing of the beard. It was a mortal sin to shave. Peter obliged them to shave. Some fled beyond the reach of his officials. Others were willing to part with their heads rather than their beards. "You had better not," said the shrewd Archbishop of Rostoff. "God will make your beards grow again: will He ever make your heads grow again?" The offence of the good archbishop has never been forgiven by the dissenters. They remember it yet, as they affectionately stroke their beards beside the Volga, and yearn for the return of the old Orthodox Russia of two centuries ago.

The Russian Church is truly national. It has grown with the nation. It has moulded the national character. It has been closely associated with all the important events of the national history. It has fostered that sacred regard for the nation which has expressed itself in the term "Holy Russia." The Russians have been taught by the Church to consider themselves the peculiar people of God. They are the *Orthodox*, and have been raised for the defence of the Orthodox religion against the heretics on the one hand and the Moslems on the other. Their wars have been holy wars—against the Poles, to protect themselves from the encroachments of Roman Catholicism; against the Tartars, to save themselves from the yoke of Mohammedanism. Parallels to their history have been found in the history of the Jews. Their deliverers have been Jepthahs and

Gideons, their Czars have been Davids and Solomons. More than ever the Puritans appropriated the events of Old Testament history to illustrate their own times, have these events been appropriated by the Russian Church. The national heroes have been canonized. Alexander Nevsky, so called because of his victory over the Swedes on the Neva, is one of their favourite saints; Dmitri Donskoi, the monarch who drove the Tartars across the Don, is held in deep veneration. National thanksgivings are celebrated, and conspicuous among them, on the 25th of December, in a cathedral specially built to commemorate the event, the grateful celebration of Napoleon's overthrow, and the retreat of his vast army across the snowy steppes, and before the burning walls of their holy city. At every point their history has been invested with a sacred significance. Religious associations are intertwined with the fibres of the national character and life.

The imitative genius of the Slav is visible in the ecclesiastical architecture. Most of the Russian churches are copies, more or less ornate, of the Byzantine model. The religion came from Constantinople. They received it, with all its doctrines and ceremonies, without alteration; what could they do better than copy the architecture of the churches in which these doctrines were enunciated, and these ceremonies observed? This faculty of imitation is seen in the realism of the Russian artistic school. The Russian artists copy from nature. The truer the copy, the more highly esteemed it is; the nearer to the standard of perfect art. That the Russians lack not creative genius we may believe, if we have only the evidence of that beautiful and fantastic structure in Moscow, the Church of St. Basil the Blessed, built by Ivan the Terrible; and terrible indeed he was with the architect when the structure was completed. He sent for him, and asked him if he could build another church exactly like it, a perfect imitation, and the architect, not perceiving the madman's design, unwittingly answered

"Yes!" Upon which Ivan had his eyes put out, that this church might remain the only one of its kind. The New Jerusalem Church of Nicon is so exact a reproduction of the Holy Sepulchre, that persons familiar with the one may easily find their way about the other. St. Basil and the New Jerusalem are exceptions. The cathedral at Taganrog is a very good specimen of Russian churches in general, and not unlike the Patriarchal Cathedral of Moscow.

The cathedral at Taganrog occupies the highest part of the town, and the centre of a public square. The western end is covered with a cupola, surmounted by a gilded cap and cross; the eastern end is ornamented by two towers, in which sets of bells ring out their full-toned and serious invitations to worship, and their clamorous rejoicings when worship has been duly solemnized and the people have received the priestly benediction. The porch, or main entrance, beside which there are four side entrances, is on the eastern side, between the two towers; and directly forward is the nave, terminating in a semicircular chamber under the cupola. There are four pillars (the orthodox number), two on each side of the nave; the spaces between them are screened off so as to form separate sanctuaries. Before one or another of these sanctuaries, on all ordinary occasions, the people assemble for worship. Each one has its altar; its iconostasis, or screen of sacred pictures; its swinging doors, through which the priest passes, backwards and forwards, in the accomplishment of his holy ministrations. The chief iconostasis, however, occupies the western portion of the semicircular chamber under the cupola. Here again are the swinging doors, and, behind them, a high altar, at which the priest officiates on special occasions. The church is full of pictures. The panels of the iconostasis, the screened portion between the pillars, the walls of the circular chamber, and the sides of the building; everywhere the eye rests upon pictures. Some are old and ugly, others are new and beautifully finished, particularly one of Alexander Nevsky; many have burning lamps suspended before them, and most are furnished with receptacles for the tapers of the devout who desire to honour any particular saint with the flame of piety. One icon, fitted into a special frame, and standing upon the floor, is worthy of close attention. It is a splendidly executed Madonna of the old kind. The face and hands only of the Virgin and Child are painted; the rest of the picture is supplied by an artistic setting of gems in the midst of beautifully chased gold and golden filigree. The dresses of both are represented by a mass of lovely pearls, and the girdles, collars, clasps, and divisions of the dresses by all kinds of precious stones, arranged with the utmost harmony—a mosaic of gems rarely seen except in the wealthier Russian churches. From the centre of the cupola, which itself internally is one great picture representing a gathering of the saints, hangs a huge silver candelabra, ornamented with innumerable prisms. The *Soleas*, or choir, is immediately within the main porch, but apparently movable to any part of the building. There are no seats. The pavement, pillars, and walls are of smooth white marble, and, both inside and out, the building has an imposing and substantial appearance.

The urban clergy differ from their brethren in the rural districts. They are well educated, strictly moral, and exercise a salutary influence over their flocks; whereas the clergy of the country are ignorant, drunken, dirty, and frequently despised. The darkness is not so dense as it was. But, generally speaking, both the priests and the people of the rural districts are in a very deplorable state. The clergy are not celibates. They can marry once. This brings them into social relations with the people. This bridges over the gap which exists between the Roman Catholic clergy and the people. The Russian priests get very near those to whom they minister, and are more *at one* with them than any class of celibates can possibly be; and the people, while they respect and even venerate them, feel free in their company, because of their common domestic joys and sorrows. The *priest*, while sufficiently prominent, does not entirely overshadow and cover the *man*. Of all the Russians none are so good-looking, none have such broad, intellectual brows, deeply intelligent eyes, frankly open countenances, finely developed physiques, as the higher order of the clergy. The long hair flowing over the capacious shoulders, the unshorn beard resting on the full chest, the gorgeous vestments in which they minister, give them a very imposing appearance. They exhibit the Russian at his very best, and give one some idea of what the nation might become under the blessings of widespread education and true liberty.

Besides the officiating priests of the churches, there is a class of ecclesiastics known as the black clergy. Monasticism was introduced early into Russia. It was of the distinctively Oriental type. We find no great monastic brotherhoods like the fraternities of the West. All the monks of Russia are of the order of St. Basil. Around Moscow, around Novgorod, at Kief, and in many other parts of Russia, are immense monasteries—cathedral, college, fortress, all in one; and here, between the pressure of Poles and Tartars, the national life and the Orthodox religion found a refuge, and survived the evil times, and commenced the happier era. Chief among these monasteries, and more closely associated with the history of the nation than any other, is the Troitza, or Holy Trinity, about sixty miles from Moscow. Pilgrims are constantly going thither. Its abbot is the Metropolitan of Moscow, its prior one of the great ecclesiastics of the Russian Church. There are many other monasteries, not so wealthy as they once were, for Peter the Great drew largely upon the estates of these sacred foundations in order to carry on his gigantic enterprises; but still in the possession of ample endowments, and supporting vast numbers who have devoted themselves exclusively to the exercises of the religious life.

Among the black clergy there are also hermits of that wild Eastern type represented by St. Simeon Stylites. They live alone, and go about almost naked, even in the extreme cold of Russian winters. St. Basil, who gave his name to Ivan's fantastic church, and whose bones rest therein, was one of these fanatics. They were regarded by the people as prophets, and, in the olden time, reproved the nobles and the Czar. Their reproofs were tolerated when those of other men would have been met by summary vengeance. And many of these raving religionaries secretly disappeared, no one knew where, after a more scathing denunciation than usual. They were made away with by a Government which, through pity for their mad vagaries, would indulge them so far but no farther. Absolutism cannot brook too much interference with its high-handed, and often cruel, ways. These hermits are not very numerous now. Sometimes the people of Moscow are startled by the sudden appearance of a wild and semi-naked figure in their streets; and they imagine, because these men are so strange, and live so much alone, that they must be invested with special sanctity.

The doctrines of the Russo-Greek Church are the orthodox doctrines of Eastern Christendom. They are not crystallized into distinctive dogmas like the doctrines of the West. The broad lines of Christianity are preserved by the acceptance of the Athanasian Creed, only refusing the later Spanish addition of *filioque*. They believe that the Holy Ghost is *of the Father* simply, and not of the Son. This belief in the *single* procession of the Spirit is the distinctive doctrinal difference between the East and the West. The philosophical and contemplative mind of the East has not been exercised in defining dogmas like the more practical mind of the West. The Church in the East remains in very much the same condition doctrinally as it was fifteen hundred years ago. Although prayers are offered for the dead, purgatory is not believed in as a clearly defined dogma. In the Cathedral of St. Michael the Archangel, within the Kremlin, rest the remains of twelve or thirteen Czars, and twice every year a special service is held to remove somewhat "that burden of sins" beneath which they lie — a tacit acknowledgment of the existence of some middle place of possible purification: and yet Nicholas, when appealed to by the synod, wrote on their memorandum "No purgatory!" They reverence highly the Virgin mother of our Lord, but they have no doctrine of Immaculate Conception. They believe the real presence of the body and blood of Christ is in the Eucharist after the ceremony of consecration, but they do not try to put their belief into words. That spirit, so common in the West, which has led men to throw their deep, inward convictions into clear, outward forms, is very rare in the East. The dreams of an Oriental seldom settle into convictions, and about most of his theories there is latitude enough to afford ample play for mysticism.

The liturgy of the Russian Church is in the common tongue. The people understand it. This is an immense advantage both to Church and people, and has largely contributed to make the Church truly national. But for the reforms of Nicon and Peter the Great, the liturgy might have been so anciently Sclavonic as to have very little meaning for the people. In other branches of the Eastern Church the liturgies are in the different national languages, but some are out of date, and almost dead letters. In Russia, however, the service is read in the vernacular. The people can follow the priest, and appreciate the appropriate responses of the choir.

One striking feature in the worship of the Russian peoples is their excessive, and well-nigh idolatrous, veneration for pictures. In Greece pictures are venerated, but not near to the same extent as in Russia. The conversion of Russia to Christianity was bound up with the introduction and influence of pictures, and, from that day to this, they have been the chief media of religious communion, and the most common objects associated with the religious life. The finishing stroke in the conversion of Vladimir is said to have been a pictorial representation of the terrors of the Day of Judgment. A mind too ignorant to read, and too lethargic to grasp abstract ideas, may be forcibly appealed to by a graphic picture, and very many in Russia must have received all they know of Christianity from the representation of its events upon the walls of their various churches. To a picture paraded in the street a man is required to uncover, and cross himself; and, some time ago, the master of an English vessel in Taganrog was actually arrested and imprisoned because he would not conform to this religious usage. The portrait of the Czar is sacred, and the neglect of the people to perform before it the customary genuflections, has led to its removal from the shop windows where it was wont to be exhibited for sale. A Russian soldier carries his picture in his knapsack; a Russian peasant, upon entering his own house, speaks to no one until he has crossed himself before the domestic saint three times. In the corner of every room (the *corner* of a room being the place of honour) the sacred icon is to be found. Whether in hut or hotel, prison or palace, steamship or railway train, every apartment has its picture, and worship may be duly performed. Without a picture, worship is almost impossible. Some face is necessary to stir the fountains of a man's devotion, and cause them to flow forth. Some representation of the Divine idea in a picture of Christ, or the Virgin, or a saint, or an angel, must be looked upon, or else his mind is a blank: he cannot adore, he cannot pray. Many of the pictures are very ugly; the hands and face painted, the dress represented by tinsel and artificial flowers. The more modern pictures, although they are tastily done, are not much sought after. The older and uglier an icon is, the more venerated it will be by the common people. The most effective pictures are those made of white porcelain. The figure is thrown out by a lamp burning *behind*, and the light and shade obtained by the varying depths of the porcelain give it a very beautiful appearance. The lamp burns *before* a painted picture. There are not many more attractive ornaments than a silver-framed porcelain icon, fixed in its shapely holder, with the subdued light shining through its sweet, angelic face.

The ceremonies of the Russo-Greek Church differ in several important particulars from the ceremonies of the Church of the West. Baptism is invariably by immersion, not once but thrice, in the name of the triune God. The Constantinopolitan Church refuses to recognize the validity of any other form of baptism. It is an ingenious task, requiring skilful execution, to immerse a babe three times without doing it any injury. It must be held in a particular manner. The palm of one hand must be so placed across the face as to cover the eyes and ears. And the operation must be quickly performed. No one may be baptized in unblessed waters. The Benediction of the Waters is a separate service, and must be gone through before the waters can be efficaciously employed for so holy a purpose as the admittance of sin-born mortals into the Orthodox community. After baptism, the priest places a Greek cross of brass, silver, or gold round the neck of the child, which it scrupulously keeps and wears to its dying day. Another, and more curious custom, is the cutting of the child's hair. The priest cuts it cross-wise, encloses it in a cruciform piece of wax, and either throws it into the font, or presents it to the child's parents as a memento of the baptism. The rite of confirmation immediately follows the rite of baptism. Those who have entered the Church by immersion in water are worthy to receive the gift of the Holy Ghost. The Eastern Church has never severed these two rites, but has kept them close together; and, as a natural consequence, permits and compels infant communion. The bread and wine are both administered to infants as well as to adults, and in a Russian service children may sometimes be the only communicants presented at the table of the Lord.

The rite of confirmation is associated with the application of chrism, or the holy oil. The child is anointed, in the form of a cross, upon the forehead, eyes, ears, nose, mouth, breast, hands, and feet, the priest saying, after each application, "The seal of the gift of the Holy Ghost." Chrism, for the Russo-Greek Church, is prepared annually in the Patriarchal Hall, Moscow. Passion Week is the time of preparation, and the ceremony is a most elaborate one, lasting nearly the whole week. The chrism is then carefully distributed among the churches according to their several needs. A small portion of the original chrism, brought from Constantinople when Christianity was first introduced into Russia, is said to be still contained in a curious pearl flagon in Moscow. The Metropolitan ingeniously perpetuates the virtue of this holy oil, notwithstanding the few drops that are annually taken from it and added to the chrism prepared for distribution, by supplying the place of these few drops by the oil newly consecrated. The original quantity by this time must have become infinitesimal, and the virtue very slight indeed.

The Russian Church, in common with the churches of the East, has retained the service mentioned in the General Epistle of James: "Is any sick among you? let him call for the elders of the church; and let them pray over him, anointing him with oil in the name of the Lord: and the prayer of faith shall save the sick, and the Lord shall raise him up; and if he have committed sins, they shall be forgiven him." This service in the West has developed into the Roman Catholic sacrament of Extreme Unction. In Russia, the priests, seven of them if possible, visit the sick person, if the sickness be dangerous, and anoint him with the holy oil, in the form of a cross, upon the forehead, eyes, nostrils, cheeks, lips, breast, and hands, each time repeating a formula of prayer for his recovery, and the forgiveness of his sins. A piece of stick, round about the end of which wadding is tied, is dipped in the oil, and with it the cross is made, the same piece never being used twice; and where only one priest can attend—and this is in the majority of cases—he must do all the anointing, and repeat the formula with each application; that is, seven times. This ceremony is never observed unless the sickness is severe.

Marriage is one of the sacraments of the Russo-Greek Church. It is a ceremony of great solemnity and importance. Several customs prevail previous to, and connected with, betrothal, quite peculiar to Russia, and in harmony with the lofty idea of womanhood which is one of the finest features of Russian life. The formal betrothal, in the lady's home, is a religious ceremony, requiring the presence and benediction of the priest. This ceremony, however, has almost fallen into disuse, because the first part of the marriage-service relates exclusively to the betrothal. No matter how poor, the bride and bridegroom are welcome to any rich man's carriage for the celebration of the happy event. Etiquette demands the concession. It would be considered most ungentlemanly to refuse. So that, once in their life, and in their most joyous hours, the luxuries of wealth are within the reach of the very poor.

I was fortunate enough to witness a marriage in the Greek Church—the church set apart for the worship of the Greeks—one Sunday evening in Taganrog. The bride was a Greek, the bridegroom a Russian. I entered the building —a small one—about nine o'clock, and took my stand near the iconostasis, and opposite the choir. The bridegroom and his groomsmen were already assembled; two priests were there—the officiating Greek priest, who was a man of refined and gentle countenance, light complexion, with auburn hair falling over his shoulders, and slenderly built, the other a dark-haired, stouter man of more ordinary appearance; a reader, who also assisted the choir, and the choir, who enlivened the interval of waiting for the coming of the bride with pleasing vocal selections. A portable altar, or *naloy*, stood in front of, and a little way from, the iconostasis. To the right of the *naloy* the groomsmen had arranged themselves; and two, who were told off for a particular part of the ceremony, anxiously passed between them and the door, in order to apprise them and the choir of the bride's appearance. The carriage-wheels were heard at half-past nine; the two helped her to alight; and as she came down the short nave, accompanied by her six bridesmaids, all choicely attired, the choir struck up a most exhilarating anthem, which, with the lights of the candelabra, the varied and beautiful dresses, the lovely tints and delicate perfume of the flowers, gave the ceremony a joyous and festive character. The bride stood at the left hand of her chosen, the bridesmaids arranged themselves opposite the groomsmen, and the service began.

First came the ceremony of betrothal, short and sweet, the chief part of which was the exchange of rings. Then came the ceremony of coronation. This is very long. Lighted wax candles, ornamented with white ribbons and flowers, were placed in the hands of the bride and bridegroom, and these candles were held during the greater part of the ceremony. It is customary to measure them after the ceremony, and see which is the shorter; for the one with the shorter candle, according to the teaching of the Russian folk-lore, will die sooner than the other. Several long prayers were offered, and very many passages of Scripture read, the most striking of which was that spiritually suggestive passage from the fifth chapter of the Epistle to the Ephesians, beginning with the verse, "Wives, submit yourselves unto your own husbands, as unto the Lord." This verse was read in a deep, full-toned bass, and from this verse the reader ascended note by note along the chromatic scale, until he brought out the concluding passage, "Let the wife see that she reverence her husband," in a loud, ringing tenor, which reverberated all through the building. The musical responses of the choir in different parts of the service, and especially the chanting of the Lord's Prayer, were most harmoniously rendered, and preserved the service from that dulness and monotony into which, by its mere length, it must otherwise have fallen. The icons in front of the crowns were kissed by the bride and bridegroom, and the crowns were placed by the priest upon their heads; the picture upon his represented the Saviour, and upon hers the Virgin Mary. Directly behind the pair stood the two special groomsmen, who, to relieve them of the weight of these crowns (for they were made of gilded metal), lifted them from, and held them over, their heads, during the remainder of the ceremony. The candles were removed, and their hands united, and tied together by the priest's stole; and they walked round the *naloy*, the priest guiding them, three times. Up to this part a wedding-service may be interrupted, if any one can show why the two should not become man and wife; but after this part the union is accomplished, and it is beyond the power of any one to sever the bond. The sacrament of the Lord's Supper was administered to the bride and bridegroom, the wine being mixed with warm water. Then followed the kissing of the family icons, the domestic saints, which, previous to my entering the church, had been placed upon the iconostasis; and the kissing of each other.

This latter kissing was a more fervent, and, apparently, a much more enjoyable exercise than the former; and the ceremony of coronation ended with the beautiful benediction of the priest, "O God, our God, who camest to Cana of Galilee, and blessed the marriage there, bless these Thy servants who have now united themselves in holy matrimony, according to Thine ordinances. Bless Thou their goings out and their comings in, prolong their days in goodness, record their union in Thy kingdom, that it may remain pure, undefiled, and unslandered for ever and ever. Amen." After this, the registers were signed in the *sanctum sanctorum* behind the picture-screen, and the concluding ceremony of the dissolving of the crowns entered upon, which was over in a few minutes, and the newly married pair left the church a little after eleven o'clock amid the congratulations and well wishes of their friends.

Services are held very frequently in the Russo-Greek churches. Their saint days number two hundred, and their complete liturgy fills twenty large volumes. The churches are always open. You may enter at any time, and will seldom see a church quite empty. There are generally a few fixing their lighted tapers before the icons, and crossing and prostrating themselves in Divine worship. The bells are rung for the ordinary services, and yet they are not rung so much as struck, for the bell itself is motionless, the hammer only swinging to and fro. The bells are of all sizes and tones, but there is no chime-ringing, no attempt at harmonious music. They have a system, well understood by themselves, but difficult to understand by a stranger. At the conclusion of the communion service, the bells peal out, big and little, in a great uproar, and there is a certain wild joyousness about the sound; it is *wild*, however; there is nothing cultivated about it, nothing sweet and refined, like the ringing of English bells in some country village on a quiet Sunday morning. Our English bells are not to be compared with the Russian bells for size. They are only pigmies. The largest bell in England, Big Ben of Westminster, weighs twenty-five tons, but the bell suspended in the tower of St. John's, at Moscow, weighs over ninety-five tons; and the great bell of Moscow, which fell from the charred beam to which it was hung, and broke out a piece large enough for two tall men to enter abreast, weighs over one hundred and ninety tons.

The singing of the Russian choirs cannot be surpassed by any in Europe. They have no musical instruments in the churches, and women are not permitted to join the choirs. The voices must be exclusively male. The Russian bass is said to be two notes lower than that of any other country, and it is certainly full and clear; while the pure soprano of some of the Russian boys is simply matchless. To attend service in one of the larger South Russian churches is a rare musical treat, and the frequent responses and tasteful, harmonious chanting are sufficient to sustain the interest to the close, even though the low, monotonous reading of the Slavonic liturgy is not at all understood. A story is told of a singing match, between two peasants, in some far-away village, where one, in the first trial, exceeded the other; but, not to be outdone, the other commenced again, and strained himself so much in the exhibition of his marvellous vocal powers, that he succumbed beneath the effort, and was carried, fainting, from the room.

Several priests take part in an ordinary service. No less than six were officiating at one time in the cathedral at Taganrog. The place was crowded with people, and blazing with tapers, and smoking with incense, and filled with vocal music. The priests passed in and out of the holy place in gorgeous, flowing, silk and velvet robes, some blue and some purple, and all richly embroidered with threads of gold. The liturgical books, and copies of the Scriptures, were set with gems and adorned with pictures, and were reverently kissed before using; and the people, without books, listened, and devoutly crossed themselves, bringing the two forefingers into contact with the thumb, and touching the forehead, breast, and right and left shoulders. Some were more intent upon their private devotions, before the pictures of their tutelary saints, than upon the reading of the liturgy and the responses of the choir; and old people, both men and women, whose limbs were stiff, and who could hardly steady themselves, were stretched prostrate, touching the ground with their foreheads, and raising themselves to look with beseeching eyes upon a painted face. Mothers, with little children, were there, teaching them how to move their tiny hands, and how to fix their lighted tapers; and, when the communion was celebrated, took them forward to the rail, to receive from one priest, in a long golden spoon, the precious drops of the Saviour's blood, and to have the moisture wiped from their lips, with a sacred cloth, by the hand of another. The whole service was very impressive. There were some who were not affected, and who went through their genuflections in a perfunctory manner, but they were exceptions. Most of the people were devout, and there were a few whose emotions were deeply stirred, and whose yearning souls were looking through eyes suffused with tears. It was a service of mystery. There was no sermon, no attempt to teach in any way, but simply to impress the great assembly with the awe, the splendour, the incomprehensible majesty of the Divine. They were in the audience-chamber of the Deity. They were in the presence of God.

When the benediction was given, and I passed out, what a change! The large square was thronged with salesmen and purchasers. Business was proceeding very briskly. There was a perfect babel; the guttural tones of the Slav mixed with the lowing of oxen, the bleating of sheep, the cackling of hens and geese; and, to crown all, out clanged the bells, noisy beyond description, adding worse confusion to the already confused ears, and driving every thought of a restful Sabbath far away. What uncleanliness! What drunkenness! What deadness! What a contrast to the scene within! From the sensual captivation, the mystery, the awe, out came the people to mix with this babel, and increase it, and forget, amid the jangling noises of a busy life, that there was a God at all.

The saints of the Russo-Greek Church are very numerous. Many of them, including the great Vladimir, are buried in the holy city of Kief. Scores of them may be seen in the catacombs of the Petcherskoi monastery. These catacombs descend through the solid rock, and the dead saints are arranged in niches and crypts, and are largely visited, and prayed to, by the devout *moujiks* from many parts of Russia. Some of these dead saints have more than a suggestion of the pious fraud about them, and some of the stories told require more than ordinary faith from the too critical stranger. There is one chamber, for instance, entirely closed, with the exception of a small window, through which the pilgrim is invited to look. Within this chamber eleven saints immured themselves, received their food through this small window, and died at their solitary devotions. To their eternal honour a lamp burns within, untrimmed and unfed, quite beyond the reach of human hands, burns miraculously; and upon this great wonder the orthodox are asked to gaze in pious astonishment, and pay handsomely for the privilege. Dead saints can be multiplied *ad libitum* when people are willing to support their living successors. Both wood and wax are plentiful in Russia. There are saints, however, who are neither woody nor waxy, and who are worthy of remembrance by the Russo-Greek Church.

Russia is not rich in martyrs. It only claims two, and they were martyred before the country was Christianized—if we may regard their deaths as a martyrdom at all. Upon the return of Vladimir from a victorious expedition against the eastern Bulgarians, and while yet in his heathenism, he determined to offer to the gods a grateful human sacrifice. The choice fell upon a young Varangian warrior. He was a Christian, and the son of a Christian. His father refused to give him up, and the people, in their disappointed rage at his apparent impiety, broke into the dwelling and murdered them both. The Church might reasonably regard one other man as a martyr, the Metropolitan Philip of Moscow. He died by the command of Ivan the Terrible, because he would not keep silence at that mad monarch's crimes. "Where would my faith be if I kept silence?" said he. "Here we are offering up the bloodless sacrifice to the Lord; while behind the altar flows the innocent blood of Christian men." With the fearless tone of a brave-hearted Christian, notwithstanding his Russian belief in the Czar's god-like authority, he said, "As the image of the Divinity, I reverence thee; as a man, thou art but dust and ashes." He was worthy of the name of saint, and his death in the narrow prison cell may not inappropriately be called a martyrdom.

Rousseau once said, "There is a dominant religion in Russia, to which the sovereign and the hangman always belong." It is a very severe remark, and would almost imply no toleration whatever in Russia of any religion beside that of the Orthodox Church. But the different races embraced under the Russian rule, and the residence in Russia of many foreigners, compels toleration to some extent of several religions. Roman Catholicism, Protestantism, Mohammedanism, and Buddhism, may all be found within the confines of the Russian Empire. Toward apostates, among her own people, and from her own Church, Russia, however, is very severe. The attempts to bring the Russian Church into the Roman communion in the sixteenth century resulted in the formation of the United Greek Church of Poland; and the persecution of these *Uniates*, as they were called, in the present century, under Nicholas, is the blackest page in Russian ecclesiastical history. The story of the sufferings of the nuns of Minsk, is one to make the heart bleed. Worse even than he had dealt with the conspirators of 1825, did Nicholas deal with these tender, innocent women. The conversion and re-admission of the Uniates to the Orthodox communion was proclaimed with rejoicing, and a medal struck in commemoration of the event; but the horrible and savage cruelties by which that supposed conversion was effected, and that farce of a re-admission brought about, were carefully concealed from the eyes of the people.

The dissenters of Russia are called Raskolniks. Under this name are included many wild sects, the remnants of heathenism, the devotees of mysticism, as well as Jewish proselytes, and the Starovers who were driven into dissent by the reforms of Nicon and Peter the Great. The Starovers are the most important schismatics. They number about eight millions. They may be mostly found on the banks of the Volga. There are wealthy men among them, and, in some parts, they have a respectable social status, and no small influence. There are two parties among the Starovers: the moderate, who are willing to accept the ministrations of the ordained priests of the Orthodox Church; and the extreme, who refuse all association with the Orthodox Church, because they believe it to be hopelessly in error. The Starovers contend that they are the true Orthodox community, and that the State Church is really in schism. They look back fondly to the old Russia, before it was troubled with Western notions and reformed by Western ideas. All these innovations are damnable. Russia has fallen from grace, and she will never recover her spiritual grandeur until she retraces her steps, and enters again the long-lost paradise.

Many attempts have been made to stamp out dissent, but all ineffectual. Means have been adopted to prevent the spread of dissent. None but the Orthodox are employed on the South Russian railways. To none but the Orthodox are many State positions open and available. Any of the Orthodox who apostatize are loaded with heavy civil disabilities. The marriage of Orthodox Russians in a Lutheran Church is not recognized, and the children born of such a marriage are considered illegitimate. Parents of the Orthodox Church, who rear their children in any other religion, can be imprisoned for not less than eight and not more than sixteen months; and parents who communicate with other churches may have their children taken from them, and the children may be consigned to the care of some one else. To be born a Russian, unless one's parents are dissenters, or believers in any other form of religion, is to be Orthodox. The safeguards against apostasy are many and strict, and those who will not be ministered to by the State clergy must make up their minds for a life of continual persecution.

Notwithstanding its long independence, the face of the Russo-Greek Church is still toward Constantinople. Thence came its religion. Thence came all the holy rites of the Orthodox community. Thence came the wife of the sainted Vladimir, the sister of the Cæsars; and, afterwards, when Constantinople had fallen beneath the Ottoman power, Ivan the Great united himself with Sophia, the last princess of the royal house of Byzantium, and thereby became entitled to the Imperial insignia of the two-headed eagle, and the coveted name of Czar. Russia has never viewed the Mohammedan possession of Constantinople with complacency. She has never reconciled herself to the fact that the Crescent, and not the Cross, shines upon the magnificent dome of St. Sophia. Constantinople is a holy city to the Russians, and the holiest place in it is its great mosque, once the temple of Oriental Christendom, and the centre of the Orthodox faith. Both the city and the temple are defiled by the presence of the Moslem. They owe a religious duty to Constantinople. The Czar is the true successor to its throne. So the Russians think, and the Russo-Greek Church confirms the thought by her traditions and desires. The heart of Russia is Moscow. As the life beats in Moscow, so follow the pulses of the whole nation. And, for that reason, the address of the Mayor of Moscow to the Czar Alexander, presented at an Imperial reception in the Kremlin, during the visit of the Czar upon his return from the inspection of the navy of the Black Sea, in the spring of 1886, was full of significance: "The representatives of the old capital of the Empire most humbly request you, Autocrat and Emperor, to accept our bread and salt and the expression of our love, and to be assured of our joy in seeing you, the Czarina, and the Czarevitch. You come to us from that blest south, where you have restored life to the Black Sea. Our hope gains wings, and strength is imparted to our belief that the Cross of Christ will shine upon St. Sophia. So thinks Moscow, and in this hope remains steadfast."

CHAPTER XII.

ON THE TRACK OF ST. PAUL.

Sacred associations—Apostolic authority of St. Paul—His character—Value of geographical observations in confirming the truthfulness of Scriptural incident—Conybeare and Howson's "St. Paul"—Voyage from Malta to Sicily—Castor and Pollux—The Euroclydon in Adria—Drifting of the vessel—St. Paul's behaviour during the storm—Ship's course from Corinth to Ephesus—Ayasaluk—Syra—Priscilla and Aquila—The shorn head—Troubles in the Corinthian Church—Alexandria Troas—The journey thither—Voyage to Philippi—Scenery—Sunrise—St. Luke—Second visit to Troas—Third visit to Troas—Affection for the Philippians—Preaching at Troas, and accident to Eutychus—Walk to Assos, and voyage down the coast—Fourth visit to Troas—Arrest and martyrdom.

To all studious Christian people, everything confirming the truth, and, by illustration, tending to elucidate the meaning of Scriptural incident, must be of great value. The association especially of Palestine with the history of the Jews, who were chosen, in the wisdom of God, to become the communicating channels of Divine revelation to the rest of mankind, and with the life of Jesus Christ, in whom Jewish history culminated and Divine revelation became complete, invest that country, its hills and dales, its lakes and rivers, its towns and villages, the manners and customs of its people—almost unchanged in the eighteen centuries which have gone by since the Saviour walked the earth—and even its flowers and fruits and animal life, with a charm such as no other country possesses, and will never fail to draw toward it the desiring eyes of all holy men and women. The Crusades are for ever past. They simply exist as a memory of mediæval times, when warfare was supposed to be worship, and when the highest spiritual service was thought to be comprised in fighting to rescue the Holy Sepulchre from the hands of the infidel. But the deeper and truer meaning of that historical period remains, and will remain so long as the Christian religion sways the hearts of men. While Palestine is pre-eminently a Bible land, it is not the only Bible land. The history of the Jews is also associated with Egypt, and Babylonia, and Persia, and they have their charm; but the chief charm, next to that of Palestine itself, must be acknowledged to belong to those countries through which the great Apostle Paul passed, and to those seas over which he sailed, in his matchless efforts to convey the glorious gospel to every part of the known world.

The most conspicuous figure in the New Testament, after that of our Lord Jesus Christ, is the figure of the ardent, learned Jew, who sat first at the feet of Gamaliel, and who sat afterwards at the feet of the crucified Nazarene. His visit to Arabia—some quiet desert place, whatever Arabia he referred to—immediately after his conversion, must have been a time of instruction, a time for the gathering together of spiritual power, a time of equipment for the work to which he had been so remarkably called. He, who had never walked the fields of Galilee, the shores of Gennesaret, the mount of Olives, the streets of Jerusalem in company with the Saviour, and who had not been present at that parting Paschal Feast, upon which the Saviour grafted the new Sacramental Supper wherein dwelt the germ of the future Church, and who, therefore, might have his Apostolic authority called in question, as it actually was, by worldly minded and contentious men, was nevertheless to have his authority established beyond all question, by special revelation and communion, in some retired and solitary place—some New Testament Horeb—that he might be not "a whit behind the very chiefest apostles."[1] "I certify you, brethren," he wrote, "that the gospel which was preached of me is not after man. For I neither received it of man, neither was I taught it, but by the revelation of Jesus Christ."[2]

No man has so extensively influenced the world for good as this man. No man has lived a more active, more heroic, more utterly self-forgetful, more patiently determined in the face of every kind of difficulty and danger, more deeply spiritual in the midst of busy worldly scenes, more loving and lovable life than this man. His many-sided character, and every side noble, lifts him high even among the servants of the Lord. Like a serene, snow-clad mountain, rising above all the smaller hills into the sky, and attracting the eyes from them to it, and yet directing the eyes still upward to their next higher resting-place, heaven itself, so the great apostle rises from the midst of his brethren; and when we look above him we look at the sapphire pavement, and the burning throne, where sits, in infinite splendour, the perfect Man, our Lord Jesus Christ.

Very much can be done to authenticate St. Luke's record of the travels of St. Paul, and to unravel the meaning of certain parts of St. Paul's Epistles, by careful geographical observation. A flood of light may be thrown thereby upon a large portion of the Scriptures, which, while confirming the truthfulness of the narrative beyond all controversy, and is this way impregnably entrenching one important Christian position, gives the Scriptures a fuller and clearer, as well as a more exact, message to all open, believing hearts. This was felt, confessedly felt, in the Introduction to their scholarly work, by the Rev. W. J. Conybeare, M.A., and the Very Rev. J. S. Howson, D.D., Dean of Chester, when they commenced writing their "Life and Epistles of St. Paul." This *Life* is far away the best that has yet issued from the press, and its value is greatly enhanced by the

[1] 2 Cor. xi. 5, xii. 11; Gal. ii. 6–8.   [2] Gal. i. 11, 12.

elaborate geographical details, and all the minutiæ of travel with which the book abounds. No labour has been spared to obtain particulars. The countries have been visited and faithfully described; the seas have been sounded, and their currents ascertained; the prevailing winds during the changing seasons of the year have been determined, and even the shape and rig of the ancient vessels, and their sailing capabilities thoroughly gone into: so that we have a picture of the apostle's life in correct perspective, with its lights and shadows, and its variable surroundings, such as no one else has given, and leaving very little to be desired.

My acquaintance with this book increased my interest in the voyage whenever we came across, or upon, the track of St. Paul. The first time we crossed his track was between Sicily and Malta. After the three months' welcome sojourn in Malta, where the healing of the father of Publius, and other sick people of the island, increased Paul's influence, and ensured kindly and even honourable treatment for him (prisoner though he was) and his fellows, "we departed," says St. Luke, "in a ship of Alexandria, which had wintered in the isle, whose sign was *Castor and Pollux*. And landing at Syracuse, we tarried there three days." It was a short voyage from Malta to Syracuse, in N.N.E. direction, and we must have cut the track almost diagonally of that large Alexandrian vessel, dedicated to the Dioscuri, the twin gods favourable to sailors, in which St. Paul reached Puteoli, by way of Syracuse and Rhegium—Puteoli, a beautiful little town at the northern end of the Bay of Naples, whence he walked to Rome. *Castor and Pollux* would be a favourite sign, or name, for vessels trading with Rome, and, indeed, with almost every city at that time. Above Syracuse stood a marble temple dedicated to the honour and worship of the twin gods. Wherever the influence of Grecian literature had been felt (and where had it not been felt in the civilized portions of the old heathen world?), Castor and Pollux would be held in deep veneration. The famous mythical account of their appearance at the battle of Lake Regillus secured for them the profound respect of the mighty city of Rome. And sailors would be ready to name their vessels after these gods, and thereby implore their protection, when they believed that

> "Safe comes the ship to haven,
>   Through billows and through gales,
> If once the Great Twin Brethren
>   Sit shining on the sails."

We are not told what was the sign of the wrecked vessel, but she also was a ship of Alexandria, and, to accommodate two hundred and seventy-six souls, besides a cargo of corn, must, like the *Castor and Pollux*, have been a vessel of large size. These two Alexandrian corn vessels, both bound for Rome, were only two among a vast multitude passing backwards and forwards between the central city of the world and its various provinces; and advantage was taken of these merchantmen by those wishing to pass from one province to another, or from distant realms to the seat of Imperial government and authority, as in the case of the centurion, Julius, who had charge of St. Paul and the rest of the prisoners.

Upon leaving Cape Passaro we came into that expanse of water called in St. Luke's narrative *Adria*. Through this sea the Alexandrian vessel drifted for fourteen days, weathering the fearful gale, the Euroclydon, in which she was caught when the fair havens in Crete were left, against St. Paul's advice, but with the concurrent judgment of the master and owner of the vessel. The Euroclydon, the stormy east wind upon the waves, swept down suddenly from the high lands of Crete, and beat so violently against the ship that she could not keep her course. They let her drive, and in two hours came under the lee of the small island of Claudia, where they found a temporary shelter, where they were able to haul in the boat which had been towing astern, and where they took the precaution to undergird the ship, to frap her, by passing ropes under her keel and round her hull, and tightening the ropes across her decks, that her timbers might be held the more firmly together, and that she might be enabled the better to bear the violence of the waves. Upon coming from under the lee of Claudia, the tempest again caught her, and they knew that if her course were not altered she would drive into the Gulf of Syrtis, among the quicksands, and inevitably go to pieces; and so they brought her round as near to the wind as possible, hoisted a sail to keep her head to the waves, and let her drift. The sky was thick with clouds, and pouring a deluge into the waters beneath. The pitchy blackness of the night oppressed their minds and increased their terror. On the third day they cast out all the spare ropes, and sails, and spars in order to lighten the ship, for, notwithstanding the undergirding, the waters had found their way through the seams, and threatened to sink her in the deep. They abandoned all hope. They expected to perish. When lo! on the fourteenth night, amid the tumult of the winds and waves, the practised ear of the seamen detected a new sound, the hoarse noise of breakers, and they knew that they must be approaching land. This discovery, while it might well have increased their dread by the greater certainty of ruin, had in it, nevertheless, a single gleam of hope—the hope that they might possibly be able to ride at anchor until the morning, and then run the vessel on some sandy shore, and escape after all. They roused themselves to activity, sounded and found twenty fathoms, sounded again and found fifteen, upon which they let go four anchors *astern*—not the usual mode of anchoring, but, under the circumstances, necessary for their safety, because, if they had anchored from the *bows*, the vessel would have swung round, and probably gone to pieces in the darkness, and they would all have been drowned. The sailors, consulting only their own safety, and under the pretence of still further securing and perhaps steadying the motion of the vessel by casting anchors from the bows, let the boat down into the sea, and were preparing to enter it and leave the ship and her cargo and passengers to their fate—a selfishly cruel thing to do—when St. Paul mentioned their intention to Julius, and told him that the departure of the sailors would mean death to the rest ; and, with that promptitude which was one of the remarkable features of the Roman soldier, he and his men immediately cut the ropes, and let the boat go. Under St. Paul's cheerful encouragement they all strengthened themselves with food, and, to increase their chances of safety, lightened the ship still more by throwing her spoilt cargo into the sea. And there they rode, tugging at their four anchors until the morning; and when the morning came they examined the land, and it was quite strange to them. Right before them, however, was a sandy creek, into which they thought they could run the ship, and cutting themselves adrift from their anchors, and letting free their rudder bands, and hoisting up their mainsail, they flew toward the shore. It was a very critical and anxious moment, and it would appear as if they had scarcely succeeded in their effort, for plunging into a place where two seas met, the bows became fixed, immovable, while the lashing waters immediately began to break the stern to pieces. And the soldiers, being answerable for their prisoners to the authorities in Rome, with that barbaric faithfulness which was another of their remarkable features, would have killed them; but Julius, the centurion, out of regard for St. Paul, hindered them, and commanded the prisoners to get to land as best they could. Some swam ashore. "And the rest, some on boards, and some on broken pieces of the ship. And so it came to pass, that they escaped all safe to land."

Adria is the stormiest part of the Mediterranean, and tempests like the Euroclydon are still met with, and are now known as Levanters. In modern times, sailors proceeding along the southern coast of Crete, like the Alexandrian vessel in which St. Paul was embarked, have had gentle south-easterly winds until they have reached Cape Matala, and then, with remarkable suddenness and velocity, while rounding the Cape, a north-easterly wind has swept down from Mount Ida, beaten the sea into white spray, and twisted the hapless ship out of her course. The heavens have been rapidly covered with dense masses of cloud, and the winds and waters have striven, as if in league with each other, to envelop man and his merchandise in general destruction. These Levanters are dreaded, and ever have been, in these seas. They are not peculiar to Crete. They will sweep from the Trojan Mount Ida sometimes, and lash the whole length and breadth of the Ægean into fury. They will descend from Mount Athos, or from the heights of Samothracia, or from the ranges of Zarex or Taygetus. Indeed, no part of the eastern basin of the Mediterranean, overlooked by high land, appears to be safe from these sudden and dangerous blasts; and the liability of certain places to these winds have sometimes determined their names, as at Cape Malea, and have furnished significant illustrations of the changeableness and impetuosity of battle in most of the ancient poems. Macaulay followed sound examples when he said—

> "So flies the spray of Adria
> When the black squall doth blow."

So exact is St. Luke's description, that we can trace the ship along her entire course, and every point in the narrative can be verified by our knowledge of the winds, and seas, and coast-line of *Adria*, and by our knowledge of the trade, and vessels, and seamanship of the people of those times. St. Luke himself was a passenger by the vessel as a companion to the great apostle, and to his presence we owe not only the exactness but the vividness of the description.

All his phrases are correct. He perpetrates no nautical blunder. He was not himself a seaman, but he belonged to a seaport town, and must have been quite familiar with shipping, and the behaviour of ships at sea. We can follow the vessel from the Fair Havens in Crete in her attempt to reach the safer and more commodious harbour further to the west in the same island, the harbour of Phenice; we can realize her rounding Cape Matala, and suddenly encountering the Euroclydon; we can watch her driving towards Claudia, and sheltering for awhile under the lee of that small island; we can see her struck again by the Levanter as she came from under the lee of Claudia, and hurried away in the direction of the quicksands of the Syrtis; and then comes in the difficult part of the narrative. But even that can be verified to the letter. The gale was from the north-east, because the vessel was driving before it towards the south-west. They brought her round as near to the north-east—that is, as near to the wind—as possible; they rigged a sail to keep her steady, and make her ride the seas, instead of falling helplessly between them; and so let her drift. She would inevitably drift westward, with an inclination toward the north, which, from the southern part of Claudia, is in the direct line for Malta; and she would drift at the rate of about thirty-six miles a day, a little more or less, according to the increasing or lessening violence of the gale. Malta is 480 miles from Claudia in this direct line, therefore, the vessel would be likely, in fourteen days, to strike Malta at or near the place now known as St. Paul's Bay. The value of these verifications are very great. They strengthen our confidence in the Biblical record. They put us in possession of a secure vantage ground where we may easily hold our own, and whence we may push out to the possession of ground of still more importance. When we are sure of one thing—the outward fact—we may with less difficulty be sure of another—the inward truth.

We cannot but notice the sound judgment and calm

demeanour of St. Paul throughout this voyage. He must have had a considerable seafaring experience previous to this, for he had already been thrice shipwrecked, and had spent a night and a day in the deep. After all, we have only a fragmentary record of his wonderful life. We have only glimpses of what he really passed through that he might finish his course with joy, and the ministry, which he had received of the Lord Jesus, to testify the gospel of the Grace of God. This voyage was not the only peril he had been in by sea, and hard experience had made him wise. When they were about to loose from the Fair Havens, he told them it was the wrong thing to do. It was a dangerous time of the year, and the winds were unsettled, and he said, "Sirs, I perceive that this voyage will be with hurt and much damage, not only to the lading of the ship, but also of our lives." But they would not hearken to him. What did he know about the sea—he, a prisoner on his way to be tried at the highest court of the Empire; he, a landsman, a scholar, a religionist, a narrow Jew! It was not likely they would hearken to him. But his advice was wise, as he reminded them when in the teeth of the tempest, and when they had given up all hope. "Sirs, ye should have hearkened unto me, and not have loosed from Crete, and to have gained this harm and loss. And now I exhort you to be of good cheer: for there shall be no loss of any man's life among you, but of the ship. For there stood by me this night the angel of God, whose I am, and whom I serve, saying, Fear not, Paul; thou must be brought before Cæsar: and, lo, God hath given thee all them that sail with thee. Wherefore, sirs, be of good cheer: for I believe God, that it shall be even as it was told me. Howbeit we must be cast upon a certain island." His words would sound strangely to them, and especially the account of his vision. Doubtless they would hear him with surprise, but his calmness, his confidence, his cheerfulness would inspire them; and when the breakers were heard, and his words seemed likely to come true, they would all the more willingly obey him, when he said, "I pray you to take some meat: for this is for your health: for there shall not an hair fall from the head of any of you." He set them the example. "He took bread, and gave thanks to God in the presence of them all: and when he had broken it, he began to eat." The reverence of the apostle would impress them. In times of great danger exhibitions of reverence are always impressive. They must have been astonished to find him so attentive to religious duty, and withal so unmoved amid the imminent peril in which they were all placed. It was a new sight to them—the evidence of a spirit which they did not possess, and which they had seen in no one else. His readiness to perceive danger, and his sound judgment thereupon, were also manifested in his advice to the centurion when the sailors would have abandoned the vessel, "Except these abide in the ship, ye cannot be saved;" and in the following of his advice by the centurion, we can observe the growing sense of St. Paul's worthiness and authority within the centurion's mind. God gave him all that were with him. Perhaps he had been praying that they might all escape death, and God gave him the lives of these people in answer to prayer. We know that He gave him power over them. They all felt his influence. He became the hope of them all. The despised prisoner, to whom they would not hearken at first, was now looked up to as a Divine oracle. The man who was on his way to stand before the judgment-seat of Cæsar was the greatest man in the vessel. And there may be a deeper meaning in the words of the angel, "Lo, God hath given thee all them that sail with thee." These shipwrecked people may have been impressed not only by St. Paul, but with the truth of his message, with the blessedness of the story which it was his business to tell, and they may have been given him as trophies of his victorious labour, as gems for his Master's crown.

Adria can be very beautiful. There was no Euroclydon blowing when we passed and re-passed its waters. The billows were heavy, and the ship rolled a little; the wind was fresh, and the skies were open. The loveliest blue tint was upon the waters. But in a storm, this wide expanse between the extremities of the two peninsulas of Italy and Greece is filled with flying foam, a seething, tempestuous mass of waters, through which only a good ship can come, and even a good ship, built in the safest modern style, comes at no small peril.

One of the finest views in the Grecian Archipelago may be had from the hills of Syra. The eye wanders over the sapphire sea studded with islands that gather about them all day long, and particularly in the morning and evening, the most delightful hues imaginable. The sea is alive with historical memories. Every island has its story. But we must not forget that across this sea, threading through the channels of these islands, St. Paul passed, and passed, and passed again, between the populous mercantile cities of Corinth and Ephesus. While other associations swarm in upon us, let the association, which, to a Christian, is dearest of all, the association of this sea and these islands with the great apostle, have its proper place. Upon this same view his eyes rested. Through these same waters he came. Two of his most successful churches lay on either side of this sea, and in his care for each, and with his messages to each, he went backwards and forwards, looking upon the surrounding scenery, which, whatever else has changed, remains the same as when he was telling his wonderful story to the world.

Syra is almost midway between Corinth and Ephesus, and lies in the direct track of boats proceeding from one to the other. They would have to pass through the channel between Zea and Thermia, immediately to the west of Syra, and then through the channel between Tenos and Mycone, immediately to the east of Syra, the island lying about fifteen miles from the former, and barely ten from the latter. And in those early times it may possibly have been a port of call. The possibility is increased by the fact that contrary winds often delayed passengers even on so short a voyage, and they were sometimes so much as a fortnight passing between the two cities. Now, by steamer, the voyage would take less than two days.

Ephesus is gone. There is no port, and only the miserable modern village of Ayasaluk to represent the ancient splendour of that crowded, wealthy city, once the emporium of Eastern commerce, and known throughout the world as "the worshipper of the great goddess Diana, and of the image which fell down from Jupiter." These Turkish huts give no more an idea of the magnificence of Ephesus, than their name *Ayasaluk* gives of the man who once dwelt there. For among, and in the vicinity of, these huts, partially buried in the accumulated soil of centuries, or submerged by the encroaching sea, we may find broken columns, mutilated sculptures, blocks of chiselled stone, the foundations of quays, and baths, and temples, telling of the greatness of the departed city; so in their name, *Ayasaluk*, we have a barbarous contraction and corruption of two Greek words, *Hagios Theologos*, the Holy Divine, the saint who wrote of Divine things, the beloved Apostle St. John. The memory of him, who leaned on the Master's bosom, and who lived for many years in this city, still lingers, although almost buried and lost, in the name of that wretched Turkish village. Corinth yet remains, but what a Corinth! only the bare, broken skeleton of what she once was. And now the trade into the Saronic Gulf is not with her, but with Piræus and Athens.

Steamers run two or three times a week between Piræus and Smyrna, calling at Syra. It is the convenient port of call. And it probably was in ancient times. For Syra was a considerable town then as now. The great apostle may have called at Syra. Of course, we have no clear evidence that he did call there, but we have clear evidence that he passed close by the island. He must often have looked upon it. He must have been familiar with its appearance, and with the view of the Cyclades around. And in boats like those now seen in Syra harbour, and skimming, under their lateen sails, from island to island—for the shape and rig of the boats, like everything else in the East, are the same now as in St. Paul's time, and even centuries before St. Paul's time—in boats like those he may have run across the Ægean, and spoken to the Greek sailors of that unknown God whom they ignorantly worshipped, but who had shown Himself and drawn near to them in the person of His beloved Son.

The first time St. Paul crossed the Ægean was in the company of Priscilla and Aquila, Jews from Pontus, but whose residence was in Rome. By a decree of the Emperor Claudius all Jews had been expelled from Rome, on account, probably, of some religious disturbances connected with a person named Chrestus; but whether Chrestus was identical with Christus, and these disturbances were owing to the introduction of the gospel into the Jewish synagogues at Rome, we cannot say. Priscilla and Aquila were obliged to leave Rome, and settled for a time in Corinth. There St. Paul met with them, and "because he was of the same craft, he abode with them, and wrought: for by their occupation they were tentmakers." How independent the apostle was! He would be chargeable to no man. He would earn his own living. But how wise was he in his independence! It was the best precaution he could take against the imputation, certain to be made, that he was a preacher of the gospel for gain, and not because he was called to be a preacher of the gospel. At Corinth, as elsewhere, he laboured with his own hands, and ate his own bread. A warm friendship grew up between the apostle and these people from Rome. Tentmaking was a profitable trade, and Priscilla and Aquila must have made money in it, because we find that they were able to accommodate the Ephesian Church in their own house.[1] On some occasion, unrecorded in Scripture, except in general terms, they must have run great risks for the apostle's sake, exposed their own lives to save his, and thereby earned the gratitude of the apostle and of all the churches.[2] And they were faithful to their Lord, for in St. Paul's latest Epistle a salutation is sent to them.[3] Very excellent people were these tent-makers, true Christians, helpers of the apostle in the three populous centres of Corinth, Ephesus, and Rome; and with these he first left Cenchrea on the short voyage across the Ægean, and in their company he looked upon the beautiful islands of the sunny sea.

At Cenchrea, where a little Christian Church had been formed, and where one of those devoted women, of whom Priscilla herself was an example, so numerous in the early Christian times, laboured as a deaconess, by name Phœbe —at Cenchrea, either St. Paul or Aquila (there appears to be a little doubt which of the two it was), being under the vow of a Nazarite, probably taken because of a providential escape from danger or death, had his head shorn in token that the vow was now ended. An insignificant matter, slipped into the sacred narrative in a casual way, it seems to be, but in reality it is not, and especially if the vow was taken by the apostle. And that is the more likely reading. For it affords evidence, all the stronger because of its apparent insignificance and casual introduction, of the apostle's attachment to the Levitical law, of his earnest desire to conciliate his countrymen, of the entire want of foundation to the charges made against him in Jerusalem, of his willingness to become all things to all men that he might by all means save some. The long locks which had distinguished his personal appearance in Corinth were gone,

---

[1] 1 Cor. xvi. 19.   [2] Rom. xvi. 3, 4.   [3] 2 Tim. iv. 19.

and, with a shorn head, he crossed these waters, and first entered the crowded port of Ephesus.

He hurried away from Ephesus to Jerusalem, but afterwards returned to that city, and dwelt there three years. It is very unlikely that he would remain three years in Ephesus without visiting Corinth, the communication between the two cities being so easy and frequent; and there are references in his Epistles which point to some such visit, undertaken for the purpose of chiding the church for its divisions and lax moral conduct, but which appears to have had very little or no effect. Apollos, an eloquent Alexandrian Jew, whom Aquila and Priscilla had instructed in Christian truth, had been over there, and also certain Judaizing brethren who regarded Peter as their head, and who had false and narrow notions of the work of Christ; and these Corinthians, not being grounded in the truth, broke themselves up into parties, and were contending one with another. There was a Paul party, and an Apollos party, and a Cephas party, and a Christ party. But this was not all, and this was not the worst. The licentiousness of the Corinthians, everywhere known, had not been utterly departed from, and was even winked at by the church authorities; and St. Paul went over to see them, and reprove them. He returned, but apparently matters were no better. He wrote them an Epistle, which is now lost; and it is not improbable that some written communication was sent to him by the Corinthian Church. At any rate, we have clear evidence of this visit, and of this lost Epistle, in St. Paul's extant writings; and it is an interesting and significant fact that the New Testament canon of the Armenian Church, one of the purest and most learned of the Eastern Churches, contains two Epistles more than ours, one an Epistle from the Corinthian Church to St. Paul, and the other a *third* Epistle of St. Paul to the Corinthians. This church caused him much sorrow. Through those smiling spaces that lie between the Grecian islands stretching across the Ægean, the apostle must have gone with a very sad heart, and these seas are associated not only with his sacred triumphs, but with his burden of pain. When recounting the numerous hardships of his apostolic life, he said—and how much is included in the words!—" Besides those things that are without, that which cometh upon me daily, the care of all the churches."

Of all the interesting places associated with St. Paul's labours none is more interesting than Alexandria Troas. For many centuries it preserved, and even now preserves, the name of Priam's ancient city, around which, if Homer may be believed, the Greeks and Phrygians fought, and from which, if we may credit the central idea of Virgil's beautiful poem, the founder of the conquering Romans came. Ancient Troy, however, the city of the Iliad, was on the other side of Mount Ida,

"in those bloody fields,
Where Simoïs rolls the bodies and the shields
Of heroes."

The fields are now peaceful enough, and the bodies and the shields have long since mingled with their common elements. The Troy of Alexander, the Troy of St. Paul, is at the western foot of many-fountained Ida, and on the very margin of the sea. Not much of it is left, but sufficient to tell of a beautiful and flourishing city. Huge masses of granite are strewn about, enormous pillars, and pavements, and foundations, many of them in the sea, and perhaps some of them never having been erected at all, for here Constantine thought to build his capital, and afterwards abandoned it in favour of Byzantium. Now the Turks call the place *Eski-Stamboul*—old Constantinople. But many of these chiselled granite masses must have formed part of the city when St. Paul was in it; for the Romans, because of its association with Troy, and consequently with their own mythical origin, granted it the privileges of a colony, and exempted its land, like that of Italy, from all taxation. Very early in the morning did I rise to see this memorable place, and again, when we returned, remained long on the bridge to gather in all the surrounding scene, and meditate upon the most important step even in St. Paul's important life, the introduction of the gospel into Europe.

The apostle and his companions, Silas and Timothy, were more than providentially led to Troas. For providential leading we understand to be the natural way a man takes, according to his own inclination or judgment, overruled by Providence to the man's good. But St. Paul was not suffered to take his natural way. He was not permitted to follow his inclination or judgment. God interfered with the apostle's purpose, and supernaturally led him to Troas. Doubtless the purpose of the apostle was to go through Phrygia and Galatia to Ephesus. But God had a larger field for him. He had opened a more effectual door. St. Paul seems not to have understood God's design. He was barred from entering Asia, of which Ephesus was the capital; he had already ministered to the churches in the central part of the Levant, and could not immediately go over the ground again; he must move westward. So he entered into Mysia. But he had no intention of proceeding through Mysia to the coast. He turned toward the north, and attempted to preach the gospel in Bithynia. Again God barred his way. He must still move westward. He must go through Mysia, and he went through, and reached Alexandria Troas, whence he could see across the flood, beyond the islands of the Grecian main, the outline of the hills of Europe.

That journey was a miracle. God's hand was in it, and in it in the same sense as in the doing of any other supernatural deed. And a greater miracle even than some which are more apparent. For a miracle that strikes us as such is generally the result of interference with, or suspension of, some physical law; or, according to the view of some, the movement of a higher and hidden law across the region of a lower and revealed law, appearing to us to be, and therefore to us practically an interference, or suspension. But here was a law governing a man's mind and heart, a man's judgment and will, interfered with, suspended, in order that the man might enter upon a larger work for the blessing of his fellow-men. The words read commonplace enough, and are passed over by many as mere geographical description; but how much is there in them! "Now when they had gone throughout Phrygia and the region of Galatia, and were forbidden of the Holy Ghost to preach the word in Asia, after they were come to Mysia, they assayed to go into Bithynia: but the Spirit suffered them not. And they passing by, *or through*, Mysia came down to Troas."

The apostle and his companions appear to have arrived at Troas in the evening, and to have immediately retired to rest. In the night St. Paul had a vision. He saw before him a man whom he recognized as from across the sea, "a man of Macedonia," and this man appealed to him. "Come over into Macedonia, and help us." Now the Lord's guidance was made plain to him. This vision was the key to his mysterious journey. He saw clearly why he had been led to Troas. And in the fulness of faith, when morning came, he embarked for Neapolis, taking with him, as well as Silas and Timothy, Luke, the beloved physician, who henceforward was his faithful companion, attending him on nearly all his journeys, and remaining with him during the anxious and dangerous time preceding his death. "Loosing from Troas," says St. Luke, "we came with a straight course to Samothracia, and the next day to Neapolis; and from thence to Philippi." It was the early morning when we passed by this ruined city, and came upon the "straight course to Samothracia," which lies between the island of Tenedos and the mainland. Vessels entering the Dardanelles always take this course, because the channel between the island of Tenedos and the mainland is deep and clear, whereas the western coast of Tenedos is troubled with shoals and is unsafe even in fine weather. The whole view lay before us, as it must have done before St. Paul on that morning centuries ago, when, called of God, and inspired by a majestic, all-conquering faith, he passed over the Grecian Sea into Europe, and planted the standard of the cross in Philippi. A small company they were, and, to human appearance, an insignificant company; four men, unknown, despised maybe, and perhaps in one of the small, slenderly built coasting vessels, sitting lightly upon the water, with its large lateen sail spread, and sweeping over the sea before a fair wind—they little looked like messengers of the King of kings on a mission which should transform Europe, and through Europe transform the world. Other men have crossed from Asia to Europe and Europe to Asia very near this place; they have had mighty armies; they have been attended by immense fleets; they have moved with all the pomp and pageantry of regal processions; they have confidently expected to establish a world-wide empire— but where are they? Their power was the earthly power, the power of Nebuchadnezzar's image, with its golden head, and its feet of iron and clay. But the power of these four men, who went over quietly and unnoticed, on an ordinary boat, in the early morning, was the heavenly power, the power of the stone cut out of the mountain without hands, small, compact, irresistible, and which is now filling the whole earth. "It shall break in pieces and consume all these kingdoms, and it shall stand for ever."

From Alexandria Troas, and along the whole of the straight course to Samothracia, the scenery is full of beauty. Eastward lie the wooded plains of Troy, stretching away to the summit of Mount Ida; the entrance to the Hellespont; the long tongue of land once called the Thracian Chersonessus, and now known as the peninsula of Galipoli; and the fertile shores of Thrace, flanked by the Rhodope mountains, and watered by the Hebrus: then, after rounding

Samothracia, under the lee of which island the apostle and his companions anchored for the night, the Thracian shore was immediately to the north, and running westward by the island of Thasos into the Strymonic Gulf. The changing scenery of this landward view is delightful, but the chief charm in the scenery is the view over the sea. Directly ahead of a vessel on the straight course for Samothracia would be the rocky isle of Imbros, and behind it, and towering above it, so as to make them appear in the distance like one island, Samothracia itself would rise majestically into the pure air, the loftiest island in the Grecian Archipelago. To the westward Tenedos would lie low in the main; and, on the rippling waters beyond, Lemnos would gather his vapours about him, "smoky Lemnos," as he is called; and yet beyond, eighty miles away, but clearly visible, the magnificent Mount Athos, loftier even than Samothracia, and, in the distance, with the rosy hues of sunrise flooding its surface and softening its form, would appear an object of incomparable beauty, and appropriately closing in this remarkable scene. This was what St. Paul beheld as he loosed from Troas and ran before the wind for the sacred isle of Samothracia.

In the early morning, as we approached the mouth of the Dardanelles, the sun was not yet above the hills, but his rays were leaping forth to herald his coming. The king of the day himself had not yet appeared, but the breath of his fiery coursers was upon the mountains, and the glittering of his golden chariot was in the sky and the wave. All round the horizon lovely colours were forming. Mount Athos robed himself first, and stood out in glory to welcome the appearance of the king, and then Samothracia, and then Lemnos, and Imbros, and Tenedos last of all, when the king upsprang from the heights of Ida, and, with his flashing eyes, filled the world with light. It was a sunrise never to be forgotten, and yet a sunrise often repeated there, and not improbably gazed upon by the great apostle, and Luke, and Silas, and Timothy.

Alexandria Troas cannot be mentioned without some reference to "the beloved physician," St. Luke. He is one of the most attractive and lovable characters in the New Testament. The modesty with which he suppresses his own name, both in his Gospel and in the Acts of the Apostles, retiring ever into the background, hiding himself behind the larger and more prominent form of others, is specially remarkable. From certain detailed portions of his Gospel, and especially toward the close of it, and from the minute account of the origin of the Christian Church contained in the Acts of the Apostles, we may fairly infer that he was in Jerusalem at the time of the crucifixion, and until after the day of Pentecost, and must have been familiar with the Saviour, and the chosen twelve. That unique incident of the resurrection, recorded by him alone, namely, the appearance of the Saviour to the two disciples on their way to Emmaus, and His conversation with them, and His revelation to them—the simple pathos and graphic recital of the story, with the careful neglect (if we may so put it) to mention the name of one of the disciples—all point to the fact that he and Cleopas were the two whose hearts burned within them while Jesus talked with them by the way. Probably he knew Saul the persecutor, before he became the companion and faithful friend of Paul the missionary. He joined him at Troas. He does not directly say that he joined him there, but leaves his readers to imply this by simply changing the grammatical construction from the third person to the first. He drops *they*, and takes up *we*. *They* came down to Troas, and *we* endeavoured to go into Macedonia. And by this modest change we trace the course of St. Luke throughout the rest of the Acts of the Apostles.

Why did he join the missionary company at Troas? He was a physician, and perhaps ministered to the apostle in in his capacity as a physician for love's sake, and for the sake of the Lord Jesus. Was he a native of Troas? We cannot say. He was not a Jew, if we may regard his Latin name, *Lucas*, as an indication of his race; and St. Paul, in his salutations to the church at Colosse, does not include him among the circumcision. The classical Greek of his writings, a Greek peculiarly free from Hebraisms, would point to the same fact. But he was doubtless a proselyte to the Jewish faith, and through that brought into contact with the teaching of our Lord Jesus Christ. He became one of His disciples, and was probably among the hundred and twenty who were first endued with power from on high. Early accounts of his life make him a native of Antioch, and tradition has bestowed upon him the fame of a painter. His graphic word-pictures may have given rise to the tradition that he used the brush as well as the pen. The apparent facility with which he wrote, and the finish of his style, as well as his calling as a physician, prove that he was an educated man; but do not prove that he was wealthy, or even in a good social position. For those proud Romans thought that it was beneath their dignity to write their own letters, and to heal their own bodies, and committed such-like work to their educated slaves. St. Luke, however, was not a slave. He was free to travel when and where he pleased. But there is nothing improbable in the supposition and statement that he was a *freedman*, one who had been a slave, and had obtained his manumission at the death of his master, or by his master's gratitude for distinguished service. To the last he was with the apostle. He shared with him his most perilous journeys. He stood by him, when others forsook him, in the dangerous days preceding his martyrdom. "Only Luke is with me."[1] That earnest desire for human friendship, that yearning for the presence of loving hearts, which, in the great apostle, almost amounted to a weakness, was fully satisfied in St. Luke. With the tenderest gratitude he called him "the beloved physician."[2]

The second visit of St. Paul to Troas, not mentioned in

[1] 2 Tim. iv. 11.   [2] Col. iv. 14.

the Acts of the Apostles, but referred to in the Second Epistle to the Corinthians, and which took place very probably after the uproar at Ephesus, and as a consequence of that uproar is specially marked by an exhibition of the apostle's longing for companionship. He could not bear to be deprived of the presence of his friends. He must have some sympathetic brother near him. We may well call this a frailty, but it is a beautiful frailty, and intensely human; and we can trace it in that pathetic reproach of our gracious Saviour, when, having taken with him, for company, for sympathy, for help, the three dearest disciples, they fell asleep, and heeded not His solitary prayer, His bitter agony, kneeling beneath the olive trees in the garden of Gethsemane. "Could ye not watch with me one hour?" said He. There was the deep, heartfelt want of man for the friendship of his fellow. Truly, He took upon Himself all our frailty, and yet He was the Perfect One. A beautiful frailty this, and intensely human; and we have it strongly manifested in the great apostle. "When I came to Troas to preach Christ's gospel, and a door was opened unto me of the Lord, I had no rest in my spirit because I found not Titus my brother; but taking my leave of them, I went from thence into Macedonia." Again he took that journey from Troas to Philippi, this time to seek Titus, to meet him on his way from Corinth, to get near his friend. To his restlessness of spirit was added restlessness of body, for "when we were come into Macedonia our flesh had no rest, but we were troubled on every side; without were fightings, within were fears. Nevertheless God, that comforteth those that are cast down, comforted us by the coming of Titus." God supplied his need, and he had joy again in human fellowship, in the presence, and sympathy, and assistance of his "own son after the common faith."

We find St. Paul again at Troas, having crossed the Ægean this time from Philippi. He was on his way to Jerusalem. He had purposed sailing from Greece to Syria, and thereby accomplishing the journey quickly; but the Jews waylaid him when he was about to embark, and to escape their toils he suddenly turned north and went overland into Macedonia. He had four companions with him in Greece. One was Gaius of Derbe, who had been with him previously in Ephesus. In his salutation to the Romans in the Epistle sent to them shortly before by the hand of Phœbe, the deaconess of Cenchrea, he calls Gaius "mine host," so that he must have been residing with him. This Gaius may possibly be the "well-beloved Gaius" of St. John's Third Epistle. Timothy, his own son in the gospel, who was doubtless well acquainted with Gaius, having come from the same locality, was another of his companions; and beside Gaius and Timothy there were two Asiatic Greeks with him, Tychicus and Trophimus, names familiar to us in apostolic history, and both faithful servants of St. Paul. Tychicus acted sometimes as amanuensis, and was the bearer of two or three epistles to different churches. Trophimus was the man observed by the Hellenic Jews in company with St. Paul in the streets of Jerusalem, who, supposing that he had been introduced by St. Paul within the precincts of the temple, raised the hubbub which ended in the apostle's imprisonment and voyage to Rome. With these four men, Gaius, Timothy, Tychicus, and Trophimus, he left Greece and came to Berœa. There Sopater joined them. They next came to Thessalonica, and were there joined by Aristarchus and Secundus. From Thessalonica they passed on through Appolonia and Amphipolis to Philippi, and there they met with the beloved physician. They were now a large company. We have quite a gathering of the saints, a cluster of remarkable men within the military city of Philippi, and the little Philippian church must have remembered their visit, and the gracious season consequent thereupon, for a long time. Why were these men gathered together from different parts? Why, having already in their company members from the churches in central Levant and the province of Asia, should they pick up *en route* other members from the Macedonian churches, and travel together to Jerusalem? The reason for this is very likely to be found in the great collection which was then being made among the Gentile churches, under the superintendency of St. Paul, for the relief of the famine-stricken Jewish churches in Palestine; and these men, travelling with St. Paul, may have been in charge of the contributions from the churches in their own neighbourhoods, delegated by these churches to carry their contributions to the mother church in Jerusalem.

St. Paul was in no hurry to leave Philippi. He lingered there, sending the company before him, with directions to wait for him at Troas, retaining only St. Luke, to whom he must have had an increasing attachment, and whose skilled ministration was perhaps necessary to him at this particular time. Philippi occupied a very dear place in his heart. No church had been so mindful of his wants. No church had shown the same loving regard for his comfort and welfare. And while other churches were troubled by false brethren, and pernicious doctrines, and immoral procedure, sometimes calling in question his own apostolic authority, this church at Philippi was pure and peaceable, and received the apostle ever as an angel of God. He had more satisfaction in this church at Philippi than any other. He had a deeper affection for its members than any other. "I thank my God upon every remembrance of you," he said; and in the conclusion of his Epistle, as if he could not find words to express his affection, he calls them "my brethren dearly beloved and longed for, my joy and crown." We cannot wonder that he lingered behind at Philippi. He could rest himself there, and obtain not only bodily, but spiritual refreshment, very necessary to him on this last journey to Jerusalem—this journey of which he said a few weeks later to the elders of the Ephesian church, "I go bound in the spirit unto Jerusalem, not knowing the things that shall befall me there: save that the Holy Ghost witnesseth in every city, saying that bonds and afflictions abide me."

He spent the Passover at Philippi, and after the Passover he embarked at Neapolis for Troas. St. Luke went with him. It was the beautiful spring-time, when the Thracian coast, and the northern islands of the Archipelago, were putting on their green vestures, and crowning themselves with blossoms and flowers. A south wind was blowing, a similar wind to that which brought them beforetime with a straight course to Samothracia; but now, having approached Samothracia from the west, and being desirous to go southward, altogether against them. It was a dangerous sea to traverse in contrary winds. To get west of Imbros, and down by the Chryse rocks, would have meant almost certain shipwreck; and yet to work east of Imbros, and clear Cape Hellas, in a contrary wind, was a very difficult matter. The only safe way was to shelter under Samothracia, and wait for the wind to change; and this they must have done. They were five days reaching Troas, a voyage which beforetime, with a fair wind, they had accomplished in two; and very glad would they be to exchange the tossing vessel for the firm land.

They stayed seven days at Troas. On the Sunday the disciples came together to break bread—an evidence that Sunday was kept as a sacred day by the early Christians; and Paul preached to them. He had to leave them on the morrow, and he continued his discourse until very late in the evening. They were in an upper room, very probably approached by a flight of stairs from the outside. The night was dark, for it was not long after the Passover, and many lamps were burning; and a young man, named Eutychus, overcome by the heat, gradually fell away into a deep sleep. He had seated himself in the *third loft*, a balcony which overhung the street, or court, and which he had chosen maybe in order favourably to see and hear the apostle, and, at the same time, benefit by the cool air. The meeting was hushed by the tones of the preacher, and the lateness of the hour intensified the silence, when, suddenly, this young man, overbalancing himself in his sleep, fell heavily to the ground below, and lay like one quite dead. Immediately consternation spread throughout the audience. But Paul ran to him and fell upon him, and embraced him, and said to the startled and fear-stricken people, "Trouble not yourselves, for his life is in him." And so it proved. Either by providential care, or the miraculous power of the apostle, the young man was picked up unhurt, and the people's hearts were comforted. The meeting continued; bread was broken, and they shared the common meal, the Christian meal, and Paul talked with them until the morning.

In the morning the ship was ready to sail, and all the missionary company embarked except the apostle. He intended walking to Assos, and joining the ship there. This would give him a little more time at Troas, and would afford opportunity for still further conversation with the members of the church while on the way from Troas to Assos. The ship had to work round Cape Lectum, and into the Adramyttium Gulf; while St. Paul could start from Troas later in the day, go direct to Assos over the good Roman road that then ran between the two cities, and be in plenty of time to join the vessel at the latter place. It was a shady road, and picturesque, winding among the oaks which are very plentiful here, and through the opening glades and vistas of which may be seen charming views of the blue waters, and the fertile island of Lesbos; and, stretching beyond the oaks, across the western foot of Mount Ida, intersected by cool streams rushing rapidly to the sea. He embarked at Assos, and came to Mitylene, the capital of Lesbos, Sappho's city; and passing southward, across the Gulf of Smyrna, entered into the channel between Chios and the mainland. Still coasting, he went round the eastern side of Samos, and, meeting with contrary winds, lay to between the promontories of Mycale and Trogyllium. When the wind changed he set forth again, landed at Miletus, sent for the elders of the Ephesian church, and delivered to them his parting, pathetic address. We can trace this voyage minutely. And by the fact that the vessel passed down the coast, always between the islands and the mainland, when, if she had been going direct from Troas to Rhodes or Patara, she might have kept to the westward of the islands, and had a clear channel, and deep seas, and a straight course all the way; and by the further fact that the missionary company left her at Patara, and embarked in a larger Phœnician ship to finish the journey, we may conclude that she was a small, ordinary coasting craft, taken advantage of by Paul and his companions to get as far south as it was possible, so as to be in Jerusalem before the day of Pentecost.

Of St. Paul's last visit to Troas we have no detailed account. It is almost impossible to trace the apostle's movements between his first and second appearance before the Imperial tribunal. It seems certain that he visited Spain, and resided there for two years; it appears equally certain that he spent some time in Macedonia and the Levant, and also in the island of Crete. That he again crossed the northern part of the Ægean is very probable, and, without doubt, he passed through Troas, because in his last letter to Timothy, written from Rome shortly before his martyrdom, and when pressing Timothy to come to him quickly, if possible before the winter, he says: "The cloke that I left at Troas with Carpus, when thou comest, bring with thee, and the books, but especially the parchments." This is also an indication of Timothy's course from Ephesus to Rome—*via* Troas, the Ægean, Macedonia, Illyricum, the Adriatic, and Brundusium, which was the quickest route, and on the great highway to Rome. When St. Paul left his cloke at Troas—or the box in which his cloke was carried, like our modern *portmanteau*, for that is what the word means—with his books and parchments, he must have been an old man. He had become "Paul, the aged." It could not have been long before his end. He may have contemplated returning to Troas for these things, in the following spring, from Nicopolis, where he had gone to winter, and where he expected to have Titus with him through the winter. Nicopolis was a quiet, although famous place, both now and afterwards, situated in Epirus, near the Adriatic seaboard; and perhaps he thought he might there escape, for awhile, from the active hostility of the Romans. Their anger had been roused by the spread of Christianity—a more formidable anger than that of the Jews. The Christians were becoming known, not as a Jewish sect, but as an independent and peculiar community. Their doctrines were distorted in the eyes of a superstitious people. Their lives were maligned by people living in the grossest sensuality. Christianity must be suppressed, and, before the winter was over, the authorities at Nicopolis had arrested the great apostle, and sent him to Rome, to appear before Nero the second time. And with the certainty of death before him —*death!* nay, rather transition, glorification, eternal life—he wrote: "I am now ready to be offered, and the time of my departure is at hand. I have fought a good fight, I have finished my course, I have kept the faith: henceforth there is laid up for me a crown of righteousness, which the Lord, the righteous judge, shall give me at that day: and not to me only, but unto all them also that love His appearing."

CHAPTER XIII.

THE SENTINEL OF THE MEDITERRANEAN.

Eastern side of the Rock in the early morning—Western side—Clear waters of the bay—Surroundings—Town—Moors—Castle—Name—Capture by the British in 1704—Siege of 1705—1727—1779 to 1783—Natural strength—Strategical position—Caverns—"Munitions of rocks"—Climate—Inhabitants—Smuggling—A soldier's conversion—Drive to Europa Point—Stranded steamer—Fauna—View from the summit—Current through the straits—Beyond the "gates."

"We can see it," shouted a voice one morning, rousing me from slumber.

"See what?" asked I, sleepily, turning over in my berth toward the place whence the voice came.

"The Rock!"

Immediately I shook myself free from the pleasant captivity of Morpheus, and drew open the port-hole window to glance as far ahead as the narrow, circular aperture would permit. I could see nothing but haze. Tumbling out of bed, and quickly dressing, I ran up the companion way, and directly before us, at a distance of about ten miles, a huge grey mass reared itself above a bank of cloud into a light blue sky. That was the Rock. As we approached nearer, its outline became more distinct; the bank of cloud rolled itself up from the base, and became a white vaporous belt round the middle of the Rock; the little village of Catalan, in an indenture of the Rock, and fronted by its strip of light sand, became visible. The white vaporous belt began to move upward, disclosing the gigantic proportions of each perpendicular layer of grey marble, upward until it wrapped the top like a turban, and upward still, vanishing in the ethereal blue, and leaving the entire 1,450 feet, straight as a wall, rugged and naked, looking from the blue heights across the blue waters, a serene, solitary, majestic, immovable sentinel.

We were now drawing near Europa Point, and the Rock was losing its serenity and solitariness, and putting on other features of majesty and strength, as we obtained this southern view. The lighthouse showed itself: the batteries began to appear: and, as we steamed round into the Bay, the western side opened up, with its sharp declivity half covered with vegetation; the town stretching along the margin of the sea, and running as far up the slope as the nature of the ground would permit; and moles and bastions of solid masonry, mounted with heavy guns, strengthening the naturally strong rocky shore, and serving, with the other defences in and about the Rock proper, to make the place impregnable.

We came to anchor in about fifty fathoms of water, outside the old mole, which is popularly known as "the devil's tongue." And the name is not inappropriate, for, if any place can spit fire, this can. The waters of the Bay are unusually clear. They are like looking into liquid crystal. The bottom can be seen, and objects easily distinguished, at a depth of eighty, or even one hundred feet. In very few waters anywhere can the fisherman drop his line fifty feet, as he can in the Bay of Gibraltar, and see the tackle and bait at that distance, and watch the various fish gather about it, and nibble at it, the big ones chasing the little ones away and then, approaching the bait cautiously themselves, touch it with their noses, look at it with their large round eyes, and swim round it as if it were a new marine curiosity.

And to the amateur fisherman, whose zest is quickened by the taste of a naturalist, fishing becomes doubly interesting when he can not only feel, but watch, the fish bite, and not only watch, but observe all his extremely cautious evolutions preparatory to the bite. These denizens of the watery world are very wary, and if we knew as much about their habits and ways as about the habits and ways of the birds and animals in our own terrestrial sphere, we might invent a new set of proverbs, and increase our stock of homely wisdom.

The Bay of Gibraltar is about seven miles long, and five broad. It has an even, semicircular shore, with high lands running completely round it, except where the short, low, narrow isthmus, known as "the neutral ground," connects the Rock of Gibraltar with the territory of Spain. This neutral ground, in time of war, may be flooded, making the Rock an island, and increasing its strength; and over this neutral ground, from caverns hewn in the solid rock, heavy guns point their ominous muzzles, ready to belch forth thunderous fire upon any army daring enough to attempt, over the isthmus, to carry the place by storm. On every side but this, the Rock of Gibraltar is washed by the sea. At the head of the Bay, standing a little way back among the hills, is the Spainish town of San Roque; and on the western coast, directly opposite the town of Gibraltar, is the other Spanish town of Algesiras, with the fortified islet of Verde at its southern extremity. Algesiras, which sometimes gives its name to the Bay, is a picturesque place, almost as Moorish as Morocco itself; and, behind it, a lofty range of hills run southwards toward Cape Tarifa. This cape, the most southern point in Europe, and the opposite African land, on which stands the town of Tangier, form the narrowest part of the Straits of Gibraltar.

The town of Gibraltar, seen from the Bay, has a semi-Oriental appearance. The light-coloured, flat-roofed, lattice-windowed houses are clustered together on the north-western slope of the Rock. Thick, low walls, mounted with guns, front the town, and terminate at its northern end, opening on "the devil's tongue," in a formidable arched gateway, whose massive gates are closed every evening at seven o'clock. Those who are in have to stay in, and those who are out must remain out, until the gates open in the morning—that is, unless special military business require entrance or exit, or one has sufficient influence to obtain a passport from the authorities. Directly above the northern extremity of the town is the old Moorish castle—the most striking and picturesque object visible, from an architectural point of view. The southern extremity of the town is abruptly broken by the *Alameda*, or public gardens and recreation grounds, from which, straggling towards Europa Point, nestling behind huge rocks and in a labyrinth of luxuriant vegetation, are detached artistic villas, occupied by officers, and merchants, and the few wealthy residents who have chosen Gibraltar for a home. Behind the town, half-way up the Rock, and more, where the sharp ascent is broken into grassy ledges, a few small houses may be seen. A towered citadel rests upon the ridge of the Rock sloping down towards the south; and upon the very top of the high northern shoulder a battery stands, and floating above it, the flag which has braved

"a thousand years, the battle and the breeze."

From this battery you may look sheer down into the Mediterranean, 1,450 feet; and down this awful precipice, a few days before we arrived, a soldier, in a fit of madness, flung himself, and was whirled away to inevitable ruin in the blue sea below. The northern end of the Rock has two sloping ledges, one about a hundred and fifty, and the other about six hundred feet from the base; and from the second ledge the precipice rises to the rounded ridge of the summit on which the battery and flag-staff stand.

The Moors have left permanent impressions in Gibraltar.

The remains of the castle, and the name of the Rock, will serve to remind future generations of their prowess and fanaticism. They are monuments of the peril which threatened Western Europe when these fierce warriors, having overrun and subjugated Northern Africa, swept into Spain, and attempted to fasten the prophet's yoke upon the Spanish people. Like a full tide riding in upon white breakers beneath a stormy wind, they rode in, strong, passionate, and apparently irresistible; but like a full tide spreading itself upon the wide strand, beaten back by rocky projections here, and running out into harmless spray and ripples there, they spread themselves, and were beaten back some of them, across the straits, into Africa again, and ran out others of them, spending their forces upon the yielding surface of society, and becoming gradually absorbed in that society which they seemed everyway likely to entirely submerge. From the Divine counsels the fiat had gone forth, "Hitherto shalt thou come, but no further: and here shall thy proud waves be stayed." The tide of Mohammedanism receded, and never flowed again on this strand, and now it flows on no other, for the crescent of the prophet is too pale and weak to influence the tides—the mere reflection of a crescent, a mirage of the skies that must disappear before the advancing light of the rising sun.

Of this Moorish castle at Gibraltar there is a substantial tower standing, evidently once the central fortress, with outlying walls enclosing a courtyard, and a zigzag line of fortifications running from the tower down to the edge of the water. More than a thousand years this dark grey masonry has been reflected in the clear waters of the Bay. The castle was built in 711, by Tarif ebn Zarca, who must have recognized the strength of the Rock both for offensive and defensive purposes; and round this fortress waged the earliest recorded struggles for the Rock of Gibraltar, when the Moors were dislodged again and again, and again and again obtained possession, until their final expulsion in 1462.

This Tarif ebn Zarca has not only left his name at Cape Tarifa, but in Gibraltar, for the name is a corruption of Gebel-Tarif, meaning the hill of Tarif; and, after rather strangely altering it to suit our English lips, we have accepted the name. Before then it was known by its ancient name of Calpe, and the opposite hill, on the African coast, by the name of Abyla, and they two were called the Pillars of Hercules, and long considered by the timid mariners of those old-world times the western extremity of the earth. When the seat of empire began to move westward, and especially during the protracted struggle between Carthage and Rome, Calpe must have been of some strategical importance. The echoes of that distant age, however, are murmuring and almost indistinct; and it is only since the activity of modern nations has opened up the world, and drawn its distant parts together, that, to a nation having possessions all over the world, and keeping up a vital commercial and political connection with them all, the strategical importance of Gibraltar has been clearly felt and seen.

Gibraltar was captured by the British in 1704, during the war of the Spanish succession, and only five weeks before the victory of Blenheim, which lifted Marlborough to the pinnacle of military fame. The Spanish fortress surrendered to the attack of a British fleet under Admiral Sir George Rooke. The attack was unexpected by the Spaniards. At the time, there were only a hundred and fifty soldiers on the Rock, but they, with the aid of armed civilians, made a gallant and desperate resistance, and only capitulated under an express understanding that they should retire with all the honours of war, and provisioned for a six days' march, and that the Spanish civilians, who remained behind, should be courteously treated, and their freedom respected and maintained inviolate. The fighting was fierce while it lasted. The Prince of Hesse-Darmstadt landed on the isthmus with eighteen hundred marines. In six hours fifteen thousand cannon balls were thrown into the town. The southern fortifications particularly suffered, and here a storming party was landed and attempted to carry the town. The Spaniards were ready for them, and opportunely sprung a mine which killed forty-two and disabled sixty; but the rest pressed on, captured a bastion, and turned the guns against their foes. The work was soon over, and the governor, Marquis de Salines, had no alternative but to make honourable terms with his enemies, and leave the fortress in their hands.

If Bishop Burnet's history may be credited, the capitulation of the fortress was hastened on by a peculiar incident which happened at the beginning of the siege. Several men ventured ashore, clambering up rocks well-nigh precipitous, and came upon a procession of all the women of the town to a shrine of the Virgin Mary, in order to beseech her favour and help in their great need. The men—a very un-English proceeding—surrounded and carried the women away to the ships, and, as the Bishop remarks, "that contributed not a little to dispose those in the town to surrender."

The capture of Gibraltar was a heavy blow to France and Spain. They immediately set about the task of regaining the fortress, and closely besieged it by sea and land for seven months; but without success. The British garrison were twice reinforced. Its most effective strength, however, never reached more than two thousand five hundred, and of these four hundred fell by sickness and in defence of the fortress; while, so terribly did sickness ravage the ranks of the besiegers, and so sure was the fire of the garrison, that in the seven months they lost ten thousand men. After a most spirited attempt, they were obliged to retreat and leave the British in possession of the Rock. More than once it was nearly taken, and most nearly when five hundred men, upon their knees, and while partaking of the sacrament of the Lord's Supper, swore to capture the fortress, or die. A goatherd guided them, unobserved, to the southern side of the Rock, through the Pass of the Locust Trees, and up the ridge into the Cave of St. Michael. There they remained until the following night. Issuing forth under cover of the darkness, they surprised the guard of the middle hill, slew them all and assisted their fellows from below to scale the Rock by means of ropes and ladders. If the stratagem had succeeded, Gibraltar might have been again under the Spanish flag; but the stratagem did not succeed. It was discovered. The Grenadier Guards marched against the small, brave band, and, at the bayonet's point, drove a hundred and fifty of them over those frightful precipices into the sea, and took the rest prisoners.

Twenty years later the Spaniards again tried to take Gibraltar. An army was assembled at Algesiras, and moved to San Roque, and, without any open declaration of hostilities, commenced the construction of earthworks and batteries in the direction of the British lines. The Spanish commander refused to give explanations. His answers were haughty. And when, at last, the earthworks and batteries were pushed forward so far as to menace the British position, the guns of Gibraltar opened fire. The Spaniards found that the British had not been idle during their twenty years proprietorship. The Rock was strongly fortified, and when hostilities were suspended upon overtures of peace being made between the two countries, the Spanish forces were no nearer taking the Rock than when they commenced the siege.

The grand siege of Gibraltar, that which most thoroughly tested the defensive capabilities of the fortress, and most severely tried the courage and fortitude of the British troops, lasted for nearly four years, from 1779 to 1783. The hands of England were fully employed with her American colonies. Spain took advantage of this circumstance to assail again the redoubtable fortress, and endeavour, by a long and mighty effort of all her forces, to wrest it from her foe. Fifty years had passed away since her last attempt, during which time the fortifications had been considerably increased and strengthened; but the Spaniards were fully aware of this, and made preparations for the siege on a very large scale. They blockaded the port. Five hundred men were employed, day and night, in the construction of batteries upon the isthmus. Their intention was to reduce the fortress by famine, and thereby compel surrender. It was hardly thought by the garrison that they could be relieved, and their enemies thought relief was impossible. As the winter wore on, provisions became scarce, and the men had to subsist on four ounces of rice per day. The ships were broken up for fuel. Chickens were artificially hatched, and capons trained to rear them. Scurvy appeared. The garrison were becoming enfeebled, when, in the night, an English vessel, laden with flour, stole into the harbour, bringing intelligence of the victory of Sir George Rodney over the Spanish fleet off the coast of Portugal, and his determination to succour them by a large supply of provisions, and a reinforcement of Highlanders. Another Spanish fleet opposed the gallant Admiral near Cape St. Vincent. A long and desperate fight ensued, and the Spaniards were signally defeated. The provisions were landed. The Highlanders joined the garrison. The sick were sent home with Admiral Rodney, who, after rendering effectual relief, left the garrison of seven thousand men to continue the defence of the Rock buoyed up with hopes of victory.

The spring and summer passed, and autumn found the garrison enfeebled by the ravages of scurvy. The disease was aggravated by the bad state of the provisions. The redoubled vigilance of their enemies made it almost impossible to obtain fresh supplies. Not only did they blockade the Bay, but xebecs (lateen sailed-boats frequently seen in the Mediterranean) and armed cruisers were constantly watching the Straits, to give immediate warning of the approach of any fleet, and to prevent daring and wary attempts at relief by single vessels. Still the men bravely held out all through the winter and to the next spring, when, fighting its way through eleven gunboats, a privateer of Glasgow, named the *Eagle*, brought the welcome tidings of coming relief by a British fleet under Admiral Darby; and the garrison was again fired with enthusiasm, while the Spaniards became aware of the futility of starving the fortress into surrender.

The following summer was employed by the Spaniards in preparing for a gigantic attack. The place could not be reduced by famine, but it should be reduced by shot and shell. So they determined; and their preparations were so costly, elaborate, and magnificent, that it seemed almost useless for the garrison to offer any resistance. They constructed ten large floating batteries. The bottoms were of thick wood; the walls were of wood and cork soaked in salt water; and, to render them still further fire-proof, spaces left between the wood and cork were filled up with wet sand. The decks were covered with rope netting, and upon the netting, for the better protection of the men, wet skins were placed. These batteries were mounted with heavy guns, some of them with ten, some of them with as many as twenty-eight; and the guns were served by more than five thousand men specially selected from the Spanish navy. Ten thousand French troops, with a thousand guns, supported the batteries, under the command of the Duke de Crillon. In addition to these naval forces, two hundred pieces of heavy cannon, and an army of forty thousand men, occupied the strong batteries of the isthmus, and the adjoining Spanish land. A brilliant early morning sortie, several months before, had considerably damaged the batteries, but they were now repaired, and in excellent condition again. When the day of attack arrived, the 13th of September, 1782, the hills of Andalusia were covered with thousands of spectators. The cannonading commenced shortly before ten o'clock in the morning, four hundred heavy guns belching forth fire against the stately Rock, answered readily by the British guns, which poured out red-hot balls upon the floating batteries, firing them time after time, and yet to no purpose. The flames were speedily extinguished. As the day wore on, and the cannonading became more furious, the masts and rigging of the floating batteries began to fall; by night, one of the immense structures was all on fire, lighting up the Bay, and directing the burning meteor shot of the garrison; another and another were soon in flames, and, before morning, the conflagration had spread to no less than six of them, exploding the magazines as the flames reached them, scattering destruction all around, and inspiring with terror those who had so far escaped. The scene was awful. Four thousand eight hundred men perished on these batteries alone, and the few hundreds who were saved were saved by the merciful and humane efforts of the British themselves, who pulled out in boats to their rescue. The Spaniards had expected the morning of the 14th of September to break upon the Spanish flag floating from the heights of Gibraltar, but the British flag was there still. And never has any other flag since then, and for long years before then, caught the early beams of the sun rising out of the blue waters of the Mediterranean.

The Spaniards were discouraged, but they fought on. Their floating batteries were destroyed, but they kept up the cannonade from the isthmus. Day by day, and often all through the night, they threw their shots at the fortress, and maintained a strict blockade of the Bay. The following February, however, brought peace; and in March, the Duke de Crillon visited General Elliot, commander of the garrison. He expressed his admiration of the bravery of the British troops, by whom he was greeted with hearty cheers, somewhat to his astonishment, until the spirit in which the men cheered was explained to him; and, upon an inspection of the fortifications, was surprised to find how strong they were, and, if well garrisoned, what were the defensive capabilities of the Rock of Gibraltar.

The Rock is a natural fortress. Its surroundings and conformation contribute to its strength more than any merely human military work possibly can, and, in ancient times, under the rudest mode of warfare, Gibraltar must have been a coveted position—coveted because dominant, and, when once possessed, easily held. The main, and almost only, disadvantage, is the necessity of provisioning from outside. The descent of the western and only fertile slope is mostly so rapid, and the soil so scanty and encumbered with so much rock, that, even if the climate were favourable, cereal sufficient for the maintenance of a garrison could not possibly be grown. There are no fresh-water springs. And the rain fall is scanty. So that the inhabitants are obliged to gather the precious drops by numerous conduits, and run them into tanks for future use. If Gibraltar fell at all, it would fall by famine in consequence of a successful blockade, which, so long as England maintains her maritime supremacy, is not likely to be. The blockade would have to be continued without reverses for a long time, because the Rock is always provisioned for three years. To storm the Rock would be impossible. Its natural strength renders this wellnigh impossible, and its elaborate fortifications make it impossible altogether. All that military genius can do has been done, not only in line after line of masonry mounted with the finest and largest guns ever made, but in gallery after gallery hewn out of the solid rock, communicating with each other, and looking upon the world outside through holes like the port-holes of a vessel; and within these galleries, their muzzles peeping through the embrasures, guns stand ever ready to breathe thunder and flame from the very heart of the Rock itself. Without doubt Gibraltar is the strongest fortress in the world.

But the value of Gibraltar as a fortress is not dependent upon its isolated strength so much as upon its strategical position. And, according to some military critics, its strategical importance has diminished with the increased facilities for communication between the East and West. They even deny its value as the sentinel of the Mediterranean, and say that it by no means commands the Straits, and appear to regard it rather as a trophy of British prowess in the past, and withal a very expensive trophy, than a present safeguard to British commerce, and an important connecting link in the chain of British empire. We have the satisfaction, however, of knowing that even if a mere trophy, it is no longer an expensive trophy, but beneath a wise administration is made almost, if not entirely, to support itself, without drawing, or drawing very little, from the revenues at home. And if the Rock does not command the Straits, in the sense of being able to fire across the Straits, and directly resist entrance to the Mediterranean, it watches over the Straits, it is the dominant position of the Straits, and any other power at Tarifa or Ceuta must be subordinate to the power in possession of the Rock, and obey the bidding of the Rock. Therefore the Rock does command the Straits, by being able, if necessary, to enforce its will at Tarifa or Ceuta, and block the passage to any ship not friendly to its sovereign. Gibraltar is one of a string of fortresses between England and her Indian Empire. Its value is seen in connection with the rest. Our expulsion from Gibraltar would weaken us in Malta, would lessen our influence in the Suez Canal, would detrimentally affect us in Aden, to say nothing of Cyprus, and the recently annexed island of Socotra; and it would lessen our hold upon the Indian Empire itself. Its value mainly depends, not upon its isolated strength, but upon its strategical position. We could not afford to lose it. It is not a citadel of merely past importance, but of present, and maybe permanent, importance. The Mediterranean is still one of the world's great highways, and so long as it remains a highway, they who stand at and overlook the entrance, and who have power to close the entrance, are so far the masters of the road; and their yea and nay cannot easily be withstood, must compel serious attention in everything affecting the vital interests of Europe and the civilized world.

In addition to the fortified chambers cut out of the rock, there are interesting natural caverns communicating with the outside world by an entrance about a thousand feet above the sea. The largest of these caverns are known as the Halls of St. Michael. From them downwards for five hundred feet natural corridors lead, sometimes widening out into caves, sometimes narrowing so much as scarcely to permit further advance; and from the lowest approachable corridor may be heard the muffled thunder of the sea breaking into a hollow down far away beneath the reach of human foot. Many of these caverns are roofed with stalactites, and present a beautiful appearance to visitors bold enough to enter them. The fortified chambers are interesting as works of human genius and skill. There are two of them, in the northern face of the Rock, and so mounted with guns as to be able to sweep, not only the isthmus, but a great part of the Bay, and the contiguous waters of the Mediterranean. These two chambers are connected with each other, and connected with the battery above, by means of a spiral stair cut through the virgin rock, and the three together form a unique fortification of that part of the Rock which is not washed by the sea.

The prophet Isaiah, speaking of the man whose soul is so stedfastly settled in righteousness that "he despiseth the gain of oppression, and shaketh his hands from holding of bribes," makes this promise, "He shall dwell on high," or, *in the heights;* "his place of defence shall be the munitions of rocks." In times of peace, and in a country not remarkable for mountain fastnesses, the force and appropriateness of this figure might easily be overlooked; but we feel its force and appropriateness while considering Gibraltar, "the munitions of rocks," the fortified heights that have successfully withstood the attacks of so many foes. As Gibraltar to the British garrison thereon, so is the Lord to His people. "The Lord is my fortress." But more than Gibraltar to the British garrison thereon is the Lord to His people. For no only shall the righteous man dwell in the heights, and have for his defence the munitions of rocks, but "bread shall be given him; his waters shall be sure."[1]

The climate of Gibraltar is very pleasant during the greater part of the year. The heat is sometimes troublesome to northerners. It is generally tempered, however, by the cool sea-breeze, and there are many shady nooks in which one may enjoy even the hottest days. The climate, while not detrimental to the health of adults, and even conducive to health, is singularly fatal to young children during the period of teething. The healthiness of Gibraltar is partly owing to the careful *pratique* regulations of the port, and to the cleanliness of the town. Almost as soon as we dropped anchor, the *pratique* boat was alongside demanding an inspection of our papers, and the papers were seized with a pair of tongs, and dexterously opened and spread out by another pair. Until assured that both crew and passengers were in good health, they would not run the risk of infection by handling anything connected with the vessel. Years ago Gibraltar had the undesirable reputation of being one of the dirtiest towns in Europe. Now it is one of the cleanest. There are three streets running parallel with each other, narrow, evenly paved with wood, and all scrupulously clean. There are no signs of offal, and the streets are not dusty, while the smooth wooden pavement deadens the sound of the vehicles, and makes driving a pleasure. The buildings are mostly lofty, throwing their shadows completely across the streets; where this is not the case, the streets are often protected by awnings; and the houses are furnished with verandahs, and latticed windows, and wide doors, Spanish houses intermingling with English, and, from the nature of the ground, overlooking each other, and giving the town a picturesque appearance.

Great variety of feature and costume may be met with in the streets of Gibraltar. The soldiers of the garrison, in

[1] Isaiah xxxiii. 15, 16.

their distinguishing regimentals, conspicuous among whom is the kilted Highlander, may be seen everywhere. The dark-whiskered, broad-faced Spaniard in his big sombrero, and with his red sash and knee breeches; the bare-limbed, scraggy and bronzed, and straight-featured, full-lipped Moor, with his turbaned head and sandalled feet; the ubiquitous Jew, proclaiming his unmistakable nationality, and as full of *the art of getting on* in a black cap and blue blouse as in any other costume; and Greeks, and Genoese, and animated Frenchmen, are walking through the streets intent upon their separate businesses. Blonde Englishwomen, in their ordinary English dresses; handsome, dark-eyed, brown-skinned Spanish ladies, with their lace shawls thrown over their heads, and drooping carelessly about their shoulders; Moors of a rich olive complexion, with eyes as dark as the Spaniard's, and features more regular and oval, and carrying always a very much more serious expression, wearing a beaded kerchief over their black hair, clad in voluminous sleeves, and a striped gown, and sandals or embroidered slippers; and others of the womenkind, may be met with in the market and shops, buying and selling, as women delight to do everywhere. These different peoples all find a congenial home, under the British flag, on the Rock of Gibraltar, and, Gibraltar being a free port, are permitted, practically without any restrictions, to carry on their peaceful callings, and observe their own peculiar customs, side by side. The market, beside the large gates, and near the old mole, is a favourable place for beholding these different peoples. They congregate here, and present a very striking scene.

Advantage is taken of the free port of Gibraltar to introduce contraband goods into Spain. The Spanish authorities are very watchful, but so easily accessible is their territory from Gibraltar that sharp-witted smugglers do a thriving trade nevertheless. When the religious intolerance of the Spaniards was more pronounced than now, and Bibles were very difficult to be had by converts to the Protestant faith, and by those wishful to read and study the Scriptures and therefore likely to become converts, Bibles were often introduced through Gibraltar by Protestant Spaniards resident upon, or visiting, the Rock. But the doors of Spain itself are being opened, tardily perhaps, yet surely, and the Bible will free Spain, as it has freed other countries, and give her power and opportunity to grow. A distinct advance has been made in the provisions for religious worship in Gibraltar. There is perfect religious toleration. The Roman Catholics have a church and bishop, and so have the Anglicans. The Jews have no less than four synagogues, and the Presbyterians and Methodists are both represented by small, but useful, communities.

Years ago religiously disposed men were not so well provided with spiritual advisers. A pleasing incident, recorded in "The Book and its Mission," occurred here, which, under God's blessing, had a signal effect for good upon the population of a much more distant part of the British Empire, the island of Ceylon. Two soldiers, having little opportunity to hear the preaching of the Word, read that Word together. The truth was revealed to one of them, and, through faith in Jesus Christ, he realized inward peace and joy. The other was desirous to obtain a similar experience. He read, and prayed, and waited, but his desire remained unsatisfied for some time. One night he and his comrade were the sentries at each end of a sallyport leading toward the Spanish lines. In the quietness of the night an officer of the garrison passed one end of the sallyport, and asked the sentry for the password, and the man, absorbed in religious meditation, gave the unexpected answer, "The precious blood of Christ." Quickly perceiving his mistake, however, he gave the proper password; but his first answer had gone down to the other end of the long passage where his comrade was keeping sentry, and where, at that very moment, he was seeking spiritual rest. The words were like a Divine message to him. The truth was in them, and he rested in the truth, and from that time rejoiced in Christ, his Saviour. His regiment was moved to Ceylon. There his adaptability for Christian work was so conspicuous that his discharge from the army was procured, and, having received in his youth a good education, he was appointed master of the principal Christian school in Colombo. He speedily acquired the Cingalese tongue, took up a partially completed translation of the Bible by a brother who had died at the task, and finished it so satisfactorily that it was afterwards published by the British and Foreign Bible Society, and spent the remainder of a very useful life as an accomplished linguist and Christian missionary in Ceylon and India.

The drive from the town to Europa Point is very enjoyable. A visitor would hardly expect to find so much of varied beauty upon the Rock of Gibraltar as may be met with in this drive. It lies along a macadamized road, in very good repair, cut here and there through huge rocks, or winding through the natural crevices of the rocks, opening up all kinds of little grassy nooks and dells, down which are glimpses of the blue sea, and the opposite Spanish land, and the high, shadowy hills of Africa. Arched gateways, well chiselled and ornamented, are thrown across some parts of the road; villas, with trellised fronts, and open, shaded windows, start up in odd corners, surrounded by a wild profusion of roses, and oranges turning golden, and velvety peaches and juicy pears ripening beneath a kindly sun; graceful palms, and prickly cacti, and century-flowering aloes adorn the hill-side, and push themselves out through broken rocks wherever there is soil enough to obtain a footing. And so the road curves in and out, presenting to the quick eye an ever-varying panorama, until it enters upon the grassy opening of the battery known as Europa Advance, where are many soldiers' homes, and where the lighthouse looks over the southern extremity of the Rock towards the African shore. Here the visitor may alight, and walk round the southern extremity, finding every rocky ledge fortified, looking over precipitous cliffs into the rippling waters, watching the vessels pass in and out of "the gates," as the Straits of Gibraltar are sometimes called, until he reaches the mouth of the Monkey cavern, into which, by an awkward turn, the path would lead him, if the military authorities had not barred the entrance by a large wooden gate. The lower path, winding nearer the shore, by which the return journey may be made, is quite as interesting. The scenery is more confined. The elaborate coast fortifications are seen to great advantage. Attention is attracted by a recently mounted one-hundred-ton gun, which can be so worked as to cover any part of the bay. The Alameda, with its pretty ornamental grounds, is passed through, and the very interesting drive completed by re-entering the shaded streets of the town.

A little to the east of Europa Point, right under the cliffs, a steamer, with her bows out of the water, and her stern buried in the tide, lay disabled, and ready, with the first fresh breeze, to go to pieces. She had run right in, during a dense fog and a dead calm, striking the rocks and immediately settling—fortunately, however, in shallow water. The crew were saved. We saw her as we approached Gibraltar, and also saw her from the cliffs above, with a gang of men aboard removing her cargo of copper ore upon the chance of floating her again, and sending her once more to sea. But the chance was a very slender one. It was a pity to see her lying down there. She looked ridiculously small compared with the towering heights against which she had come, not driven by a gale in the full expectancy of striking those heights, but steaming all innocent of her danger, and with the impression that the waters were deep and her course was clear.

The fauna of Gibraltar, as might be expected on a comparatively barren rock of its size and shape, is not very varied. But the few species of animal life found there are not molested, and consequently rapidly increase. Rabbits are numerous. Woodcocks and wild pigeons may be met with. But the speciality of the Gibraltar fauna is the monkey, the only place in Europe where the monkey is found wild. It is a small, snuff-coloured monkey, closely akin to its tribe across the Straits, from whom probably it first came, and, by the appearance of a pair nestling in the arms of a Spaniard walking through one of the principal streets, a tractable creature, and easily trained to obey the commands of man. Walking down the path from the Monkey cavern at Europa Point, I observed a bright green lizard slip from under a cactus, and over a rock, into the bush beyond. The rapidity and ease of its movement on the perpendicular face of the rock, which was almost as smooth as polished marble, were surprising; and brought to my mind the rendering of the Revised Version of one of the four wise little things mentioned by Agur, the son of Jakeh: "The *lizard* taketh hold with her hands, yet is she in king's palaces." May not this rendering obtain support from the fact that the lizard's feet are like human hands, and that she is able to *take hold* of the smoothest surfaces, even the polished stones of king's palaces, and run over or rest upon them? And may not the exceeding wisdom set forth by the lizard be tenacity, clinging power, and the consequent ease acquired in the accomplishment of purposes?

The view from the summit of the Rock is very fine. Looking northward, over the isthmus, the fertile valleys of Andalusia, with two rivers winding through them, and emptying themselves into the bay, and far away in the distance the spurs of great hills, dotted with snow, rising and closing in the scene, present a noble landscape to the gratified vision. Looking southward, across the sea, the mountains of Africa appear—Ape's Hill, with its majestic rounded form, the centre and most conspicuous of them all, reminding one of the "broad-shouldered" mountain farther back, great Atlas, who

"turns the rolling heavens around."

Looking westward, across the bay, the eye alights upon the high Spanish land behind Algesiras terminating in Cape Tarifa, and measures the straits between Cape Tarifa and the African coast, through which the ships are moving in and out, and beyond which widens the vast expanse of the western ocean. Looking eastward, the beautiful Mediterranean stretches out as far as the eye can see, a flashing sapphire pavement beneath the azure dome of heaven. What more of beauty can the eye desire than this? Sea and land combine to furnish a magnificent prospect, and historical association steps in to crown the view by engaging the mind in a pleasant reverie upon bygone times.

The current of the Straits of Gibraltar is always inward from the Atlantic to the Mediterranean. This inward current upon the surface is balanced by an outward current beneath the surface. Before the discovery of this outward under current the Mediterranean was a scientific puzzle. Salt water is supplied by the upper current at the rate of seventy two cubic miles every year. The rivers supply six cubic miles of fresh water every year; and, if the quantity lost by evaporation be set down at twelve cubic miles, a liberal estimate, there is still an excess of sixty-six cubic miles per annum, to be accounted for somehow, and to be accounted for with no perceptible increase, and with no alteration in the specific gravity of the waters. The outward under current is the satisfactory explanation. Dr. Maury says, "Unless there was some escape for all this solid matter which has been running into the sea . . . for ages, it is very clear that the Mediterranean would long ere this have been a vat of strong brine, or a bed of cubic crystals." The outward under current has been ascertained and tested by experiments. But a well-authenticated and curious incident of two hundred years ago proves the existence of the current. A Dutch brig, laden with oil and alcohol, was chased by a French corsair, the *Phœnix*, and sunk, by a single broadside, in the Straits of Gibraltar between Cape Tarifa and Tangier.

She went down as far as the under current, and there her cargo kept her floating, although submerged; and the under current drew her westward, and finally threw her ashore twelve miles westward of the place where she went down. The surface current would have drawn her eastward, and the motion of the submerged vessel in the directly opposite direction is clear evidence of the opposite under current by which the waters of the Mediterranean preserve their equilibrium.

We left Gibraltar in the evening. The grey shadows were creeping over it, and over the African hills; and, as we entered the "gates," the western sky before us was reddening in the setting sun. There was not much of redness. It was quickly gone. The twilight rapidly deepened into darkness, and there flashed out, on either hand, the African light of Cape Spartel, and the European light of Cape Trafalgar.

CHAPTER XIV.

OLD ENGLAND.

Fire on the Spanish land—Sagras Point and Cape St. Vincent—Sea fowl—Land seen through the haze—Healthy breeze—Bay of Biscay—Old England—The Lizard Lights—Coast of Cornwall—Falmouth Harbour—Home.

WE approached Cape Trafalgar as the shadows deepened into the night. A huge fire was blazing beyond the hills on the Spanish land, and casting a lurid glare far over the firmament. Some large building was being steadily consumed. We could mark the rise and fall of the fiery element by the wavering illumination of the sky, until the gradually fading hue told us, as we steamed westward, that the element had done its work.

Sagras Point and Cape St. Vincent came out clearly in the grey light of the morning. The waves were tumbling upon the rocks that line the bay between the two promontories and covering them with snowy foam. The convent crowning the high cliffs was sharply outlined against the pure sky. The waves were booming in the caverns of Sagras, and the sea-fowl had left their homes to search for their morning's meal. Right off St. Vincent—the scene of the victory of Sir John Jervas, and the Cape whence his family, the Earls of St. Vincent, take their name—the troubled waters, swept by a stiff north-easterly breeze, met the calmer seas sheltered by the high lands; and there, where the commotion was greatest, the birds were assembled in large numbers, wheeling in the air with outspread wings, rocking uneasily on the restless tide, and expressing their satisfaction with the morning, and its prospects, in a discordant screaming chorus only understood by themselves.

As we rounded Cape St. Vincent we met the stiff northeasterly breeze, and found it necessary to rig a weather sail on the bridge in order to comfortably look ahead, and enjoy the sight of the sea and the shore. We soon left the shore so far to the eastward as only to distinguish a hazy line, rendered still more hazy by the intervening sunshine and flying spray. The majestic Rock of Lisbon was subdued by the distance into a soft, rounded object, a seemingly unsubstantial mountain that might any moment fade away. The Berlings, surrounded with foam, were but dimly visible; and next day, in similar weather, Cape Finisterre loomed through the haze a very uncertain end of the land. It would have been difficult to say where the land ended and the sea began. The weather was enjoyable. It was a healthy breeze. It reddened the cheeks, toned the nerves, tightened the muscles, gave elasticity to the limbs and a glow to the heart; and it was a luxury to feel the dipping of the boat, and watch her bows rise and fling the water from her like a live thing. And the enjoyment was not all ours, or the sea-fowls' either, for, not far away, six columns of water were rising from the deep, blown from the nostrils of as many whales, who had left their northern home for a sporting holiday in these summer seas.

The mighty billows were rolling into the Bay of Biscay from the Atlantic, and the good ship was swung hither and thither as she ploughed her way home. What a magnificent swell the seas have in the Bay of Biscay! There is nothing like it in the Mediterranean, or the Black Sea; and when you enter the English Channel you leave it behind. In these other places the seas are shorter. You lose the long curve between the crest of one billow and another. They do not impress you with the same sense of irresistible majesty. Like the strong and healthy pulsations of the ocean's great heart these magnificent waves swept along, and we rose and fell upon the ocean's bosom as if we were the merest trifle. Lighter than the lightest feather we seemed; simply a speck, and hardly visible in the interchanging mountains and valleys of that watery world.

By Sunday morning we had crossed the Bay of Biscay and were nearing the shores of old England. The morning broke amid flying clouds, and we were uncertain whether the lines ahead were other clouds appearing above the horizon, or the cliffs of the "West countrie." Presently the familiar Lizard lights flashed through the dawn, and all at once we appeared quite near the land. We were not so near as we seemed. The Lizard lights are rather deceitful. There are two of them, both powerful electric lights, and sending out their brilliant shafts to an immense distance; but they have the sustained brilliance, almost throughout the entire length of the shafts, peculiar to all electric lights, by which the sense of distance is disturbed and well-nigh destroyed. Soon the lights were extinguished, and the morn advanced and revealed the homely features of the sweet Cornish land—the broken, serpentine cliffs of Kynance; the abrupt declivities of Mullion; the rounded shoulder of Godolphin; the far-away, thin, semi-circular margin of Mount's Bay; and right ahead, up the coast, Pendennis Castle jutting out, and protecting the entrance to Falmouth Harbour.

Standing out from Falmouth Harbour toward the Channel was a pilot boat, in the direction of which we bent our way. The men aboard guessed our intention, and were soon alongside; and, quickly strapping together my bags and portmanteaus, and snatching a few hasty farewells, I was soon on the clean deck of the trim little craft, watching the *Treloske* steam away. There was scarcely any wind. The sea was smooth as glass, and blue as sapphire. The capacious sail was set, and we slowly swung about, and glided lazily through the opening, with the slopes of Pendennis on one side, and the tiny white hamlet of St. Mawes on the other. The harbour opened out, and stretched away, serene and lovely, toward the woods of Tregothnan, rich with autumn tints, and sweeping down to the very edge of the water. The quaint old town of Falmouth overlooked the shipping; and soon I had jumped ashore, and was giving an account of myself, and the contents of my baggage, to the kindly disposed custom-house officer, who had a right to make the inquiries, and to a few "old salts" who were inquisitive enough to listen at the door. The railway train was steaming in the station almost ready to depart, and by eleven o'clock that same morning I was welcomed within my own doors in " Ye loyalle and antiente boroughe of Saint Ives."

THE END.

INDEX.

A.

ABDUL HAMJD, II., 161, 202
Abydos, 120; bride of, 128; fortifications of, 129
Acalephæ, 225
Achmedie mosque, 158
Adria, 359, 361-2, 366
Ægean Sea, origin of the name, 42; view in north of, 74
Ægospotami, 132
Africa, Coast of, 25, 404
Agrarianism in Russia, 314, 321
Alexander the Great, 125
Alexander I. of Russia, 254, 256-9
Alexander III. of Russia, 311, 324, 354
Alexandria Troas, 371-4, 377-8, 381-4
Algesiras, 387, 392
Almeria, 22
Almsgiving in Turkey, 206
Andros, 58
Aquila and Priscilla, 368, 371
Arabia, its condition in the seventh century, 194
Archilochus, 53-4
Assos, 382
Athos, Mount, 40, 78, 84, 362, 375
Ayasaluk, 367

Azov, Sea of, 233; flat land around, 249; shallowness of, 250; ice accident on, 251; city of, 267; captured by Peter the Great, 269

B.

Bajazet, Sultan, 184
Beaticus Bay, 41
Belisarius, his triumph, 169
Bells in Russia, 347
Berlings, 9, 408
Besika Bay, 75, 130
Biscay, Bay of, 3, 408
Black Sea, 221
Bon, Cape, 25
Bosphorus, 118, 137; deep waters, 140; castles of, 141; palaces, 143
Boulair, 135
Burnt column of Constantinople, 174

C.

Caiques, 188; English seaman's use of, 189
Caliphate, assumption of, by Sultan of Turkey, 200
Carthage, 25
Carveoiro, Cape, 11

412   INDEX.

Castor and Pollux, 62, 358
Catalan, 385
Cenchrea, 369
Central Asian route, 272; Turkish attempt to open it, 272; attempt of Napoleon, 273
Cemeteries, 142
Cerigo, 42
Chanak, 120
Charles XII. of Sweden, 249
Chickens, 237
Church of the Fountain, 161
Claudia, 359
Constantinople, its water ways, 117; railway system, 118; isolation of, 118; suburbs of, 142; moonlight view, 144; morning view, 146; origin of, 147; situation of, 148; description of, 149; streets of, 175; dogs of, 176; beggars of, 177; bazaars of, 178; fortifications and sieges, 180-7; Russian desire for, 353
Contrast between Greeks and Russians, 284
Conversion of soldier, Gibraltar, 401
Corinth, 366
Cornish coast, 2, 409
Corunna, 4
Cossacks, 268; origin of, 278; their position in Russia, 279; love of music, 279; loyalty, 317
Crete, 259, 362, 383
Crimea, 227; Tartars of, 229; English in, 231; fortifications of, 231
Cuttle-fish, 15
Czar, veneration for, 315, 324; danger of, 323

D.

Dardanelles, 118-35
Deli, myth concerning, 47; oracle of, 47; confederacy of, 48; religious festivities of, 49; palm tree in, 50; sacredness of 51; earthquake in, 52
Delphi, its oracle, 47, 147, 166
Dervishes, dancing, 217; howling, 218
Dhroskies, 285
Dolma Bagtché palace, 160
Don, river, 271; bridge over, 271
Dragon-fly, 238
Dress of the Russians, 285

E.

Eastern Church, its peculiarities, 39
Elizabeth Alexeiovna, wife of Alexander I. of Russia, 256-9
English fleet, injury to, 130
Ephesus, 366-7
Eremite of Cape St. Angelo, 38
Espichel, Cape, 11
Eumæus, 113
Euroclydon, 359-63
Europa Point, 386, 402-3
Eutychus, 381
Euxine Sea, 222

F.

Falmouth, 409
Family life in Russia, 288
Fanar, 161
Finisterre, Cape, 6, 408

G.

Galata, 162; its round tower, 163-4; its bridge, 174
Gallipoli, 133
Gata, Cape de, 23
Genoese, 163
Giant's grave, 139
Gibraltar, Bay of, 386-7; town of, 387; name, 390; captured by British, 390; sieges of, 391-5;

INDEX.   413

fortress, 396; strategical importance of, 397; caverns of, 398; climate of, 399; people of, 400; religious accommodation of, 401; scenery of, 402-4; fauna of, 403; current through the Straits of, 405
Golden Horn, 187
Government in Russia, 298-301
Grain tract of South Russia, 264
Greeks, appearance of, 90; costume of, 91
Gyarus, 59

H.

Habits of the Russians, 286
Hamals of Constantinople, 163
Harbours of refuge, 10
Hellespont, 118-35; sea-fowl in, 119
Homer, 33, 70
Hoopoes, legend concerning, 223
Horses in South Russia, 266

I.

Icaria, 64
Imagination, Phenomena of, 8
Imaum-ul-Islam, 201
Imaums, 215
Imbros, 78, 375
Impiety, punishment of, 59, 62
Islam, its origin, 192; its divisions, 198; its geographical boundaries, 192, 272; national embodiments of, 199; influence upon the policy of the Sublime Porte, 201; doctrines of, 203; duties of, 205; restrictions of, 208; indulgences of, 209; paradise of, 214; influence upon Turkish life and character, 219; in Spain, 389

J.

Janizaries, origin of, 133; turbulency and destruction of, 170-4; fighting of, near Azov, 268
Jews in Russia, 306, 314
Job, Patriarch of Russia, 329
John, the Apostle, in Patmos, 64; teaching on the sea, 65; appearance of Christ to, 66; the Divine, 367
Julius Cæsar, 126
Julius, the Centurion, 361

K.

Kertch, 233
Kief, 327, 350
Kingfishers, 265
Koran, 205, 210
Krapotkine Alexander, 322
Kremlin, 329, 340

L.

Labouring classes in Russia, 283, 294
Laconia, Gulf of, 32
Leander, 121
Leander's tower, 190
Lemnos, 76, 375
Lightning, sheet, 244; forked, 245
Lisbon, Rock of, 9, 408
Lizard Point, 409
Locusts, 238-44
Luke, the Evangelist, descriptive power of, 363, 373; character and calling of, 376-7
Lundy Island, 2
Lycurgus, 33

M.

Mahdi, 203
Malea, Cape, 36, 42, 362.
Marmora Island, 119, 136.

Marmora, Sea of, 135; islands of, 136
Marriage service in Russia, 344-7
Matala Cape, 362-3
Matapan Cape, 31
Mediterranean, colour of, 24; depth of, 24; volcanic region of, 26; bed of, 27
Megarians, 147
Michael, the first Romanoff, 275, 330
Milo, 44
Miltiades, 54
Mirage, 47, 246
Mitylene, 71, **73**, 382
Mohammed, his birth, 195; his personal appearance and character, 195; life at Mecca, 196; at Medina, 197
Mohammedanism. *See* ISLAM.
Mohammedan women, 175, 211-3
Monks of the Archipelago, 58; of Mount Athos, 84; of Russia, 338-9
Moore, Sir John, 4
Moorish Castle, Gibraltar, 388-9
Mosquitoes, 237
Muezzins, 215
Muscovy, 277, 328-9
Mycone, 56, 366

N.

Napoleon I., 5, 249; designs upon British India, 273
Navarino, 30
Naxia, 55
Nelson, Lord, 17
Newport, South Wales, 1
Nicholas, Czar of Russia, 256, 321, 340
Nicon, Patriarch of Moscow, 331, 352
Nicopolis, 384

Nihilism, 303; origin of the name, 304; moderate and advanced, 307-8; organization, 309, etc.
Nika riots, 167
Novgorod the Great, 319, 326
Novo Tcherkask, 270, 278, 317

O.

Official class in Russia, 282
Old Seraglio, 151-2
Olga, Princess of Russia, 327

P.

Pantellaria, 27
Paros, its marble, 53
Passaro, Cape, 359
Patmos, **64**
Paul, his apostleship, 356; his character, 357; Conybeare and Howson's Life of, 358; wisdom and influence, 364-5; desire for companionship, 378
Pelicans, 235
Pera, 162
Peter the Great, 269, 280, 320; ecclesiastical reforms of, 332-4
Peter, Metropolitan of Moscow, 328
Petrels, 15
Pherecydes, 113
Philaret, Archbishop of Rostoff, 274, 330
Philippi, 373, 378-9, 380-1
Phœbe, of Cenchrea, 369
Phosphorescent waters, 28
Pigeon mosque, 159
Pilgrimage to Mecca, 207
Pittacus, 73
Polycrates, 67
Porpoises, 226
Psyra, 69
Pugatchef, 321
Pythagoras, 68

R.

Ramadan, 206
Raskolniks, 306, 352
Religious intolerance in Russia, 352
Romanoffs, 274-5, 329
Rostoff, 270; wool and grain trade of, 271
Rurik, 277, 319, 327
Russian conspiracy of 1825, 254-6, 321
Russian foreign policy, 302
Russian industries, 292-8
Russo-Greek Church, origin of, 326; clergy of, 337; doctrines of, 339; liturgy of, 340; picture worship of, 341; ceremonies of, 342-4; service of, 347; singing in, 348; saints and martyrs of, 350; its yearning toward Constantinople, 353

S.

Sagras Point, 14, 407
Salamansky's circus, 270
Samothracia, its grandeur, 79, 82; worship of the Cabiri, 80; deluge, 82; view from, 83; storms of, 362; and St. Paul, 373-5
Samos, 66
San Roque, 387, 392
Sappho, 72
Scio, 70
Scopas, 53
Scutari, 190
Selamlik, 160
Seraskierat, 164
Serpho, 45
Sestos, 120; fortifications of, 129
Sharks, 71
Sicily, 28
Sierra Nevada, 20
Signals, universal code of, 12

Simonides, 61
Siphanto, 45
Slavery, 211
Smyrna fleet, miscarriage of, 19
Spain, influence of Roman Catholicism in, 23
Spanish fishermen, 4
Sparta, laws of, 34; city of, 35; laconism of, 68
Spartel, Cape, 406
St. Angelo, Cape, 36
Starovers, 334, 352
St. Bartholomew's Hospital, 107
St. Basil the Blessed, church of, 335
Stenka Radzin, 321
St. Ives, 3, 410
St. John's Eve, its bonfires, 110-3
St. Sophia, mosque of, 145; origin of, 153; building and architecture of, 154; furniture and ritual of, 155; conversion to a mosque, 156; "bloody hand" in, 157; external appearance of, 158
Students in Russia, 311
Sturgeon, 234
St. Vincent, Cape, 13, 407-8
Sulieman the Magnificent, 159
Sultana Validé mosque, 175
Symplegades, 138
Syra, 46; view from, 63; town of, 86; harbour, 88; people of, 89; cafés in, 92; wineshops of, 93; market, 94; English in, 96; gardens of, 98; churches of, 101-5; funeral in, 108; Sunday in, 109; and St. Paul, 366; port of call, 367
Syrtis, Gulf of, 360, 363

T.

Taganrog, 250; streets of, 252; gardens of, 253; palace of the

Czar, 254; visit to Czar's palace, 259-62; railway line to Rostoff, 262; cathedral, 336; service in cathedral, 348
Tamerlane, 184, 267
Tartars, 319, 328
Taygetus mountains, 31, 362
Tchin, 281, 307, 310, 315, 320
Tenedos, 75, 130, 375
Tenos, 56, 366
Thasos, 78, 375
Therapia, 139
Thermia, 60, 366
Timothy, 373, 383
Trafalgar, Cape, 17, 406
Troy, plains of, 75; Mount Ida, 362
Tumuli, 263
Turks, entrance into Europe, 127; boatmen, 132
Turtle, 25, 71

U

Ulema, 214
Uniates, 351

V.

Vigo, 7
Virgin Mary, worship of in Tenos, 57
Vladimir, 227, 229, 327

W.

Whales, 4, 408
Women in Russia, 289-92, 312
Women in Turkey, 175, 211-3
Wrecked steamer, 403

X.

Xerxes, 122

Y.

Yenikalé, Straits of, 233

Z.

Zarex mountains, 44, 362
Zea, silk manufactured in, 60; its strange law, 61, 366

www.ingramcontent.com/pod-product-compliance
Lightning Source LLC
Chambersburg PA
CBHW022105290426
44112CB00008B/553